WOODSTOCK CHAMBERLAINS' ACC

The Oxfordshire Record Society

WOODSTOCK CHAMBERLAINS' ACCOUNTS, 1609–50

Edited by Marjorie Maslen

VOLUME 58

1993

ISBN 0 902 50922 5

Produced for the Society by
Alan Sutton Publishing
Far Thrupp, Stroud, Glos.
Printed in Great Britain.

CONTENTS

FOREWORD

An edition of the Woodstock Chamberlains' Accounts was proposed in 1970 by Mrs. Conny Schwarz, who, during the next few years, prepared an annotated transcript. Other commitments prevented further progress, and in 1982 she magnanimously handed over the material for others to use. The society wishes to record its gratitude to Mrs. Schwarz for her initial work and for her co-operation and encouragement since. Mrs. Maslen has been able to make use of the transcript and notes in preparing her own edition of the accounts.

The society is grateful to Woodstock Town Council, which granted access to, and allowed publication of, its manuscript, and to the Marc Fitch Fund and the University of Otago, New Zealand, for grants towards publication costs.

Oxford, December 1993   Christopher Day
General Editor, O.R.S.

EDITOR'S PREFACE

I wish to acknowledge here the work of Mrs. C. Schwarz, whose involvement in the project is outlined above in the foreword.

My thanks go to the University of Otago, New Zealand, for giving me research time and money, and in the history department to the research assistants, and to Mrs. Flora Kirby for willing work on the word processor. In Oxford I received encouragement, guidance, and help from Dr. Molly Barratt at her various places of work in the Bodleian Library, the Oxfordshire Archives, and the Woodstock archive room. I am also grateful to the other archivists and librarians in the Bodleian Library and the Oxfordshire Archives who provided information, especially when asked for from 12,000 miles away. I owe much to my husband and daughter for their support and practical help. Finally, the volume could not have been produced without the work of the General Editor of the Record Society, Mr. Christopher Day, and I am duly grateful.

LIST OF ABBREVIATIONS

Common abbreviations are used for months, towns, counties, and personal names

acct(s).	account(s)
B	Woodstock Borough Muniments
B.L.	British Library
Bodl. Lib.	Bodleian Library, Oxford
Cal.	Calendar
Cam. Soc.	Camden Society
cttee.	committee
D.N.B.	*Dictionary of National Biography*
E.H.R.	*English Historical Review*
O.R.O.	Oxfordshire Record Office, now Oxfordshire Archives
O.R.S.	Oxfordshire Record Society
P. R.O.	Public Record Office
rec(s).	record(s)
reg(s).	register(s)
T.R.H.S.	*Transactions of the Royal Historical Society*
V.C.H.	*Victoria County History*

INTRODUCTION

For a small borough Woodstock has a remarkably fine collection of records ranging from the late 15th century to modern times. Few throw as much light on the activities of the town at a particular period as the chamberlains' book for 1609–50.

The manuscript, B 79, is still kept with the borough records in the town hall. It is paper but with parchment wraps, in this case made from a medieval music manuscript. That was contemporary practice, and the borough court books are similar. The covers were probably added after the accounts had been written up, as some entries in the inner margins of the manuscript are now hidden by tight sewing; 17th-century scribbles on the covers suggest that it was done fairly soon. The folios are numbered 1–211 plus 18a and 24a, and are of uniform size, 21cm. by 56cm. They are worn on the right hand corners but otherwise are in good condition, testifying to continuity and care in custody. Blank folios are indicated in the edition.

On its cover the manuscript is called 'A booke of the chamberlins accomptes, and of the rentes of the boughroughe of Newe Woodstocke'. It contains the accounts for 1609–50, two rentals (1609–13 and 1614–18), an account of dole money paid from 1615 to 1621, and a record of a council meeting in March 1636, preceding the 1636 account. All the records in the book have relevance to the finances of the borough. Checking and collecting the rents was among the chamberlains' most important work for the town, and the many alterations and additions to the rentals show this, particularly between 1609 and 1613. The details of the dole money follow the 1622 account and seem to be a record made by the town clerk after the death in that year of the donor, Sir Thomas Spencer of Yarnton, perhaps to ensure that the town knew what to claim from his heirs. The dole money was distributed by the mayor and until 1646 the chamberlains' accounts did not deal with its receipt and distribution, only with the money spent to secure payment from the Spencers. The brief record of a March meeting of councillors in 1636 dealt with the constables' accounts, as well as giving some of the orders made for the town, useful information in the absence of a council order book for this period.

The chief interest of this edition lies in the chamberlains' accounts from December 1608 to December 1650. They are fuller and more informative than other early financial records which have survived for the borough. The one surviving earlier account for the single year from Michaelmas 1517 to Michaelmas 1518[1] is useful for comparison, but belongs to the period before the corporation had acquired all the money and reponsibilities seen in the seventeenth century. Then there is a long gap in the accounts until the 1609 to 1650 series, and again after 1650 until 1738, when there is a second series up to 1812. The mayor's book, Borough Mun. B 81, called the ledger book in the chamberlains' accounts below, contains the annual audit from 1534 to 1812, but the entries are brief: until 1619 only the town's debts and liabilities were given, with thereafter the final totals of the chamberlains' accounts. It supplements the accounts printed here, particularly as it gives more detail of audit decisions, but it does not supplant them. These early-seventeenth century accounts, therefore, give us the first opportunity to see in detail how the Woodstock borough finances worked. They provide an historical record of the town under the early Stuarts and in the civil wars, and add to our knowledge of town reactions in that troubled period.

The chamberlains' accounts were made up at the end of the year from other records, none of which are now extant. For example, their own daily accounts, and those of the town crier and the constables, as well as such items as an almanack, are known only from occasional mentions in this book, but were obviously the basic materials. Fortunately, other contemporary records have survived in Woodstock's well-stocked archive room. They include the ledger audit book already mentioned, earlier and later rentals, records of freemen's admissions and of council business, property deeds, original and enrolled, and lists of inhabitants, musters and taxes. In addition there are court books of various dates between 1588 and 1635 for the portmoot and frankpledge courts, as well as for Woodstock's own sessions court. Information from these as well as from state and ecclesiastical records has been used for this edition, though not exhaustively. Through probate records, for example, it is possible to find out more about local people mentioned, and some identifications are provided in the footnotes and appendix. The chamberlains' book will itself prove a quarry for other researchers.

The evolution of the accounts and of the chamberlains' office can be traced throughout the 16th century. Chamberlains were not mentioned in the 1453 grant of incorporation, and they may have been comparatively new officers when they appeared in the first surviving account of 1517–18. In that account the two chamberlains had money in hand 'of the last yeres proffet the first accompt', but whether this previous account was the chamberlains' first account or the first time those particular men accounted is not clear. The town had had more money to manage since

1453 when Henry VI granted its charter of incorporation and an income from the borough quit rents, from Le Pool marsh, and from fines, forfeitures, waifs, strays, felons' goods and other royal perquisites. The charter granted as well the assizes of bread and ale and other victuals, and confirmation of the fair of St. Matthew (21 Sept.), dating back to the 13th century, and of St. Mary Magdalen (22 July), which had been held since the 14th century, both fairs now for four days.[2] In the same year townsfolk endowed the chantry of St. Mary which Henry VI established in Woodstock chapel, and the new corporation was closely involved with the management of the land and shops belonging to it.[3] In 1488 the mayor and corporation acquired more such obligations when Thomas Croft made them trustees of the lands he left to St. Margaret's chantry in Woodstock chapel and for the two poor men who were to pray there,[4] apparently the beginning of the almshouse.

Despite all this, the role of the chamberlains was limited at first because the mayor took the rents, waifs and strays and other perquisites, and paid the fee farm rent of £2 13s 4d to the Crown for Le Pool.[5] Other property was similarly farmed out throughout much of the 16th century to individuals, who were responsible directly to the council.[6] At the audit of the 1517–18 account, held in 1519, the chamberlains accounted for only 55s 2d of the borough revenues, but their responsibilities for repair of the town's roads and property were there, as later, and the connexion with the chantry. The account was brief. They took in money from a few rents only, i.e. 20s from Le Pool, 4s from a shop under the guildhall and 2s 4d from the Spittle House close in Old Woodstock; 6s 10d came from making freemen and 22s were left over from the previous account. They paid out 2s 7d on the hedges of Spittle House close, 9s on the stocks and cucking stool, 4s on the chantry lands, and 2s 11d on wages to repair the highways, 12d similarly for the prison wall work and for lime, and 20d for crests for the guildhall; they were allowed 13s 4d for losses to the lessees through damage to Le Pool by the king's men and their horses. Their total expenditure was 34s 6d, and so they had 20s 10d in hand for the next year. The ledger audit book (B 81), which was begun in 1534, shows that the chamberlains were presenting such limited accounts regularly for the next fifty years.

By the late 16th century there were changes. The chantries were dissolved in 1547, but the town bought the chantry house, which Croft had endowed, for the town almshouse in 1551. In 1565, by grant from Queen Elizabeth, they acquired some of the houses and rents which had belonged to St. Mary's chantry, so that they were once again dealing with property which earlier townsfolk had given for the community.[7] The town obviously hoped to benefit from thriving local trade and by the same grant in 1565 was allowed to hold a new Friday market, in addition to the Tuesday market dating back to the 12th century, and two new fairs of St. Nicholas (6 Dec.) and Lady Day (25 Mar.), each for four days. The stallages and tolls added to the town's revenues.[8] The grant of the wool beam at the same time was similarly designed to increase trade and help the town, and the mayor received all the profits from the weighing of wool and yarn in the market. In 1576 there was further encouragement when Woodstock was made a staple town, where anyone could buy and sell wool and yarn.[9] In 1585 more charity obligations came with Richard Cornwell's endowment of the grammar school, and in the next decades the town embarked on moving the almshouse away from the original church site and enlarging it.[10] Most important for the chamberlains' role was that by reforms in 1580 the mayor was given a fixed stipend of £10 a year and the chamberlains took over the revenues he had been collecting, including the profits of the wool beam, and they now paid the fee farm and quit rents to the Crown.[11] This revolution in council affairs meant that the chamberlains' status and responsibilities were enhanced and that their accounts must have become fuller and more like those we see in the early 17th century, when they accounted for all the borough revenues. Because of these changes the Woodstock chamberlains' accounts are clearer and easier to understand than those of other local corporations like Abingdon, Banbury, and Oxford, where different officials each presented their own separate accounts at the audit.

In the 16th century and in these accounts for 1609–50 the two chamberlains were elected at the audit in December, not as in the 19th century with the mayor in September.[12] They were chosen from the common council, the senior elected by the common council, or more precisely in these accounts, those who were at the audit, while the junior was the choice of the mayor; he would move up later to be senior. Although elected annually, chamberlains frequently served a number of years, as several careers in the biographies below show. George Noble, for example, was chamberlain for some fourteen years in all. The *cursus honorum* was envisaged in the 1580 constitution as a progress from tithingman, churchwarden, and constable, though these offices could be by-passed on payment, to chamberlain, alderman and, for some, mayor.[13] Those who reached the office of chamberlain were of some standing in the local community, tradesmen or others who could bear the expense of serving. They were unpaid and had often to reach into their own pockets for the money for the accounts before the revenues came in, since there was usually only a small amount handed over in ready cash as a running fund at the beginning of their year. Not much is shown in these accounts as to how the two divided their duties. The junior chamberlain presented a small account of eight items in 1610, and in 1636 he held the book recording gifts and rewards. In 1646 their accounts are entered separately and, as might be expected, the senior chamberlain dealt with the major revenues. There does not seem to be as clear a division of duties as a larger town like Oxford was perhaps obliged to have.

The town clerk was almost as important in the development of the accounts. He was recorded in Woodstock in 1498[14] and would have been needed to deal with all the responsibilities and records arising from the 15th-century incorporation. As the senior permanent official he could exert influence over 'amateur' chamberlains, particularly when, as in these 17th-century accounts, he was a man of standing in the community and closely related by marriage to the leading families. We can see that many of the functions of the town clerk had developed in the 16th century. He is mentioned in the reformed constitution in 1580 and in 1589 he was specifically ordered to write up the 'mayor's book', i.e. the ledger audit book, though he presumably had been doing that already. He had to keep the records in the town chest, for which both he and the mayor had keys.[15] In the ledger book in 1598 Thomas Rawlins, the town clerk, dealt with the mortmain for the school and almshouse, as well as looking after the town's records.

We owe the accounts below almost entirely to the town clerk Edmond Hiorne, who took over the position from Rawlins, his father-in-law, in December 1607.[16] A year later he began writing up the chamberlains' accounts in this book, and during his long tenure of nearly forty years he put his own stamp on them and gave them a more orderly and settled character. In a very real sense the accounts are his as well as the chamberlains'. Hiorne collected receipts and some of the money, cast up and wrote the accounts for the chamberlains and signed them as they did; he then entered the audit account and other records in the ledger book. He also wrote up the court records of the town and records for Woodstock manor of which he was deputy steward. He belonged to the new breed of town clerks, meticulously keeping his records and maintaining a watchful eye on the finances and policy of the town in all spheres. He was not always in the town office. He journeyed in the county and to London on town business. He sat in the courts, was a justice of the borough, and saw to legal transactions, although, like other Woodstock town clerks up to the 19th century, he was not trained in law; expert legal advice came from the recorder of the borough.[17] It is, though, the scrupulous care taken over the layout of the accounts and in writing them up and ensuring they were agreed and signed which reveals the dedicated professional clerk in Hiorne. He undoubtedly 'worked over' the accounts. Looking at the ledger book for his first year, 1608, we can see him trying to find out where and when payments were made and establishing the practice of entering and signing the receipts. It was probably his thinking that led to the transfer of most church business from the town accounts after a few years. For example, in 1608 he wrote in the ledger book that the Whitsuntide money from the Whitsun sports or revels, which at that time was handed over to the chamberlains, was 'cleerly gotten to the use of the Church'; it disappeared from the chamberlains' accounts after 1615 and from 1617 appeared in the churchwardens' accounts.[18] The accounts in the 1630s show how he liked to present the finances, grouped under headings such as wine, school, or repairs. The change can be appreciated by comparison with the first account of 1609.

The importance of his position can be gauged from the fact that it was he who was blamed for handing over the town armour to the royal forces in 1642. He was brought before the House of Commons to be reprimanded by Speaker Lenthall, who was also the recorder and member for Woodstock. Hiorne's loss of the clerkship in the Civil War purge of 1645 must have hurt, but he remained in the town and on the council. He voted against making Richard Croke, the deputy recorder, a freeman in 1652, perhaps because of Croke's connexion with parliamentary commissioners who destroyed the royal manor and park in 1649. Hiorne was restored to office in 1662, but in 1663 he retired in favour of George Ryves, his granddaughter's husband. He lived on in Woodstock until his death in 1669. Though his own father was a yeoman and his brother a blacksmith, his marriage had brought him gentry connexions and his will shows that his daughter Ann had married a Fleetwood, from a leading local family from the park.[19]

Only a few years of the accounts of his successor, John Williams, have survived. He was the son of an earlier mayor, Thomas Williams, one of the wealthiest bakers and innkeepers in Woodstock in the 1630s.[20] John Williams, too, was deeply involved in town affairs. He was admitted freeman in 1635, worked his way through the system as churchwarden in 1640, constable in 1641, and lessee of the common meadow from 1640. He was set, one would have thought, to become chamberlain and alderman in time; instead it looks as if he was diverted to the town clerk's office at a time of crisis in 1645. He differed in politics from Hiorne, but was equally concerned to preserve the interests of the town. His style of writing up the accounts differed in that he did it on a day and month basis, but they are full from 1648 and show the restoration of accountability after the

Civil War with, for example, the recovery of rents and the making of back-payments in the last years of the 1640s. Williams served the town throughout the Commonwealth period, apparently supporting the regime: he named a son Oliver. Though the chamberlains' accounts have not survived for these years, the ledger audit accounts show that they were presented and were entered by him. In 1662 he was dismissed, along with his brother-in-law the mayor, Alexander Johnson, in the new purge of corporations.[21] He died before Hiorne, in 1663, and, perhaps because of the troubles of the 1640s and 1650s, he left only £184 10s, rather less than his father, who died worth £464 15s 11d in 1636.[22]

Woodstock was one of the towns where the town clerk was paid for his work. In December 1607 the ledger book records that it was agreed that Edmond Hiorne should be paid 26s 8d a year for life. The accounts below show that he also received 13s 4d for attendance at the assizes in Oxford twice a year, when he reported on the town's sessions court, and 5s for writing and casting up the chamberlains' accounts, a total of 45s a year. That remained the payment until Williams became town clerk. He received just 26s 8d a year, perhaps as an economy measure and because Hiorne continued to deal with the courts for a time. There would in addition be certain fees received in the courts, but those form no part of the chamberlains' accounts.

We learn something about the working conditions for the town clerks and the council in the 17th century from these records. The town office had been built by Rawlins at the back of the town clerk's house near the church and opposite the town or guild hall.[23] Both he and Hiorne rented the house from the council at first, but in the 1618 account Hiorne is recorded buying the freehold. In 1609 he purchased a lock for the office door and in 1621 two iron-plate bolts. In 1630 the office was repaired and new slates put on. In 1640 Hiorne had a new table and four joinery stools and a new wainscot cupboard installed, with red leather for the cupboard and 36 yards of matting as well as leather for the seats. At the same time a table of fees for the office was written out. The town chest contained the records of the town such as the ledger book and bonds and deeds, and in 1609 Hiorne had likewise bought a lock for it. In 1621 the chest was said to be in the care of alderman Thomas Meatcalfe, and was again furnished with a lock and key. This is presumably the chest now in the present town hall. For the audit the town clerk and chamberlains moved over to the town hall, though on a rare occasion in 1643 the chamberlains' accounts were audited in the town clerk's office. The town or guild hall was also the place where the town courts were held.

Other officers appearing in the accounts were mainly those who collected money for the town and those receiving wages or stipends. Hence, in the receipts section the chamberlains accounted for money received each year from the sergeant at the mace and the tollman. The sergeant, although elected annually at the same time as the mayor in September, kept his office for life. They collected the stallage money and paid some to the chamberlains, but kept part, the proceeds from the St. Mary Magdalen and St. Nicholas fairs, for their emoluments. Sometime between 1635 and 1637 the council decided to pay them a wage of £1 10s instead, and for a few years the stallages were collected by the tollman for a wage and paid over to the town. By 1645 the sergeant was again collecting stallages, but for a wage on the new basis. Other business also brought them into the accounts: in 1633, for instance, for the repair of the great silver-gilt mace which it was their duty to carry on ceremonial occasions. The tollman was also the crier of the court and keeper of the town hall, where he looked after the fire buckets. In 1609 he was Edward Longe, a lastmaker, who had been given his office as crier for life in 1608.[24] Longe was also the church clerk, and this probably explains why he was paid in the early accounts for looking after the bells and graves. As tollman he paid over the sums he collected from tolls for the first twenty five years. Sometime after 1635, perhaps after Longe's death in 1636, there was another change in policy: this time, in contrast to the stallage arrangement, a set sum or 'farm' of £8 a year was paid in by the new tollman, declining to £4 by 1650.

Under expenses the chamberlains accounted for the stipends and fees of the higher officers such as the recorder, town clerk, and mayor, and also for wages to lesser officers. The warders at the fairs, for example, were paid 8d each per fair, a rate which did not vary throughout the period. The town scavenger, Raphe Lucas, received 6d a quarter in the 1630s and 1640s and a besom. Lucas was a useful character who also 'swept up', as it were, the poor in his capacity as the beadle of beggars from 1632. That seems to have been a new office, created in response to Charles I's book of orders, urging action on the poor.[25] From then on the chamberlains accounted for the purchase each year of red and blue cloth, later a more sober grey, for the beadle's coat and cap.

It is in the disbursement section that the town's two constables can be found, engaged with many aspects of the borough's administration. They collected fines and estreats for the court, looked after prisoners, and were responsible for the town armour and much of the work with musters and trained bands which appears in these accounts. Sometimes payments were made to them for their own levies as in 1622 and 1636, and they

were frequently reimbursed for their expenditure on the poor and
vagrants. They were elected annually at the leet court and their own
accounts should have been presented before the quarter sessions court.
Such overlap of duties and officers was common where there were several
bodies responsible for the same problem, generally the poor at this time.
For this reason the collectors for the poor sometimes appear in these
accounts although as parish officers they are usually to be found in the
churchwardens' accounts. In 1633, indeed, they were elected at the audit
meeting. The surveyors of the highways likewise had payments made to
them. They were elected in the leet court and worked under an agreement with the council, as described later in the 1650s, to repair the borough roads.[26]

Some town officers, who were elected in the courts and made presenta-
tions there, were only occasionally mentioned in the accounts because
they had no regular payments to receive or make. References to the
leather sealers and the tasters and weighers occur only when their seals or
scales and measures had to be replaced. Tithingmen, essential in the
courts, make only an incidental appearance when in 1611 one was
assaulted. A full range of the officers is more easily seen in the court
books.

The officers of the account were responsible to the commonalty of
Woodstock borough, comprising a common council of twenty councillors
and five aldermen including the mayor, and the other freemen, numbering
some 40–50 in lists surviving from 1608 to 1630.[27] The common council,
the town's governing body, was largely made up of leading businessmen
and notables. The mayor and aldermen headed the council and supervised
its finances. Under the 1580 constitution the mayor must have served as
chamberlain. He was elected annually from the aldermen but was usually
re-elected for a second year, and because of the smallness of the group
would often have other turns at the office, as the appendix below shows.
When aldermen were long-lived the office was monopolized by a few.
The mayor's own expenditure on town business appears in the accounts,
particularly that on entertainment and on the poor and on prisoners in
Oxford castle. In 1631, again apparently in response to the book of orders,
he was given 6s a quarter to distribute to the poor, instead of making payments at will. His stipend of £10 was spent on the two dinners held after
the leet courts, but in 1641 the accounts show that the town took economy measures and discontinued his stipend in favour of paying the actual
cost of the dinners, which in the following years was indeed cheaper.
High Wycombe in neighbouring Buckinghamshire did the same in a similar economy campaign in the 1640s.[28]

Grander men from outside also had a place in the borough accounts. Most important from the 16th century were the recorder and the high steward, who were regarded as giving status to the town. The recorder was a lawyer who provided the borough with legal expertise. New Windsor, on which Woodstock's privileges were modelled in 1453, tried hard and in vain in the 17th century to acquire one, but Woodstock had James Bury as recorder by 1551.[29] The recorder was paid £3 6s 8d a year, and on occasion collected it in person in December; he took an oath and had a formal patent of office, as shown in the 1622 account. He was in the commission of the peace for the borough, and he or his deputy were supposed to be present at the court of sessions and the leet and to form a quorum with the mayor for the court of record.[30] He was consulted on such matters as the procedure to be followed in 1611 when the mayor died in office, about school matters in 1638, and about the Spencer dole money in 1640. The recorder usually represented the town in Parliament. Sir James Whitelocke, who held both offices, maintained in his biography that this was customary. He also pointed out that there could be tension over this between them and the high steward.[31]

The high steward's role was more ceremonial, but he was a grander personage and provided the political patronage regarded as vital for the town. He was not paid a fee, but each year the town sent wine, sugar, or a taste cake at Christmas, and payments to his servants, regularly recorded in the accounts. In the early years he was chosen from among leading local landowners. Thus, Sir Henry Lee of Ditchley (d. 1611) was followed by Sir Thomas Spencer of Yarnton (d. 1622). Philip, 1st earl of Montgomery and 4th earl of Pembroke, was high steward for the remainder of the accounts. Although not a local landowner he was steward of the royal park and powerful in the royal household, of which he was Lord Chamberlain from 1630. From at least 1614, according to Whitelocke, he and his brother William, 3rd earl of Pembroke, tried to bring Woodstock under their influence so as to secure the election of their nominees. In the 1620s they succeeded in gaining at least one of the two places for their candidate, and the 4th earl allegedly overturned the town's choice in 1640, procuring the election of William Lenthall and Sir Robert Pye to the Long Parliament.[32]

The borough, of course, spent money on writs and returns for those and earlier elections and on correspondence with its members, though the actual election costs would be paid by the candidates and their patrons. The accounts also show that it sent gifts to other local and influential families such as Crown lessees of the park lodges and park rangers, and to local Catholic gentry, like the Brownes of Kiddington, who were high in Stuart favour. In 1641 gifts went to Robert Dormer, 1st earl of Carnarvon, son-in-law of the Earl of Pembroke and steward through him of Woodstock manor; he died in the royalist cause at Newbury in 1643. The borough also sent, in 1641, to 'Old Subtlety', the Puritan Lord Saye and Sele. It was, however, too early to presume that the town was picking sides.

The process of the 17th-century audit, for which the chamberlains' accounts were prepared, can be studied in the ledger audit book and in these accounts. The ledger book shows that in the 16th century the audit had originally been taken near St. Catherine's Day (25 Nov.), whereas in these accounts in the early 17th century it was held on or near St. Thomas's Day (21 Dec.), and from the mid century accounts were often audited in the subsequent year. Payments came in at various dates in the year, but the major town rents were paid at Lady Day (25 Mar.) and at Michaelmas (29 Sept.), and that meant the town accounts had to be presented yet later. Incidental expenses were accounted for up to the end of the accounting year. The Civil War delayed the audit of 1642 and 1643 until March 1644, and from 1645 the accounts were audited in January or February of the next year, but the year of account still ran from December to December. The December date meant that the accounts took in part of two mayoral years since the mayor was elected in September and took office at Michaelmas. Perhaps this gave some greater check on the accounts since the second mayor audited part of his predecessor's expenditure, but the reason is more likely linked to the gathering in of income at the end of the year.

The audit was held before the mayor and such of the aldermen and members of the common council as were present. In the 16th century the chamberlains brought their box with them to the audit and in 1590 they had to take out a bond for the money they handled, but neither boxes nor bonds are mentioned in these 17th-century accounts. The mayor and town clerk and occasionally others signed the accounts in the audit book, while the mayor, town clerk and chamberlains signed the presented accounts. Corrections were made to the accounts, some at the writing up and others at the audit. Where it looks as if there was an audit correction, it has been indicated in this edition. There are also later notes added when, for example, debts were paid; these again are indicated below. There are sometimes obvious mistakes in addition and in 1610 the rents were omitted as an item, but not in the final reckoning. It is not always possible to explain what happened since there may have been allowances made at the time of account. Accordingly, no corrections have been made to the manuscript totals in this edition.

The object of the accounts was to record receipt and expenditure during the year and in particular the amount still to be collected or to be handed over by the chamberlains at the end of the year, the usual charge and discharge of medieval and contemporary accounting. At the audit the new chamberlains were made responsible for the receipt and expenditure of the annual income, and for the collection or payment of debts owed to and by the town. They were charged with the collection of all the rents on the rent roll, but were allowed for unpaid rents in their disbursements. Unpaid debts appeared in a separate item of debts owing to the town and there was another section for debts owed by the town. Debts to the town included unpaid rent, like that owed year after year by the Whittons for the Great House, or admission fees or payments for sealing charters. Debts owed by the town included money borrowed by the town or owed after the account to their officers, as well as capital on which there were charges for sermons or charities, i.e. the town's liabilities. To know if the town was living within its means, therefore, it is necessary to know not just the annual expenditure and receipt, but also the extent of debt and liability: how much it had borrowed or had in money out on loan at interest or was liable for from endowed funds for the poor or for sermons. In certain years the debts and liabilities were equivalent to almost half the receipts, but the debts did not have to be repaid at once and were sometimes wiped out by a bequest or use of an endowment as in the case of the school money below.

The town relied a great deal on the goodwill of its townsfolk and officers. The council would collect money at its meetings, as for a constable's levy in 1636. Like other towns it raised loans from townsfolk for unusual expenditure: in 1603 the borough borrowed £21 10s from twenty one local people, which was still being paid back in the early accounts in this book. The mayor and chamberlains made payments for the town out of their own pockets and by 1614 the town was paying interest on such debts. The officials in turn were in a position to secure preferential treatment in taking town leases of the corporation meadow, Le Pool, or of the Hampton Poyle leys. Local businessmen acted as town bankers. William Rayer took the £50 school bequest money on loan in 1612 and paid the interest over for the schoolmaster's salary. He also financed town expenditure over a number of years and the loan money eventually went in the time of his son in 1640 to pay the debt which the town had incurred to them both, while the town took on the payment to the schoolmaster out of current funds. The accounts show that the interest rate was ten per cent until 1626 when it droppped to eight per cent and the schoolmaster got only £4 from that source. It was at that time that Thomas Rayer was summoned before the archdeacon's court because he refused to pay more than 8s on his father's bequest of £5 for a sermon, on the grounds that he could no longer obtain the higher rate himself.[33]

The chamberlains rarely had money to hand over to the town at the end of the year but it is not a situation unique to these accounts or this town. In 1584, admittedly an exceptional time because of the reorganization, the town had owed £67 17s 8d, and in the 19th century the commission of enquiry into corporations showed it spending more money than it received, a position it shared with a number of other towns.[34] It did not necessarily mean that matters were bad in the town, as long as local businessmen had confidence in the corporation. In these accounts the town had a profit in ten of the thirty-six years, as shown in the table of totals. The deficit was above £14 in only six years (1612, 1613, 1621, 1622, 1642, 1648), and can be explained by higher expenditure on enlarging the almshouse in 1612, repayment of debt in 1613, the new commission of the peace in 1621, repair of highways in 1622, the war in 1642, and the attempt to secure the Yarnton dole money in 1648.

Until 1640 the annual receipts were between £50 and £60. A third to a half (c. £25–30) came from the quit rents and property which had been granted by the two monarchs and from houses purchased with the money given for the school. Some rents were lost when property was sold off, as to Edmond Hiorne in 1618, but there were also additions, as in 1626 when the town increased its rents by charging for encroachments on the waste by tenants who built out into the roadway. Larger entry fines compensated for low rents, as in the case of Hampton Poyle leys, rented for 1d a year but with entry fines of £10 in 1614, £15 in 1619, and £18 in 1636. Revenue from the rents of the wool beam (24s), and from the stalls and tolls at the markets and fairs (£10–12) made up about a fifth of the total. It was the increase in these two sources, from a rise in rents after 1640 and through the reorganization of tolls and stallages from 1636, which brought the annual borough income to c. £90 in the early 1640s. Receipts from court fines and for sealing deeds were only ever irregular and small, and payments for admissions to freedom did not bring in more than £4 or £5, if that, in a year. Nonetheless, they could be a helpful windfall, for instance in 1619 when eleven freemen were admitted. Until 1616 the corporation also had the money from the Whitsuntide revels.[35] As in many other towns, no rate money was collected for the town accounts, and when the constables made their levies and the collectors of the poor gathered in their money they accounted to other bodies. It is salutary to remember that the chamberlains' accounts do not show us all the finances of the community.

Endowments for education, for the poor, and for sermons were in the words of a 19th-century commentator 'blended with those of the corporation'.[36] This state of affairs came about in the 16th and early 17th centuries when the town received the various bequests which enabled it to provide and maintain these social services. The most notable charity in the accounts is seen in the various sums for the school from the legacy of Richard Cornwell (d. 1585). He was a London skinner, but he came from Woodstock. His father seems to have been the Robert Cornwell of Woodstock who died in 1545 and left his young son Richard some silver spoons, but his grandfather, William Cornwell (d. 1552), who had been mayor of Woodstock and was an executor of Robert's will, endowed him with a house in Woodstock, which may have helped him on his road to fortune.[37] Richard bequeathed £300 for a free grammar school to be established in his home town; £100 was for the schoolhouse and £200 was to buy lands for the school and the schoolmaster. The White Hart and another house in Oxford Street, and land in Hensington were purchased.[38] The rental of 1609 shows that the town managed them for the schoolmaster's income and housing. Another part of the bequest seen in the accounts, the Doleman or Dolman annual payment for the schoolmaster, was collected twice a year as an £8 rent charge from Frethorns manor in Childrey, near Wantage (Berks.). It came from the final settlement made in 1599 by John Doleman, who had married Richard Cornwell's widow, Mary. He died in 1607 and it was his son, Thomas (d. 1649), who paid it in these accounts.[39] The £50, already noticed as lent out, to Sir Henry Lee and then to the Rayers until 1640, was another part of the settlement, providing part of the schoolmaster's salary. In 1616 a cousin of Cornwell's, Thomas Fletcher, also a London skinner and member of a Woodstock family, left £4 to the schoolmaster out of his £12 bequest to the town, money which it was finally agreed in 1623 should be paid by the Skinners' Company of London at their hall.[40] It does not appear in the accounts until 1642 when the town paid it because it could not be obtained from London, but from 1645 it occurs regularly in the receipts and disbursements. The schoolmaster's salary was covered by the bequests, but the corporation would have had to pay some money from its own funds for the maintenance of the schoolbuildings, which would only partially be met by the 6s 8d quit rent they received from the White Hart. It was much the same situation as in the 19th century when it was felt that not enough return was gained from the property.[41]

The town's poor often received bequests in local wills of bread and money which rarely appear in the town accounts, because they were distributed at the funeral,[42] but there were some long-term gifts. The most regular appearing in the accounts was from 1629, when the town received £5 for the poor of the almshouse from the town clerk's father, Edmond Hiorne senior, yeoman; the borough undertook to pay 8s a year to the almshouse poor.[43] The later accounts show the receipt and expenditure of the £4 given to the poor at the five sermons which Thomas Fletcher endowed in 1616, as well as the £4 for the preachers. Then there was the charity of dole money given in his life-time by Sir Thomas Spencer (d. 1622) of Yarnton, and eventually paid also by his heirs. Neither of those latter two bequests, however, were distributed through these accounts until the mid 1640s. Two other bequests from men born in Woodstock likewise came into the later accounts: John Chadwell's gift of £20 in 1638, of which £10 was held by the town and the interest used for the poor, appeared in 1639 and 1640; and Henry Hopkins's bequest, made in 1643, of £5 for bread to be distributed every Good Friday.[44]

Loan money to help young tradesmen and artisans was another form of legacy favoured in towns to encourage the industrious. In 1600 Dr. John Case had left £40 to be lent to four tradesmen, and although the loans were not accounted for by the chamberlains he is referred to in 1621. Richard Nash left £100 in 1637 for a Whitsuntide sermon and loans to eight burgesses for six-year terms, but because of the war and the investment terms notice of the loans only came into the receipts in 1648. Capt. Thomas Warburton's £100, bequeathed for three-year loans to burgesses in 1641, likewise appeared in the 1647 account.

After the Reformation townsfolk retained their concern for their own commemoration and for the upkeep of the fabric and services of Woodstock chapel. The town rented the churchyard from the rector of Bladon, and in 1637 expressed due gratitude to Sir Gerard Fleetwood for his lady's gift of a velvet cushion and a pulpit cloth. Money bequeathed to the chapel was, when managed by the mayor and corporation, noted by the chamberlains or at audit. The provision of extra sermons was a typical 17th-century concern shared by Woodstock residents. The first two accounts below detail money spent on sermons endowed by Margery Nurse, widow of a former chamberlain. Longer-term endowments of annual sermons were made by two former mayors, William Meatcalfe in 1608 and Thomas Browne in 1621, as well as by Thomas Fletcher in 1616, and by Richard Nash of Old Woodstock in 1637.

Throughout most of the period charity money was only a minor part of the revenues, but it became more valuable to the town when it was trying to restore the revenues in the late 1640s. The Civil War was disastrous for town finances, though Woodstock seems to have managed better than Banbury,[45] and kept accounts going throughout the worst years,

1643–6. In 1643, however, the receipts as a whole were down by a quarter and rents were in arrears. In 1644 only a third of the revenues received in the pre-war period were collected and many disbursements were not made. This was shown up in 1646 when the fee farm and quit rents for the previous two years were paid and five years' back payment to the recorder, William Lenthall. The town was still chasing rent arrears in the last years of the decade but had restored much of the traditional finance by 1650. In that year the town showed a healthy receipt total of £105, though receipts from stallages and tolls were low and a third of the revenue came from the charity money passing through the accounts.

It is from the way the chamberlains and other officers spent the money that we learn most about the life of Woodstock and the corporation's dealings with local inhabitants, the wider community of the county, and the government of the realm. Like every other town the mayor and officers had to keep affairs running smoothly for themselves and to meet government demands. The upkeep of town property was a prime charge and the sections on town repairs tell us not only about the guild or town hall and the town clerk's office, but also about the little house, which had a bed in it and seems to have served as a town prison, in addition to the cage, which is frequently mentioned. The cucking stool and the stocks were in use and had to be mended. The sergeant had his chains and whipping post. The town paid for cleaning the bays or sluices at the mill, as well as for the upkeep of the roads. Generally the chamberlains dealt directly with the workmen for the particular task, as the long lists of day payments at the standard 17th-century rate of 10d or 12d a day show. For some jobs they had annual contracts, as with the town surveyors, or with Thomas Screevin for the repair of the glass in the civic buildings, or with Edward Longe for care of the clock. Salaries, stipends, gifts and entertainment costs, particularly for wine, took up a high proportion of the income but this was on a par with other towns. They would undoubtedly have defended this expenditure as proper and necessary for the dignity of the town and the defence and maintenance of privileges which helped its economic survival. Payments were made for law suits and to central government officials when the council was defending the town's chartered rights and liberties or pursuing the Spencers for the dole money. Modern historians see the maintenance of social harmony behind the payments for the maypole and in the observance of what has been called the 'Protestant Calendar', with celebrations on November 5, and on the king's accession and at royal births and weddings.[46] There was also the fasting enjoined by both king and parliament in times of distress that became more frequent than rejoicings as the period wore on.

Through the entries we see the many visits which made the town a social centre, among them the arrivals of the king and his household, tax commissioners, justices, recruiting officers, and preachers. In other entries the social conscience of the 17th century as well as its problems is apparent in the money spent on more unwelcome visitors, the vagabond poor and 'travellers'. We read of Bohemian soldiers, of Irish poor gentlefolk, of a blackamoor wench, of a man whose tongue had been cut out by the Turks, and of other genuine and rogue poor. Maimed soldiers frequently passed through and were given money by the borough officers, who also paid to the high constable's fund for them. Money was sent for the maintenance of the Marshalsea, the debtors' prison in London, and for poor prisoners in Oxford castle. The town was tender of its own poor, and names of those in the almshouse become familiar as they are tended in sickness or given shrouds at death. A few bastard children regularly appear, in the care of locals or occasionally in the almshouse. The school was an important responsibility. There is nothing in these accounts about teaching in the school, but there is a great deal of information about the hiring of schoolmasters and the upkeep of the school and the master's house. Through the school the town got not only education for its children but also a useful member of the community in the person of the schoolmaster. Symon James, the master up to 1632, was particularly active. He was admitted a freeman of the borough in 1605, and appointed schoolmaster and made a member of the common council in 1608. He was also the licensed attorney in the borough court, and was witness and overseer of many local wills and inventories. He was a member of the governing circle, not only through his work but also through his family, by which he was related, probably through his wife Elizabeth,[47] to Edmond Hiorne the town clerk. His connexions were typical of that inner circle of borough families whose members featured in positions of authority in these accounts.

Throughout the accounts there is evidence of the pressure of the central government on the provinces. Proclamations,[48] with the cherished views of the king on tobacco, fasting, alehouses, schemes for wool and the merchant adventurers, for gold and trade and much more, came into the town in James's reign, followed by yet more, and the books of orders and other measures, from Charles I. In the 1630s Laud's influence with the king stopped the town's combination lectures. There were numerous demands for money to finance the Stuarts' wars and projects, bringing collectors down to the town and creating correspondence with the Privy Council. There were payments for parliamentary elections. Eventually the town was dragged into the Civil War as a royal garrison, with devastating consequences for its economy and well-being.   The accounts then become testimony to the determined effort to keep Woodstock functioning amid its traumas: the problems of collecting the income and paying stipends and dues, the attacks by contending forces, the presence of hundreds of soldiers, the care of the sick and wounded, the adjustment to parliamentary rule and taxation.   The final impression is of the council's success in managing its affairs so that by 1650 it was clear that the borough and its finances would survive the crisis.

[1] B 83/1, p. 102. It was audited in 1519, hence Ballard's date of 1519: A. Ballard, *Chronicle of Royal Borough of Woodstock* (Oxf. 1896), 20.

[2] *Cal. Charter R.*1427–1516, 125–7. For a full discussion of the charter see *V.C.H. Oxon.* xii. 372 sqq.

[3] *Cal. Pat.* 1452–61, 51; *Valor Ecclesiasticus Temp. Hen. VIII* (Record Commission 1810–34), ii. 185; B 83/1, pp. 3–4; cf. *V.C.H. Oxon.* xii. 406, 410. Woodstock is a chapelry of Bladon: *V.C.H. Oxon.* xii. 406.

[4] *Some Oxon. Wills*, ed. J. Weaver and A. Beardwood (O.R.S. xxxix), 37–38.

[5] e.g. B 81, f. 6v, mayors discharged in 1573 for fair, stallage, and fee farm.

[6] e.g. ibid. ff. 1v, 3r (chantry lands).

[7] *Chantry Certificates and Edwardian Inventories of Church Goods*, ed. Rose Graham (O.R.S. i), 23; *Cal. Pat.* 1563–6, 440; *V.C.H. Oxon.* xii. 410.

[8] *Cal. Pat.* 1563–6, 440. Note that below the fairs are only warded for one day, presumably through lack of trade.

[9] Act 18 Eliz. 1, c.21.

[10] The new site has been identified as Nos. 76–8 Oxford St.: *V.C.H. Oxon.* xii. 346, 420.

[11] See Ballard, *Woodstock*, 43–59, for details of the documents; and *V.C.H. Oxon.* xii. 374.

[12] B 81, *passim*; *Rep. Commissioners on Municipal Corpns.*, H.C. 116, App. 1, p. 141 (1835), xxiii.

[13] See appendix below for biogs.

[14] B 83/1, p. 35.

[15] Ibid., p. 115; *V.C.H. Oxon.* xii. 382.

[16] B 83/1, p. 91; and see appendix, biogs.

[17] *Rep. Com. Mun. Corpns.* (1835), pp. 141–2.

[18] B 81, f. 22v; O.R.O., Woodstock churchwardens' accounts, p. 6.

[19] *Journals of House of Commons*, ii. 792; B 81, f. 44r; O.R.O., MS. Wills Oxon. 33/2/28. His will does not say which Fleetwood his dau. married. For the Croke episode see notes to the 1650 account below.

[20] See appendix, biogs.

[21] B 81, f. 44r; B 76/1, ff. 1–6v.

[22] See appendix, biogs.

[23] *V.C.H. Oxon.* xii. 353.

[24] See appendix, biogs.

[25] See below, 1631 n. 6; 1632 n. 5.

[26] B 83, p. 93. For the leet courts see B 77/2; 78/2.

[27] B 96, ff. 9sqq.

[28] *First Ledger Book of High Wycombe, 1475–1734*, ed. R. W. Greaves (Bucks. Rec. Soc. 1956), xiii.

[29] He witnessed a local will in that year: MS. Wills Oxon. 180, f. 182v. This is an earlier ref. to a recorder than noted in *V.C.H. Oxon.* xii. 383. Windsor gained its first charter in 1277, but was not formally incorporated until 1466, later than Woodstock. For this and Windsor's attempts to secure a recorder see *First Hall Book of…New Windsor 1653 to 1725*, ed. S. Bond (Windsor Borough Hist. Recs. 1968), xiv.

[30] See below in 1621 for a commission; and *Rep. Com. Mun. Corpns.* (1835), p. 141.

[31] See below, 1609 n. 29.

[32] See V. Rowe, 'Influence of Earls of Pembroke on Parl. Elections, 1625–41', *E.H.R.* (1935), 242, 250; M. F. Keeler, *The Long Parl. 1640–1641*, (Philadelphia 1954), 60.

[33] See below; E. Marshall, *Early Hist. of Woodstock Manor and Environs* (Oxf. 1873), 187–8, citing the archdeacon's court recs.

[34] *Rep. Com. Mun. Corpns.* (1835), p. 143.

[35] See above; O.R.O., Woodstock churchwardens' accts.

[36] *Rep. Com. Mun. Corpns. (1835)*, p. 143.

[37] MS. Wills Oxon. 179, f. 96v; 180, f. 122v.

[38] For the arrangements and purchases see his will in P.R.O., PROB 11/ 29 Brudenell; and Bodl. Lib. made-up vol. for Oxon. of *Reps. of Commissioners Appointed...to Inquire Concerning Charities and Educ. of Poor...1815–39, vol. xxvi*, 489–90. The property is identified as Nos. 8–12 Oxford St. in *V.C.H. Oxon.* xii. 343, 416.

[39] *Rep. Com. Char.* 490. John Doleman inherited the manor from his father Thos. (d. 1575), a wealthy clothier of Newbury. His son Thos. (d. 1649) sold it in 1646 but apparently was held responsible for the rent charge to the end of these accts.: *V.C.H. Berks.* iv. 89, 274; P.R.O., PROB 11/47 Pyckering; *Berks. Wills* (Index Lib. viii, Brit. Rec. Soc. 1893).

[40] *Rep. Com. Char.* 491, 494.

[41] *Ibid.* 491.

[42] They can be traced through Oxon. wills. There is a note of the receipt by the council of two such bequests in 1607 in B 81, f. 21v.

[43] See appendix, biogs. His will is in P.R.O., PROB 11/156, f. 86, and there is an inventory for his Great Tew personal property only in MS. Wills Oxon. 33/2/28. His eldest son was John, a black-smith of New Woodstock.

[44] See below under appropriate year for refs. for these and following bequests; and Padgetts Book (B 97), with record of charity bequests.

[45] See *Banbury Corporation Recs.: Tudor and Stuart*, ed. J.W.S. Gibson and E.R.C. Brinkworth (Banbury Hist. Soc. xv, 1977).

[46] See D. Cressey, 'Protestant Calendar and Vocabulary of Celebration in Early Mod. Eng.', *Jnl. Brit. Studies* 1990, 31 sqq.

[47] Possibly the dau. of Edm. Hiorne sen.: see his will above.

[48] They have been checked against listings in *Stuart Royal Proclamations*, i, ed. J.F. Larkin and P.L. Hughes (Oxf. 1973); ibid. ii, ed. J.F. Larkin (Oxf. 1983).

EDITORIAL NOTE

Punctuation and capitalization have been modernized, as has the orthography of the letters c and t, i and j, u and v, which have also been given their modern placings. Side headings have been transferred to the body of the text, and other material in the margins has been indicated as [marginated] in the accounts. Sums have been tabulated on the right-hand side, a practice that sometimes occurs in the original and that makes for easier reading. Ease of use has also determined the employment of bold-face type for headings and of italic for sub-headings.

The text contains all entries found in the manuscript, but the words 'item', 'received', and 'paid' are omitted where they can be inferred from the context. The year, which is often found in entries, has also been omitted except where there is a risk of ambiguity.

Some entries have been abbreviated. The headings, after the first one, have been shortened to the date of the account and the names of the chamberlains. Since the mayor's name is given only occasionally in the heading it has been omitted here but can be found in the appendix of office-holders. The recurring payments for stipends are also shortened, but they are given in full at the first occurrence or when there is any alteration. Dates have been abbreviated.

Latin days and months have been translated into English, as occasionally happens in the original. Modern spelling is used to distinguish them from those in which the clerk used contemporary spelling. Latin words such as *vidue* for 'widdowe', as used in the English rendering in the accounts, have also been translated.

Common abbreviations and personal names have been extended, except in the appendices. The extension of some commonly used words in the accounts proved more difficult, as in the case of the sum total at the end of each account, which might be 'summa totalis', 'summe totale', or, as adopted here, 'summ totall'. The abbreviation 'pd' has been given the common extension 'paied'. *li* has been altered to £ or lb throughout. The contemporary usage of 'Oxon' for Oxford has been retained.

The first rental in the book (ff. 19r–23v) was heavily altered and is not easy to present in transcript. The information has therefore been abstracted and laid out in tabular form so as to show the sequence of tenants.

The usual editorial conventions such as square brackets for editorial insertions have been observed.

MANUSCRIPT SOURCES USED IN THIS EDITION

In the borough muniments in Woodstock town hall

B 7/19   rental, 1652
B 77/2   court book, 1618–35
B 78/1   court book, 1588–95
B 78/2   court book, 1607–13
B 78/3   court book, 1613–22
B 79   chamberlains' book, 1608–50
B 81   ledger or audit book, 1534–1812
B 82   council bye-laws, 1580
B 83/1   miscellaneous Woodstock documents, including earliest rental and chamberlains' account
B 96   miscellaneous Woodstock documents, including rental and lists of inhabitants
B 97   Padgetts book: records of charity donations
Deeds   references as given in footnotes: 13(2)/7 (deed); 31/11 (fine); 44/3/1 (deed)

In the Oxfordshire Archives (O.R.O.), County Hall, Oxford

Clerus   Canon Oldfield's index to the Oxfordshire clergy (previously in the Bodleian Library)
MS. Wills Oxon.   Wills and inventories of the Oxford diocese
Woodstock churchwardens' accounts, 1611–1783

In the Public Record Office (P.R.O.), London

PROB 11   registered copies of Prerogative Court of Canterbury wills (P.C.C.)

BURGUS NOVE WOODSTOCK in Com' Oxon'
A true note of such money as John Glover and Richard Meades receaved into there handes as chamberlains of the said boughrough from the xvjth day of December Anno Domini 1608 untill the accompte of the said boughrough vizt the xxith daye of December Anno Domini 1609[1]

	£	s	d
[Marginated] Not receaved[2]			
Delivered to them at the accompte one bonde of Roberte Paynes of Cassington for	0	50	0
One bonde of Thomas Gee for	0	10	0
One bond of William Butterfeildes for	0	40	0
One bond of Edward Longes. [Marginated] Received 20s.	0	40	0
[Marginated] Received			
One bond of Roberte Symons and John Slatter for	0	52	6
There is one clocke [cloak] taken from the Egiptians delivered to them and allso 2 silver ringes gilte, which are to be sould.			
To them in reddy mony at the last accompte	0	20	0
[Marginated] Not receaved. They are to receave			
Of Thomas Screeven for extreates[3]	0	5	0
Of Mistris Phillipps for the rent of her house	0	3	0
Of Mr Whitton for his house	0	0	15½
Of John Powell for his admission	0	20	0
Of Drewe [John deleted] Gregorye for his admission	0	40	0
Of William Meatcalfe which his father gave to the towne[4]	0	40	0
[Marginated] Received			
23 January 1608[/9] for the admission of Henry Ledbrock carrier	0	30	0
4 February one cloake supposed to be Mr Farrers of Oxon'[5]	0	0	0
Of Thomas Bradford a prisoner as money stolen from Richard Durrand a player to the Lord Chandoes[6]	0	7	0
For William Raunson and Randall Richardsons admissions	0	3	4
Of Joseph Harris for a little mare with bridle and sadle which was Water Howells mare[7]	0	20	0
Of Thomas Williams one other mare of his	3	6	8
[f. 1v] For Nathaniell Nobles seale of his fine,[8]	0	4	0
At Whitsontide as mony then gotten	7	18	0
Of Mr Doleman	8	0	0

Of Edward Long cryer for the tole of the beafe and sheepe soulde in the markett since the last accompte as appeereth by his booke	3	0	11
Of George Noble for the Kinges parte upon an information[9]	0	2	6
Of William Kinge for the like	0	2	0
Of Mr Maior for a peece of tymber brought to the towne at Whittsontide	0	10	0
Of the serjant for stalladge	8	8	7
Upon the rentrole for the rentes of the towne	27	2	$7^1/_4$
For a cloke of the Egiptians	0	10	0
As mony paied Bell more than bargained	0	5	0
Summ totall of the receiptes [£67 18s 1d deleted]	67	3	1
Leied out for the towne	61	4	$10^1/_2$
Remayninge to the towne	5	18	$3^1/_2$
They paied	0	18	$3^1/_2$
So leaft in theire handes	5	0	0

[f. 2r] Fellons goodes remay[ning]
John Glover hath one cloke and 2 ringes one platter and Walter Howelles sworde and the black booke.
Mr Maior hath one redd sadle and a bridle. Edward Rudgate[10] one payer of shewes, 1 pistoll, 3 yeardes and halfe a quarter of russett fustian, 3 dozen of buttons, 3 skeynes of silke, one pere of hangers, with a bodkine, one halter, 2s in mony taken of one Vahan[11] [Line of cancellation through above entries]
Joseph Harris hath certene pewter platters and 3s.

The accompt 21 December 1609

John Glover and Richard Meades elected chamberlains and then delivered to them	5	0	0
One bonde of Roberte Paynes for	0	50	0
One bonde of Thomas Gees for	0	10	0
One bonde of William Butterfildes for	0	40	0
One bonde of Edward Longes for	0	20	0
They are to receave of Thomas Screevin for extreat	0	5	0
Of Mistris Phillipps for rentes	0	4	6
Of Mr Whitton for rent lately behinde	0	2	7
Of John [Roger deleted] Powell for his admission	0	10	0
Of Drewe Gregory for his admission	0	40	0
Of Widdowe Tanner for her rent	0	6	8

Debts due from the towne[12]

To Mr Browne and his Lady Day rent paied	0	20	0
Richard Meade	0	20	0
William Ball	0	20	0
John Woodrooffe	0	10	0
John Norman	0	10	0
To Robert Spitle	0	2	6

[f. 2v] [blank]

[f. 3r] The accompte of John Glover and Richard Meades chamberlaines of the said boughrough for all such moneys as they have leied out for the said boughrough from the xvjth daye of December Anno Domini 1608 untill the xxith day of December Anno Domini 1609

2 January paied to Roberte Bruce as mony appoynted to be payed him at the last accompte	0	4	0
10 January for the inrolinge the indenture of bargaine and sale for Mr Brownes[13] house to the clarke of the peace for this cowntie of Oxon	0	5	0
15 March for 2 inditmentes versus Bradford and Bridges[14]	0	3	0 .
For a lock for the office dore	0	4	0
21 December 1608 to Seare for mending of Charles Barneshewes shewes	0	0	5
For a sugar loffe 9s 6d and a cake 9s sent to Sir Henry Lee	0	18	6
For mending the churchporch	0	0	12
Geiven to 2 souldiers by Mr Maiors appoyntment	0	0	12
23 January for mending the schoolehouse and penniles bench[15] with new crestes	0	0	12
For mending a locke at the almshouse	0	0	3
To Edward Rudgate for expences for dyett and for sending 2 prisoners to Oxford, vizt Bridges and Bradforde	0	8	3
[an item of 2s deleted]			
For mending the cooking stoole	0	0	6
4 February paied Mr Mayor as geiven to 4 souldiers	0	0	12
Sent Mr Scott the preacher a quarte of sacke	0	0	12
11 March. [Deleted] Robert Robinson for mending the leades of the crosse with soder 6s 6d and paynes about same worke For soder 6s 6d, wood 2s 6d and workemanshipp about the mendinge of the leades of the highe crosse 2s	0	11	0
Paied to Robinson the ploomer for his wages for this yeere ending at Michaellmas 1609	0	5	0
10 March to Mr Mayor for Mr Recorders dinner and certeine neighbours to beare him company, being 8 in number	0	16	1
For wine at the same dinner	0	2	3

[f. 3v] For wyne sent to John Raunson his house for his son at his sermon	0	0	21
19 March geiven to one Thomas Lewes upon a breefe by Mr Maiors appoyntment	0	0	12
For nayles to mende the crosse	0	0	4
24 March to the ringers for ringing on the Kinges hollyday[16]	0	4	0
For iron worke about the office dore	0	2	1
To Mr Wattson for Mr Warde his paynes about the armour	0	2	0
6 April to Mr Thomas Meatcalfe for the bringing of the £4 from Mr Doleman due at Our Lady Day	0	2	0
5 April for a potle of sack and a pottle of clarrett wine geiven to the commissioners for the Prince his ayde[17]	0	3	6
For suger then to that purpose	0	0	6
7 April to Thomas Bradshewe maior for his fee due at Our Lady Day 1609	5	0	0
12 April for Mr Recorders supper cominge to the sessions 10s and for his horsemeate then 5s 3d	0	15	3
To Mr Recorders men for ale then	0	0	6
Geiven to Mr Recorder in wyne then a potle of sacke and a potle of clarrett	0	3	6
Geiven to Mr Recorder then for his paynes	0	10	0
12 April paied Mr James to more then his ould wages due at Michaelmas[18]	0	26	8
20 April to Sir Henry Lee, the lord cheife barron, and other justices at the seasinge of the subsidy for wine and sugar[19]	0	4	6
Last day of April for wine and sugar geiven to Sir Tayler for preaching	0	2	1
2 May to the churchwardens for their charge at Wittny, John Bradshawe and Thomas Williams[20]	0	3	4
7 May to Mr Garnons of Christ Church for preaching twice in one daye in wyne and sugar	0	0	13
For the chardge of the house built at the almeshouse for Walkers people, with the fier wood and other necessaries besides meate and drink	4	11	11
26 May to Screevin for glasing worke donn about the schoole-house as appeareth upon his bill	0	3	1
16 June to Mr Feodary in comming to the town about the Princes ayde for wine and suger[21]	0	0	12
[f. 4r] To Mr Taylor for his second sermon heere in wine and suger	0	2	2
18 June wine and suger to twoe preachers in one daye	0	3	6
23 June to the Queenes players in rewarde	0	5	0
2 July paied for wine and suger for one preacher	0	0	13
8 July geiven to 2 cripples by Mr Brownes appoyntment	0	0	8

Paied for sending Debanck and Howell to the goale more then receaved[22]	0	0	3
26 July for wine when Mr John Jeames preached	0	2	0
For wine at his seconde sermon	0	0	20
For ringinge upon St Jeames daye	0	4	0
For ringinge 5 August	0	4	0
To a preacher that supped at Mr Brownes	0	0	6
8 August to 2 souldiers that were stayed, in reward	0	0	16
12 August to Bell of Abington for paynting the church	6	10	0
To Pulchoe for 2 daies worke in poynting the church windowes and for the lyme and heare	0	3	0
1 September delivered to Mr Maior 4s which he paied to Goffe to goe to Clifton upon Dunsmore	0	4	0
For a twiste for the office cheste	0	0	5
5 August to William Hickes for worke donn about the bells	0	0	12
8 September for 2 daies worke, lyme, heare and crestes bestowed upon the penniles bench	0	4	8
23 September for wine to Mr Odill at his sermon for the widdowe Nursse[23]	0	0	12
26 September for a bell rope for the saunctbell	0	0	18
2 October for Goffe goeing to Dunsmore the second time	0	3	0
For a messenger sent to Winchcombe	0	2	0
4 October for a new scabbard and clensing Howells sworde	0	0	14
8 October to Richard Shad for fetching Mr Dolemans mony	0	2	6
To Mr Maior for his fee	5	0	0
To the shreife for the feefarme and the acquittance	0	53	8
October to Mr Jeams towardes his wadges	0	26	8
[f. 4v] 14 October paied for wine for a preacher	0	0	12
For wine sent for to Mr Maior	0	0	12
20 October 20 bushells of lyme for the guild hall	0	13	4
6 bushells of heare for the same	0	3	0
To Pulchoe for 6 dayes work for plausteringe	0	6	2
3 November to Turner 2 daies for himselfe and boy	0	3	0
To Corbott for his yeers wadges then ended for mending the clock	0	6	0
For wyer and oile about the clock	0	0	4
Paied the chantery rent at Michaelmas	5	6	8
For the acquittance	0	0	12
Mr Recorder his fee due at Michaelmas	3	6	8
For ringing on 5 November	0	4	0
For mending the flud gate at the bayes	0	2	0
17 November clarke of the markettes dinner and wine[24]	0	5	4
Geiven to him in rewarde	0	6	8
17 November a lock for towne cheste for towne clark	0	3	0

For a brasen powndwaite	0	0	10
To the towneclark for 2 inditementes at Oxon' at the quartersessions when Debanck was executed	0	3	0
[Deleted] For a lock for the office dore	0	4	0
For an inditment and expences leid out at Oxon' against him that stole Mr Farrers clocke [cloak]	0	3	0
To John George of Ledwell which our towneclarke promised him upon the apprehension of Debank and Howell[25]	0	20	0
22 November to Robinson the ploomer for his halfe yeers wadges for the leades of the church	0	2	6
To Thomas Screevin for glasing and sodering worke donn in the church and at the guild hall	0	9	4
For wine to Mr Edward Jeames when he preached	0	0	12
Paied 6d a weeke for 54 weekes ending upon Tewsday 19 December 1609 for the nursinge of Nicholas Glovers base childe[26]	0	27	0
To Turner for plaustering at the hall	0	0	18
20 November geiven to Bell the painter in earnest for paintinge the tymber work about the hall for 15s	0	0	18
17 November paied Edmond Hiorne towneclark for his fee due at Michaelmas	0	40	0
To the churchmen of Bladon theire composition mony[27]	0	3	0
To Bell the painter for paynting and coolleriing the new building at the hall	3	0	0
[Marginated subtotal]	56	5	7

[f. 5r] 17 December 1609 for wine for Mr Odill preachinge for the widowe Nurss	0	0	12
To Mr Maior the same day as mony geiven by him to diverse poore souldiers and other poore people	0	11	6
To Edmond Hiorne as mony which he paied for the Princes ayde more then he receaved	0	5	2
To Longe for his wadges and other things which he hath leied out for the towne as in his bill[28]	0	17	2
For allowances to be deducted out of the rent role, for widdowe Tanners house 6s 8d, for Mr Whittons house 15¹/₂d, for Mr Browns house 6d, for Mistris Leakes pales 12d	0	9	5¹/₂
To Edmond Hiorne towneclark for the keeping of the chamberlaines accomptes and the writing of them	0	5	0
For 4 pownde of grease for the bells for this laste yeere	0	0	16
For clensing the highwayes at the bayes	0	0	12
18 December 1609 to Mr Undershreive his fee upon the electing of Mr Recorder for our burgess for the Parliament[29]	0	6	8
To Mr Maior his dinner and his mannse about the same business	0	12	6

To Mr Rayer and myselfe for the chardge of Walkers house more than I and he receaved of the constables	0	19	2¹/₂
To be allowed unto me out of the rent role for Mistris Phillipps her house	0	0	18
Paied to Mr Rayer for wine for the communicates unpaied by Mr Noble[30]	0	4	1¹/₂
For mending the hammer of the clock 6d, for mending the holes in the church upon the graves 8d	0	0	14
For one newe payre of guyes	0	2	6
[Marginated subtotal]	4	16	5¹/₂
[Marginated] Summ totall [corrected in ms. from £61 2s ¹/₂d]	61	0	14¹/₂
[Marginated] Summ	61	4	10¹/₂

[f. 5v] Allowaunces deducted

Due out of widdowe Tanner her rent	0	6	8
Out of Mr Whittons greate house	0	0	15¹/₂
Out of Mr Brownes dwelling house	0	0	6
For mistris Leakes pales at her dore	0	0	12

[1] The full heading. For this edition the headings in subsequent accts. are shortened.

[2] Most bonds and debts are carried over from earlier years, i.e. Gee and Gregory occur 1605; Butterfeild 1606; Slatter and Symons of Bladon, and Paynes 1607; Powell's and Longe's admissions, Phillips's rent and the Egyptian, i.e. gipsy, goods 1608: B 81, ff. 21r–3v. For the resolution of problems over the Whittons' rent, which go back to 1596 and continued to 1626, see ibid. f. 13r, and below in 1626. The tenant here was Hen. Whitton: below, rental.

[3] Estreats. Described Dec. 1608 as amercements by his father Blith's appointment, presumably his father-in-law and perhaps the Thos. Blith listed as rent payer 1598: B 81, f. 23v and B 96. This may link Screeven, founder of a firm of Oxfordshire glaziers, with John Blithe (d. 1612), Oxf. pewterer: MS. Wills Oxon. 4/2/58; and explain why he was buying pewter in 1610, below.

[4] See P.C.C. PROB 11/111, f. 20. The father, Wm. Meatcalfe, mayor, died in office in 1608: see appendix, biogs.

[5] John Farrer of New Inn, Oxf.: B 78/2, f. 65r, 3 Feb. 1608/9. The cloak was obtained by false pretences by his former servant, Wm. Bridges of Oxf., labourer, for whom see below.

[6] Thos. Bradford of Ludlow (Salop.), sawyer and former servant of the Players' Company 'coming to Buck towne', was arrested when he fled back to Woodstock after the theft, which took place at the Bell: ibid. f. 66r, 4 Feb. 1608/9. 'Lord Chandoes': Grey Bridges, Lord Chandos of Sudeley.

[7] Wal. Howell of Winchcombe (Glos.), butcher, taken for horse theft: B 78/2, f. 84v, 23 July 1609. He sold the horse to John George of Ledwell, smith, for £2.

[8] See B 78/2, 24 Apr. for the final concord for two dwellings.

[9] Criminal suits were often initiated on the information of a common informer, who sued on behalf of the king as well as himself: see G. Jacob, *Law Dictionary* (1782). For Noble's subsequent career on the council, see appendix, biogs.

[10] Edw. or Edm. Rudgate (d. 1617), constable and later sergeant at the mace: see appendix, biogs.

[11] Fras. Vahan of Presteigne (Salop.), 'a rogue': B 78/2, 6 Sept. 1609.

[12] In 1603 the town borrowed £21 10s from these and other townsmen: B 81, f. 19v. The debts were not completely repaid until 1615: see below.

[13] Ald. Thos. Browne (d. 1621). For deeds of surrender of his house at the park gate to the use of the town see B 81, ff. 22v–4v; for disputes see below 1612–13.

[14] See above, nn. 5, 6.

[15] The schoolhouse was in the church. Penniless bench appears below in 1631 among guildhall

expenses; in other towns it was often outside the church as at St. Martin's, Carfax, Oxf.
[16] Anniversary of accession of Jas. I.
[17] A feudal aid for knighting the king's eldest son, Prince Hen.: *Cal.S.P.Dom.* 1603–10, 494. It and the aid below in 1612 were the first requested since Hen. VII's reign.
[18] In Sept. 1608 it was agreed he was to be paid £2 next Michaelmas and £10 yearly for four years from 25 March next, and then was to have the house and garden he dwelt in and £14 a year: B 81, f. 23r. See also above, Intro.
[19] Collection of subsidies granted by Parl. in 1606 was still proceeding : *Cal. S.P.Dom.* 1603–10, 305, 504. Sir Hen. Lee (d. 1611): high steward of the borough and lieut. of the manor. Lord Chief Baron of the Exchequer: Sir Lawr. Tanfield, Lee's nephew by marriage, M.P. for the borough 1584–1601, and recorder by 1598: *Hist. of Parl.: House of Commons, 1558–1603*, ed. P.W. Hasler (London 1981), i. 227; iii. 475–6; *V.C.H. Oxon.* xii. 383.
[20] The bishop's visitation was held alternately at Witney and Woodstock: ex inf. Dr. D. M. Barratt.
[21] Mr. Feodary: officer of Court of Wards and Liveries, responsible for valuing Crown tenures and deciding liability for payment of feudal aid for the prince's knighting: Jacob, *Law Dictionary*.
[22] Rob. Debanck *alias* Johnson: taken in possession of a stolen horse and lock-picking instruments: B 78/2, f. 84r, 23 July 1609. For Howell see above. Costs below of going to Clifton upon Dunsmore (Warws.) and Winchcombe relate to these cases.
[23] Margery Nurse (d. 1609) left money for four sermons: MS. Wills Oxon. 47/2/2.
[24] The royal clerk who controlled markets while the royal court was there and also came later in the year to check weights, measures, and prices: *Stuart Proclams.*, i, no. 10, n. 1.
[25] See above, n. 7.
[26] John Turtle *alias* Glover, son of Marg. Turtle and Nic. Glover. For maintenance orders see B 78/2, e.g. 10 Dec. 1607, 17 Apr. 1608. For the child, eventually admitted to the almshouse, see below and index.
[27] Probably payment made for right to bury in the cemetery attached to Woodstock chapel: see below in 1611.
[28] Edw. Longe, lastmaker: see appendix, biogs.
[29] Sir Jas. Whitelocke (d. 1632), recorder of Woodstock 1606–21, was elected M.P. 6 Dec. 1609 since 'it was ever usual with them to elect thear recorders burgeses': Whitelocke, *Liber Familicus*, ed. J. Bruce (Camden Soc. 1858), 16, 19. Sir Thos. Spencer (d. 1622) of Yarnton, was the other member: W.R.J. Williams, *Parl. Hist. County of Oxf.* (Brecknock 1899, 198–9).
[30] Ant. Noble, curate: see appendix, biogs.

[f. 6r] 21 December 1609 to 22 December 1610, John Glover and Richard Meade, chamberlaines

[Receipts]	£	s	d
Delivered to them in reddy mony at the last accompte 21 December 1609	5	0	0
One bonde of Roberte Paynes for	0	50	0
One bonde of Thomas Gees for	0	10	0
One bonde of William Butterfeildes for 40s [Marginated] Received 11s, remains	0	29	0
One bonde of Edward Longes for	0	20	0
For William Meatcalfe his fyne	0	4	0

Monyes to be receaved without bonde

Of Thomas Screevin for extreat	0	5	0
Of Mistris Phillipps for rent	0	4	6
Of Mr Whitton for rent lately behinde	0	2	7
Of John Powell for his admission	0	10	0
Of Drewe Gregory for his admission	0	40	0
Of Widdowe Tanner for the rent of her house	0	6	8

Debtes owinge by the towne

Due to Mr Alderman Browne besides his rent paied for his meade at Our Lady Day next	0	20	0
Richard Meade	0	20	0
William Ball	0	20	0
John Woodrooffe	0	10	0
John Norman	0	10	0
Robert Spittle	0	2	6

Money receaved by the chamberlaines to be accompted for

At the accompte in redy mony delivered to them	5	0	0
William Meatcalfes seale for his fine[1]	0	4	0
Of one Browne for drunckennes[2]	0	3	4
Mony gotten at Whittsontide	6	13	4
For George Noble and Thomas Bruce theire admission 3s 4d [each]	0	6	8
Of Mr Doleman for one yeeres anuytie at Michaelmas	8	0	0
Of Thomas Gee upon his bonde	0	10	0
Of Robert Ducock and John Doe for their admissions	0	38	0
Of William Butterfeild upon his bonde	0	11	0
Of Steephens the tayler for his admission[3]	0	10	0
Of Mr Whitton for his seale of his fyne	0	4	0
Of John Norman and Richard Reade for theire admissions [?each]	0	3	4
Of Robert Payne upon his bonde £4 12s whereof spent in chardges more then was allowed 17s 4d and the principale chardge was 24s 8d	0	50	0
[f. 6v] For nayles of he that sould pewter to Thomas Screevin[4]	0	0	22
For stallages	8	0	5
Of Longe for tole in the beafe and kett	0	49	8
Summ receaved[5]	64	16	0¼
Summ of that leyings out is	65	6	7½
So remayninge due to the chamberlains	0	10	7¼

[Signature of Edm. Hiorne]

22 December 1610 Joseph Harris and Thomas Meatcalfe are elected chamberlains

Debtes due to the towne

One bonde of William Butterfeildes for	0	29	0
Thomas Screvin for extreates. [Marginated] paied by extreat.	0	5	0
Mistris Phillipps for rentes behinde	0	4	6
Mr Whitton for rentes behinde	0	4	9
John Powell	0	10	0
Drue Gregory	0	40	0
Bryan Steephens	0	20	0

Debtes owing by the towne

To John Norman	0	10	0
To Robert Spittle. [Marginated] paied by extreat.	0	2	6
To John Glover. [Marginated] paied by extreat.	0	2	3
To pay Mr Browne 40s which he hath payed before hand at Our Lady Day next	0	0	0
To pay William Ball 28s 4d for his halfe yeeres rent at Our Lady Day next	0	0	0
To Joseph Harris[6]	0	12	5
[Marginated] Delivered to me	0	36	0
Delivered to Joseph Harris in reddy mony	0	46	0

[f. 7r] 22 December 1610 receaved upon extreates
Of Hed 12d, Widowe Spitle 2s, Abbott 2s, Bignill 2s 6d, Screvin 6s, [J. Harris deleted], Ed. Rudgate 18d, Henry Rudgate 18d, Edward Long 12d, Raph Durbridg – he oweth 14d, William Edwardes 18d, John Lowe [Long deleted] 4d, Joseph Harris 6d, John Norman 12d, William Meatcalfe 2s 6d, Mr Rayer 12d, William [Meatcalfe deleted] Bradshewe 8d, Thomas Williams 2s 4d, John Bradshewe 12d, Shad 3d, John Doe for Seare 2s, Richard Meades 20d, Jerome White 12d, Mr Bradshew 12d, John Ackly 12d, Mr Flye 2s 6d, John Tayler 8d, William Hickes 6d, Hugh Hamond 6d, Water Parker 6d, Godfery 6d. William Bradshewe receaved after of Farrmers which he paied to Joseph Harris 7s.

[f. 7v] [blank]

[f. 8r]   [Disbursements]

24 December 1609 to Mr Browne for timber bestowed upon the bayes and other ymplements for same	0	2	0
For wine to Mr John Raunson for 2 sermons	0	2	8
For one cake 9s and one sugerloffe 9s 10d sent to Sir Henry Lee at Christmas 1609	0	18	10
For one cake sent to Mr Thomas Spencer then	0	9	0
Rewardes geiven to souldiers 21 December to 24 February	0	4	6

WOODSTOCK CHAMBERLAINS' ACCOUNTS 11

For wine and ale at Mr Maiors at the eating of a taste [cake] at Christmas 1609	0	3	4
To Drewe for dressing of armour	0	3	0
Geiven in rewarde to Sir Henry Lees servantes upon Twelfe Day	0	22	0
To a preacher at Mr Maiors at Christmas 1609	0	0	10½
To William Hickes for mending the bells and the clock	0	0	6
For goodwife Crawlye for reliefe in sicknes	0	0	8
For wine and other expenses at Mr Maiors at Sir William Spencers funerall sermon[7]	0	3	0
For wine when Mr Oliver Witington preached	0	2	0
For oyle for the clock and bells	0	0	8
For wine to Mr Odill at widowe Nursses sermon	0	0	12
For making of 4 coates for Richard Coles children	0	2	0
For wine to Mr Scott at Mr Abrams sermon[8]	0	0	12
For makinge goodwife Toe her coate more then receaved	0	0	8
For a rope for the second bell	0	3	0
For ringers and oyle 24 March	0	4	4
For wine to the clarkes of the assise by Mr Towneclarke	0	0	14
For soder and workmanshipp upon the schoolehouse	0	2	10
To Robinson the ploomer for his wadges due 25 March	0	2	6
For wood for heating of irons	0	0	12
For sending for Mr Dolemans money on Our Lady Day	0	2	6
To Mr Thomas Bradshewe his fee due at Our Lady Day	5	0	0
To Hugh Corbott for a newe watch for the clock 12s and for his wadges due at Our Lady Day 2s 6d	0	14	6
For wine at Mr Bradshewe his dinner at Our Lady Day	0	5	9
For wine at Mr Grigsons sermon	0	3	0
For wine at Mr Maiors on Easter Day	0	3	0
For wine and suger for Sir Henry Lee and the lord cheife baron for subsidy[9]	0	4	0
[Marginated subtotal]	11	5	3½
[f. 8v] To Mr Jeams for the increase of his allowance at Our Lady Day	0	26	8
To Mr John Bradshewe and Edward Rudgate churchwardens for their chardges at Wittny at the visitation	0	5	1
To Mr Bradshewe maior for the keeping of a nagg that was sould to John Glover	0	13	6
For paving work in the church	0	0	12
To Mr Wattson highe constable for maymed souldiers	0	6	6
For wine for Mr Potter and Mr Raulinsons sermons	0	3	0
To Drewe for mendinge the towne peeces and for oyle for the same	0	2	6
For a scowringe stick for one of the peeces	0	0	4

For musick at the bring home of the elme from Combe on May Day as a maypole by Mr Maiors appoyntment	0	3	2
For a preachers horsemeat at Mr Maiors	0	0	6
For bowling of the great bell clapper	0	10	0
To Mr Browne as money due from the towne	0	40	0
For iron worke at the church and guild hall	0	0	16
For wine and suger at Mr Suttons sermon	0	3	6
For wine at severall tymes for communions	0	5	2^1/$_2$
More for wine for one Mr Rogers a preacher	0	0	21
For makinge the eye of the great bell claper	0	3	0
For wine at Mr Taylers sermon	0	2	0
For takinge downe the sumerpole	0	0	9
Expences upon 2 men of the garde at theire cominge for a certificate of the estate of our towne	0	7	10
For wine for Mr Jeams and Mr Tayler preaching at theire cominge to the Acte[10]	0	3	10
For worke about the office	0	5	8
To Roberte Bradbury of Chricherton in Norfolk a collector for the same towne beinge drowned	0	5	0
To the poor and to maymed souldiers from 12 February last to 12 July by Mr Maiors appoyntment	0	7	7
For wine and suger when Mr Jeames his two brothers preached	0	4	0
For wine at Mr Raunsons sermon	0	0	22
To the ringers on St Jeames Day	0	4	0
For wine and aiel at Mr Maiors to a strainger a preacher 16d and geiven to him in mony 5s	0	6	4
For grease for the bells on St Jeams day	0	0	4
To Long for oyle and candles for the clock	0	0	7
For suger spent at Whitsontide at the church accompt	0	0	6
To Vardam for a bawdrick for the treble bell	0	2	6
To the ringers 5 August	0	4	0
To the ringers at the Queenes cominge	0	0	18
To the Kinges cominge, to the clark of the Kinges houshould for his fee 10s, for the trumpiters to attend him 10s, and to the Kinges littermen 6s[11]	0	26	0
[Marginated subtotal]	10	11	3^1/$_2$
[f. 9r] To the amners men[12] for sealing the church dore for not ringinge at the Kinges goinge away	0	3	6
To the Kinges trumpeters	0	6	8
To Mr Thomas Meatcalfe for wardsmen on St Matthews Day	0	2	0
For wine to the commissioners at the last subsidy	0	0	21
For wine to Mr Maior for a preacher	0	0	21
To Mr Raunson maior his fee at Michaelmas last	5	0	0
For fetching Mr Dolemans mony at Michaelmas last	0	2	6

To Mr Jeams at Michaelmas last towards his allowance	0	26	8
For wine at Mr Maiors feaste	0	0	12
To Richard Lowe for keepinge of the bace childe[13]	0	9	4
Wine at Mr Thomas Meatcalfes at Mr Garnons sermons	0	4	6
For his diet for 2 meales and for his horsemeate	0	4	0
For the whole chardge of the building the portch over the prison dore at the guild hall	8	6	6
For stuffe and workmanshipp bestowed about the repairinge of Mr Jeames his house	0	31	0
The whole chardge of the coockingstole	0	17	0
To Corbett for his whole yeeres wages for looking to the clock, endinge at Allhallowtide last	0	6	0
For ringing and oyle 5 November	0	4	6
To John Symons for makinge a newe stock and new wheele for the great bell and for hanging her up	0	15	4
For nailes and iron worke for the same	0	6	10
For a haspe and staple for the seller dore	0	0	6
For wine at maiors that nowe is	0	0	12
For a loade of strawe for the almeshouse	0	8	0
For nailes hinges and hookes for the same house	0	0	16
For fouer daies for 1 man thetchinge there	0	4	0
To Edward Hewett carpenter for 2 daies worke there	0	0	20
22 November for the clarke of the markett and his men and Mr Maior and his neighbours to beare him company 8s, wine 12d, to the clarke in rewarde 6s	0	15	0
To the almesfolke for ealming [feeding] and serving the thetcher at the almeshouse	0	0	8
For mendinge the stockes and pillory with the timber work-manshipp and nayles	0	2	0
To Mr Rayer for planckes for the great bell wheele 7s and to Joseph Harris for the stocke 18d	0	8	6
Paied Mr Recorder for his fee due for one whole year at Michaelmas last	3	6	8
Chauntry rent and 12d for acquittance [same period].	5	7	8
For the fee farme [same period], acquittance 6d	0	53	10
[Marginated subtotal]	34	1	8
[f. 9v] To Richard Lowe 6d a wicke for 1 whole yeere endinge 22 December 1610	0	26	0
Paied Mr Towneclarkes fee for year ending Michaelmas	0	40	0
To the chirurgion that came to the lame man at John Dubbers	0	4	6
For a statute booke for the towne[14]	0	2	4
For the timber, workmanshipp and iron worke about the towneclarkes seate	0	24	4

To the poor and maimed souldiers from 1 July last till 22 December	0	9	2
[Marginated for next 8 items] Richard Meades his accompte 43s[15]			
Paied Richard Meades 20s the towne owed him	0	20	0
To the churchmen at Bladon	0	3	0
To a poore souldier	0	0	4
For a peece of timber for the holloway	0	0	8
For Mr Morsse[16] and Mr Maior and his neighbours to beare him company at the Kinges coming	0	17	0
To 3 poor people	0	0	12
For carryinge of stones from Mr Whittons quarry to the pentise over the litle house dore	0	0	6
Paied to Grubson by Mr Browns appoyntment	0	0	6
[End of bracketed items]			
Geiven to Grubson for goodwife Irons	0	0	6
To Robert Robinson for his halfe yeeres wadge ending at Michaelmas last	0	2	6
For a shrewde for a poore childe that died at John Tomlins house	0	0	14
To Screevin for culleringe the newe porch 4s 6d and for glasinge at the church and Mr Jeams his house as appeareth by his bill	0	9	10
To Edward Longe for his wages and other monye leied out by him as appeereth by his bills	0	17	3
To Edmond Hiorne towneclarke for keepinge and writing the chamberlains accompte	0	5	0
Allowances to be deducted out of the rentrole, for Mr Whittons greate house 15½d, for the house where John Coombes the carrier lat dwelt 12d and for the house Mr Browne dwelleth in 6d	0	2	9½
[Marginated subtotal]	9	8	4½
[Marginated total]	65	6	7½

---

[1] Between John Whitton (d. 1643), *alias* Darlinge, and Meatcalfe for five dwellings in New Woodstock: B 78/2, 11 Dec. 1609: below, rentals. For Whitton family see *Hist. Parl. 1558–1603*, i. 227–8; *V.C.H. Oxon.* xii, index.

[2] Edw. Browne of Eynsham: B 81, f. 24r; and see below in 1611.

[3] Bryan Stephens: B 81, f. 24r. Admissions below are recorded in B 83, pp. 87 sqq.

[4] Hiorne's note in B 78/2 on 5 Apr. explains that he bought them from the town out of the goods of the man who sold the pewter to Thos. Screeven; and see above in 1609.

[5] Does not include 16s for a horse and packsaddle recorded in B 81. The assized rents, which are not listed in the receipts, are presumably included to make this total.

[6] 'As payed for fyfteenes': B 81. Parl. granted a subsidy of one tenth and one fifteenth in 1609–10: Act, 7 Jas. I, c. 23.

[7] Of Yarnton, d. 18, bur. 19 Dec. 1609: Yarnton parish regs.; *Parish Collections Made by Ant. Wood and*

Ric. Rawlinson, ed. F.N. Davis (O.R.S. xi, 1929), 361–2.
[8] i.e. Wm. Meatcalfe (d. 1608): see appendix, biogs.
[9] For subsidy see Act, 7 Jas. I, c. 23. Provisions for appointment of commissioners and meetings with local men are made in the Act.
[10] Possibly a ref. to the Oxf. Univ. 'Act', at which degree candidates publicly defended their theses, or to Act Sunday when two new Doctors of Divinity preached: Oxf. Univ. Statutes, (London 1845), ed. G. M. Ward, i. 57.
[11] The court seems to have been at Woodstock from c. 22–25 Aug. and in early Sept.: J. Nichols, Progresses of King James the First (London 1828), ii. 365; Cal.S.P.Dom. 1603–10, 629; Cal.S.P.Ven. 1610–13, 40.
[12] Almoner of the king's household. See below, 1611, where the town pays the almoner's counsel.
[13] Nic. Glover's child: see above, 1609.
[14] Perhaps the collections of statutes issued for the guidance of justices in 1609: see B. W. Quintrell, 'Making of Chas. I's Book of Orders', E.H.R. (1980), 555
[15] The junior chamberlain.
[16] Royal clerk of the market.

[f. 10r] 22 December 1610 to 14 December 1611, Josephe Harris and Thomas Meatcalfe, chamberlains

Debtes owing to the towne	£	s	d
[from Butterfeild, Phillipps, Whitton, Powell, Gregory and Steephens as on f. 6v above]	[5	8	3]

Debtes owinge by the towne

Inprimis due to John Norman	0	10	0
Due to Joseph Harris	0	12	5

Mony receaved by chamberlains

Inprimis delivered to them in reddie monye	0	36	0
Receaved of Mr Browne 10s for the payment of his le poole rent at Our Lady Day next and he was allowed 20s which the towne owed him and 10s the towne owed to Woodroffe which made up his 40s for Our Lady Day rent next	0	10	0
Of William Butterfeild upon his bonde	0	7	0
Of Damery and Warren for the seale of theire 2 fynes	0	8	0
Of William Bradshewe for extreates which he geathered of Farmers	0	7	0
Of Edmond Hiorne towneclarke 24s 4d he did geive the towne and also did geive his seate to the towne	0	24	4
Of George Noble for his fine	0	4	0
Of Water Parker and others for eatinge of flesshe in Lent[1]	0	0	18
Of Mr Knotsford for breakinge the peace upon Bodely[2]	0	0	18

Of widdowe Fleminge for a composition for the towne to graunte Mr Hollowayes house to Edmond Hiorne towneclark and for the seale thereof[3]	0	20	0
Of Edmond Hiorne for his fine from her	0	4	0
Of Henry Price for breaking the peace upon John Norman tythingman[4]	0	2	4
[f. 10v] Of Edward Browne [the like] upon Robert Bruce[5]	0	2	4
At the church accompte at Whitsontide last as monye gotten then	9	10	0
Of Archer the tayler for his admission[6]	0	20	0
Of William Castell for an extreate	0	5	0
Of Ned Abbott for the like	0	15	0
Of Edmond Hiorne which he paied for 3 inditmentes which the towne before had paied him	0	3	0
For a seale for Collingwoodes recovery[7]	0	4	0
Of Longe for tole in the beafe markett, at Our Lady Day faier 11s 7d, on Magdalen faier 4s 4d, St Mathewes faier 13s 6d, on St Nicholas faier 5s 4d, and for severall markett daies 20s 3d.	0	55	0
Of Rudgate for stallages	8	12	8
Upon the rentrole	26	15	7¼
Of John Bradshewe 4s 6d as mony taken upon one George Bennett a fellon in the goale[8]	0	4	6
For a horsse nowe in Mr Bradshewes handes which was taken as a waife[9] [no sum]			
Of one Moslie for a fyne for disordering himselfe in the faier[10]	0	5	0
Of Mr Doleman for one year's annuity due Michaelmas	8	0	0
Summ totall receaved besides the money for the horse	63	17	9¼
The somme of the layinges out is	73	6	9½
So remayninge due to Joseph Harris chamberlaine	9	9	0¼

14 December 1611 the said chamberlains were dischardged and were newly elected for the next yeere

Debtes which the towne doe owe

To Joseph Harris [£9 5s deleted]	4	6	8
To John Norman 10s	0	10	0

Debtes due to the towne

From William Butterfeild	0	10	0
From Mistris Phillipps for rentes behind	0	4	6
From Mr Whitton for rentes behind	0	6	9½
From John Powell for his admission	0	10	0
From Drew Gregory for his admission	0	40	0

From Bryan Steephens for his admission	0	20	0
Sir Henry Lee owing upon his bonde[11]	55	0	0
From John Archer for his admission	0	20	0

Due at Michaelmas 1612
[Entry cancelled, cf. above] Mr Bradshewe oweth for a gelding

taken as a waife	3	0	0

Mr Evans accepted of 18d per annum for the churchyeard at
Michaelmas only[12]

[f. 11r] At the accompte 14 December 1611
Whereas it is entered in the liger[13] in the chest that there is due at
this accompt £9 to Joseph Harris he hath nowe receaved in reddy
mony £3 for a horsse which Mr Bradshewe paied for, and 20s
more which was paied in reddy money then out of extreates, and
also he is to receave of widdowe Aspoole 13s 4d for extreates,
[interlined] and which William Bradshewe undertooke to pay her.
So the towne oweth him but £4 6s 8d.

[Signature of] Ed. Hiorne

[different hand] 16 December 1611 Sir Henry Lee barronett payed
£5 of the £55 for his interest due at Michaelmas 1611 which is
delivered to Joseph Harris. Paied for a pynt of sack out of it to
Mr Maior and Mr Browne.

[f. 11v] [Disbursements]

Inprimis geiven to one Mr Cottford a preacher in rewarde 5s and for his diet and wine 4s 7½d	0	9	7½
For a cake and sugerloffe to Sir Henry Lee knight and for another cake and suger loffe to Mr Spencer sent to them at Christmas 1610	0	39	3
Geiven in reward at Mr Spencers. To Mr Gadbury 3s 4d, to the butler 5s, the clarke of the kitchine 2s 6d, the cooke 3s 4d, the porter 12d, the groome 2s, William Hickes 12d,[14] the fuiler 12d	0	19	2
Geiven in rewarde at Sir Henry Lees	0	20	5
For wine and suger when Mr Jeames preached	0	2	4½
For a clothe for the communion cupp	0	0	12
For wine for a preacher that dined at Mr Brownes	0	0	18
In wine and suger at Mr Raunson his funerall[15]	0	4	0
Geiven to poore people at sundry times untill 10 February	0	0	14
Paied to Richard Lowe 6d a wick towardes the keeping of Nicholas Glovers base childe from 22 December 1610 untill Monday 22 Aprill 1611, being 22 weekes	0	11	0
To Joseph Harris 12s 5d due at the last accompte	0	12	5

To be deducted out of the rent role as mony which was allowed by the towne at the last accompt which they owed, 30s to Mr Browne, 28s 4d due to William Ball, 20s to himselfe and 8s 4d which was set on of Mr John Glovers debt	0	58	4
To a pursefant that brought a packett of proclamations for the dissolvinge the parliament[16]	0	2	6
For a quire of paper for the collectors booke	0	0	4
To churchwardens of Bladon for theire composition mony	0	3	0
Paied for carrying a man from John Dubbers house to Begbrock which lay sick at his house from before Michaelmas to Candlemas	0	0	12
Wine to Mr Raunson at his dinner when he preached	0	0	21
For wine when the parson of Bladon preached	0	0	13 1/2
For a bellrope to Symonns of Bladon[17]	0	4	0
To him for an other bellrope	0	3	0
To Wheeler for 1 dayes worke about the clock and for nayles bestowed in the church	0	0	16
For wine and suger at Mr Recorders being heere at Ould Woodstock and Hensington	0	5	9
For suger at Mr Bradshewes on Easter Day	0	0	12
To the ringers on Our Lady Day	0	2	0
Fetching Mr Dolemans £4 at Our Lady Day and Michaelmas. [Total corrected in MS.]	0	5	0
[f. 12r] To William Rayer, Frauncis Garter and Benedict Norwood for diginge of stone in the churchyearde for the amendinge the highwayes. [Deleted] 3 dayes at 10d a day	0	8	4
2 April paied to Lowe for the keepinge of the said childe for 4d a wick that was behind unpaied at Michaelmas last	0	10	0
To Amsden for on dayes worke about the wales at the almshouse	0	0	12
To Hickes for makinge newe boultes and irons for the correction of the poore which remayne with William Bradshewe[18]	0	2	6
To Mr Rayer maior 4s which he gave to poore people and to Mr Browne and Mr Bradshewe at severall tymes till 14 August [Marginated] receaved 14 August [Total corrected in MS.]	0	9	11
For worke done about the holloway as followeth. To Ned Bluett for sawinge 4d. To Warren and Hibbard and one boy for 5 daies work 12s 6d. To Coles for throwinge stone out of the church-yeard 12d. For 2 postes and 2 railes 18d. To Wheeler for one daies work 12d, Norwood and Private for 1 daies work 20d, Ray and Privat for sawinge 8d. For 8 peeces of tymber 8s. To Warren for 5 daies work 4s 6d. To Hamond and Greene for digging of stone in the churchyeard 7s 10d. To John Kent for carrying of stone from the churchyeard to the hollowe way 6s 2d.	0	45	2

For stringes for the drum	0	0	18
For work about the sumerpole to Wheeler	0	2	0
For 2 shirtes for a poore boye at the almeshouse	0	2	0
For wine and suger. To Mr Tayler 4s 8d. At Mr Nasshes to Mr Recorder 4s 6d. [Deleted] wine at the church accompte 2s 4d. [Total corrected in MS.]	0	9	2
For work about the bells. To Hickes and Pettybone for newe mending the bell clapers 16s, for 3 newe bauderickes 5s, for rearing the stock of the bells and other iron work about the bells by Mr Maiors appoyntment 6s.	0	27	0
To a pursefant for bringeinge 2 proclamations with writtes, one for silver, the other for the oath of allegance at twoe severall tymes	0	5	0
To Mr Rawlins for his chardge at Deddington to deliver the subsidy bill to the commissioners[19]	0	2	0
To Durbridge for a chaine for the prisoner[20]	0	3	4
For wringinge on St James his day 4s, on 5 August 4s	0	8	0
For two wardsmen on Magdalen day faier day	0	0	12
For 3 wardsmen at Our Lady Daie faier	0	0	18
To Longe for the ringers 4 August	0	2	0
Paied for tymber and workmanshipp about the beere	0	0	15
For tymber and workmanshipp about the pownde gate	0	0	15
To Mr Maior as monye geiven by him to the poore	0	2	5
Paied for expences in eatinge the 2 buckes which the Prince bestowed on the towne.[21] For 2 bushels of wheate 8s, 10 pownd of shewett 3s 4d, 2 pownde of pepper 5s, 14 pownde of butter 4s 8d, milke 6d, egges 6d. For bakinge, the baker havinge the branns 8d. White paper 1d. To Brookes the cooke for his paines 5s.[22] To the keepers for theire fee 10s. For wine £3 14s 6d. For expences at the last 2 pasties which came from Mr Berries 3 pownd of butter 12d, 2 pownde of shewett 8d, egges 2d, pepper 6d, paper 1/2d. To Meadowes the cooke for paynes 12d. For wine 5s 10d.	6	17	0 1/2
[f. 12v] To Robbins the ploomer for his wages for one whole yeere endinge at Michaelmas 1611	0	5	0
To Durbridge for ironworke about the forebell	0	7	0
To Wheeler the carpenter for work about the same	0	3	0
For one borde about the same bell	0	0	9
Paied for a seale to seale pottes and waightes	0	3	4
To 2 wardsmen at St Mathewes fayer	0	0	12
To Turner the slatter for workemanshipp about the chauncell gutter 3s 8d. For 5 bushells of lyme 3s 4d, a peck of heare 2d, 24 greate nayles for the same worke 22d	0	8	8
October for wine for Mr Jeames when he preached	0	0	20

	£	s	d
Paied for expences of diett and horsmeate for an ould preacher which did lye at John Taylers house	0	4	0
For a plancke to mende the bayes 18d. For a carpenter for one dayes worke about the same 10d, a staple 1d [Total corrected in MS.]	0	2	5
To Hugh Hamond for 12 pownde of soder, 10 pownde of leade and for his workmanshipp about the leades upon the tower	0	17	0
To Mr Maior as mony geiven by him to the poore	0	2	5
To Tomalyn	0	0	3
To Symons the carpenter for mending the great bell	0	0	12
To the ringers 5 November	0	4	0
Geiven to Mr Mosse clark of the markett 10s for his dinner and Mr Maior and the rest of the neighbours to beare him company 11s 4d and wine 4s 8d	0	26	0
For a new rope for the greate bell	0	3	0
For paringe the markett busshell and pecke	0	0	2
To Corbott for one yeeres wages for mending the clock ending Michaelmas	0	6	0
1 December for worke about the parsons seate and for mending diverse seates and making newe formes in the church. For the carpenters worke 8s. For nayles 18d, a hundred of oaken bordes 7s 6d, 2 oaken planckes 2s, a plate of iron 4d, certeine other peeces of tymber 22d.	0	21	2
Mr Recorder fee for one yeere ending Michaelmas	3	6	8
Chauntry quitt rent £5 6s 8d [same period], acquittance 6d.	5	7	2
Undershreeve fee farme [same period], acquittance 6d	0	53	10
To Edmond Hiorne towneclark for fee [same period]	0	40	0
For keeping and writing the chamberlains accompttes	0	5	0
To Longe for his wages for looking to the clock and wringing the bell and other laying out as appeereth by his bill	0	18	4

[f. 13r] To Edmond Hiorne towneclark as mony leied out by him for the towne in Michaelmas term. To Mr Recorder for a fee 10s. To Mr Blunt for a search in the crowne office 6s 8d.[23] To Mr Johnson the almoners cownsell for his hand to a reporte to avoide a plea 10s. To the clark of the Exchequer for the search of the inquisition of John Normans death 3s 4d.[24] For the coppye of the inquisition 16d. For the clarkes hande of the crowne office to the same coppy 2s. To the master of the crowne office for his fee for the expurgation of the proceedinges upon the number role 6s 8d. To Mr Blunte the attorny for making the record thereof 3s 4d. To Mr Fuller the master of the extretes in the Exchequer for a search and coppy of the extret 2s. To my lorde cheife barrons porter 12d. To my lord cheife barrons clark for takinge my affidavit 2s 6d. To Mr Fuller for the constant 4s and for his fee 6s. To Mr Pember clark of the amercementes of thassises 2s. To the shreeve 13s 4d, for Mr Bradshewes amercementes. For a bag to carry my writinges in 12d. For my expences and

my horse 14 dayes 46s 8d. To the shreeve for a coppy of the extret of his
chardge 18d.   6   3   4

To be deducted out of the rent roll for the house which William
Tanner late held, which nowe Mr James houldeth 20s. Quitt
rent for Mr Brownes house 6d. Rent of Mr Whittons great house
15$^{1}/_{2}$d and for his house which was John Groomes[25] which nowe
Mr Gadbury hath 12d. For the churchyearde which William
Metcalfe houldeth and which Mr Evans claymeth 3s.   0   25   9$^{1}/_{2}$

Paied to Richard Lowe for keepinge of Nicholas Glovers bace
childe from 22 Aprill till 16 December beinge 34 wickes at 10d
a wick   0   28   4

To Mr Rayer for the rent of Richard Coles his house for 2
yeeres at Michaelmas 1611 at 16s per annum 32s   0   32   0

[Deleted] Summ totall   55   10   11$^{1}/_{2}$

[Signature of] Edm. Hiorne

Paied to Mr James 53s 4d towardes his £10 per annum and
more £5 which he should have had for the interest of £50 in
Sir Henry Lees hande due at Michaelmas 1611   7   13   4

To Mr Rayer maior for his fee for one yeere   10   0   0

[Deleted] Summ totall   73   14   3$^{1}/_{2}$

Summ totall   73   6   9$^{1}/_{2}$

[Signature of] Ed. Hiorne

---

[1] James I was particularly anxious to enforce Lenten rules against meat eating, and it fell to the justices to seek out offenders. For the court cases see B 78/2, 27 Feb. 1611.

[2] Wm. Bodeley, cutler. The fine was used to pay watchmen at the fair: ibid. 4 Mar. 1610/11.

[3] For final concord see ibid. 15 April 1611. For Hiorne's purchase in 1618, see below.

[4] Discharged on submission and payment of fine: B 78/2, 17 Apr.

[5] Browne, an Eynsham baker, 'confesssed that he being droonck did strike the said Bruce with his dagger': ibid. 19 Apr.

[6] Wm. Archer, tailor, admitted 11 July 1611: B 81, f. 24v and B 83, p. 89.

[7] Fras. Collingwood: B 81, f. 24v.

[8] A Worcs. labourer taken at Deddington fair for theft: B 78/2, 18 Nov. 1611.

[9] A note in B 81, f. 25r records that Bradshewe was to have the horse which was valued at £4 for only £3 by consent of the neighbours; and see p. 17.

[10] John Moslie of Broad Campden (Glos.) confessed to drawing his sword and threatening actions 'being as he thinketh drunk', and was discharged on payment of 6s 8d: B 78/2, 23 July, 5 Oct.

[11] See also below. Lee was involved in the disposition of Cornwell's bequest for the school and by 1606 held on loan at 10 per cent £50 of legacy money which John Doleman had handed over in 1599. See Intro. and note of bond in B 81, f. 21v.

[12] The town's agreement with Edw. Evans, rector of Bladon, is noted in B 81, f. 25r; and see above.

[13] i.e. audit book (B 81): see above, Intro.

[14] Possibly 'ould Hickes', called on for information about the Spencer dole in 1640 below.

[15] John Raunson, glover, elected mayor in Oct. 1610, died in office 21 Jan. 1611: see appendix, biogs.

[16] Dissolved 9 Feb. 1610/11: Stuart Proclams., i, no. 114.

[17] John Symons of Bladon, carpenter (d. 1638): B 78/2, 3 Apr. 1609; and Bladon parish register.
[18] i.e. the 'idle poor'. In 1611 the town had 'three pair of guives for prisoners, one newe longe chaine to tye a prisoner with...and certain irons and boults for the whipping post...and one little staple for the said chain': B 81, f. 25r. For whipping and the stocks see B 78/2, 11 Apr.
[19] See appendix, biogs., for Rawlins.
[20] A note in B 81, f. 25r that exemplifications upon the 'rescuing of a prisoner' from the sheriff were deposited with Hiorne may be a connected with this entry and with payment below to the sheriff.
[21] Prince Hen. was in Woodstock, said to have been 'recently given him', by 9 Sept. 1611: Cal.S.P.Ven. 1610–13, 207. Cf. Marshall, Woodstock, 629.
[22] Probably Chris. Brookes of New Woodstock, said to be a cook in recognizances of 1618 in B 77/2.
[23] Probably Ric. Blount, member of the Oxf. circuit: Members Admitted to the Inner Temple 1547–1660 (London 1877).
[24] There is no indication as to why the town wanted Norman's inquisition and it has not been found.
[25] John Coombes, carrier: see rental below.

[f. 13v] 14 December 1611 to 19 December 1612, Joseph Harris and Thomas Meatcalfe, chamberlains

[Receipts]	£	s	d
Debtes due and owinge to the towne			
From William Butterfeild 10s, Mistris Phillipps for rentes 4s 6d, Mr Whitton for rentes behind 6s 9½d. For admissions, John Powell 10s, Drue Gregory 40s, Bryan Steephens 20s, John Archer 20s.	5	11	3½
Debtes owing by the towne			
To Joseph Harris as a remaynder at his last accompte	4	6	8
To John Norman at said accompte	0	10	0
Money receaved			
Of Sir Henry [Lee] for the use of his £50 [Deleted £5]	7	0	0
Of Mr Bradshewe for 4 asshes at the crosse at the townes end	0	12	0
Of Mr Doleman for his annuity	8	0	0
Of Tayler for rent due at Our Lady Day	0	45	0
Of Mr Maior for a fyne for all the rentes due upon Taylers lease[1]	10	0	0
Of Screevin for a fyne for the barne called the wooll barne in his backside[2]	10	0	0
Of Mr Rea, Jenckins, Underill and Symons, for breach of the peace[3]	0	14	0
The church accompte at Whitsontide	6	10	0
[Deleted] of Longe for tole till 11 July	0	43	5

[Deleted] of Symons for a fine for breach of the peace upon Hugh Hamond	0	4	0
[f. 14r] Of Edmond Rudgate for stallages	8	14	1
One dagger remained with Mr Rayer out of which he hath payed 2s to Roger Sturges[4]			
The peese which John Archer fownde was geiven by the towne to Sir Thomas Spencer			
Of Edward Longe for tole in the beafe markett [Deleted] 49s	0	51	1
Upon the rent role for rentes due this yeere	26	15	7
Of Mistris Hord as mony geiven by her towardes the almeshouse[5]	0	40	0
Of John Norman constable upon the extractes [estreats] remayninge with him	0	19	6
For lyme of Mistris Dumford 6s 2d, of Edward Longe 14d, of Joseph Harris 14d, of Mr Evans 14d, of Thomas Meatcalfe 14d	0	9	8
For the makinge of freemen	0	8	4
More for making of freemen	0	4	0
Summ receaved [Deleted £86 10s 1d]	87	4	5
The layinges out is	109	9	11
So the towne oweth to Joseph Harris	22	5	6

[f. 14v] [Disbursements]

Inprimis one suger loff wayinge 10lb, 16s, one cake to Bignill 10s. Sent to Sir Thomas Spencer at Christmas 1611 in rewardes to the officers there 25s 10d	0	51	10
To Wheeler for one dayes work and nayles to mende the certaine bell in the church	0	0	14
For making widdowe Toes and a pore boyes coate	0	0	20
A shrewde for widdowe Cripps	0	2	6
Paied to Raph Durbridge for mending the clock	0	2	0
To Warren for him and his boy for workinge 2 dayes about the holloway	0	2	8
Geiven Mr Recorder for a fee in Sir Henry Lees sute 10s.[6]			
Layed out by Mr Browne in Bestes sute at London 6s 6d, at Sir Thomas Spencers house in rewards about same 2s 6d, at Oxon' at the heereinge of the same 6s 8d.[7] In wine upon the clarkes of thassisse 2s 8d.	0	28	4
To the ringers 24 March	0	4	0
Oyle for the bells 2d, packthreed at the hall 1/2d	0	0	2 1/2
Payed to John Bradshewe to pay 2 wardsmen	0	0	16

	£	s	d
6 April to Mr Recorder for his paynes in cominge to the towne about our vittlers busines 20s. Wine and diet for him and the company at that tyme 30s 4d[8]	0	50	4
Bringing Mr Dolemans money at Our Lady Day	0	2	6
For a loade of thornes to hedge the almeshouse close	0	6	6
To Hickes for lockes and worke about the church by Mr Maiors appoyntment	0	2	6
To Norwood, Garter and Anthony for mending the high way at the mill	0	3	4
Delivered to Lowe as mony to be spent about the church	9	10	0
For gunpowder to scower the towne peeces	0	0	4
To Drewe for scowringe the armor	0	5	0
For 20 yeardes of wier for the clock 20d and for 4 ropes for the church and almeshouse 12d	0	2	8
To Thomas Screevin by the churchwardens appoyntment for mendinge of the glasse windoes in the church 30s 1d, to him for mending the glasse windowes about the towne hall 16s 3d	0	46	4
To Mr Maior and Mr Bradshewe as mony geiven by them at severall tymes till 11 July	0	3	8
For wine, suger and rewardes spent at gentlemens meetinges and upon preachers at sundry tymes till 11 July. For a pynt of sack at Sir Henry Lees payment of his £5, 6d, at Mr Docter Laudes sermon 2s, at Sir Thomas Spencers cominge 3s 9d, for wine 9 March for the neighbours 18d, more at the eating of the taste cake 18d, to the preacher that came from Chippingnorton in wine 2s 4d, at Mr Bradshewes on Easter Day 5s 4d, to Mr Tayler in wine 12d, to Mr Ascue in wine 12d, to a preacher in wine and rewarde that lay at Screevins 4s 2d.	0	23	1
To Mr Maior his fee at Our Lady Day	5	0	0
Due to me Joseph Harris at the last accompte	4	6	8

[f. 15r] Worke and expences laied out about the almeshouse.
To Amsden for 5 dayes to dig stone in the backside 4s 2d, to Greene for 7 dayes for like 5s 10d. To Norwood, Garter and Anthony for 3 dayes apeece for like in the churchyeard 5s, for pulling downe the almeshouse 2s 6d, for 3 dayes work a peece 5s. For nayles 2d. To Wheeler for 4 dayes work 4s, Greene for work 4s 2d, Amsden for 4 dayes 3s 4d. To Norwood, Garter and Anthony to dig the flower in the churchyearde 14s. To Warren for 7 dayes work 7s, his boy 7 dayes 4s 8d, Jo Damery for 7 dayes 7s, Huggins and his boy 20d. To widdowe Smith for 2 peeces to make lintorns 2s 6d. To Amsden for 6 dayes worke 5s, Greene 5 dayes 4s 2d, Warren 5 dayes 5s, his boy 5 dayes 3s 4d, Jo Damery for 4 dayes 4s, Hugins for 5 dayes 5s, his boy 5 dayes 3s 4d, Amsden for 5 dayes 4s 2d, Greene 5 dayes 4s 2d, Batt 5 dayes 4s 2d, Anthony for his boy 5 dayes 3s 4d. To Kent for carrying of stone and morter 23 loades 11s 6d. For one cowle 2s 6d, nayles 2d. To Garter, Norwood and Anthony for filling the pitt in the churchyearde 3s 4d.

To Garter for digging of morter 5d, Warren for 4 dayes work 4s, Damery for 5 dayes 5s, Dameryes man 4 dayes 4s, Huggins for 5 dayes 5s, for his boy for 4 dayes 2s 8d. For grease, candles, oyle, leather, nayles used by Long in the church 2s 3d. To Kent for 10 lodes carriag of stone, morter and tymber 5s. For morters carriage and for ale at Woodrooffes⁹ and at Rudgates 2s 10d. To Warren 3 dayes 3s, his boy 3 dayes 2s, Damery for 2 dayes and a halfe 2s 6d, his man 3 dayes 3s, Huggins 3 dayes 3s, his boy 3 dayes 2s, Amsden for labor 6s 6d, Batt for 5 dayes 4s 2d, Greene for 8 dayes 7s. To Privat and Ray for sawyinge 3s 4d. To Gee for a mantle tree 16d. To Amsden for work 3s 4d. To Kentes for 2 loades carriag 12d. To Abbott and Ray for sawyinge 6s 8d. To Wheeler for 4 dayes 4s. For 3 peeces of tymber 40s. Delivered to Wheeler for nayles 15d. To Robert Symons for carriage of tymber from Kirtlington 5s. To Wheeler for a windowe 3s and 7 dayes work 7s. To Garter 1 dayes work 10d. For sawyinge at Kirtlington, for beare upon the carters and workmen 12d, to Norwood 3d, to Greene for 1 day 10d, for 2 saplinges 6s, for nayles to the slatter 6d, to Wheelers for 4 dayes 4s, Widdowes for 4 days 4s, Kent for 5 carriages 2s, to Garter 2 dayes 20d, Warren for 2 dayes 2s, his boy 2 dayes 16d, Dameryes man for 2 dayes 2s. For a loade of lyme 15s 6d. To Abbott and Privat for sawyinge 7s. For nayles 6d, 2 dozen of crestes 5s, 2 crestes 5d. To Muckell for slattinge worke 28s 9d. To Grubson to carry water 2d. For mosse 3s 2d. To Dameryes man for mending the pownde wall 2s. To Butcher for nayles for the almeshouse 11s [and] 3s 6d. To the twoe Wheelers for 45 dayes work at 12d per diem 45s. To Private and Abbott for sawinge 2s, to Kent for carrying tymber sawed to the almeshouse 6d. To William Hickes for £19 of iron 6s. For nayles 3s 1d, 1 borde and 2 peeces of bord and pynwood 18d. To Warren and his boy for masons worke there 5s 10d, to Wheeler for 8 dayes work 8s, [f.15v] for the use of his barrowe 6d. To Amsden and his wife for thetchinge 1 day 18d. For nayles 21d. To Warren and his boy for 4 dayes worke 3s 4d, to Norwood for 2 dayes 20d, Thomas Jackson for 1 day 10d. A pole, nayles and a staple 9d. To Wheeler for 2 dayes 2s. To Hickes for a key and mendinge a lock 6d. To Amsden for him and his wife for thetchinge 2s 6d. To Mr Rayer for tymber 23s. For beere spent amongest the workmen at the almeshouse 12d. To Abbott, Pryvate, and Raye for sawing 6s. For 2 mantletrees 3s. To Richard Shad for 3 peeces of tymber about the almeshouse 9s. To Mr Rayer for 6 thousand of slatt £3, eves 10s, for holing 14s, carriage 25s, 12 hundred of lath 12s 4d. To Huggins and his boy for 5 daies about the almshouse wale 6s 8d, besides the mucke there and the fillinge of the hole to Parrott for 5 dayes to serve them then 2s 6d. To Amsden for dygging stone 3 dayes 2s 6d. The whole chardge of the almeshouse.

[Deleted £31 17s 1d]   32   0   1

For ringing 5 August   0   4   0
For wine when Mr Raunson preached   0   0   20

For expences at Mr Recorders being heere when Sir Thomas
Spencer was chosen our high steward 26s and geiven to Mr
Recorder in mony then for his paynes 20s. To Mr Bradshewe
for 3 bushels of oates for Mr Recorders horsses at 2 severall
tymes 8s.[10]   0 54 0

For beare to the ringers on St James Day   0 0 12

For beare to the carpenters at the setting upon of the bells   0 2 0

To the ringers at the Prince his cominge 22 August   0 0 12

For expences for Mr Mosse his dinner at the Kinges last cominge
17s 8d, to him in rewarde 10s and to his men 18d   0 29 2

For ringing at the Kinges, Queene, and Princes goeinge from
Woodstock at 3 severall tymes   0 3 0

For expences about the eating of the buck which the Prince
bestowed on the towne. For one bushel of meale 4s 8d, 10
pownd of butter, 3 pownd of suet 4s 6d, egges 4d, pepper,
cloves and mase and sinimont 18d, paper and candles 11d. To
Paynter the keeper[11] and his man in rewarde 6s. For baking the
pasties 12d, wine then spent 16s 4d.   0 35 3

[f. 16r] Spent upon the Kinges servantes at the Kinges beinge last
here.[12] To the Kinges trumpeters 10s, to the Prince his
trumpeters 10s, to the Queenes littermen 6s 8d. Spent in wine
upon the gardes and other the Kinges servantes and officers
13s 4d.   0 40 0

To 2 wardsmen at St Mathewes Day   0 0 16

To 1 poore geathering man by Mr Brownes appoyntment   0 0 8

To Shad for bringing Mr Dolemans mony at Michaelmas   0 2 6

To Robert Wells for goinge to Cassington   0 0 4

For wine to a preacher that dined at Mr Nasshes and to the
undershreeves deputy   0 3 8

To Mr Rayer mayor for mony leied out by him   0 5 7

To Corbott for keeping the clock till Michaelmas   0 6 0

For ringing 4 November [sic]   0 4 0

Payed for diet for Mr Mosse when he last sate as clark of the
markett 10s, to him in rewarde 10s and for wine and suger
then 15d   0 21 3

To Warren for poynting the tower   0 4 4

To Huggins for poynting of the church   0 5 0

To Mr Glover maior for mony geiven by him to the poore   0 3 2

Payed to Edmond Hiorne for his expences at Deddington at the
seasing of the lady Elizabeth's ayde[13]   0 2 6

For wine to a preacher that dyned at Mr James his house   0 0 20

To Hopkins at Bladon for our composition   0 3 0

For lides and bordes for the schoolehouse windowes   0 3 4

To Durbridge for ironworke for the same lides   0 4 0

For two wardsmen at St Nicholas Day	0	0	16
For expences at the Prince his funerall.[14] To Mr Evans for his paynes 10s, for the dinner 15s, for wine 4s 10d	0	29	10
Mr Recorder his fee	3	6	8
Quitt rent for one year £5 6s 8d, acquittance 6d, a quart of wine and payment 12d	5	8	2
To Mr Glover maior his fee	5	0	0
[f. 16v] To Edmond Hiorne towne clarke his fee	0	40	0
For keeping and writing the chamberlains accounts	0	5	0
To Longe for his wages, ringing the bell, lookinge to the clocke and other thinges as appeereth by his bill. For his wages 12s, the leades 2s 6d, a grave 6d, oyle 22d, a proclamation 2d, mendinge the ropes 8d, mendinge the church porch 3d	0	17	11
To Richard Lowe for the keepinge of Nicholas Glovers child for one yeere untill 16 December 1612, 52 weekes at 10d a weeke	0	43	8
For diet and lodging for a poore man that was robbed at Gorrell gate	0	0	14
Fee farme 53s 4d, acquittance 6d	0	53	10
To John Norman as appereth by his bill[15] for sendinge to Wootton with horsse and man 3d. Spent at Deddington 12d, with a creeple to Wotton 6d, for a horse to Deddington 10d	0	2	6
For dyet for a preacher that did lye at Mr Glovers house 14 December 5s, wine 2s	0	7	0
To Hickes for mendinge the clock	0	0	22
To Mr Glover maior for money geiven to the poore	0	4	4
To Mr James the schoolemaster his mony for this yeere at Michaelmas last besides the rent due from Mr Noble 46s 8d[16]	7	13	4
To Mr Evans for the rent of the church yeard	0	0	18
For a paper booke for the chamberlains accompte	0	0	4
To Thomas Screevin for glasinge at the hale 3s 5d and at the church 2s 2d	0	5	7
To be deducted out of the rent role for the wooll barne 5s, Tanners house 20s, Mr Whittons rent 15¼d and 12d, Mr Brownes house 6d. Bignells backside [deleted]	0	27	9½
Payed for Richard Coles his rent to Mr Rayer for this yeere	0	16	0
Summ totall	109	9	11

[1] For Hampton Poyle meadow. For leases see rental below.
[2] B 31 (11), 3 Mar. 1612; and see rental below.
[3] Thos. Rea, gent., and John Underhill, yeo., both of Severn Stoke (Worcs.) apparently attacked Wm. Jenckins or Jenkes of Yarnton, while Wm. Symons 'drewe bloode' upon Hugh Hamond: B 78/2, 2 June, 6 July, 2 and 19 Oct.

[4] Sturges, a barber, was paid 'for curing Hickes his head' and the dagger was left with Rayer after the fray: ibid. 21 Oct. 1612.
[5] See also below. Dorothy Hord, widow, gave the money in her lifetime and also left £5 in her will of 23 July 1617 to be distributed at the rate of 12d dole at her funeral to the most honest poor people: MS. Wills Oxon. 30/3/6.
[6] Perhaps related to the school money which Sir Hen. had held on bond and for which there is a settlement at the end of this account.
[7] A suit about Browne's property at the park gate granted to the town in 1608. See below in 1613.
[8] For innholders and victuallers licensed on 8 Apr. see B 78/2.
[9] John Woodroofe's house in Old Woodstock: B 78/3.
[10] Presumably Edw. Bradshewe, landlord of the Bull by 1613: see rental below.
[11] Edw. Paynter, keeper of Hensgrove in Woodstock park: see B 78/2, 21 Feb. 1610/11.
[12] The full court was at Woodstock 26–31 Aug. when the prince made the king an entertainment 'with devices' and 'the greatest and best ordered feasts as ever was seene': Nichols, *Progresses*, ii. *460-*2; *Cal.S.P.Dom.* 1611–18, 138, 147.
[13] i.e. feudal aid levied when the king's eldest dau. was married to the Palsgrave Fred., Elector Palatine; the commission for the levy was sent out from Woodstock 30 Aug.: *Cal.S.P.Dom.* 1611–18, 140; *Progresses*, ii. *462, 467–87.
[14] Prince Hen. d. 6 Nov. 1612. The rumour that he was poisoned at Woodstock was discounted: *Cal.S.P.Dom.* 1611–18, 154–5; *Progresses*, ii. 467 sqq.
[15] As constable to 21 Oct. 1612: B 78/2.
[16] The schoolmaster's salary came from a number of sources as explained in the intro. above. This sum seems to be made up of the £5 interest money and the rent from the White Hart, occupied by local clergyman Ant. Noble.

[f. 19r] A Rente Roule of all the rentes within the said boughrough made the twentith daye of Januarye...1608...in the tyme of Thomas Bradshewe maior, William Ryly, Thomas Browne, William Rayer and William Flye aldermen and Edmond Hiorne towneclark and John Glover and Richard Meades chamberlains of the said boughroughe as followeth[1]

Property[2]	tenant (a) and occupier (b) on 20 Jan. 1608[/9][3]	changes made by 20 Dec. 1613[4]
RENTES *due to the towne upon lease* Due at Our Lady Day [25 March] and Michaelmas [30 Sept.]		
Upper part of Le Poole £4	a. & b. Mr Thomas Browne, alderman [d. 1621]	
Another part of same meade £4	a. & b. Mary Phillipps, widdowe of John Phillipps, alderman [d. 1608]	
Ditto £2 16s 8d	a. & b. William Ball [ironmonger d. 1615]	
Ditto £2 16s 8d	a. & b. Widdowe Munck	

Property[2]	tenant (a) and occupier (b) on 20 Jan. 1608[/9][3]	changes made by 20 Dec. 1613[4]
Butclose 5s 6d	a. [John] Pyman late alderman [d. 1596] b. in occupation of Salloman Fly son of William Fly alderman[5]	a. & b. Salloman Flye [woolman d. 1616] own occupation
Little garden plot between wooden bridge and Gyles Coles house fronting upon the hollowaye 2s	a. & b. Robert Bignell, baker [d. 1624]	
[f. 19v] Churchyeard rent 3s	a. & b. William Meatcalfe alderman late deceased [d. 1608], nowe in tenure of William Meatcalfe his youngest son [woollendraper d. c.1644]	
Tenement new built on Cornemarkett Hill with the backside adjoyning 6s 8d Lease of seaven score years or thereabouts still to come	a. & b. William Meatcalfe the son	a. & b. wherein he nowe dwelleth [sentence re lease crossed out]
His dwellinge house next unto the parke gate 6s 8d	a. & b. Thomas Browne alderman, demised unto him, his son and daughter for three lives	
Messuage or tenement in the streete next the parke gate 5s 4d	a. Phillipp Jeames b. John Hamond labourer	a. & b. Edmond Hiorne[6] [margin] a [whole entry deleted by 1613 but appears on f. 20v under chantry quitrents]
Tenement upon the holloway leading to Le Poole next unto the Piggin house 5s	a. & b. Richard Dodman [carpenter d. 1610] wherein he dwelleth	

Property[2]	tenant (a) and occupier (b) on 20 Jan. 1608[/9][3]	changes made by 20 Dec. 1613[4]
Tenement next unto the church adjoyning the towne office 10s	a. & b. Edmond Hiorne nowe towneclerk [d. 1669] wherein he dwelleth	
Tenement and certeine lande in Hensington Feild adjoyning to the lane leading towardes Hensington, called the White Hearte. 46s 8d to the chamberlains for the schoolmaster's wages and to the towne 6s 8d	a. & b. Mr Anthony Noble, clerk [d. 1617]	
Tenement and backside in woollmarket streete 16s	a. John Dubber, shewmaker b. in occupation of Thomas Screevin, glasier	a. & b. Thomas Screevin [d. 1637]
Wooll barne adjoyning backside of above 15s	a. & b. John Dubber	a. & b. Thomas Screevin, 10s[7]
Shopp and seller newly built adjoyning his house in the hogmarkett or beafe markett 2s	a. & b. William Bradshewe [mercer, d. 1616] son of Raphe Bradshewe, mercer	
[f. 20r] Mawlte house adjoyning to the river neere unto the bayes 5s	a. & b. Thomas Browne alderman	
House and garden lying between the White Harte and the house of Symon Jeames nowe schoolmaster. No lease in writing. 26s 8d	a. & b. Christian Tanner, widdowe of William Tanner [d. 1608]	[entries in first two columns deleted by 1613]. [margin, not deleted] 20s. This rent allowed gratis to Mr Jeames more than his £14[8]
Wooll beame 20s	[no tenant given]	And 1s 1613. [margin] stet. 24s which is due at Our Lady Day 1614[9]

Property[2]	tenant (a) and occupier (b) on 20 Jan. 1608[/9][3]	changes made by 20 Dec. 1613[4]
Hampton Poyle meade 1d	a. & b. Richard Tayler for 3 years and after 45s a yeer for 7 years beginning at Our Lady Day	[margin] Discharged and sold to Mr Rayer for £10 which he paid to the towne[10]
Summ [1610]		Summ [1613]
£20 8s 11d minus 2s 3d		£21 7s 10d
21 Dec. 1610 [signature of] Ed. Hiorne		20 Dec. 1613

CHANTERY QUITT RENTES
To be paid at Our Lady Day and Michaelmas

Tenement called Magdalen House adjoyning to the hollowaye 5s	a. & b. Gyles Coles his dwellinge house	
House in Oxford streete near Robin Hoodes elme 20s	a. & b. Bridgett Spittle widdowe her house	
Tenement in Hoggmarket streete 10s	a. William Bradshewe [mercer d. 1616] b. wherein John Bradshewe his brother nowe dwelleth late the lande of John Ryly [d. 1611]	a. & b. John Bradshewe [mercer d. 1614] his dwellinge house
Tenement in the Beafemarkett streete 13s 4d	a. William Fly alderman b. wherein Hugh Hamond [pewterer] nowe dwelleth	a. Salloman Fly 10s b. Hugh Hamond and b. more of John Ackly for grownd between Hickes house and Acklyes which Mr Fly houldeth 3s 4d

Property[2]	tenant (a) and occupier (b) on 20 Jan. 1608[/9][3]	changes made by 20 Dec. 1613[4]
Tenement in Oxford streete otherwise called Sheepemarkett streete 3s	a. Frauncis Collingwood [woolman d. 1613] b. wherein William Hickes smith nowe dwelleth	a. Widdowe Collingwood [Joan Collingwood]
Tenement in Oxford streete adjoyning on south side 12s 4d	a. Frauncis Collingwood b. wherein John Gibbes nowe dwelleth	a. Humfrey Silver b. wherein William Wheeler nowe dwelleth
[f. 20v] Tenement in Black Hall Lane 4s 6d	a. & b. Richard Hawkins wherein he dwelleth late land of Abraham Dawnter [weaver d. 1605]	a. Edmond Hiorne b. wherein Richard Hawkins dwelleth[11]
Ditto 4s 6d	a. Robert Chamberlaine b. wherein widdowe Fleminge dwelleth	a. George Noble [cooper] b. wherein William Muckell dwelleth
Tenement on south side of William Bradshewes shopp in the woollmarkett 8s	a. & b. Elizabeth Rathbone wyddowe wherein she dwelleth	
Tenement in the streete next the parke gate 8s	a. Widdowe Fleminge b. wherein William Holloway gent. nowe dwelleth	a. Edmond Hiorne[12]
Tenement	a. [Phillipp Jeames in leases on f. 19r]	a. & b. Edmond Hiorne wherein John Hamond lately dwelt
Summ [1610]		[1613]
£4 8s 4d		£4 8s 8d
21 December 1610 [Signature of] Ed. Hiorne		20 December 1613

CHANTERY QUITT RENTES
To be paied at Michaelmas only

Property[2]	tenant (a) and occupier (b) on 20 Jan. 1608[/9][3]	changes made by 20 Dec. 1613[4]
Dwellinge house nowe in parke gate streete over against the church 3s 4d [Mundyes]	a. & b. Frauncis Collingwood	a. & b. Thomas Browne alderman for his two tenementes which he bought of widdowe Collingwood, the one called Mundyes and the other called Maynardes, 3s 4d and 18d. [Total] 4s 10d [and see below f. 21v]
House leading along Blakhall Lane 2s 4d	a. & b. Robert Bignill [baker d. 1624]	[margin] a stet
House called The Crowne, and close adjoyning to the parke walle 18d	a. & b. John Glover [innholder d. 1643]	
Tenement in [blank] lane 16d	a. Frauncis Collingwood b. in occupation of John Abbottes sawier	a. Widdowe Collingwood b. in occupation of Edward Longe [lastmaker d. 1635]
Two tenements lying by the holloway 12d. 6d a peece	a. Thomas Paynter [d. 1619] b. one in occupation of Bennett Paynter his son [glover d. 1646] b. the other in occupation of John Parker	a. John Kirby[13]
[f. 21r] Tenement in Oxford streete 7d	a. Bartholomew Edginge b. wherein Nicholas Glover [d. 1620] nowe dwelleth	

Property[2]	tenant (a) and occupier (b) on 20 Jan. 1608[/9][3]	changes made by 20 Dec. 1613[4]
Tenement and other premises in Oxford streete 3s	a. Thomas Grove gent. b. wherein Thomas Godferye [glover d. 1627] nowe dwelleth	
Great house[14] in the streete at Oxford townes end 15¹/₂d	a. Henry Whitton gent. b. wherein William Raunson and John Gadbury gent. nowe dwell	a. John Whitton [d. 1643] b. wherein Edward Evans [rector 1610 to 1621] and John Gadbury gentlemen dwell
Tenement adjoyning to Mr Henry Whittons house 12d	a. John Whitton gent. b. wherein John Combes carrier nowe dwelleth	b. late Combes[15] Mr Gadbury nowe houldeth [margin] There is 12d a yeer concealed a long tyme since
Dovehouse close in Ould Woodstock adjoyning to the weste side of the parke wall neere Old Woodstock gate and adjoyning to easte of the highway from Woodstock to Wootton 6d	a. & b. Mr Jerome Nasshe [d. 1623] lately pulled down by him	
Tenement next unto the church 1d	a. & b. Symon Walker, sonne of Thomas Walker, grandchild of Raphe Walker	a. & b. George Noble cooper where he nowe dwelleth
House in Oxfordstreete 1d	a. & b. Raphe Durbridge [Dudbridge, blacksmith, d. 1615]	
Tenement in Oxfordstreete 1d	a. & b. John Cooper	

Property[2]	tenant (a) and occupier (b) on 20 Jan. 1608[/9][3]	changes made by 20 Dec. 1613[4]
Tenement in High streete 1d	a. William Ball [ironmonger d. 1615] b. nowe the land of Thomas Symons	
Summ [1610] 16s 2¹/₂d		[1613] 16s 5¹/₂d
21 December 1610 [Signature of] Ed. Hiorne		20 December 1613

[f. 21v] QUITT RENTES to be payed at Michaelmas

House at the parke gate 6d	a. & b. Thomas Browne alderman	[entry deleted][16] [In margin] Extinguished
Chawcers House 18d	a. & b. Mary Phillipps her house	a. & b. Jerome Kyte gent. [d. 1631] his house
Puttgally 6d	[not in existence until 1612: see end of rental]	a. & b. Jerome Kyte
Dwellinge house in Parke gate streete 10d	a. & b. Thomas Meatcalfe [woollen draper d. 1629]	
Dwellinge house on Hoggerill hill 1d	a. & b. Symon Collier, late Christofer Battons [Batsone d. 1609] his father-in-law	
The garden and court before the door 3s 4d		a. & b. Symon Collier [margin] 20 Dec. 1613 agreed that he that dwelleth there shall pay 3s 4d per annum which is behind for two years
Tenement in the Coperyeware streete	a. John Whitton alias Darling b. wherein John Lowe cooper dwelleth	a. William Meatcalfe [d. c.1644] [margin] More every Good Friday 6s 8d to the poor

Property[2]	tenant (a) and occupier (b) on 20 Jan. 1608[/9][3]	changes made by 20 Dec. 1613[4]
Dwellinge house in Parkegate streete 18d	a. & b. Frauncis Collingwood [d. 1613]	a. & b. Thomas Browne for one of the houses he bought of Collingwood [entry deleted by 1613; see Maynardes on f. 20v]
Tenement in Oxon' streete near the Corne market hill 6d	a. Thomas Browne alderman b. wherein Margery Fletcher widdowe nowe dwelleth	
Dwellinge house against Corne markett 7d	a. & b. William Rayer alderman [d. 1619] his dwellinge house	
Tenement 12d	a. Mr Alexander Crosly b. nowe in occupation of John Dubber shewmaker	
Tenement over against the Crosse 3d	a. Town of Bister b. Josephe Harris, mercer, alderman [d. 1635]	
House over against the Crosse 3d	a. & b. William Ryly . alderman	a. Leonard Ryly b. wherein Nicholas Tayler dwelleth
Tenement hereto adjoyning 3d	a. [William Ryly] b. nowe in occupation of Nicholas Taylor	a. & b. Widdowe Ryly wherein she dwelleth [whole entry deleted by 1613; see entry below]. [margin] a
Tenement in Glovers and Shewmakers streete 5d	a. [Tenant not given] b. Robert Bruce and William King shoemakers	[Entry deleted by 1613]
House 5d	a. Silvester b. Water Parker dwelleth in	
House 3d	[see Ryly above]	a. & b. Widdowe Ryly wherein she dwelleth

Property[2]	tenant (a) and occupier (b) on 20 Jan. 1608[/9][3]	changes made by 20 Dec. 1613[4]
[f. 22r] Dwellinge house in Shewmakers streete 5d	a. & b. William Dunford[17]	a. & b. Salloman Fly his dwellinge house late Dunfords
Tenement in Shewmakers streete 6d	a. & b. John Raunson glover [d. 1610] wherein he dwelleth	a. William Rayer alderman [d. 1619] b. where William Ranson dwelleth
House in Shewmakers streete 1¹/₂d Pales and porch before her dore 12d	a. & b. Mistris Leake widdowe [Ann d. 1615] a. & b. ditto	pales and porch 6d
House 3d	a. John Gregory b. wherein Thomas Abbott sawyer [d. 1613] dwelleth	a. Frauncis Gregory esq. b. wherein William Butterfield [tailor d. 1624] nowe dwelleth
Range of housing next unto Oxford Townes end 14d	a. Hugh Weller for b. William Wells house 2¹/₂d Richard Lowes house 2¹/₂d John Archers house 2¹/₂d John Seelyes house 2¹/₂d Hugh Wellers close 4d	a. William Rayer alderman by lease of Hugh Weller for b. Widdowe Welles Richard Collingwoods Alexander Hedes John Seelyes Hugh Wellers
House at Oxford Townes end 3d	a. & b. John Slatter of Hensington [d. 1635]	
Tenement in the sheepemarket in Oxford streete called Blundells lande 3d	a. Edmond Hiorne towneclark b. nowe in the occupation of William Edwardes [tanner]	
Tenement called The Rose and Crowne in Oxford streete 6d	a. William Rayer alderman b. Thomas Williams baker [d. 1636]	

Property[2]	tenant (a) and occupier (b) on 20 Jan. 1608[/9][3]	changes made by 20 Dec. 1613[4]
Copped hall in the sheepe markett in Oxford streete 1½d	a. & b. Richard Wright joyner wherein he dwelleth near Durbridge the smith his house	a. Widdowe Collingwood b. Richard Write late dwelleth
Tenement in Oxford streete near Robbine Hooddes elme 1½d	a. Thomas Browne alderman b. wherein John Ackly dwelleth	
Dwellinge house in Oxford streete 5d and pales 2d	a. & b. Benedict Norwood [d. 1643] own dwellinge	
House in Oxford streete 3d	a. William Rayer alderman b. for Edward Barnes house	
House in Oxford streete 3d	a. William Rayer alderman b. John Tayler	b. Widdowe Tayler
[f. 22v] House in Oxford streete 5½d	a. Robert Symons b. in tenure of Androwe Jarves [or Iarnes][18]	b. Rudgate [deleted]; widdowe Phillipps [added]
House in Oxford streete 3d	a. John Ryly [d. 1611] b. in occupation of Bartholomew Edginge glover	a. Widowe Ryly [margin in latin] Enquire about it
House in Oxford streete 3d pales and porch 6d	a. & b. John Norman [butcher d. ?1653]	
Tenement by the holloway 2½d	a. Robert Chamberlaine b. wherein Thomas Jackson [alias] Loaders[19] dwelleth	a. Nathaniel Noble b. wherein John Collingwood dwelleth
Tenement in Crowe lane 1½d	a. Frauncis Collingwood b. wherein John Abbott dwelleth Late land of Ascole of London painter	a. Widdowe Collingwood b. Widdowe Bowlandes [margin] Enquire
Bakehouse 2d	a. & b. Robert Bignell [baker d. 1624]	
Dwellinge house 3d	a. & b. Thomas Paynter	

Property[2]	tenant (a) and occupier (b) on 20 Jan. 1608[/9][3]	changes made by 20 Dec. 1613[4]
The Bull over against the Crosse 5s 6d	a. Richard Raves b. wherein Thomas Bradshewe maior dwelleth	a. & b. Henry Bradshewe
House over against the guild hall 6d 3d a peece	a. Mr. Henry Standard b. Jerome White [sergeant d. 1618] and Richard Shad	
House in the beafe markett 4d oven 2d	a. Thomas Browne alderman b. wherein William Hitch dwelleth	
Dwellinge house 1½d pales at the door 4d	a. & b. Richard Peeters woolman [d. 1610] own house	a. & b. Widdowe Peeters
Tenement by the holloway 1½d and ground to sett his side wall upon next unto the streete 3d	a. Roberte Seare [cordwainer d. 1609] late Barneshewes land	a. John Doa [shoemaker]
House over against the High Crosse 18d	a. William Flye alderman b. wherein Edward Rudgate [shoemaker d. 1617] dwelleth	a. Salloman Flye [d. 1616] b. wherein Drewe Gregory dwelleth
His shopp 1d	a. [William Flye] b. wherein Drewe Gregory cutler nowe dwelleth	a. [Salloman Flye] b. wherein Pepper Cooper [cooper] nowe dwelleth
[f. 23r] Dwellinge house in Oxon' streete 3d	a. & b. Michael Nursse [butcher d. 1609]	a. & b. widdow Bradshewe late Mr Nursses
Dwellinge house in Beafe markett streete 1½d	a. & b. William Bradshewe [mercer d. 1616]	
Tenement near the guildhall in woollmarkett 6d	a. Alexander Crosly b. wherein Roger Sturgis [barber] nowe dwelleth	b. wherein Thomas Heathen [sergeant d. 1642] dwelleth
Tenement in Petty Johns lane towards the backgreen 4d	a. William Porter [d. 1622] b. wherein Symons carpenter dwelleth	

Property[2]	tenant (a) and occupier (b) on 20 Jan. 1608[/9][3]	changes made by 20 Dec. 1613[4]
Peece of garden adjoyning same house 0d	Due to the towne, not demised as yet to any person	
Tenement in Petty Johns lane 1/2d	a. & b. William Rayer [d. 1619] late purchased of John Whitton	
Tenement in Oxford streete 1d	a. Thomas Metcalfe b. wherein Frauncis Garter nowe dwelleth	
House in the woollmarkett 3d	a. Thomas Russell of Sawford b. wherein John Heath dwelleth	b. wherein Nicholas Glover [d. 1620] dwelleth
Tenement 3/4d in the Cooperye markett	a. & b. Thomas Meatcalfe late William Glovers	
and garden plot adjoyning 1 1/2d	a. & b. Thomas Meatcalfe	
Tenement and barne in the backgreene next the parke wall 1 1/2d	a. & b. William Meatcalfe	
Tenement at the Parke gate streete 1 1/2d	a. Thomas Meatcalfe b. wherein Alexander Head dwelleth	a. Edmond Hiorne b. wherein Randall Richards dwelleth
Tenement 1 1/2d	a. Thomas Meatcalfe b. wherein Water Parker fydler dwelleth	b. wherein William Bradshewe dwelleth
House by Robin Hooddes elme in Oxford streete 12d	a. & b. John Tomlins	
His pales before his door 4d	a. & b. Richard Meades [yeoman d. 1620]	

Property[2]	tenant (a) and occupier (b) on 20 Jan. 1608[/9][3]	changes made by 20 Dec. 1613[4]
Peece of ground adjoyning to the north house of a tenement of Newe Colledge in Oxon' over against John Normans house 6d	b. in occupation of Robert Winter [sadler d. 1635]	
[f. 23v] Certain pales before Nicholas Stayners streete door on Oxford streete 1d	a. & b. Robert Symons	
Yeardes of Hampton Poyle 1d	a. & b. Richard Taylor three yeeres and after for five	[deleted by 1613; see Rayer in leases f. 20r]
Two tenements at the bridge foot 2¹/₂d	a. Thomas Paynter [d. 1619] b. in the townes gift nowe in tenure of widdowe Gyles and Henry Price dishmonger	a. John Kirby
Tenement upon the the hollowaye 4¹/₂d	a. Mr Jerome Nashe b. wherein Michael Pulchoe nowe dwelleth	
Tenement at the parke gate called The Talbott 3d	a. Jerome Nashe b. whereof Mr Alderman Fly payeth for his house 2d	

Summ [1610]

[deleted] 29s 0s 1³/₄d
[margin] 28s 0s 9¹/₂d

22 December 1610

SUMM TOTAL 1610[20]
[deleted] £27 2s 7¹/₄d
[changed to] £26 15s 7¹/₄d

22 December 1610
[Signature of] Ed. Hiorne

Property[2]	*tenant (a) and occupier (b)* *on 20 Jan. 1608[/9]*[3]	*changes made* *by 20 Dec. 1613*[4]
		Due from Mr Kyte for his newe wall and for settinge upp his putgally neere his brewehouse 6d, which was agreed on befoure Mr Recorder 6 April 1612 as appeereth by a note upon the fyle.
		Summ [1613] 29s 3³/₄
		20 Dec. 1613
		SUMM TOTAL 1613[21] £28 2s 3³/₄

From Mr Doleman of Chilray £8 per annum at Our Lady Day and Michaelmas equally

[1] This rental has been rearranged into a table in order to show the alterations made over the years more clearly. It was made 20 Jan. 1608/9, but the first totalling up was not entered and signed until 21 Dec. 1610. Three years later, Edm. Hiorne altered the previous dates and totals to bring the rental up to date on 20 Dec. 1613. He may have made the changes to individual holdings as they occurred or in 1613. Hiorne had in 1608 one rental and in 1611 seven rent rolls in his hands which were to be redelivered, presumably to the chamberlains: B 81, ff. 22v., 25r.

[2] Property and rents on 20 Jan. 1608/9 are shown in first column.

[3] The tenants of the town (a), and their sub-tenants the occupiers (b), as entered on 20 Jan. 1608/9, are shown in the second column. Occupations and dates of death shown in square brackets are supplied by the editor from information in the accts., wills and inventories, freemen's admissions in B 83, and the recognizances in B 77/2.

[4] The third column shows changes to the rental by 20 Dec. 1613. Where there is no entry in this column, there has been no change to the tenant and occupier listed for 1609 in the second column.

[5] For the Fly family and its property see Borough Mun. deed 13/2/7, by which William settled tenements on Salloman in 1611. Salloman died first, on 18 Sept. 1616, and in his will, in deed B 44/1, left Butt close and other property to his father to settle his debts. His father d. *c.* 1623: he was no longer listed among the aldermen then.

[6] Hiorne paid £10 for the farm of the property in 1613: see 1613 acct., f. 17v.; and 1618 acct., f. 45v.

[7] Screevin took over in 1612: see 1612 acct., f. 13v.

[8] See Widow Tanner's rent of 6s 8d in 1609 on f. 2r, and the 20s deducted by 1611 from the rents on f. 13r.

[9] Let to Ric. Shad by 1613: see 1613 acct., f. 17r.

[10] By 1612: see 1612 acct., f. 13v.

[11] By 1613: see 1613 acct., f. 17v and n.6.
[12] By 1611: see 1611 acct., f. 10r and n.3; 1618 acct., f. 45v.
[13] By 1611: see 1613 acct., f. 17v and n.2.
[14] The arrears are noted in the early accts. up to 1625. Hen. Whitton was nephew and heir to Geo. Whitton (d. 1606). John Whitton, Geo.'s illegitimate son by his servant Alice Darling, was Geo.'s heir in Hensington. See also the 1610 acct., n.1. For Evans and Gadbury, see 1613 acct., f. 27r.
[15] By 1610: see 1610 acct., f. 9v.
[16] Sold to the town: see 1609 acct., f. 3r and n.13.
[17] Described as yeoman of Ditchley in the bond for payment by Fly on 8 Feb. 1609/10, but as gent. of New Woodstock in 1627 in Borough Mun. 44/1.
[18] Jarves seems more probable and there was an And. Iarves in Woodstock in 1617: B 96. However, an And. Janes was admitted in 1581: B 81, f. 18v. Both names occur in probate recs. for Woodstock.
[19] Alias given in 1601 rental: B 96.
[20] Deleted sum is the same as the rents received in the 1609 acct. and the new sum that for rents in the 1611 acct. The rents are not given as an individual item in the 1610 acct..
[21] The same as rents in 1613 acct.

[f. 17r] 19 December 1612 to 20 December 1613, Josephe Harris and William Bradshewe chamberlains

[Receipts]	£	s	d
Debtes due and owinge to the towne			
William Butterfeild oweth upon 1 bonde	0	10	0
Mistress Phillipps for quitt rent	0	4	6
Mr Whitton for quitt rent	0	9	1
John Powell for his admission	0	10	0
Drewe Gregory oweth for his admission	0	20	0
Bryan Steephens for his admission	0	20	0
John Archer for his admission	0	20	0
Widdowe Collingwood oweth £4 upon a bond which Mistris Hoord gave to the towne and which was due at Midsomer 1613.[1] The bond remains with Mr Rayer	4	0	0
Debtes which the towne doth owe at the last accompte			
To Joseph Harris	22	5	6
To John Norman	0	10	0
To John Bradshewe	0	4	0

Md William Rayer alderman is to have Taylers rent of 45s per annum during his whole lease. He paied £10 which was accompted for at the laste accompte.

Md delivered to Robert Bignill and William Edwardes collectors for the poore in reddy mony which they are to accompte for	0	10	0

Md Thomas Screevin did undertake to keepe the church and
the hall in glasinge for 12s per annum from this day.

Md allso Hugh Hammond undertooke to keepe the leades of
the tower for 12d per annum from this day.

Md the wooll beame was then lett to Richard Shad from Our
Lady Day 1613 till Our Lady Day 1614 for   0   24   0

[f. 17v] Mony receaved by the said chamberlaines to the use of the towne from the said 19 December 1612

Delivered to the chamberlains at the last accompt	0	30	0
In reddy mony at Whitsontide 1613	9	0	0
For 3 fynes for Kirby[2]	0	12	0
For the admission of Busby the barber[3]	0	13	4
By Longe for tole of the beafe markett 19 December 1612 till 20 December 1613. [Total corrected in MS. from £3 14s1/2d]	3	2	21/2
For the admission of Thomas Rayer and John Stone	0	17	4
£10 which Edmond Hiorne paied for the farme of John Hamondes house[4]	10	0	0
Of Mr Doleman for one years anuitye	8	0	0
[Deleted] Mr Noble for rent of his house	0	46	8
Of Mr Ray[er] for the interest of his £50 for one yeere endinge 20 June 1613[5]	5	0	0
For breache of the peace made by Thomas Heathen	0	0	12
Receaved of Edmond Hiorne towneclark, for fynes for the sealinge of certins fynes yet to be sealed due to the towne at 4s a seale, for Salloman Fly from his father 4s, Mr Dunford from Salloman Fly 4s, Richard Hawkins from his sister 4s, Edmond Hiorne from Richard Hawkins 4s, Richard Pyman from widdowe Collingwood and others 4s.[6]	0	20	0
The seale of one fyne from widdowe Collingwood to Humfry Silver	0	4	0
Of Edmond Rudgate for stallages for year ending 20 December	8	7	4
Rentes of whole towne, yeere ending Michaelmas 1613	28	2	31/4
Of widdowe Collingwood £4 which Mistris Whorde gave to the towne	4	0	0

[ff. 18r, v, 24 and 24a] [blank] [For ff. 19r–23v, see above, pp. 28–42]

[f. 25r] [Disbursements]

For Beastes sute and the discharge of amercementes out of the Exchequer and to
the clarkes of the assises. In Hillary terme 1612 to Mr Recorder for his fee 10s.

To Mr Lutwich the attorny for his fee 5s 6d. For the towneclarkes diet and his horsemeate 9 dayes 27s 6d. In Easter term to Mr Underill 2s 6d, to Mr Fowler 2s 6d, to his man 6d, to Mr Lutchwich 6s 8d, to Mr Spiller for rulinge the petition 9s 4d, to his man Corbut 12d. Trinity term to Mr Lutwich 6s 8d, for the essoyne 10d, for a pynt of sack 6d. At Oxon' assises 13 July payed to Beaste for a composition for Mr Brownes house £6 13s 4d, for the judge for the fine 10s, for drawinge the fine and for a deede of release and bonde 5s, for a coppy of the quowarrant 6d, to the baylife that made the same 12d. For expences at Oxon' at the sealinge the bookes 12d. Expences at Mr Maiors at the payment of the mony 20d. For the towneclarkes expences at Oxon' aboute the same 2s 6d. Geiven to the clarkes of thassises for dischardge of Mr Maior for his appeerance that assises 3s.

	11	11	6
Paied to this accomptant Josephe Harris as monye dewe to him from the towne at the last accompte	22	5	6
To him for the interest of the same monye	0	35	0
Geiven to Sir Henry Browne[7] one cake at Christmas 1612 10s, and in rewardes at the same house 20s	0	30	0
To Sir Thomas Spencer one cake 10s, one suger lofe wayinge 12lb 2 oz, 18s 7d, rewardes 25s 8d, same place	0	54	3
For wine and beare spent by the neighbours at the tastinge of the taste cakes	0	2	0
To Mr Maior mony to poore 19 December to 14 August	0	21	3
For James Dissells shrewde and threed, 3 ells	0	2	4
Wine to a preacher which laye at Meades house	0	0	20
Wine geiven by Mr Maior to a messenger that came for the extreates out of the Exchequer	0	0	14
In March for wine and suger geiven to Sir Thomas Spencer when he tooke muster here[8]	0	3	10
4 March for wringinge	0	2	0
25 March 2 wardsmen	0	0	16
[f. 25v] To William Hickes for mending the clock	0	5	0
To Shad for fetching Mr Dolemans mony at Our Lady Day	0	2	6
Wine upon Captaine Warde by Mr Maior his appoyntment	0	0	12
Wine and suger geiven to Mr Woodward when preached here	0	2	11
Geiven by Mr Maior and the neighbours 11s for a breakfaste upon Sir Henry Browne in April	0	11	0
25 April payed to Ducock by Mr Maiors appoyntment for chardges leid out by him	0	4	0
27 April paied to Drewe for mendinge of the towne armor 12s whereof 5s was deducted out of his 20s which he oweth so paied him	0	7	0
To Butterfeild for mendinge the paule	0	0	18
Geiven to a Turke by Mr Maiors appoyntment to make up his collection 6s 8d	0	0	22

9 May wine to a preacher that dined at Mr Kites[9]	0	0	20
To a preacher by Mr Maior and the neighbours consent 6s 8d and wine 12d	0	7	8
In May to Corbott by Mr Mayor and Mr Rayer theire appoyntment for mendinge the clock 26s 8d, oyle 2d	0	26	10
Geiven in rewarde to a messenger that brought a writt and proclamations concerninge halfe penny tokens	0	0	18
Wine geiven to Mr Tayler when he preached	0	3	2
Paied to Butterfeild by Mr Maiors appoyntment for mendinge of Mr Whittons auncient[10] which was torne	0	0	12
Beare spent at the church accompt at Whitsontide	0	0	12
Wine geiven to Mr George Spencer when he procured woode against Whitsontide	0	0	12
Expences upon widdowe Coles[11] when she was in prison	0	0	3
For 2 wardsmen on Mary Magdalen faiere	0	0	16
For ringers at St James Day	0	2	6
Delivered to Shad for 2 belropes 20 July	0	6	0
Payed Mr Rayer for wine due to him at the church accompte,[12] parcell of the 22s 6½d then due to the churchwardens John Norman and John Lowe	0	19	2
To ringers 5 August	0	4	0
Wine to preacher at Henry Rudgates funerall[13]	0	2	2
[f. 26r] 11 August wine and suger to Mr Recorder 2s 2d, a busshell of oates sent to him 2s 6d.	0	4	8
13 August paied to Mr Osbaston undershreive for Sir William Clark the fee farme	0	53	10
14 August wine to preacher that dined at Meades	0	0	20
For a shrewde for Joane Bowland	0	2	4
To Mr Maior for his fee for yeere ending Michaelmas	10	0	0
For wine and suger spent at Mr Maiors when Mr Roolles preached in August	0	0	23
Wine and suger then to a preacher that dined at Meades his house	0	0	20
For 3 wardsmen upon St Mathes fayer	0	2	2
To William Wheeler for mending the treble bell	0	0	12
To him for mending the tressells at the schoolehouse	0	0	6
For worke done about the almeshouse	0	0	16
To Mr Gadbury for a bord for the same use	0	0	12
To Mr Maior mony geiven by him to poor till 13 October	0	5	9
To Mr Evans rent of churchyeard endinge Michaelmas	0	0	18
Wine, suger, ale upon Mr Doctor Tucker and his chapline	0	7	11
Wine and sugar to a preacher 16 October	0	0	20
[Deleted] which dined at Mr Thomas Metcalfes 16d			
Wine and suger upon Mr Trewluck when he preached	0	2	1

	£	s	d
To Mr Ainger by Mr Maiors appoyntment to send a messenger to London to Sir Thomas Challoner for his monye	0	5	0
For oyle for the bells	0	0	2
To the ringers 5 November	0	4	0
Quitt rent £5 6s 8d, 6d acquittance, quart of wine 12d	5	8	2
Mr Recorder his fee for this yeere ending Michaelmas	3	6	8
[f. 26v] To Richard Lowe for the keepinge of Nicholas Glovers base childe from 16 December 1612 untill 23 December 1613 being 53 weekes at 10d by the weeke	0	44	2
To Edmond Hiorne towneclarke fee 40s and keeping chamberlaines accompte 5s	0	45	0
To William Hickes for a lock for the clockhouse dore and nayles for the bells	0	0	17
Geiven Mr Mosse clarke of the markett in December 1613, 10s in rewarde, his diet and wine and the neighbours to beare him companye 17s 5d	0	27	5
To 2 wardsmen on St Nicholas fayer	0	0	16
Sendinge of Isabelle Robinson to the house of correction in December 1613[14]	0	2	6
To Richard Warren composition money due to Bladon	0	3	0
For a shrewde for widdowe Cowles	0	2	5

To Mr Chesterman[15] in Michaelmas terme for the chardge of
the quowarranto against Mr Rayer for beinge crowner. To
Mr Recorder for his advise 10s. For the coppy of the
quowarranto 4s 4d, for the imparlance 7s, for the atturnyes
fee in the Crowne office 6s 8d.[16] For Mr Chestermans fee
3s 4d. To him for Bestes fine, vizt pro bre' con' 2s 6d, pro
fine inde 6s 8d, pro indorsmentes [?magistri] Thelwall 14d, pro
pixid 1d, pro ded pot 9s 2d, pro return' bre' con' 2s, pro return'
ded pot 16d, pro custod' brevium 3s 8d, pro argent receaved 10d,
pro chirographo 5s 8d, pro clerico 3s 4d, pro feod' 6s 8d.[17] For a
horse for sending the charter to Wittny 14d. To Mr Browne
about Bestes sute which he leyed out when he was arrested at
Bestes sute 20s.

	£	s	d
All amountinge to	4	15	7
To Mr Raye[r] for the rent of Richard Coles his house for this yeere endinge at Michaelmas laste	0	16	0
To Mr James for his allowance for one whole yeere endinge at Michaelmas last: £5 at Our Lady Day and £7 at Michaelmas of which £7 40s was the first payment of his £14 per annum agreed upon to be paied him after.	12	0	0

[f. 27r] To be deducted out of the rentrole. For the house
wherein Mr Evans and Mr Gadbury dwell 15^{1}/$_{2}$d.
[Marginated] Mr Whitton hath owed this rent for a longe tyme.
For the house where John Combes late dwelt in which
Mr Gadbury hath as his kitchine 12d. And 24s for the wooll
beame which Richard Shad is to pay at Our Lady Day 1614
for 1 yeere then endinge.   0   26   3^{1}/$_{2}$
Paied to Longe for his wages and ringinge the bell and other
thinges as appeereth by his bill, for the clock and the bell 12s,
keepinge cleane of the leades of the church and the hall 2s 6d,
oyle for the clock and the bells 2s 6d, leather for mendinge the
bellroppes 4d   0   17   4
To John Bradshewe which the towne owed to him at the last
accompt   0   4   0
To Mr Maior for mony leied out by him to poor   0   4   4
To Mr Rayer for a dagger for the towne   0   2   0
To Thomas Screevin for keepinge the hall and the church in
glasse only 12s, for the keepinge the leades of the church
(all but the tower) 6s 8d for this yeere endinge at this accompte.
He is yeerely during his life so to be paied.   0   18   8
To Hugh Hamond for keepinge the leades upon the tower for
this yeere endinge at this accompte 2s. And he is to be so
yeerely paied during his life.   0   2   0
For sendinge for Mr Dolemans mony at Michaelmas   0   2   6

Summ totall leid out   99   2   10^{1}/$_{2}$
Summ of the receiptes is   80   9   5^{3}/$_{4}$
So remayninge due to the accomptantes   18   13   10

[f. 27v] 20 December 1613 at the accompt houlden at the hall William
Bradshewe and Thomas Williams were elected chamberlains

Debtes due to the towne

Mr Whitton oweth for rentes   0   11   4^{1}/$_{2}$
John Powell upon his bonde   0   10   0
Drewe Gregory for his admission   0   15   0
Brian Steephens for his admission   0   15   0
William Archer for his admission[18]   0   15   0
Thomas Aynger oweth 5s which the towne lent him   0   5   0
Mistris Phillipps for rentes   0   4   6

Debtes which the towne oweth

Due to Joseph Harris chamberlyn   18   13   10
More due to John Norman   0   10   0

Receaved by the newe chamberlains

Md delivered to the said newe chamberlains in reddy mony at
the said accompte. [Marginated] receaved 　　　　　　0　31　0

¹ See above in 1612.
² For John Kirby's fines for dwellings by the Holloway see B 78/2, 18 Oct., 21 Dec. 1611, 25 Jan.
1611/12.
³ Edw. Busby, admission paid 22 Feb. 1612/13: B 81, f. 25v.
⁴ Next to the park gate. Hiorne bought up the lease in 1618: acct. below; *V.C.H. Oxon.* xii. 351.
⁵ The £50 was school money on loan: see above, Intro.
⁶ For Fly's fine from his father Wm. see B 13(2)/7. For the fines of Hawkins and Hiorne, Pyman,
Joan Collingwood and Silver see B 78/2, 20 Aug. 1612, 5, 8 June, 8 Nov. 1613.
⁷ Sir Hen. Browne (d. 1638) of Kiddington. He and Sir Peter, who succeeded him in 1639, were
noted recusants: B. Stapleton, 'Catholic Regs. of Dom. Chapel of the Browne-Mostyn Fam. at
Kiddington, 1788–1840', *Catholic Rec. Soc.*, xvii (1915), 455–7.
⁸ Formal musters, which had lapsed in 1603, were resumed in 1612; in 1613 there was fear of a
Spanish invasion: L. Boynton, *Elizabethan Militia, 1558–1638* (London 1967), 209 sqq.
⁹ Jerome Kite, Kyte or Keyt, gent. (d. 1631) held Chaucer's House: rental below; and see appendix,
biogs.
¹⁰ His ensign or standard: *O.E.D.*
¹¹ Joyce Coles, widow, suspected of witchcraft against Ald. Bradshewe on inf. of Eliz. Smith and Jane
Bradshewe, 29 May 1613: B 78/2. There is no conclusion, presumably because she is the widow
Cowles for whom a shroud is provided below.
¹² Probably communion wine.
¹³ His status came from being sergeant-at-the-mace: see appendix, biogs.
¹⁴ Set up in Witney in 1611: Bodl. MS. Top. Oxon. d 211, f. 88.
¹⁵ Jas. Chesterman of Oxf., gent., active in county legal affairs, related to previous town clerk and
associated with Woodstock from at least 1611: B 78/2, 17 Apr. 1611, and below.
¹⁶ Perhaps a challenge to his right to act as coroner within the borough from the king's court of the
verge when in Woodstock. Imparlance = petition in court for a day to consider the defence: Jacob,
Dict.
¹⁷ Payments for writs, their return into court, for money and fees. Probably writs *contra formam* and
dedimus potestatem. The latter was used to speed process: ibid. For Eubele Thelwall, later Master in
Chancery, see Foster, *Alumni*. The MS. reading of the word before his name is not certain.
¹⁸ See above in 1611, n.6.

[f. 28r] 20 December 1613 to 23 December 1614, William Bradshewe and Thomas Williams, chamberlains

[Receipts]	£	s	d
Debtes owing and owed [as on *f. 27v*]			
Monyes receved by the chamberlains			
Delivered to them in reddy monye at the accompte	0	31	0
Of Mr Doleman at Our Lady Day	4	0	0
And at Michaelmas	4	0	0
For a seale for Bartholomewe Edginge his fine from Bigges and Bowden¹	0	4	0

Delivered to them in reddy mony at Whitsontide	5	0	0
Of Longe for the tole [for the year]	0	57	5
Of Mr Rayer interest of £50 for the yeere ending 20 June	5	0	0
Of Edmond Rudgate for stallages for yeere	8	0	10
Rentes of towne for one yeere	27	0	19
Of Pawle Samone 6s, William Dainnell 3s 4d, Abraham Miller 12d, for composition monye for informers actions[2]	0	10	4
Of Nicholas Midwinter for breaking the peace upon Roberte Bruce[3]	0	0	12
[f. 28v] Richard Shadd for rente of wooll beame for one yeere ending Our Lady Day	0	24	0
For a horsse which was taken upon John Amosse	0	33	4
For the peste house soulde to John Collingwood	0	7	4
Of Stowte for a composition for the informers sute[4]	0	3	4
Mr Glover hath one grey trotting coult which was sould by one Christofer Freeman of Wallingborowe in the county of Northampton to one Mr Oliver Aschcombe of Lyford in the county of Barkes for 5 nobles. Praysed at 30s	0	30	0

Mr Ashcombe was promised by me to have back 3s 4d which he gave in earneste to Freeman.
[Marginated] Disavowed at Magdalen faier 1614.

Summ totall receaved	63	4	2
Summ totall leid out	65	19	1
Remayninge due to the chamberlins	0	54	11
Besides Mr Raye[r] demaundeth for Coles his rente	0	16	0

Debtes which the towne oweth

23 December 1614. Md at this accompt the towne oweth to Mr Harris maior which he is to have interest[5] from this day	20	10	10
Md more due to Mr Rayer for Richard Coles his rent for the last yeere	0	16	0
Md more due to William Bradshewe from the towne upon his accompte. It is entred in the ledger 50s but he receaved 20s	0	30	0

Debtes owed to the town

[as f. 27v but Thomas Aynger omitted]

Md John Archer hath undertaken to keepe Nicholas Glovers base child at 16d a wick till his 15s be paied.

Md at the accompte 23 December 1614 there was delivered in reddy mony to Thomas Williams and William Bradshewe chamberlins	0	28	0

[f. 29r] [Disbursements]

22 December 1613. [Deleted] To Richard Lowe for keeping
Nicholas Glovers base child 5s.

22 December to a messenger that brought a writt with proclamations concerning working of clothes truly	0	2	6
24 December geiven by Mr Maiors appoyntment to the towne of Bissiter towardes the newe erecting of burned howses	0	5	0
25 December wine to Mr Ingolsbe that preached	0	0	22½
1 January [1614] for 3 cakes 30s, one shugerloffe waying 10lb 2 oz at 18d the pownde 15s 2½d, of which the said sugerloffe and one cake was sent to Sir Thomas Spencer, our high steward, one cake to Sir Henry Lee, the other cake to Sir Henry Browne	0	45	2½
3 January in rewardes at Sir Thomas Spencers 26s 4d and at Sir Henry Lees 21s	0	47	4
Spent at Mr Maiors in wine and suger at the eating of the taste cakes	0	3	3
9 January geiven by Mr Maiors appoyntment to a messenger that brought a writt with proclamations concerninge feltes	0	2	6
2 March payed for wine and suger by Mr Maiors appoyntment geiven to Sir Henry Lee and his lady	0	5	8
13 March for wine and suger to Mr Doctor Searchfeild when he preached heere	0	2	1
To a poore preacher in rewarde 3s, in wine 12d	0	4	0
15 March for a bellrope to Tyms 3s 4d, a bauderick 14d	0	4	6
26 March to Mr Maior 3s which he gave to the shreeve for the warrant to chuse our burgesses[6]	0	3	0
15 March to Mr Maior [as] geiven to poore people	0	5	0
30 March wine and suger sent to Mr Whittons to Mr Recorder	0	2	1
24 March to the ringers	0	3	0
25 March to 2 wardsmen in the fayer	0	0	16
[f. 29v] 8 April to Mr James half yeeres stipend	7	0	0
[To him]other half yeeres stipende	7	0	0
To Richard Shad going for Mr Dolemans mony at Our Lady Day and Michaelmas [sum corrected from 3s 6d]	0	5	0
10 April for wine geiven to Sir Thomas Spencer and Mr Culpepper at theire being at the Bull[7]	0	2	0
13 April to John Glover maior, fee to Lady Day	5	0	0
Josephe Harris maior, fee at Michaelmas	5	0	0
20 April 14 postes and 8 rayles bestowed in and about the causewayes and highe wayes 6s and to Symons and his boy for 1 daye to worke them 18d	0	7	6
28 April a loade of thornes for almeshouse hedge 4s, carriage 2s 6d, John Kent and Simon Ray to hedge it 20d	0	8	2

8 May wine and suger to Mr Hamonn that preached heere and dined at Mr Maiors	0	2	1
10 May John Parker by Mr Maiors appoyntment for the newe headinge of Mr Whittons drum	0	8	0
12 March [sic] Edmond Hiorne 2s he gave to the clarkes of thassise, a quarte of sack 12d	0	3	0
9 May. [Deleted] 10d a wick to Richard Lowe 1 February to 9 May 15s			
20 June for a shrewde for goodwife Bowman	0	0	22
More in mony to those that stripped her	0	0	6
22 June To Mr Glover maior as geiven to maymed souldiers and poor people [16s deleted]	0	0	6
23 June for a shrewde for goodwife Toe	0	2	2
25 June to Mr Glover maior as geiven to poore	0	6	2
12 July to Mr Chesterman for Mr Bluntes fee our atturny in the crowne office for the quo warranto	0	6	8
25 July to twoe wardsmen at Mary Magdalen fayer	0	0	16
28 July to Edmond Hiorne towneclark at Oxon' summer assises to the clark of thassise to dischardge Mr Maiors appeerance 2s, for the inditmentes against Mose [Amosse] and Gaunte 3s, for a quarte of wine to the clarkes of assise 12d	0	6	0
[f. 30r] To him for a booke in paper for the portmouth courte	0	3	0
29 July to Hugins the mason for mendinge the hall wall in Drewes backside	0	0	16
30 July to a messenger that brought a lettre to the towne from the cownsell concerninge the gratuity to the Kinges majesty[8]	0	2	6
1 August to a messenger that brought a writt and proclamations concerninge the dyinge of clothes	0	2	4
For a shrewde for Ann Gardner and in mony geiven to them that looked to her	0	3	0
5 August to the ringers	0	4	0
Geiven to John Amosse upon his coming out of goale	0	0	12
Paied to Edmond Rudgate for chardges bestowed upon John Amosse and his fellowe Gaunte	0	6	6
1 August for a breakefaste for 2 of the garde that came to understande the state of the towne before the Kinge came 2s 4d, theire horsmeat 3s 4d. For ringinge at the Kinges cominge 2s, and at his goeinge away 12d	0	8	4
24 September for chardges bestowed upon John Hewes the cuttpurse and for sending him to the goale[9]	0	11	6
25 September to Mr Glover maior as geiven to poore	0	4	6

	£	s	d
To him as mony geiven to poore folke at the almshouse in bred and drinck, vizt to goodwife Parrat, old Dissell, Bowmans wife, Freemans wife, Coles his wife and to those that watched them in their sicknes	0	3	0
26 September geiven to a messenger that brought a writt with proclamations for fells and woolls[10]	0	0	18
[f. 30v] 22 September to 2 wardsmen at St Mathewes fayer	0	0	16
Geiven to Elline Collins our Whitsontide lady one aperne cloth by Mr Maiors appoyntment[11]	0	2	0
20 September paied to William Hickes for mendinge the bellclaper and a sturropp for the bell and makinge cleane the clock	0	3	0
5 November to the ringers	0	4	0
27 November to Huggins for digging stone and for mendinge the wall of the bayes and the pownde wall	0	3	0
To Ned Blunt carpenter mendinge the bayes flud gate	0	0	8
Delivered to Richard Shad churchwarden at severall tymes. Paied to John Durbridge for worke done about the bells 4s. To Richard Shad when he went to Readinge with the bell 20s. Which he paied to Abraham More the bellfounder 15s. For the carriage of the bell to Oxon' and for beare at the loadinge and unloadinge 5s. For William Bradshewes chardges being chamberlyn to lye at Readinge at the castinge the bell 10s. At the visitation at Michaelmas 4s 2d. At the busshopps visitation in May 10s.	3	8	2
25 August geiven to Mr Mosse the clarke of the markett in rewarde at the Kinges cominge 10s, to his man in rewarde 2s 6d, in diet for him and the neighbours to beare him company 14s 6d. When he came in November 10s, for dyet for him and the neighbours 11s.	0	48	0
September for a shrewde for Mille Parrate	0	2	8
25 August geiven in rewarde to the Kinges trumpiters at the Kinges beinge heere 10s, for beere bestowed upon them and the garde by Mr Maior 4s[12]	0	14	0
[f. 31r] Paied to Richarde Lowe for keepinge of Nicholas Glovers base childe, 52 wickes at 10d a wick	0	43	4
To Thomas Williams for the keepinge of John Amosse his horse	0	3	0

Paied for wine for the townes use from May till 4 December.
7 quarters of sacke and 5 quarters of clarrat 11s 8d, a quarte of sacke and a quarte of clarrett 20d, one quarte of sacke, 2 quartes of white and 1 quarte of clarrett for Mr Price at Mr Brownes 3s.
Wine at Mr Mosses being heere at the Kinges coming 5s.
3 potles of clarrett, 3 quartes and 1 pynte of sacke for the garde and trumpiters 7s 6d. 1 potle of sack and 1 potle of clarratt for

the garde at theire dinner at the Bull 3s 4d. 1 potle of sack and
1 potle of clarrat to the justices 5 September 3s 4d. 1 quarte of
sack and 1 quarte of clarrat to a Scottishe preacher 20d. A quarte
of sack and a quart of clarrett for a preacher at Mr. Maiors that
now is is 20d. For a potle of sack and a potle of clarret
14 October to the justices at the generall muster 3s 4d. A potle
of sack and a quarte of clarret at Mr Mosse his last beinge heere
2s 8d. A quarte of sack for Mr Evans when he preached and
dined at Mr Maiors 12d.   0   45 10
For suger spent at the drinkinge thereof   0   6   8
2 November to Mr Robbs Sir Henry Lees undershreeve fee
farme for this yeere   0   53   4
10 November quitt rent £5 6s 8d, 6d acquittance, 12d wine
at the payment. [Marginated] receaved £6 10d   5   8   2
Mr Recorder his fee   3   6   8
2 December to Edmonde Hiorne town clark for fee 40s,
keeping the chamberlains accomptes 5s   0   45   0
Paied for a bell stock for the newe bell   0   3   4
[f. 31v] To Thomas Screevin for this yeers stipend for keepinge
the hall and church in glasse only 12s, and for keepinge the
leades of the church (excepting the tower) 6s 8d. He is to be
paied yeerely at the accompte and to have it during his life.   0   18   8
To Hugh Hamond likewise for the keeping of the leades of the
tower for this yeere   0   2   0
To Edward Longe for his wages for settinge the clock and
ringinge the bell 12s, makinge cleane the church leades and the
hall leades 2s 6d, oyle and grease for the clock and bells 2s,
leather and threede for mendinge the bellrops 14d, nayles to
hange the bell 10d, making 2 graves for John Lucas and
Christofer Bowmans wife 12d   0   19   6
To twoe wardsmen of St Nicholas Day last   0   0 16
10 December 1614 to a messenger that brought a writt with
proclamations concerninge the merchantes charter   0   0 12
20 December to Mr Harris maior as mony geiven to poore
people and maymed souldiers   0   6   0
To William Hickes for irone work about the litle house dore   0   0 12
10 November to John Symons carpenter for takinge downe the
newe bell and hanging him upp 5s 6d, and to twoe bellfownders
in earneste for the casting of the bell 5s a peece 10s   0   15   6
1 August. [Deleted] For a breakfast at the Bull by Mr Maior

Summ totall   65   19   1

[ff. 32r–32v] [blank]

[1] 19 Mar. 1613/14 between Edginge and Thos. Bigges and John Bowden for a tenement in Oxford St. occupied by Nic. Glover: B 78/3.

[2] See actions brought by John Taylor of Leafield, 18 July–28 Nov: ibid.

[3] Ibid. 28 Sept., 28 Nov.

[4] Geo. Stowte: ibid. 15 Aug.

[5] Interest was ten per cent: f. 34v [item crossed out].

[6] i.e. Jas. Whitelocke and Sir Phil. Carye, the high steward's nominee, for the 'Addled' Parl., 5 Apr.–7 June 1614: Williams, *Parl. Hist.* 199; *Liber Familicus*, 40.

[7] Presumably Mr. Wal. Culpeper who also came in 1608 to administer the oath of mayoralty: B 78/2, 3 Oct.

[8] Parl. failed to give Jas. I a subsidy and he asked towns for a gratuity for payment of his debts in Ireland and the Low Countries, and for the navy: *Acts of P.C.* 1613–14, 491–5; for £5 given see below in 1615.

[9] See below in 1615.

[10] The proclamation was made 26 Sept. and its reception in Woodstock was presumably later: *Stuart Proclams.*, i, no. 141, p. 317.

[11] Equivalent of the later 'Queen of the Revels' at Whitsuntide festivities: Ballard, *Woodstock*, 80; *V.C.H. Oxon.* xii. 331.

[12] The king was at Woodstock 25–9 Aug.: *Cal.S.P.Dom.* 1611–18, 241; Nichols, *Progresses*, iii. 10–11. He was also said to have been in Woodstock 14–29 Sept.: Marshall, *Woodstock*, 169.

[f. 33r] A true rent role...made 29 September 1614...in the time of John Glover maior of the said borough, William Bradshewe and Thomas Williams chamberlains[1]

Rentes due by lease at Michaelmas and Our Lady Day	£	s	d
Thomas Browne alderman for 1 parte of Lee poole	4	0	0
Mary Phillipps widdowe for an other parte thereof	4	0	0
William Ball for an other parte thereof	0	56	8
Widdowe Munck for an other parte thereof	0	56	8
Salloman Flye for the Butt Close	0	5	6
Robert Bignill, garden plott at the wooden bridge	0	2	0
William Meatcalfe for the church yearde	0	3	0
[and] his dwellinge house at the Cornemarkett	0	6	8
Thomas Browne alderman for his dwellinge house	0	6	8
Thomas Gee for his dwelling house	0	5	0
Edmond Hiorne for his dwelling house next the church	0	10	0
Anthony Noble clarke for his dwelling house called the White Harte and lande in Hensington feild 53s 4d of which the quitt rent was 6s 8d, the other 46s 8d is to the scholemaster	0	53	4
[In margin, added by 1618] There is but 6s 8d due to be paied only for the quittrent for that the scholemaster hath the rest to himself [2]			
Thomas Screevin for his dwelling house 16s, and the wooll barne in his backside 10s	0	26	0
William Bradshewe for his shopp and seller newe built	0	2	0

Thomas Browne alderman for his mawlt house	0	5	0
[Crossed out] Summ Totall [1614]	19	18	6
Summ Totall 21 Dec. 1618	17	11	10

Chauntery quitt rentes to be paied at Michaelmas and Our Lady Daye

Gyles Coles for his dwellinge house	0	5	0
Bridgett Spitle widdowe for her dwelling house	0	20	0
Ann Bradshewe widdowe for her dwellinge house	0	10	0
Salloman Flye for Hughe Hamones house	0	10	0
John Ackly for a peece of grownde between Hickes and him	0	3	4
Joane Collingwood widdowe for William Hickes his house in the Sheepe streete	0	8	4
Humfry Silver for William Wheelers house	0	7	0
Edmond Hiorne for Richard Hawkins his house in Blackhall Lane	0	4	6
George Noble for William Muckells house next to it	0	4	6
Widdowe Rathbone for her dwellinge house	0	8	0
Edmond Hiorne for Mr Hollowayes house	0	8	0
and his house called Hamondes in Parkegate streete	0	5	4
Summ totall [1614]	4	14	0
[Summ total] 21 December 1618	4	14	0

[f. 33v] Chauntry quitt rentes due at Michaelmas only

Mr Browne alderman for his newe built house in the Park gate street, late Collingwoodes, sometymes twoe tenementes, the one called Maynardes, the other Mundyes place at 3s 4d and 18d rent	0	4	10
Robert Bignill for his dwellinge house	0	2	4
Mr Alderman Glover for his house and close called the Crowne	0	0	18
Joane Collingwood widdowe for Edward Longes house	0	0	16
John Kerby for Bennet Paynters and John Parkers twoe houses, 6d a peece	0	0	12
Bartholomewe Edginge for his dwellinge house	0	0	7
Thomas Grove gent for Thomas Godferyes house	0	3	0
John Whitton gent for his greate house wherein Mr Evans and Mr Gadbury dwell 15$\frac{1}{2}$d and of him for a tenement which Mr Gadbury useth as a kytchine 12d	0	2	3$\frac{1}{2}$
Jerome Nasshe gent for a close in Ouldwoodstock called the Dovehouse close lyinge betweene the higheway and the parke wall	0	0	6
George Noble for his dwelling house	0	0	1

Widdowe Durbridge for her dwellinge house	0	0	1
John Cooper for his tenement in Oxford streete	0	0	4
Thomas Symons for William Balles house	0	0	1
Summ totall [1614]	0	17	11½
Summ totall 21 December 1618	0	17	11½

Quitt rentes to be paid at Michaelmas only

Jerome Kyte gent for his house called Chaucers	0	0	18
More for his newe wall betweene his malt house and the river 6d per annum for 21 yeeres from the 6 Aprill 1612 graunted him by lease per all at Mr Whitlockes requeste our recorder. [Margin] The trees and the lop of the trees excepted to the towne.	0	0	6
Thomas Meatcalfe for his dwellinge house	0	0	10
Symon Collier for his dwellinge house 1d and for the garden and plott before the dore 3s 4d [Margin] 21 Dec 1618 this 3s 4d is deducted for that it lyeth waste to the towne[3]	0	3	5
William Meatcalfe for John Lowe his house Md allso he is yeerely to pay for that house on Goodfryday to the poore of Woodstock 6s 8d	0	0	2½
Thomas Browne alderman for widdowe Fletchers house	0	0	6
William Rayer alderman for his dwellinge house	0	0	7
Mr Alexander Crosley for John Dubbers house	0	0	12
The towne of Bissiter for Mr Alderman Harris his house	0	0	3
Leonard Ryly for Nicholas Taylours house	0	0	3
Silvester for Walter Parkers house	0	0	5
Widdowe Ryly for her house next to John Normans	0	0	3
Mr. Henry Bradshewe[4] for the Bull	0	5	6
[Running total for quit rents on f. 33v for 1614]	0	15	2½
[Substituted running total, for 1618]	0	11	10½
[f. 34r] Salloman Flye for his dwellinge house late Mr Dunfordes	0	0	5
William Rayer alderman for William Raunson his house	0	0	6
Widdowe Leake for her house 1½d and for her pales and portche at her dore 6d	0	0	7½
Frauncis Gregory esq for William Butterfeildes house	0	0	3
William Rayer alderman for Wellers lande vizt for widdowe Wells her house 2½d, Richard Collingwoodes 2½d, Hedes house 2½d, Seelyes 2½d, and the close 4d	0	0	14
John Slatter for Archers house at the townsend	0	0	3
Edmond Hiorne for William Edwardes his house	0	0	3
William Rayer alderman for Thomas Williams house	0	0	6

Joane Collingwood for her house called Copped hall	0	0	1^{1}/$_{2}$
Thomas Browne alderman for John Acklyes house	0	0	1^{1}/$_{2}$
Benedict Norwood for his dwellinge house 5d and for his pales 2d	0	0	7
William Rayer alderman for widdowe Barnes her house	0	0	3
Him for widdowe Taylours house	0	0	3
Robert Symons for widdowe Phillipps house	0	0	5^{1}/$_{2}$
Widdowe Ryly for her nowe dwellinge house	0	0	3
John Norman for his dwelling house 3d and for his pales and portche 6d	0	0	9
Nathaniell Noble for John Collingwoodes house	0	0	2^{1}/$_{2}$
Joane Collingwood for widdowe Bowlandes house	0	0	1^{1}/$_{2}$
Robert Bignill for his backehouse	0	0	2
Thomas Painter for his dwellinge house	0	0	3
Mr Henry Standard for Jerome Whites and Richard Shaddes house 6d vizt 3d a peece	0	0	6
Thomas Browne alderman for William Hitch his house	0	0	6
[Margin] 2d bated⁵ for that the oven is taken away			
Widdowe Peeters house 1^{1}/$_{2}$d and for the pales 4d	0	0	5^{1}/$_{2}$
John Doa for his dwellinge house	0	0	4^{1}/$_{2}$
Salloman Fly for Drewe Gregories house 18d and for Peppers shopp 1d	0	0	19
Widdowe Bradshewe for the house late Michael Nursses	0	0	6
William Bradshewe for his dwellinge house	0	0	1^{1}/$_{2}$
Alexander Crosly for Thomas Heathens house	0	0	6
William Porter for Newalls house	0	0	4
William Rayer for his dwelling house	0	0	0^{1}/$_{2}$
Thomas Meatcalfe for Frauncis Garters house	0	0	1
Thomas Russell for Nicholas Glovers house	0	0	3
Thomas Meatcalfe for Nicholas Mitchells house ³/₄d and for the garden plott thereto adjoyninge 1^{1}/$_{2}$d	0	0	2^{1}/$_{4}$
Him for Brathertons house	0	0	1^{1}/$_{2}$
Him for William Bradshewes house	0	0	1^{1}/$_{2}$
[Running total for f. 34r for 1614]	0	12	11^{1}/$_{4}$
[Running total for f. 34r] 21 December 1618	0	12	9^{1}/$_{4}$
[f. 34v] William Metcalfe for his tenement and barne in the backgreene	0	0	3
John Tomlins for his dwellinge house	0	0	12
Richard Meades for his house and pales	0	0	4
Roberte Winter for a peece of grownde at the north ende of newe Colledge house wherein Robert Winter dwelleth which he houldeth at the townes curtacy	0	0	6

[Margin] Discharged for the towne hath 3s 4d per annum for
the newe house

Roberte Symons for the pales before Nicholas Stayners house	0	0	1
John Kerby for widdowe Gyles and Henry Prices house	0	0	2¹/₂
Mr Jerome Nasshe for Michaell Pulchoes house	0	0	4¹/₂
More of him for John Dissells house at the parke gate	0	0	1
Of Mr Alderman Flye for his dwelling house	0	0	2

Summ   0   31   1¹/₂

Md Hampton leyes are lett to Mr Rayer for certeine yeers yet
to come. Allso Richard Shad is to pay 24s at Our Lady Day
1615 for the rente of the woolbeame for this yeere then
endinge. And Mr Doleman of Childry payeth yeerely £8
which is to be paied to the schoolemaster. Allso the £50 in
Mr Rayers handes is to be ymployed towardes the
schoolemasters stipende of £14 per annum.
Md allso William Porter hath waled in a litle peece of garden
grounde adjoyninge to Nualls house and payeth no rent for it,
it is the townes land.

Summ totall of the rentes of this borough 23 December 1614⁶   27   0   19 ¹/₄

[Entry crossed out] Md. at this accompte the towne is
indebetted to Mr Joseph Harris maior which the towne is
to geive him interest for, a £10 in the hundred.   20   10   10

*A note of armor of the boughrough taken at the accompt the 23 December 1614 and deliv-
ered to Thomas Rayer and Richard Shadd constables*

Twoe coslettes furnished remayninge in the hall. 2 callivers
furnisshed.⁷ One muskett furnisshed without flaske and
tutchbox.⁸ Three swordes and 3 [five crossed out] daggers.
On lether belte. Twoe headpees, and one jack⁹ for a horsmon
without sleeves. Pike newe bought and one ould pike in the
hall. William Raunson hath one dagger in his handes.

[Margin]
Rentes increased 21 December 1616 at the accompte

Robert Winter is to pay yeerely at Michaelmas 3s 4d for 40 yeers for the voyde grownd adjoyninge to his backside	0	3	4
Edward Carden is likewise to pay at Michaelmas 3s 4d for 40 yeers for his newe shopp by his house	0	3	4
Bartholomewe Edginge is yeerly to pay for his newe plaes [pales] before his dores at Michaelmas only [6d crossed out]	0	0	4
Mary Tame widdowe for the rent of the Spitlehouse Close	0	0	2

John Tomalyn is to pay
[end of margin entry]

The totall some of all the rentes (with the newe increase upon this marjant) is at
Michaelmas 1617 besides the woolbeame   27   8   9¹/₄

[An entry in centre of page] 21 Dec. 1618   0   9   8

¹ Sub-totals are emended in the rental for 21 Dec. 1618, but the final grand total on f. 34v is for 1617
and is the same as the rents received in the acct. for that year.
² By 1618 the sums 53s 4d and 46s 8d have been crossed out in the main entry and 6s. 8d. substituted
in the column of payments. The change is reflected in the sum total for 1618.
³ The 3s 5d in the column of payments has been crossed out and 1d. substituted. This is reflected in
the running total for 1618.
⁴ Mr. Jos. Harris substituted before 1618.
⁵ By 1618 4d has been substituted for the 6d. in the column of payments. This is reflected in the
running total for 1618.
⁶ The same save for ¹/₄d as the rents in the acct. for 1614.
⁷ Muskets.
⁸ A tinderbox for the lock of a musket.
⁹ A jacket, usually leather, for a jackman or soldier.

[f. 35r] 23 December 1614 to 18 December 1615 Thomas Williams and William Meatcalfe chamberlains

	£	s	d
[Receipts]			

Debts owing to towne

Mr Whitton rentes 11s 4¹/₂d, John Powell upon his bonde
10s. For admissions Drewe Gregory 15s, Bryan Steephens
10s, Mistris Phillipps rentes 4s 6d.

Debts owing by towne

Debts owing by the towne. To Mr Harris maior £20 10s 6d,
Mr Rayer for Richard Coles rent 16s, William Bradshewe 30s.

Monye receaved by the said chamberlyns

Delivered to them in reddy monye at the accompt	0	28	0
Of Mr Doleman	8	0	0
Delivered to them in reddy mony at Whitsontide	5	0	0
Of Longe for tole. [Marginated] query 2s	0	59	7
Of Edmond Rudgate serjant for stallages, one yeere	7	16	1
Of Mr Rayer interest of £50 to 20 June	5	0	0
Rentes of the towne for one yeere	27	0	19
Of Richard Shad rent of wooll beame to 25 March	0	24	0

Of Symon Collier for shrewd of asshes at his dore	0	5	0
Of Mr Evans for a litle windfall in Mr Nobles hedge	0	0	8
Summ	58	14	11

[f. 35v] [blank]

[f. 36r] [Disbursements]

23 December 1614 to Drewe Gregorye for a flaske and tutchbox for the towne	0	0	12
For wine for a preacher that dyned at William Raunces on St Stephens Day[1]	0	0	12
1 January 1615 for one cake geiven to Sir Thomas Spencer 12s, and for one other cake, geven to Sir Henry Browne 8s. One suger loffe sent to Sir Thomas Spencer waying 11lb, 16s 10d. In rewardes to Sir Thomas Spencers servantes 28s 4d: to Mr Gadbury ussher of the hall 5s, Thomas Judge buttler 5s, the cooke 5s, the clark of the kitchine 3s 4d, the porter 18d, the groome 3s, the fuiler 18d, William Hickes 18d, the boy in the stale 6d, Robert Hancock that invited the towne 2s. To Mr Gregories servantes when Mr Maior dined there 9s 6d[2]	3	14	8
For makinge of 2 smockes for Joane and Ann Cope of an ould sheete	0	0	6
For wine and suger for a preacher that dined at Mr Brownes in Christmas	0	2	0
8 January for a quart of sack for a preacher that dined at Mr Maiors	0	0	12
7 February to William and Christofer Wheeler for mendinge the bayes	0	2	6
29 January wine to a preacher at Mr Meatcalfes house	0	0	20
2 February to a preacher 5s. For wine sent for him at Mr Kytes and Mr Browns 20d.	0	6	8
11 February the towne did geive out of theire stock £5 to the Kinges Majesty for a gratuity by meanes of a letter written to the maior and comminaltie from the Privy Cowensell and was paied to Sir Thomas Spenser knight one of the collectors thereof for the cowntie of Oxon[3]	5	0	0
[f. 36v] To the clarkes of the assises 2s at each assise and for wine to them 16d	0	5	4
For wine for Mr Hull when he preached	0	2	0
5 March wine for Mr Harwood when he preched	0	0	12

Worke donne about the holloway. To Thomas Huggins and his 2 sonns for 5 daies 8s 10d, to Frauncis Garter to serve them 4 dayes 3s, for bordes, tymber and nayles spent about the

	£	s	d
mendinge of the woodden bridg which the ploomers brake downe 8s 2d and the carpenters worke 3s	0	23	0
28 March for worke about the almeshouse. To William Wheeler for 3 daies about Grubsons chamber and for twistes and nayles 3s 6d. Rafters and a side peece 4s 8d, bordes for Joane Cope her dore 2s, 1 loade of strawe 6s 8d, 6 hurdles and to the thetcher for Grubsons house 2 dayes and a halfe 4s	0	20	10
To Mr James stipend and fetching Mr Dolemans monye	14	5	0
For wine and suger geiven to Sir Thomas Spenser and Sir Michaell Dormer at 3 severall tymes when they came about Painters busines [Sum corrected from 6s 18d]	0	7	6
Mr Joseph Harris maior yeers fee	10	0	0
Wine and sugar at Mr Maiors and Mr Brownes at severall tymes when preachers dined	0	4	4
For worke done about the free schole, the towne office, and Mr Jeames his house. To Batt for 17 dayes about the schole and the office 17s. 13 dayes and a halfe at Mr Jams his house 13s 6d. For mosse 10s 2d, lyme 11s 4d, lath and nayles for the same workes and pynns 5s 6d.	0	57	6
To Muckell for a loade of slattes for same	0	8	4
[Marginated subtotal for f. 36r]	30	14	10
[f. 37r] 30 May wine, sugar for preacher, dyned at Mr Maiors	0	0	20
11 December to Mr Harris maior as geiven to poor people 24s 6d. To poore by Mr Brownes appoyntment 20d.	0	26	2
For warding 4 fayers, 2 wardsmen a day 8d a peece	0	5	4
Wine, suger sent to preacher to Mr Nasshe his house	0	0	20
27 August to Mr Osbaston the undershreeve for a post fyne for Mr Brownes house at the park gate 10s, the acquittance 6d	0	10	6
Geiven to Mr Culpeppers clarke for writinge to Mr Bassett about Thomas Heathen[4]	0	0	6
Wine for a preacher that dined at Mr Maiors	0	0	20
24 September for wine for Mr Hull dyninge at Mr Maiors when he preached	0	0	12
To William Randle for carryinge of rubble into the highewayes and lanes	0	2	6
1 October wine for Mr Hull at Mr Maiors when preached	0	2	0
10 October delivered to Richard Shad constable when he went to trayne at Blackheath[5]	0	12	0
Payed to Drewe Gregory for dressinge the towne armor	0	7	0
29 November geiven to Mr Mosse the clark of the markett in reward 10s for wine, diet and fyre for him and the neighbours to beare him company 14s 10d [sum corrected from 29s 4d]	0	24	10
3 December wine sent to Mr Whittons for Mr Standard when he preached	0	0	20

For suger spent at Mr Maiors upon preachers and strayngers	0	3	8
[Marginated subtotal for f. 37r]	5	6	8
[f. 37v] Geiven in rewardes to twoe messengers that brought proclamations with writts	0	2	6
Paied to William Archer for keepinge of Nicholas Glovers base child 36s 4d, to Richard Lowe 20d 3 January	0	38	0
To Mr Osbaston the undershreeve, fee farme	0	53	4
Quitt rent, acquittance 6d, wine 12d	5	8	2
Mr Recorder his fee	3	6	8
Edmond Hiorne towneclark fee and keeping accompte	0	45	0
[Marginated subtotal]	15	13	8
To Thomas Screevin for mending the glasse about the guild halle for one yeere endinge at this accompte	0	6	0
Wine for Mr Morris that dyned at Mr Evans	0	0	20
Geiven to Mr Christofer that brought a writt with proclamations	0	2	6
Summ totall leid out	61	11	10
The receiptes by them receaved	58	14	11
So remayninge due to them	0	56	11

[Signature of] Edm. Hiorne towneclark

18 December 1615 Debtes owing by the towne

To Joseph Harris maior £22 11s 10d. To Mr Rayer for Richard Coles his rent 32s. To William Bradshewe 30s. To William Meatcalfe 56s 11d. Summ	28	10	9

Debtes owing to towne [as on f. 35r]

18 December 1615 William Meatcalfe and John Norman were elected chamberlyns for the next yeere. Delivered to them in reddy mony	0	25	0

[f. 38r] Md John Hewes of Bullwich in County of Northampton vittailer was comitted to Oxon' goall for suspicion of felonye for stealinge of a purse in Woodstock fayer and at the last sommer assises he was acquited upon proclamation. Yet his chardge was 11s 3d to sende him to the goale, besides my chardges and attendance at the assise. He had a cloke was sould at this accompt to Richard Shad for 13s 4d and a sword 5s and a sadle at 18d which was geven to Edmond Rudgat serjant.	0	18	4
Md more there was one litle nagg delivered to Richard Shad, which he lent to Richard Browne, whoe let the cuttpurse take him from him at the castell yeard and Richard Shad and he were amerced at 6s 8d	0	6	8

[1] Perhaps Wm. Raunson: B 96, list of 1617.
[2] Fras. Gregory, esq., of Hordley (in Wootton), lawyer and later J.P. for the borough.
[3] Above in 1614. Spencer was high steward.
[4] Edw. Bassett, gent., probably of Woodstock park: B 78/3, 25 Oct. 1615.
[5] Part of the effort to improve the local militia which intensely concerned the council c. 1615: Boynton, Militia, 216. See note in rental above, p. 59, of armour in the town in Dec. 1614.

[f. 38v] 18 December 1615 to 21 December 1616, William Meatcalfe and John Norman, chamberlains

	[Receipts]	£	s	d

Debtes owing to the towne

[By Whitton, Powell, Gregory, Steephens, Phillipps as on
f. 35r], John Pepper upon his bonde 20s and 6s 8d,
George Barnsley by his bonde 15s.

Debtes owing by the towne

[To Harris, Rayer, Bradshewe, Meatcalfe as f. 37v]

Mony receaved by the said chamberlins

	£	s	d
To them in reddy mony at the laste accompte	0	25	0
Of Mr Doleman	8	0	0
Of Edward Longe for tole	3	13	5
Of Mr Rayer for interest of £50	5	0	0
Rentes of the towne	27	0	19
[f. 39r] Of Richard Shadd for rente of woollbeame	0	24	0
Of George Barnsly upon his admission of freedamshipp[1]	0	5	0
Of Robert Bruce, Thomas Lowe and John Batt junior 20d a peece for theire admissions	0	5	0
Of William Lyddam for his admission	0	0	20
Of John Pepper at his admission 6s 8d, of John Durbridg for his admission 18d, out of which paied to Screevin for glasinge 12d so remains	0	7	2
Of Francis Pyman for his admission	0	0	20
Of Jeams Joffes of Oddington for breakinge the peace upon Robert Bruce[2]	0	2	0
Of Edmond Rudgate for stallages	7	7	0
Of Mr Browne for a seale for a fyne from Mr Whitton of Nedd Whites close[3]	0	4	0
Of Mr Hull for seale for a house sould by Mr Whitton[4]	0	4	0
Of John Pepper in parte of his 20s	0	6	8

Summ totall of alle the receiptes	55	8	2
Summ totall of all the layinges out is	62	0	21
So remayninge due to the chamberlins	6	13	7

Md at a court houlden 27 May Richard Browne had a horsse
delivered to him praysed at 40s by William Metcalfe,
Thomas Rayer and Richard Shad, which was forfayted by one
Nicholas Hamlen, for that he did not answere to Richard
Browne in a plea of debte. He promised Mr Harris maior to
deliver the horse or 40s to the towne when it should be
demaunded.[5]

[f. 39v] [Disbursements]

Paied to Richard Shadd constable for sendinge of 3 persons to Bridwell[6]	0	5	0
For a suger loffe sent to Sir Thomas Spensers at Christmas 1615 wayinge 9lb 3 quarters, 15s 6d. To Thomas Williams for twoe cackes [cakes] then sent, one to Sir Thomas Spenser, the other to Sir Henry Lee 22s. In rewardes to Sir Thomas Spensers servantes at Christmas 1615 29s 8d as appeereth in my almanack of 1615. In rewardes to Sir Henry Lees servantes 29s 6d.	4	16	8
To William Bradshewe which the towne owed him upon the last accompte	0	30	0
Geiven to the clarkes of the assises at the twoe laste assises	0	4	8
To Mr Harris maior for his stipend £5 at Lady Day, to Mr Rayer £5 at Michaelmas	10	0	0
Richard Shadd going to Mr Doleman twice for his £8	0	5	0
Paied for a shrewde for goodwife Gilberte 2s 6d and for Roger Norwood 2s	0	4	6
To Mr James for his stypend ending Michaelmas	14	0	0
To Huggins the mason for mendinge and pitchinge the hollowaye about the woodden bridge[7]	0	3	10
[Marginated subtotal for f. 39v]	31	9	8
[f. 40r] To William Archer keepinge of Nicholas Glovers base child yeere endinge 8 November, 16d the wick	3	9	4

For wine and suger as followeth. Wine and suger the Sonday after 12th Day [for
a preacher?] that supt at Mr Brownes 20d, his horsmeate and beare at Mr Glovers
22d. To a preacher the Sonday before Candlemas Day 20d. To Mr Hull in
wine on Midlelent Sonday 20d. To Mr Bowne for wine the Monday in Easter
wick 20d. To a preacher 14 Aprill in wine 12d. For wine and suger to the justices 26 Aprill 3s 4d. To Mr Evans in wine 4 May 20d. To a preacher that dined
at Mr Browns on Holly Thursday in reward 5s, wine for him 8d. To a preacher
the Tusday in Whitson wick in wine 20d. To Mr Hull on Trenity Sonday in
wine 20d. To the justices in wine 10 June when they sate about armorye 3s 4d.

To a preacher 7 July 20d. To Mr Evans for wine 11 August when he preached 10d. For wine for Mr Doctor Lawde 18 August 2s 6d. Same day to Mr Hull in wine 20d. Wine to the justices 27 September 3s 4d. For Mr Jobe 29 September 20d, suger sent by Mr Harris maior at the spendinge of the said wine 5s. Wine for Mr Mason that preached 6 October 2s 1d. To a preacher 13 October in wine 20d. Wine for Mr Doctor Lawde on St.Symon and Judes Day 20d.

Summ totall	0	48	11
[Marginated subtotal for f. 40r]	5	18	3

[f. 40v] Geiven to pore people by Mr Meatcalfe chamberlyn, by the aldermens appoyntment 7s, by Mr Harris in his maioralty 18s 10d   0 25 10

Leid out about the newe makinge of the dyall, and about the newe flurrishinge of the crosse. For a drinckinge upon the free mason and John Cooper when they came first to see the dyall 12d. To the free mason and his man for squaringe and framinge the stone and settinge up 18s. To a messenger to goe to Oxon' for the paynter 6d, for his owne paynes in cominge on the fayer day 12d. For 33lb of sheete lead to coover the topp of the diall stone 5s 6d. To Mr Rayer for 12lb of lead to melt in the holes of the diall and for wood to melt it and lyme 2s 6d. To John Durbridge for 4 irone corkes, 1 iron crosse 12s. To Dyamon the paynter for cullaringe the postes and rayles of the crosse 6s 8d, more to him 7s 6d, besides 12s 6d otherwise geiven by Mr Eevans 5s, Mr Nasshe 2s 6d, Mr Martyn 2s 6d, and Edmond Hiorne 2s 6d. To the 2 Wheelers, carpenters, for settinge upp the scaffold and pullinge downe the same, with others helpe 5s 6d. To John Cooper for his paynes 20s. For iron and nayles for the same 22d. For 10lb of lead to Thomas Screevin 20d.   4 3 8

Paied and leid out to Mr Mosse the clark of the markett as followeth. For his diett at Mr Glovers at the Kinges cominge[8] 13s 10d, for a gratuity then 10s, to his clark 12d, for wine for the jury and the neighbours at the dinner 4s 2d. In rewardes to the Kinges and Queenes trumpiters at the same tyme 20s. For wine spent upon them and other the Kinges and Queenes servantes at the same tyme 22s 8d. To Mr Mosse as he sate as clarke of the markett 25 November for his dinner 9s, besides 3s the high constables paied.For wine 2s 8d. To him for a gratuity 10s.   4 13 4

[Marginated subtotal for f. 40v]	10	2	10
[f. 41r] Paied to Huggins for mendinge the pownde wall	0	0	6
To 2 watchmen at 4 faiers	0	5	4
To a messenger for bringinge of 2 proclamations in Easter wick	0	2	6
To Mr John Weston undershreeve to Mr Reade for fee farme endinge Michaelmas and acquittance	0	53	10
Quitt rent £5 6s 8d, acquittance 6d, wine 12d	5	8	2
To Mr Recorder for his fee	3	6	8
To Edmond Hiorne towneclark for his fee 26s 8d, attendance at the assise 13s 4d, keeping the chamberlyns accomptes 5s	0	45	0

To Thomas Screevin for mendinge the glasse about the
guildhall one yeere endinge at this accompte   0   6   0
[Marginated subtotal]   14   8   0
Geiven to a souldier by Mr Maiors appoyntment 18 December
1616   0   0   3
To be deducted out of the rentrole for Mr Peeters his rent
5¹/2d, for Mr Whittons great house 15¹/2d, for Mr Gadburyes
kitchine 12d.   0   2   9

Summ totall of all the layinges out is   62   0   21

[f. 41v] Md the accompte was houlden at the hall before
William Rayer maior 21 December 1616 at which accompte
William Metcalfe and John Norman were newly elected
chamberlyns for the yeere followinge.

Debtes owing by the towne

To Mr Harris £24 16s 10d. To Mr Rayer maior 32s.
To William Meatcalfe £9 15s 6d. Summe   36   4   4

Debtes owing to the towne

Mr Whitton for rentes 14s ¹/2d. John Powell upon his bill
10s. Widdowe Gregory 15s.⁹ Bryan Steephens 15s. Mistris
Phillipps for rentes 4s 6d. John Pepper for his admission
13s 4d. George Barnsley upon his bond 15s. [Marginated
by last two]. John Powells bill and these bondes delivered to
the chamberlins.
Summ totall   4   6   11¹/2

Md at this accompte all the armor which Thomas Rayer
constable had (savinge 1 muskett which he will see delivered)
unto Thomas Heathen and William Butterfeild constables.
They have a note thereof delivered to them under my hande.

Md the extreates of the 2 last sessions are delivered to Thomas
Heathen and William Butterfeild to geather all but what are
crossed with this lettre a.

21 December 1616. Md at this accompte there was delivered to
the chamberlynes in reddy mony   0   25   0

Md the ould extreates for 6 sessions are to be collected and newe extreated.

---

¹ Edw. Carden, also admitted freeman this year, paid nothing in return for keeping the town armour
for three years: B 81, f. 26v.
² See B 78/3, 25 Mar. 1616.
³ Ibid. 14 Apr. 1616.

68 WOODSTOCK CHAMBERLAINS' ACCOUNTS

Ibid. 16 June.
[5] Ibid. 27 May.
[6] At Witney.
[7] The hollow way was so deep that there was a bridge across it at the end of Browne's lane: see below; *V.C.H. Oxon.* xii. 337.
[8] 22–9 Aug., 2–6 Sept: Nichols, *Progresses*, iii. 186–9; *Cal.S.P.Dom.* 1611–18, 391–2; ibid. 1580–1625, 556.
[9] Drewe Gregory's wife: B 81, f. 27r.

[f. 42r] 21 December 1616 to 20 December 1617 William Meatcalfe and John Norman, chamberlains

[Disbursements]	£	s	d
Paied for 2 cakes 22s, one sent to Sir Thomas Spenser, other to Sir Henry Browne at Christmas 1616. For one sugerloffe wayinge 9lb sent then to Sir Thomas Spenser 13s 6d. To Sir Thomas Spensers servantes in rewardes 29s 8d, to Sir Henry Brownes servantes in rewardes 13s.	3	18	2
Geiven in rewarde to the clarke of the assises at Lent assises 2s and in wyne	0	3	0
Sending for Mr Dolemans mony at Our Lady Day	0	2	6
Geiven to 2 messengers that brought 2 proclamations, one concerninge woolls, the other for farthinge tokens	0	5	0
To Mr Mosse the clark of the markett in rewarde and for his dinner at the Kinges cominge in September[1]	0	15	0
More in wyne and suger to him at that tyme	0	0	16
To the Kinges trumpiters in reward 12s 6d, to the littermen 5s, in wyne for trumpiters and them 12s	0	29	6
In rewarde to Mr Mosse the clarke of the markett when he sate at Woodstock 28 November 10s, and for his dinner and for wyne 13s 6d	0	23	6
Wine. To [preachers] Mr Evans 2 sermons in one day 22 December 1616 12d, Mr Hull on Christmas Day [1616] 20d, Mr Potter on Twelfe Eave [1617] 20d, Mr Evans on Candlemas Day 12d, Mr Raunson 9 February 20d, Mr Potter 23 February 20d, a preacher that dined at Mr Nasshes 9 March 20d, Mr Potter 16 March 20d, a [preacher that] preached 3 March and dined at Mr Nasshes 20d. To Mr Whitlock that supped at Mr Whittons 30 March 20d, for him the next day 20d, Mr Hull that preached on Easter Day at night 20d, Mr Doctor Potter 18 May 20d.	0	20	4

[f. 42v] [Preachers] John Normans unkle that preached 29 June 20d, a preacher that day that supped at Mr Browns 20d, Mr Chafyn that preached 20 July 20d, Mr Potter 27 July

20d, Mr Evans 10 August 6d, Mr Whitlock 16 August 20d,
Mr Doctor Lawde and Mr Recorder same day 3s 4d,
Mr Fletcher[2] the last of August 20d, Mr Hull that day 20d,
Mr Jo. Jeames 7 September 20d, Mr Landon 12 October 20d,
Mr Chafyn 19 October and dyned at Mr Brownes 20d.

0	20	6

Work. Paied to William Wheeler for mendinge the pillory and
for a bord for same 8d. To John Batt and his brother for
slattinge work done at the schoolehouse and the cage 3s 6d.
For 2 bushells of lyme and slatt pins 19d, 1 hundred of slattes
and eaves for same 18d. For 1 freestone creste for the cage
10d. For lath nailes 5d. For a horse to fetch the mosse and
slattes 6d. To Mr Browne 12d which he paied for mendinge
the bayes. For 2 crestes for the scholehouse 8d.

0	10	8

For two wardsmen for 4 fayers, 8d per diem a peece

0	5	4

For a sheete for Nicholas Glovers base child when it went to the
almeshouse 2s 6d. For a shrewde for Amy Lucas her child 15d

0	3	9

To Mr Rayer maior geiven to diverse poore people this yeere

0	16	1

To Mr Rayer maior his fee for his yeere

10	0	0

To Mr Batson the undershreeve for the fee farme for yeere
endinge at Michaelmas 53s 4d, acquittance 6d

0	53	10

Quitt rent £5 6s 8d, acquittance and wine 18d

5	8	2

Mr Recorder his fee

3	6	8

Edmond Hiorne towneclarke fee,drawing accompte, keeping
the book hereof

0	45	0

To Mr Jeames for his stypend

14	0	0

To be deducted out of the rentrole 23s 4d which Mr Jeames
claymeth due to him out of the lande belonging to the free
schoole in which he dwelleth

0	23	4

[f. 43r] To be deducted out of the rentrole for the rent of
Mr Whittons greate house 15$\frac{1}{2}$d, and his kitchine which
Mr Gadbury houldeth 12d, more for the peece of grownde
upon hoggerill hill latly graunted to Symon Collier 3s 4d and
for the quit rent of Roberte Winters grownde adjoyning to his
house 6d, for that he payeth 3s 4d per annum for a lease
of 40 yeere yet to come 6d.

0	6	1$\frac{1}{2}$

[Marginal total]

50	17	9$\frac{1}{2}$

[f. 43v] [Receipts]

To them in reddy monye at the laste accompte

0	25	0

Of Mr Doleman

8	0	0

Of Mr Rayer maior for interest of £50

5	0	0

Of George Barnsly upon his bonde 15s for his admission and
3s 4d for his buckett

0	18	4

Of John Pepper upon his bonde	0	13	4
As fellons goodes upon the prisoner that stole sheepe from Spillesbury and was taken at Hensington	0	7	0
Of John Pepper for a paire of stolen shewes	0	0	18
Of Christofer Smith for his admission	0	0	20
Of Mary Taine for the seale of her fyne acknowledged by Richard Pyman[3]	0	4	0
Of Edward Longe for tole this yeere	0	55	3
Due to the towne for stallages which Edmond Rudgate receaved to the townes use before his death and which he confessed to be due upon his death bed £5 20d.	0	0	0
Of Jerome White serjant for stallages since the death of Edmond Rudgate from 7 October untill 20 December 1617	0	54	4
Rentes of the towne for one yeere	27	8	9¼
Of widdowe Shad for the rent of the wooll beame for one yeere endinge at Our Lady Day 1617	0	24	0
[Marginated total]	50	13	2¼
Due to the chamberlins	0	4	7½

[f. 44r] An accompte at the hall 20 December 1617

Debtes owinge by the towne[4]

Due to Mr Rayer maior £9. To Mr Harris £27 6s. To William Metcalfe £11 5s 4d. For which they are to have interest from this day. Summ	47	11	4

Debtes owinge to the towne

Mr Whitton for rentes 16s 4½d. John Powell oweth 10s. Drue Gregory 15s.[5] Bryan Steephens 15s. Mistris Phillipps 4s 6d. Edmond Rudgat oweth for stallages which he received before his death £5 20d. Summ	8	2	6
16 December 1618. Roberte Busby oweth 20s, Humfry Silver oweth 20s[6]	0	40	0

[f. 44v] [blank]

[1] 6–10 Sept.: Nichols, *Progresses*, iii. 435–6.
[2] Perhaps a relative of Thos. Fletcher, the benefactor who left money to the town this year.
[3] For Spittle House close in Old Woodstock field see B 78/3, 19 Jan. 1616/17.
[4] The increased debts are explained in B 81, f. 27r as: to Rayer for money laid out for town use; to Harris and Meatcalfe as existing debt and interest. Harris's debt was paid out of Hiorne's £30 for his house fine, the rest appear below with interest.
[5] Late deceased: B 81, f. 27r.
[6] Both for admissions.

[f. 45r] 20 December 1617 to 21 December 1618, William Meatcalfe and Thomas Rayer, chamberlains

[Receipts]	£	s	d
Of Mr Doleman	8	0	0
Of Mr Rayer for interest of £50	5	0	0
Of Thomas Heathen serjant for stallages [one year]. [Marginated]			
Lost by Jerome White for 2 dayes stallages 19d and 23d.[1]	7	9	1
Of Edward Longe for the tole	0	56	5
Rentes of the towne for one yeere	24	18	1¹/₄
Of widdowe Shadd rent of the wooll beame	0	24	0
Of widdowe White for an ould asshe digged upp at Symon Colliers dore and for the lopp of twoe other litle trees thereby	0	7	0
Of Thomas Love for the shrewde of the trees in the almeshouse backside and of the tree before the almeshouse dore	0	25	0
Of Thomas Heathen and Richard Reade for the shrewde of Robbine Whodes elme in Oxford Street	0	26	0
[f. 45v] Of William Holloway gent for the shrewde of the elme before Mr Brownes dores	0	6	8
Of Merriall Tayler for the shrewde of a litle elme before Thomas Gees dore	0	2	6
Of William Archer for the shrewde of the elme at John Lowes the coopers dore	0	15	0
Of Humfry Silver for his admission besides the 20s he oweth at Our Lady Day	0	20	0
Of Henry Bradshewe gentleman for his admission	0	0	20
[Marginated total]	54	11	5¹/₄

Md at this accompte 21 December 1618 before William Fly maior and the aldermen and common cownsell Edward Hiorne towneclarke paied for the fee farme of his dwellinge house next the churche (havinge 52 yeeres to come of a lease thereof) £30 in monyes and the ould rent of 10s per annum. Allso he paied before £10 for the fee farme of John Hamondes house and extinguisshed a lease of 25 yeers to come therein and payeth yeerly the ould rent of 5s 4d. Allso he paied before £3 to the towne for the fee farme of Mr Hollowayes house besides £30 paied to Fleminge and a lease of 7 yeeres a foote and the ould rent of 8s payable yeerely. Which three houses they sealed one feoffment to Edmond Hiorne and his heiers for ever under theire comon seale for the considerations aforesaid.

[Signature of] Edmond Hiorne

[f. 46r] [Disbursements]

Inprimis paied for one suger loffe wayinge 10lb 13oz at 16d the
pound 14s 4d, and 1 cake 12s sent to Sir Thomas Spencer at
Christmas 1617. Rewardes to his servantes then 27s 10d.
One cake 10s sent then to Sir Henry Browne, one to Sir Jerrat
Fleetewood 10s.[2]   3   14   2

Geiven in rewardes to a pursephant that brought a proclamation
for gold and silver lace 2s. Another messenger that brought 2
proclamations the one concerninge Sir Walter Rawly and
the other about hott waters 3s. Another messenger that
brought a proclamation concerninge wayne cartes 2s, an other
that brought a proclamation about pedlers 2s, another that
brought a proclamation concerning pynns 18d.   0   10   6

Paied for wine and suger as followeth. A quarte of sack for Mr Hull on
Christmas Day 1617 12d. Wine to a precher that preached the Sondy after and
dyned at widdow Collingwoodes 20d, a preacher 4 January [1618] that dyned at
Mr Nasshes 20d, a precher 11 January that dyned at Mr Nasshes 20d, a precher
15 March that supped at Mr Brownes 21d. Wine and suger to Mr Recorder 27
March that dyned at Mr Nasshes 2s 3d. Wine to Mr Hull 29 March that then
preached and dyned at home 21d, to a preacher 12 April that dyned at Mr Kytes
21d. A pynt of wine to a messenger 17 April 6d. A pottle of clarrett wine to Mr
Fletcher last day of April 18d. Wine for Mr Doctor Lawde 3 May 21d, for Mr
Rawnson that preached 10 May 21d, for a preacher last day of May that dyned at
Mr Nasshes 21d, for Mr Coventrie that preached 7 June 21d, 26 July to a
preacher Mr Doctor Standard 21d, to Mr Taylor that preached twice 2 August 3s
6d, wine and suger to Mr Recorder the last of July at morninge and eveninge 3s
7$\frac{1}{2}$d. Wine to Mr Hull preached 30 August 21d, to Mr Humfryes preached 6
September, and to another preacher the same day 3s 6d, for Mr George
Woodward 27 September 21d, for Mr Doctor Lawde 22 November 21d.
In toto   0   44   7$\frac{1}{2}$

[f. 46v] Geiven to the poore by Mr Rayer maior 13s 6d and
by Mr Fly and Mr Browne 3s 10d   0   17   4

Paied for a shrewde for widdowe Meadowes 3s, ould Gilbert
21d, widdowe Norwood 2s 9d, Richard Pryvate 2s 1d, widdowe
Wilsden 3s. In toto   0   12   7

Geiven to Richard Coles in his sicknes by Mr Flyes
appoyntment   0   2   0

Paied for William Glovers base child, for the makinge of his
coate besides 3s which geiven out of Mr Fletchers mony[3]   0   3   0

To wardsmen at the 4 fayers   0   5   4

Paied for severall workes done for the towne this yeere. For the litle house, hall
dore, planckes and iron for the same by Mr Rayer his appoyntment 8s 11d. To
William Wheeler for worke done about the litle house inner dore and for a bolte
for the same 16d. To him for a borde for the pownde gate and for his paynes 2s. A

staple 6d. For a dayes worke for 2 carpenters and a boy 2s 6d. Iron worke done by John Durbridge and Cruelins for the litle house 2s 3d, for nayles 4d. For an oaken bord and tymber about the pillorye 3s 4d. To William Wheeler for halfe of a hundred of 10 penny nayles, a hafe peny worth candle 5$^{1}/_{2}$d for the litle house. In 8 penny nayles for the pownde 4d. For oyle and thredd 6d. For work done at the bayes, to John Symons for his worke and Thomas Gees by Mr Brownes appoyntment 4s 8d, to Thomas Lowe for planckes and ledges 4s, iron to Mr Harris and Durbridg to worke it 6s 10d, 2 uprittes of oake 3s 4d. To Huggins for mendinge the scholehouse chimny 12d. To Frauncis Garter for 2 dayes work and to Benedict Norwood for one dayes worke to shrewde the trees about the towne 3s. To Booten and Huggins for 7 daies work a peece about the holloway and pitchinge at the bridge to turne the water and for digginge of stones 14s, for a laborer to serve them 3 dayes 2s 3d. To John Slatter for his teeme to carry stone and gravill for same 4s. For tymber to Mr Gadbury and William Wheeler to mende the holloway 4s 6d.

In toto	3	10	0$^{1}/_{2}$
[f. 47r] To Mr Rayer maior fee at Our Lady Day	5	0	0
To Mr Flye maior fee at Michaelmas	5	0	0
To Mr Osbaston undershreeve feefarme this yeere and acquittance	0	53	10
Quitt rent this yeere £5 6s 8d, acquittance 18d	5	8	2
To Mr Recorder his fee for this yeere at Michaelmas	3	6	8
To Edmond Hiorne towneclark, fee, assizes, accomptes	0	45	0
To Mr Jeames for his stipende	13	0	0
To Mr Evans for 3 yeeres rent for the churche yarde at 18d per annum, endinge at Michaelmas 1618	0	4	6
Paied for printinge of verses in the memoriall of Mr Cornewell and Mr Fletcher 3s, to the joyner for the frames to them 12d, to John Cooper for gildinge and bewtifyinge them 3s 4d. To Morgan for carryinge of letters to Mr Fletcher for the towne 4d.[4]	0	7	8
To John Archer for a loade of slattes for the newe buildinge 7s 6d. To Bridgett Davy for a loade of mosse 4s. For the carriage thereof from Fewden 2s 6d. 2 hundred of longe lath 2s 4d, a pecke of pynns 9d, a thousand of lath nailes 16d, 3 hundred of fourpenny nayles 12d, other nailes 1d. For 9 bushells of lyme to Mr Alderman Rayer at 8d a bushell 6s. 3 crestes 7d. To Turner for his worke and his sonnes 9 dayes at 18d per diem 14s 6d. 5 peckes of heare 7d.	0	40	4
Paied to Mr Mosse the clark of the markett for a gratuity in December 1618 10s, for his diett 12s 6d, wine and suger for him 2s 2d	0	24	8
To be deducted out of the rentall for Mr Whittons dwellinge house 15$^{1}/_{2}$d, and for his kitchine 12d	0	2	3$^{1}/_{2}$
[Marginated subtotal]	52	12	8$^{1}/_{2}$

For bordes, iron worke, and workmanshipp about the repayring of the coocking stoole	0	2	14
For canvas to bynde the table of verses sent to Mr John Fletcher 9d and to the carrier 6d	0	0	15
Wine for a preacher on Sonday before Christmas [1618]	0	0	21
Summ totall	52	18	0½
Summ totall of this yeeres receipts	54	11	5¼
Remayninge to the towne	0	33	4½

[In latin] By me Edmond Hiorne the common clerk there

[f. 47v] The accompt holden 21 December 1618

Debtes owinge by the towne

To Mr Rayer £9 18s, William Metcalfe £12 7s 4d.

Summ	22	5	4

Debtes owinge to the towne

By Mr Whitton 17s 7½d, John Powell 10s, Bryan
Steephens 15s, Mistris Phillipps for rentes 4s 6d, Edward [sic]
Rudgates executors £5 20d,[5] Robert Busby 20s, Humfry

Silver 20s. Summ	9	8	4

William Meatcalfe receaveth allowance of 6s 8d paied for Richard Shadd. Allso
John Norman receaveth allowance of 10s lett to the towne heeretofore.[6] Both
are leafte to be considered untill the nexte meeting to be allowed or disallowed.

[f. 48r] [blank]

[1] Jerome White, the third sergeant-at-the-mace in these accts., d. 18 Feb. 1618, and Thos. Heathen was chosen in his place: B 78/3, n. at end of 9 Feb. court. Jerome's wife Alice is the widow White below.

[2] M.P. for Woodstock 1625; said to have been ranger of Woodstock park 1611: Williams, *Parl. Hist.* 199; *V.C.H. Oxon.* xii. 440.

[3] Perhaps an error for Nic. Glover whose child had been maintained since 1609. For Fletcher's bequest see above, Intro.: this is the first ref. to payment from it.

[4] Probably John Fletcher: see above. For the benefactors see above, Intro.

[5] Edm. Rudgate (d. 1617), previous sergeant-at-the-mace: see appendix, biogs.

[6] In 1619 he was owed 5s, to be paid out of his rent: B 81 f. 28r; see below in 1619.

[f. 48v] **21 December 1618 to 22 December 1619, William Meatcalfe and Thomas Rayer, chamberlains**

[Receipts]	£	s	d
Of Mr Doleman of Childrye, Berks	8	0	0
Of Mr Rayer for interest of £50	5	0	0
Of Thomas Heathen serjant for stallages	8	8	3
Of Edward Longe toleman for the tole	0	51	6
Rentes of this boughroughe	24	18	1½
Of Alice Shad widdowe for rent of the wooll beame	0	24	0
John Grainger glasier for his admission	0	0	20
Of John Sea joyner for his admission	0	40	0
John Dissell for his admission	0	0	20
Richard Phillipps for his admission	0	0	20
William Whiting for his admission	0	0	20
Richard Skey for his admission	0	0	20
[f. 49r] Thomas Woodward for his admission	0	50	0
Henry Whiteside for his admission[1]	0	30	0
Richard Plumpton joyner for his admission	0	40	0
Richard Reade as mony taken upon one Thomas Rogers taken upon felonye	0	14	0
Edward Hull sadler for his admission	0	40	0
John Durman in parte of payment of his 20s for his admission	0	10	0
Summ totall of all the receiptes for this yeere	61	14	2½

[In latin] By me Edmond Hiorne

[f. 49v] [Disbursements]

Leied out and paied for the reperations which was done about the bayes this yeere as followeth. To Edward Parsons for carryinge of 3 loade of stone from Handborowe quarry 6s, more for carriag of 6 loades of stone from Phillipp Hawthorns house to the bayes 18d. To Randall and Richardes of Shipton for 4 loades carriage of stone from Shipton quarry 6s 8d. For the same stone 2s. To Randall for 3 loades carriage of stone 4s 10d, for 2 loades of stone and carriage 4s 4d. To Richardes for 2 loades of stone and carriage 4s 4d, to Phillipp Hawthorne for 6 loades of stone 10s. To Mr Browne for 16 bushells of lyme at 8d a bushell 10s 8d, for 18 bushells of lyme to Edmond Hiorne at 8d a bushell 12s, to Mr Glover for 1 bushell of lyme 8d. To Jo. Damery for his man and himselfe for 3 dayes worke at 14d a day 7s, to Richard Warren for 3 dayes worke 3s 6d, to Richard Huggins for 3 daies 3s 6d, to Phillipp Hawthorne for 3 dayes 3s, to George Greene for 1 day 12d, to John Doa for 2 dayes 2s, to Edward Richardson for 3 dayes 3s. To Anthony Richardson and Greene for clensing the bayes 2s 6d. To John Damery for 5 daies worke for himselfe and his man at 14d per diem 11s

8d, to Richard Warren for 6 daies worke 7s, to Richard Huggins for 6 daies worke 7s, [f. 50r] to John Cotton for 6 daies worke 6s, to Phillipp Hawthorne for 6 daies 6s, to Edward Richardson for 6 daies worke 6s, to George Greene for 2 daies worke 2s, to William Hawthorne for 2 daies worke 2s, to John Doa for 6 daies worke 6s. For 3 loades of stone at Handborowe 18d. To John Damery for himselfe and his man for 3 daies worke at 12d per diem 6s, to Richard Booden for 3 daies worke 3s, to Richard Huggins for 3 daies worke 3s. To John Tomalyn for the carraig of 8 loades of stone 2s, carriag of 2 loades of stone from Handborowe 2s. To Pope for the same stone 22d. To Randall for carriage of one loade of stone from Shipton and the stone 2s, to Richardson for the like 2s. To John Doa for 6 daies worke at 9d per diem 4s 6d   8   9   7

For a suger loffe wayinge 9lb at 16d a pownde 12s and for a cake 12s which were sent to Sir Thomas Spencer at Christmas 1618. In rewardes geiven to his servantes 29s 8d.   0   53   8

In rewardes to diverse pursephantes that brought proclamations with severall writtes   0   14   6

Paied for wine at severall tymes to severall uses for the towne. Sent to the justices 22 February 2 quartes of sack and 1 quarte of clarrett 2s 8d. 7 March for 1 quarte of sack to a preacher that dined at widdowe Collingwoodes 12d. Wine sent to Mr Whitlock 22 March 10d, to the justices in Easter wick 3s 4d, to Mr Hull 4 April 20d, Mr Humfryes when he preached the same day 12d, to a preacher that dined at Mr Evans 16 May 20d, to Mr Taylor 23 May 20d. Wine and suger to Mr Recorder 22 July 2s 2d. Wine to a preacher that dyned at widdowe Collingwoodes 8 August 20d, to a preacher [f. 50v] that supped at Mr Brownes 20d, to 2 messengers that came to Mistris Dinglies 2 September 12d,[2] to Mr Hull 19 September when he preached 20d. Sent to Sir Thomas Spencer and the justices 23 September 3s 6d. Sent to Mr Mayer for a preacher last day of October 12d.   0   27   4

Paied to Mr Maior as geiven by him to poore people   0   22   1

Payed for workes done for the towne this yeere. To Huggins and his sonne for wallinge one daye about the bayes 22d. Halfe a loade of mosse for the towne hall 3s 6d, one loade of mosse and for the carriage, for the hall 4s 10d. Slatt pinns 2s 3d, heare 15d, 1 loade of slatte 7s 6d, lyme for the hall 10s 4d. To Thomas Turner for newe ceaping of the hall beinge 22 hundred and a halfe at 22d the hundred 41s 3d. To John Cooper for measuringe it 6d. Lath and nailes for the same worke 7s. 2 cartes to carry rubbell stone upon the topp of the bayes and for one workman to attende them 6s 6d. One loade of strawe to thetche the almeshouse 6s 4d. Robert Nurth for 2 dayes and a halfe in thetchinge the almeshouse 2s 4d, for ealminge and servinge him 22d. To Jo. Durbridge for iron worke about the stockes, the hall and the litle house and the cage, as appeereth by his bill 7s 8d. For oaken planckes and tymber for the cage 2s. To John Symons and his man for theire worke about the cage 18d.

For one quarter of bayes for the pike 7d.   5   9   0

To Mr Harris for the rent of the churchyarde for one yeere ending at Michaelmas 1619	0	0	18
[f. 51r] To 2 wardsmen at 4 fayers	0	5	4
To Mr Flye maior his fee for one yeere	10	0	0
To Mr Gostelowe,³ Sir Edward Fenners undershreeve, for fee farme 53s 4d, acquittance 6d	0	53	10
Quitt rent £5 6s 8d, acquittance 18d	5	8	2
Mr Recorder for his fee	3	6	8
To Edmond Hiorne towneclark for his fee 40s and making town accomptes 5s	0	45	0
To Mr Jeames for his stipend	13	0	0
To Mr Maior as monye geiven to the kinges servantes and for wine to be spent upon them at the Kinges beinge heere⁴ by the consent of all the common cownsell	0	40	0
Geiven to Mr Mosse the clark of the markett in gratuity at the Kinges beinge heere 10s, to his man 2s and for Mr Mosse his dinner 5s, more to him 6 December 1619 10s and for his dinner and wine spent upon him and upon the neighbours to keepe him company 12s	0	39	0
Paied to Edmond Hiorne towneclark towarde parte of his expences in answeringe for the towne upon the escape of the rouges [rogues] out of the cage at the Kinges being last heere	0	20	0
To Mr Chesterman 13s 4d a terme for 4 termes endinge in Michaelmas terme 1619 for the quo warranto brought against the towne by Mr Atturny Generall	0	53	4
To Thomas Screevin glasier for glasinge worke done about the schoole. For 46 foote of newe glasse at 5¹/₂d a foote 21s 1d, for newe leading of 12 foote of ould glasse at 3d a foote 3s, for 14 newe gnarrells 12d, for glasinge the hooles over the windowes 3s 6d.	0	28	6
[f. 51v] To Thomas Screevin for glasing worke done about the townehall. For 40 broaken panes in the nether hall 3s, 55 in the upper hall 4s, newe bandinge, leadinge, soderinge, scowring of all the windowes in the hall, being 150 foote at 1¹/₂d a foote 18s, for 12 foote of newe glasse at 5¹/₂d a foote 5s 6d, all amownting to 29s 6d. But he is to have but 25s 5d and 8d for nailes to sett upp the glasse.	0	26	0
To be deducted out of the rentrolle as followeth: For Mr Whittons dwellinge house 15¹/₂d, for his kitchine 12d. [Three lines deleted and total corrected from 5s ¹/₂d]	0	2	3¹/₂
Geiven by Mr Maiors appoyntment to the prisoners in the castell at Oxon' against Christmas 1619	0	2	0
To Mr Recorder halfe a pownde of suger sent with his wine at 2 severall tymes	0	0	9

Summ totall of all the payments and layinge out	67	8	6¹/₂
Summ totall of the receiptes is	61	14	2¹/₂
Remayninge due to the chamberlins	5	14	4

[In latin] By me Edmond Hiorne

[f. 52r] Debtes owinge by the towne 22 December 1619

To Mr Browne £4.⁵ To Mr William Metcalfe £10 13s 8d.

Debtes due to the towne

From Mr Whitton 19s 11d. John Powell upon his bill 10s.
Bryan Steephens upon his admission 15s. Mistress Phillips
rent 4s 6d. Edward Rudgates executors £5 20d. John Durman
upon his bonde 10s. Gyles Hooper upon his bonde 30s.

Due to John Norman 5s to be paied him out of his Lady Daies rent next.

[f. 52v] [blank]

¹ See appendix, biogs.
² Probably Audrey, wife of Edulphe Dinglie or Dingly (d. 1624): MS. Wills Oxon. 296/4/48.
³ Presumably Ric. Gorstelow, undersheriff in 1614 also: J. M. Davenport, *Oxon. Lords Lieut., High Sheriffs, and M.P.s* (Oxf. 1888), 61.
⁴ By 25 Aug.: Nichols, *Progresses*, iii. 564.
⁵ 'which he paid for the passage of the business concerning the guifte of Mr Thomas Fletcher of London': B 81, f. 28r. See above, Intro.

[f. 53r] **22 December 1619 to 22 December 1620, Thomas Rayer and George Noble, chamberlains**

[Disbursements]	£	s	d
Imprimis paied for a cake and a sugerloffe sent to Sir Thomas Spencer at Christmas 1619, the cake 10s, the suger loffe 15s 7d. Geiven in rewardes to his servantes at that tyme 30s 2d.	0	55	9
The expences of the neighbours that wente to Bandbury upon the Comission of the Inquire of Tythes and Impropriations¹	0	18	0
For a cake which was sent to Sir Jarratt Fleetewood at his marriage	0	10	0

For a greate staple for the litle house dore 3d, a key for a horslock for the same dore 3d, to Jo. Durbridge for mendinge the lock of the same dore 18d. To Richard Hugins for one dayes worke about the pownde 12d, for a loade of stone for the pownde and for the carriag thereof 10d. John Norman for fetchinge 2 loade of stones and one loade of gravill for the hall dore 3s, for fetchinge one loade of gravill, and for 1 loade of stone bought of him, and for carryinge one

loade of stones out of the comon acre 2s 4d. Richard Huggins and Booden for digginge 3 loades of stone and 2 loades of gravill with some parte of a day to begin to dig upp the streete at the hall dore 16d. Richard Huggins for 3 dayes work and to Richard Booden for 2 dayes worke with halfe a dayes worke betweene them at the gutter at the hall dore 5s 5d. One loade of broade free stones at Shipton pitt for the markett stone 3s and for the carriag thereof 18d and for digginge of one loade of ruffe stone for the same work 6d. Richard Huggins for 3 dayes work 3s and to Frauncis Garter for 1 dayes worke 8d. 3 bushells of lyme 2s, nyne cowles of sande fetchinge from the ryver 3d.   0 26   4
[Marginated subtotal for f. 53r]   5 10   1

[f. 53v] To Thomas Williams for 2 asshen planckes containinge 32 foote and a halfe to make rayles for the frame of the table in the scholehouse 3s, for 2 square peeces to make the postes to the same frame 18d. John Sea joyner for the makinge and nayles thereunto 4s 1d. To William Hobbs the ploomer of Oxon' for work done about the 2 gutters betweene the chauncell and the tower and the schoole house, for 18lb and a halfe of soder at 20d per lb and for his workemanshippe and his boyes 18d, drinck and candles 4½d and for a laborer to attende them 4d. In the whole 16s 8½d.   0 25   3½
Paied for wine as followeth. A quarte of sack and a quarte of clarrett to Mr Weston 20d. A quarte of sack and a pottle of clarrett sent to Mr Recorder[2] to Mr Nasshes 8 November and in beer 2d, 2s 6d, to him in wine and suger 19 March 20½d, in wine and suger 13 August 3s 4½d. Wine and suger sent to the Bull to Sir Thomas Spencer and other justices 2 March 4s 1d. Wine to Mr Thornebury a preacher 11 March 20d, Mr Inglish a preacher 19 March 20d, Mr Wright a preacher 26 March 20d. Wine and suger sent to the Bull to the justices that sate about alehouse bussinesses 21 April 2s½d, more then bestowed upon them at the same tyme by Mr Fly then maior in wine 20d.[3] In wine to Mr Raunson a preacher of May 7 20d, a straunge preacher about the same tyme 20d, Mr Heardson a preacher 21 June 20d, Mr Collingwood a preacher 25 June 20d, Mr Wright the preacher 2 July 20d, Mr Doctor Potter the preacher and to his kinsman at theire 2 sermons 23 July 3s 4d, Mr Wattkins a preacher 30 July 20d, Mr Woodward and Mr Tayler at theire 2 sermons on 6 August 3s 4d, Mr Hull the preacher 27 August 20d, Mr Heardson a preacher on Michaelmas Day 12d, for his sermon 1 October 20d, Mr Potter a preacher 2s, Mr Urneson a preacher 15 October 20d, to the justices at the Bull about the benevolence 19 October 20d,[4] to Mr Potter and Mr Robbs at theire 2 sermons 2s 8d, Mr Herdson for his sermon 10d, Mr Raunson 12 November 20d, a preacher of Hart Hall and Mr Raunson 1 day 2s.   0 55   6½
[Marginated subtotal for f. 53v]   4   0   10

[f. 54r] Geiven in rewardes to messengers for bringinge of proclamations as followeth: About plantinge of tobacco 11 January 2s, 23 March concerning light gold 2s, 4 April concerninge hote presses for cloth 2s, concerninge starch 12d, concerninge pirattes 24 May 2s, 29 July concerning tobacco pips 2s, concerninge titles of land 2s 6d, concerninge the parliament 2s 4d, 9 July concerninge the disordered use of tobacco 2s.   0 17   10

To 2 wardsmen at 4 faiers	0	5	4
Paied as mony geiven to poore people as followeth. To Mr Fly maior as mony geiven by him to certeine maimed souldiers upon theire passes and to certeine trumpeters of the Palsgraves and to diverse poore people at severall tymes in his maioralty 26s 6d. By George Noble to diverse poore people besides by Mr Flyes appoyntment at severall tymes 5s 9d [and] for a shirte for a boy in the almeshouse 16d. To diverse poore people by Mr Rayer at the appoyntment of Mr Fly maior at severall tymes 4s 9d.	0	38	4
Paied for shrewdes as followeth. For widdowe Gellyes 7 August 2s 6d, Henry Samborns wifes 2s 3d, Nann Cox and to the poore women that leyed her forth 2s 6d	0	7	3
Paied for an inditement at the summer assises against Henry Hiorne for breakinge prison out of the litle house	0	2	0
For sendinge upp the writinges to London to Mr Chesterman concerninge Mr Fletchers geifte and for wax and for sendinge one other lettre to Mr Recorder concerninge the burgesses	0	0	7
Geiven to Mr Mosse the clerke of the markett as a gratuity in November 10s, and paied for wine and his dinner at Mr Maiors and for the neighbours that did beare him company 14s 2d	0	24	2
[Marginated subtotal for f. 54r]	4	15	6
[f. 54v] Paied to Mr Pokins the high constable of Wootton hundred for the maymed souldiers, marchalsy, and house of correction 13 June, 16s 10d. Allso paied him 26 September 3s 6d as due to the mustermaster.[5]	0	20	4
To Mr Fly maior for his fee £5 and Mr Glover £5	10	0	0
To Sir James Whitlock 8 November his fee one yeere	3	6	8
To Edmond Hiorne towneclark his fee and drawing and presenting the towne accomptes	0	45	0
To Mr Candishe undershreive[6] to Sir William Cope fee farme for one yeere 53s 4d, and acquittance 6d	0	53	10
To Sir Robert Lee, knight recevor for the Cownty of Oxon, quitt rente £5 6s 8d, acquittance 18d	5	8	2
To Mr James his stipende	13	0	0
To John Norman 5s appoynted at the laste accompte to be allowed him of his rente	0	5	0
To be deducted out of the rentrole for the rent of Mr Whittons greate house 15½d and for his kitchin that Mr Blunt hath 12d.	0	2	3½
Geiven by Mr Glover maior to the prisoners of the castell of Oxon' at Christmas 1620	0	2	6
For a pynt of wine to the Prince his messenger that came with a lettre about the election of a burges[7]	0	0	6
For wax to seale the indenture for burgesses	0	0	1
[Marginated subtotal for f. 54v]	38	4	4½

Summ totall of all the layinges out	52	10	9¹/₂
Summ totall of all the receiptes	49	17	7¹/₄
So remayninge due to the chamberlins	0	53	2¹/₄

[f. 55r] [blank]

[f. 55v] [Receipts]

Of Mr Thomas Doleman for one yeers annuity for the maintenance of the free school	8	0	0
Of Mr Rayer for interest of £50 also to be ymployed towards the annual stipende of the schoolemaster[8]	5	0	0
Of Thomas Heathen serjant at the mace for stallages	7	8	0
Of Edward Longe toleman for the tole	0	29	9
Rentes of this boughroughe for one yeere	24	17	10¹/₄
Of Alice Shadd widdowe for rentes of the wooll beame	0	24	0
Of Thomas Warde for his admission to his freedom 20s besides 20s to pay more at Michaelmas 1621	0	20	0
[f. 56r] Of Christofer Smith and Richard Phillipps for a fyne for an uprore in the night tyme made by them[9]	0	2	0
Of Edward Silver for a fyne for a contempte made by him to the constables in the execution of theire office[10]	0	0	12
Of William Butterfeild, William Bradshewe and widdowe Carden, 5s a peece for victualing without licence[11]	0	15	0
Summ totall of all the receiptes	49	17	7¹/₄

Debtes owinge by the towne 22 December 1620

To Mr Thomas Browne £4 8s. To Mr William Metcalfe £11 4s 8d. To Mr Thomas Rayer 52s 8d.

Debtes due to the towne 22 December 1620

Mr Whitton for rentes 22s 2 ¹/₂d. For admission John Powell 10s, Bryan Steephens 15s, John Durman 10s, Thomas Warde 20s. Mistris Phillipps for rentes behinde 4s 6d.

[f. 56v] [blank]

---

[1] Possibly in connexion with grant for 10 yrs. on 5 June 1620 to Sir John Sparrow *et al.* of 50 per cent of all income from compositions for concealed tithes: *Cal.S.P.Dom.* 1619–23, 149.

[2] Still Sir Jas. Whitelocke, who received many honours in 1620: *D.N.B.*

[3] See B 78/3, 24 Apr., when six victuallers were imprisoned for three days with 20s fines for being unlicenced.

[4] To pay for increasing involvement in the wars of his son-in-law the Palsgrave, i.e. the Thirty Years' War: *Acts of P.C.* 1619–21, 291 sqq. The summoning of Parl. and the Palsgrave's trumpeters referred to below were all part of the war effort.

[5] The first record in the accts. of payment to the county for the muster master, the professional soldier sent to train the militia. For him see Boynton, *Militia*,106, 180.
[6] Hugh Candishe of Banbury: Davenport, *Oxon. Lords Lieut.* 61.
[7] Woodstock is said to have been granted to Prince Chas. 19 Feb. 1617: Marshall, *Woodstock*, 177. Whitelocke and Carye were again members for the Parl., which was summoned 13 Nov. 1620 and sat 30 Jan. 1621–18 Dec. 1621: *Handbook of Brit. Chron.*, ed. E.B. Fryde *et al.* (R.H.S. 3rd ed. 1986).
[8] This extra information is also given in subsequent accounts in the MS. but has been omitted in this edition.
[9] See B 78/3, 12 Apr. 1620.
[10] 'For refusing to ayd the constable to attach Pulchoe': ibid. 24 Apr., 12 Oct.
[11] Ibid. 14 Apr. Widow Carden was Ann, widow of Edw. (d. 1619): MS. Wills Oxon. 78/1/34.

[f. 57r] 2 December 1620 to 22 December 1621, Thomas Rayer and George Noble, chamberlains

[Receipts]	£	s	d
Of Mr Thomas Doleman	8	0	0
Of Mr Thomas Rayer for interest of £50 to 20 June	5	0	0
Of Thomas Heathen serjant for stallages to 22 Dec.	7	15	1
Of Edward Longe toleman for the tole to 22 Dec.	0	35	9
Rentes of this boughroughe to 22 Dec.	24	17	10¹/₄
Of Alice Shadd widdowe for rentes of the wooll beame	0	24	0
For the admission of William Seare barber[1]	0	0	20
For the admission of Mathewe Toms barber	0	26	6
For the admission of George Frauncis 5s. And he paied 3s for his buckett to the chamberlins. And is to pay 15s more quarterly.	0	5	0
[f. 57v] Of Roberte Phillipp for a fyne ymposed upon him by Mr Maior[2]	0	2	0
Of Christofer Smith for a fyne ymposed upon him for victualinge without licence[3]	0	10	0
Of Richard Yate as a fyne ymposed upon him for misusinge Richard Reade and his wife[4]	0	2	0
Summ totall of all the receiptes	50	19	10[¹/₄]

Debtes owinge by the towne at this accompte[5]

To Mr William Meatcalfe £12 16s 8d. Mr Thomas Rayer £29 16s 9d. Mr Thomas Browne £4 16s.

Summ	47	9	5

Debtes owinge to the towne at this accompte

Mr Whitton oweth for rentes 23s 5¹/₂d. John Powell 10s. Bryan Steephens 15s. Mistris Phillipps 4s 6d. John Durman

10s. Thomas Warde 20s. George Frauncis 15s. Thomas
Williams for a horse 30s. Ned Hull for Plumpton 5s.[6]
Summ   6   8   5

[f. 58r] [Disbursements]

For a cake and a suger loffe of 12lb 4oz, the cake 10s, the suger loffe 16s, which
was sent to Sir Thomas Spencer for a newe yeers guift at Christmas 1620. To his
officers in rewardes then 32s 2d.   0   58   2
For a cake sent to Sir Henry Lee the same tyme 10s, in rewardes to
his servantes then 24s. For muskadine at the eatinge of the tastes of the said
cakes 2s.   0   36   0
Geiven by Mr Maior in rewardes to the Kinges Majesties messengers which
broughte diverse proclamations as followeth. For prohibitinge scandalous speech
about state government 2s, prohibitinge eatinge of flesshe in Lent 2s 6d, pro-
clayminge Sir Gyles Mumparsons a rebell 12d. To Mr Hunte that brought 3
proclamations at one tyme 3s 6d. One concerninge publique greevances 2s 6d.
To a messenger that brought the subsidy booke 22d. One proclamation concerninge licentious speech 2s. One concerninge transportation of grayne 2s.
Twoe concerninge proroginge the Parliament 5s. One concerninge revivinge
the Parliament 2s 6d. All amowntinge to   0   24   10
Paied for a cake which was geiven to Sir Jarrat Fleetwood
2 February   0   10   0
To 2 wardsmen at 4 faiers   0   5   4
[f. 58v] Workes. Paied for workes done for the towne this yeere. To Silver
for makinge twoe iron plate boltes for the towne office dore 2s 6d. To
Richard Huggins mason for mendinge the pownde wall 6d. For stones for
same 6d. A lock and a key for the towne cheste that Mr Thomas Meatcalfe
keepeth 2s 4d. To Symons and his man for mendinge the seller dore 6d. A
bord and 2 ledges 10d, nailes 6d. For a hinge and a haspe to John
Durbridge 18d. Three newe ladders for the town 14s 8d as followeth, for an
elme 6s 4d, carriage 2s, sawinge 20d, for makinge them 4s, wood to make
the rowndes 3s. The stubbs were sould to John Say for 2s 4d which beinge
deducted the 3 ladders cost as aforesaid. Paied to George Drewe[7] for trim-
minge the towne armor, for makinge of a britche to one of the muskettes
and for twoe scoweres 8s. In earneste to Raphe Steephens of Blechington
for pitchinge our towne gutter at 2d a yarde 4d. To Thomas Gee and
another for fittinge twoe wasshinge stockes for use of the towne 6d. Newe
makinge and settinge upp 12 paire of postes and rayles upon the causeways
at the holloway and at the piggion house land, beinge three dayes worke and
a halfe for Wheeler and his boy, with the timber to make the rayles and
postes 13s 9d. To Crowdson for mosse used about the schoole 2s. For the
carriage thereof 16d, hundred of newe slattes in the same worke 14d, halfe a
pecke of pinns and nayles 5d. 7 bushells of lyme spent about the rippinge,
wasshinge and plastering of the same house and halfe a bushell of heare 4s 11d.

For Crowesons worke and his boy 5 dayes and a halfe at 16d per diem 7s 7d. To George Noble for twoe crestes used about this worke 7d. To Lyddam for glasinge the upper windowe in the schoole and mending one of the nether windowes beneath 4s 6d. To Frauncis Garter for digginge downe Mr Kytes stones and the way in the lane there 10d 9 Auguste.

[f. 59r] To Henry Whiteside for twoe horslockes which he boughte for the towne 2s 4d. For wood to heate the irons for markinge the towne ladders 2d. Diginge of 50 loades of stones for the townes use 16s 8d [Marginated: query]. To John Norman for the carriage of 13 loades of the same stones 6s 6d. For 39 foote of oaken bordes used about the mendinge the wooden bridge at the holloway at 1d a foote 3s 3d. One oaken rafter of 18 foote in length. 2 other oaken rafters and one oaken planke to lyne the sills and to make upright postes, a topp rayle and braces 4s, all for same bridge. To Hickes a dozen of spikes used about same 9d. To Silver for halfe a hundred of tenn peny nayles and halfe a hundred of eight peny nayles about same 8d. For Symons and his man for theire worke about same 2s 11d. A peece of tymber to make a crosse sill in the midle of the bridge 2s. To Symons for squaringe a peece of tymber to make the coockinge stoole 6d. For same tymber beinge 21 foote in length 4s. Oaken tymber to make the chaier and for nayles 19d. Sawinge same 6d. To Symons and his man for one dayes worke and a halfe with 3d in beare 3s. All which perticular woorkes for the towne for this yeere doe amounte to   5   18   0

Wyne. A perticular note of all the wine that hath beene spent by the towne this yeere as followeth: Upon Mr Dorrell the preacher 13 December 1620, 1 pynte of sack 12d. Mr Coventre 14 January 1621 a quarte of sack and a quarte of clarrett 20d. Mr Recorder 14 January a quarte of sack and a quarte of clarrett 20d. Mr Hearson 21 January a quarte of sack 12d. A preacher of Harthall 4 February a quarte of sack and a quarte of clarrett 20d. Mr Heardson 11 February a quarte of sack 12d. Mr Philpott 18 February a quarte of sack and a quarte of clarrett 20d. Upon the justices [f. 59v] which sate heere about recognizances for alehouses 22 February 1 quarte of sack, one quarte of clarrett 20d. Mr Hunte 15 February one quarte of sack and a quarte of clarrett 20d, Mr Potter the same day one quarte of sack 12d, one pynte of sack 6d, Mr Potter 4 March 1 quarte of sack and 1 quarte of clarrett 20d. A preacher 11 March 1 quart of sack 12d, Mr Wright a preacher 18 March a quarte of sack and a quarte of clarrett 20d. A preacher 25 March 3 pyntes of sack and a pynte of clarrett 22d. Mr Hull upon Easter day 1 pynt of sack and 1 pynt of clarrett 20d. Mr Heardson 20 April a quarte of sack 12d. Mr Browne 30 April a quarte of sacke, a quarte of clarrett 20d. Mr Potter 7 May 18d. Sir James Whitlock in May in sack and clarrett 2s 10d. 13 May a preacher a quart of sack and a quart of clarrett 20d. Mr Tayler 27 May for preachinge 2 sermons that day in wine at dinner and supper 2s 8d. [Wine upon] Mr Joabe 10 June 20d, 17 June upon a preacher of Exiter Colledge 20d, Sir James Whitlock in June a pottle 16d, Mr Browne 14 June 20d, Mr Hull preachinge 1 July 2s 8d, Mr Doctor Whetcombe 15 July 20d, Sir James Whitlock 19 July 16d, Mr Doctor Laude 22 July 20d, Mr Fleetwood and Mr

Coolinge 6 August in wine and suger for theire 2 sermons 2s 4d. [Wine upon] Mr Hull 12 August 20d, Mr Wattson 19 August 2s 8d, Mr Doctor Evans that preached heere at the Kinges beinge heere 12d, a preacher 8 September 12d, a preacher of Newe Colledge 16 September 20d, Mr Coventree in September 20d, a preacher in September that came from Harte Hall 8d, Mr Browne 7 October 20d, Sir James Whitlock 22 October 20d, Mr Heardson dyninge at Mr Maiors 20d. More over 3 April in wine sent to Sir Thomas Reade and Mr Gregory and other justices sittinge about alehouses and collectors accomptes 2s 4d. Mr Doctor Case his kinsman 1 quarte of clarrett and suger 12d.[8]

	3	9	4
[f. 60r] Paied for a shrewde for Cate Meaddowes with 2d geiven to Grubson for her paynes 2s 7d, for a shrewde for Bridgett Davye 2s 11d, for Bowman 2s 2d.	0	7	8
Geiven by Mr Maior himself and by his appoyntment paied by Thomas Rayer chamberlyn to diverse poore people this yeere 10s 8d. And by George Noble 13d	0	11	9
Geiven to ould Lowe and ould Dissell by Mr Maiors appoyntment 14d	0	0	14
To Mr James schoolemaster his stipende	13	0	0
To Mr Maior as leied out at Chippingnorton at the firste asseasement of the subsidies 4s. To Edmond Hiorne as leyed out by him there at the second asseasment of the subsidies 3s 3d.[9]	0	7	3
To Mr Almont[10] high constable of Wootton hundred for the Marchalsye, maymed souldiers and the house of correction and muster master for this yeere	0	20	4
To Edmond Hiorne for his chardges which he layed out 11 dayes at London about the settlinge of the £12 per annum of Mr Fletchers guifte	0	44	0
To him which he gave to Mr Anslowe[11] clark of the assise for recordinge Mr Maior his appearance at the assise and in wine to him	0	3	4
Geiven by Mr Maior in rewarde to the Kinges trumpiters at the Kinges beinge heere 10s.[12] To Mr Walker the clarke of the markett of the Kinges housould in rewarde 6s. Spent at Mr Maiors upon him, the kinges trumpeters and upon the guarde, that dined at Mr Maiors and in wine 9s.	0	25	0
To Morgan for carryinge of severall letters for the towne busines, about Mr Fletchers busines, our commission and to our newe recorder 6d [and] 4d.[13] To a messenger that brought a warrant for payment of the Kinges rent at Readinge 4d.	0	0	14
To Sir James Whitlock knight our recorder his fee for this yeere endinge at Michaelmas 1621, beinge his laste payment	3	6	8
[f. 60v] To Mr Glover maior his fee	10	0	0

To Mr Batson undershreeve to Sir Richard Baker the fee farme 53s 4d, acquittance 6d	0	53	10
To Sir Robert Lee knight the kinges receavor for quitrent £5 6s 8d, acquittance 18d	5	8	2
To Edmond Hiorne towneclarke fee, assizes, accomptes	0	45	0
Geiven to Mr Mosse the clarke of the markett 22 November as a gratuity 10s. For his chardges and the neighbours to beare him company 14s 8d.	0	24	8
Deducted out of the rentrole for the rent of Mr Whittons greate house 15½d. And for his kitchine that Mr Blunte hath 12d.	0	2	3½
To Mr Richard Ockly my lord chauncelors secretary for the renewinge of the comission of the peace £10 4s.[14] To his brother for his paynes 5s. For the incerting of Sir Thomas Spencers name and Mr William Lenthall's name our newe recorder £5 15s 4d.	16	4	4
For 2 crestes for the almshouse 6d, a peck of lyme 2d, the workman 2d, a planck of 9 foote for the wooden bridge 9d. Md the planck of 9 foote is accompted before into the 39 foote at 9d, so that this some is but [sum corrected]	0	0	10
For burnt wine bestowed upon Mr Recorders man	0	0	18
To Garter for lopping of two ashes and cutting other wood for the poore people in the almeshouse 6d. To Tomalin for carrying of it up to them 8d.	0	0	14
Delivered by Thomas Rayer for the use of the towne from the 26 January as followeth, for pouder, match, fustian, the hire of a horse and a new pike which cost 5s 6d, with 12d delivered by Edmond Hiorne to William Hicks and 18d laid out by him for the bringinge downe the pick from London all cominge to	0	26	8
Summ totall of all the receiptes	50	19	10
Summ totall of the disbursementes	77	18	5
So remayninge due to the said accomptantes	26	18	7

[Signature of] Edm. Hiorne towneclark

[1] By apprenticeship to Rog. Sturgiss 2 Feb. 1617: B 78/3.
[2] Ibid. 7 Feb., 25 Apr. 1621: for threats to burn a house and for stealing wood.
[3] Ibid. 26 Feb. 1620/21.
[4] For assault: ibid. 29 Sept. 1621. He was a butcher.
[5] Meatcalfe's was paid 1622, £13 16s 8d of Rayer's on 25 Mar. 1622: B 81, f. 28v. For Browne's money see below, 1625 n. 11.
[6] Hull was surety for payment of Ric. Plumpton's fine of 5s in June 1620: B 78/3, 7 June, 12 Oct.
[7] *Alias* Gregory: see appendix, biogs.
[8] John Case (d. 1600), former Fellow of St John's Coll., Oxf., and canon of Salisbury. He apparently made his money practising medicine. Born in Woodstock, he left the town £40 to be loaned to four tradesmen burgesses: *D.N.B*; B 97, p. 12.
[9] Two subsidies were voted this year on account of the Palatinate: *Cal.S.P.Dom.* 1619–23, 225.

[10] Probably Rog. Almont of Kidlington (d. 1640): MS. Wills Oxon. 113/1/39.
[11] Possibly Ric. Onslowe: *Lincoln's Inn Admission Reg*, i. 92.
[12] By 26 Aug.: Nichols, *Progresses*, iv. 713–4.
[13] Wm. Lenthall, related by marriage to a previous MP and recorder, Lawr. Tanfield of Burford, whose estate there he subsequently purchased. For Lenthall see above, Intro.
[14] The commission was renewed for the addition of the new recorder. For Woodstock's commissions of the peace see *V.C.H. Oxon.* xii. 393.

[f. 61r] 22 December 1621 to 21 December 1622, Thomas Rayer and George Noble, chamberlains

[Receipts]	£	s	d
Of Mr Thomas Doleman	8	0	0
Of Mr Thomas Rayer for interest of £50	5	0	0
Of Thomas Heathen serjant at the mace for stallages	7	18	11
Of him for the standinge of the coontrye bakers under the highe crosse after the rate of 12d a peece for everye quarter 10s, and for the standinge of certeine priviledged butchers upon an yeerely composition[1]	0	10	0
Of Edward Longe toleman for the tole [sum corrected in MS. from 34s 6d]	0	43	2
Rentes of this boughroughe	24	17	10$^{1}/_{4}$
Of Alice Shad for rent of the wooll beame	0	24	0
Receaved at the last accompte in reddy monye delivered to the chamberlyns	0	2	6
[f. 61v] To be allowed to the towne as mony payed out at the last accompte for the digginge of 50 loades of stone 16s 8d, whereof 13 loades were delivered in to the townes use. Due to the towne out of the said 16s 8d	0	11	11
Of Thomas Williams paied for the wastes committed by him in the comon poole by cuttinge up of willowes	3	0	0
Of the widdowe Norman for the like offence	0	30	0
Of Jerome Longe and Thomas Snape for theire admissions besides 3s 4d for theire buckettes a peece, 20d a peece	0	3	4
Receaved at the hall 23 February which was collected upon the extreates	0	24	0
More as mony collected 2 March	0	3	0
Of James Nickoles baker for his admission 10s, besides 3s 4d for his buckett	0	10	0
Of Henry Whiteside, Roberte Belcher and John Yonge 20d a peece for theire 3 admissions besides 3s 4d a peece for theire buckettes which Thomas Rayer hath	0	5	0
More of John Yonge for his admission 10s and is to pay 10s more at Midsommer nexte	0	10	0

Of John Durman as due for his admission	0	10	0
Of John Tassill as due for his admission which he was to pay by 5s a quarter	0	20	0
Summ totall of all the receiptes	59	2	8

[f. 62r] [Disbursements]

Inprimis paied for guiftes and rewardes, geiven by the towne at Christmas 1621 as followeth. For a cake 10s and for a sugerloffe 13s sent to Sir Thomas Spencer our highe steward, rewardes geiven then to his servantes 30s 2d. For a cake sent to Sir Henry Lee 10s, rewardes then geiven to his servantes 24s 4d. For one cake sent to Sir Jerratt Fleetwood then 10s. All amowntinge to	4	17	6
For expences for the entertainement of Mr Lenthall our recorder at his coming to take his oath 10s and for wax to seale his patente 1d	0	10	1
For a newe paper booke for enteringe the towne recordes and courtes	0	4	0
To Thomas Screevin for mendinge the windowes of the towne hall	0	6	0
To Mr Glover maior his fee due at Our Lady Day 1622	5	0	0
For expences in the entertaynement of Mr Recorder when he came to the towne 1 April	0	8	0
To John Say for turninge 38 pynns and boringe the holes in the beames in the hall to hang the buckettes on and for settinge them upp	0	3	0
To John Viall for makinge a seale to seale leather	0	0	2
To Thomas Robinson for making cleane the bayes and clensinge the greate hole wher the water standeth	0	0	12
For a planck 5 foote longe, 4 inches and a halfe thick to make a stepp at the ende of the bridge at the holloway and masons and carpenters worke	0	0	16
To Edward Kemps wife[2] of Hampton 3s 4d asseased by the towne of Hampton out of our 15 yeardes towardes the reparations of the churche of Hampton	0	3	4
[Marginated subtotal]	11	14	5
[f. 62v] In rewarde to Mrs Willson, Mr Cornewells daughter the fownder of our free schole, by Mr Maiors appoyntment with the consent of the neighbours 10s, and bestowed in wyne, beare and cakes upon her 20d	0	11	8
To the ringers for ringinge at the death of Sir Thomas Spencer[3]	0	2	0
Geiven to widdowe Pryvattes daughter to buy salve for her arme	0	4	0

9 September paied for expences for the entertaynement of Mr Recorder with diverse of the neighbours to accompany him 9s 6d. For wine at the same tyme 2s. The same day for wine sent to Mr Justice of Chester 3s 4d.

0	14	10

For expences and rewardes at the eatinge of the one buck and a halfe buck 16 September which my Lord of Montgomery sent to the towne upon theire electinge him to bee theire Highe Steward, as followeth. To William Todman⁴ for his fee for 1 buck 10s and to his man Sattin 12d. To Ned Painter for his fee for the halfe buck 5s and to his man 6d. For wine and beere spent upon them when they brought it in 18d. For twoe bushells of wheate 14s. For wine and suger sent to the keepers at the eatinge of the venison 12d. For expences upon the cooke and others that came to him at the makinge of the pasties 13d. To Megg Hamond for helpinge the cooke 6d. For 8 pownd of sheepe shewett 2s 2d, 15lb of butter 5s, egges 16d, 1lb and a quarter of pepper 2s 11d. Geiven to the cooke for his paines 5s. To Mr Maior and Thomas Williams for bakinge the 8 pasties 2s. For paper for the pasties 1¹/2d. All amownting to

0	53	1¹/2

To Edmond Hiorne towneclark, which he leid out in his jurny to carry the townes letter to my Lord of Montgomery when they elected him our high steward

0	16	0

For one quart of sack geiven to Mr Crytche⁵ the undershreeve by Mr Maior at Michaelmas

0	0	12

Paied to Mr Crytche undershreive to Sir Frauncis Stoner knight fee farme 53s 4d, acquittance 10d

0	53	14

To the receavor for the cownty of Oxon' at Readinge for the quitt rent £5 6s 8d, acquittance 18d

5	8	2

Of William Hitche upon the payment thereof.

0	0	4

[Marginated subtotal for f. 62v]

13	0	15¹/2

[f. 63r] To Mr Harris maior his fee at Michaelmas

5	0	0

To Mr William Lenthall esq our recorder his first fee

3	6	8

To Edmond Hiorne towneclarke fee assises, accomptes

0	45	0

Geiven in rewarde to Mr Mosse, clarke of the markett 6 November 10s, wine and other expences to entertaine him and the neighbours that bare him company 15s

0	25	0

To one that brought a lettre about the benevolence⁶

0	0	3

For wine spent at the eatinge of the taste cake made for Sir Jarrat Fleetewood

0	0	14

In rewardes by Mr Maior and his appoyntment to diverse messengers for bringinge of proclamations at severall tymes as followeth. For 2 proclamations concerning the dissolvinge of the parliament and about the 6 clarkes office 3s 4d. One proclamation in February about flesshe killinge and dressinge in Lent 2s 8d. For 1 proclamation concerning starche 2s. For a proclamation concerninge gold 3s 19 June. For a proclamation about Eastland marchantes 2s. For 1 proclamation about woolls, blockwood and cloth 2s 6d. For 2 proclamations about marriners and about waggon cartes 2s 6d. To a messenger that brought the lettres of benevolence 27 Auguste 19d. For 2 proclamations concerninge tradinge into America and garbling of spices 3s.

Amowntinge to	0	22	7
To twoe watchmen for warding at fower fayers	0	5	4
To Mr James schoolemaster his stipend	13	0	0
For wine sent to the townehall on St Steephens day to Mr Recorder when he tooke his oath 2s, and at dinner 5s 4d	0	7	4
For three newe casementes for the schoolehouse windowes 10s and for the freemasons worke 12d and in leadinge in of the hookes to hang them	0	11	0
[Marginated subtotal for f. 63r]	27	4	4

[f. 63v] For monyes geiven to poore people at severall tymes by Mr Glover maior and by Mr Harris maior and by the chamberlins as followeth. To Mr Glover geiven by him 3s 6d. To a poore Irishe wooman 8d, 2 sowldiers that came from the Palsgrove 6d, Privattes dawghter in the almeshouse 6d, a poore souldier that was borne at Hoockenorton 4d. To Mr Glover as geiven by him to poore people and souldiers 8s 8d. To a poore traviler that had his toung cutt out by the Turkes 6d. To Mr Glover as geiven to Bohemia souldiers at severall tymes 4s. To a poore minister that came out of Ireland 4d. To Mr Glover as geiven by him at severall tymes 8s. To poore people at 3 severall tymes 6d. To Mr Glover as geiven by him at severall tymes 7s. To a poore greate bellied wooman 3d. To a poore Irishe wooman by Mr Glover 6d. To Mr Harris maior as geiven by him to poore people 12s 10d. More to souldiers by Mr Glover 9d, and by George Noble 8d.   0   48   6

Paied for wine geiven by Mr Maiors appoyntment to diverse uses for the credite of the towne as followeth. Wine and beere sent to Mr Justice of Chester the last of July 10d. Wine to Mr Potter when he preached 12d, Mr Dorrell that preached 27 January 20d, Mr Browne at his first readinge of prayers 18d.[7] Mr Mason that preached 3 March 2s 2d. Sent to the justices 17 March that sate about alehouses 20d. Wine and suger geiven to Mr Recorder 28 March 2s 6d. Wine for Mr Woodward when he preached 20d. Wine and beere for Mr Collingwood when he preched 7 April 18d. Wine for Mr Potter that preached 14 Aprill and for a messenger that brought a letter about the benevolence 2s 6d. For [preachers] Mr Bird 22 May 20d, Mr Woodward 12d, Mr Reeves 24 June 20d. Sent to Mr Justice of Chester 25 June 16d. For a minister of Salsbury that preached 2 sermons 2s 8d. Sent to the justices that sate about subsidies 20d. For Mr English that preched 28 July 20d. For Mr Potter, Mr Hull, Mr Trulock, Mr Browne that preached 7 severall sermons 13s 4d. Sent to the justices that sate about the benevolence 20d, to Mr Justice of Chester at 2 severall times 5s 3d. All amowntinge to   0   48   11

[f. 64r] Paied for pitchinge of the newe gutter in the high streete and the markett hill, and before the schoole house, as followeth. For the carriage of 59 loades of stone out of Hensgrove beinge 9 daies worke at 4s per diem 36s. To Denmore for digginge the same stones at 3¹/₂d a loade 17s 2¹/₂d. Geiven to the carters in beare at severall tymes in the carriage of those stones 18d. To a laborer to helpe to fill the carte 3 dayes 2s. To Mr Nasshe for the carriage of 14 loades of gravill at 8d the loade 9s 4d. To Archer for digginge that gravell 2s 3d. For 23 loades of stone at Mr Whittons pitt at 4d a loade and for digginge the same stone at 4d the loade 15s 4d. To Mr Nasshe for 6 loades of stone at 8d a loade 4s. To him more for 3 loades of stone with the carriage 2s. To Mr Nasshe, Templer and Slatter for carrying of 72 loades of gravell more from Mr Nasshe his pitt at 8d a loade 48s. Mr Nasshe for the same 72 loades of gravell at 4d the loade 24s. More for 27 loades of stone from Mr Whittons pitt at 8d a loade 18s. For 9 loades of gravill from Yearnneton pitt at 16d a loade, and a peny a loade for the digginge thereof 12s 9d. For bread and beare geiven to Mr Nasshe his men while they were bringinge of 10 loades of gravill which Mr Nasshe gave to the towne 6d. For beare for the carters at severall tymes when they carried the stones 12d. To severall laborers to helpe to carry stones, rubbell and gravell and to helpe to fill the cartes beinge in all 7 dayes worke 5s 6d. To Thomas Robinson for digginge of gravill 8 dayes and for 1 dayes worke in the streete 9s. To Archer for 2 dayes and a halfe to digge gravell 22¹/₂d. To Archer for 2 dayes to digge gravill with Thomas Robinson 2s. To Lucas for digginge gravell 2 dayes and a halfe 2s. For a showle and an iron rake that was broken in this worke 16d. To the masons for pitchinge the maine gutter conteyninge 25 pole in length and halfe a yarde beinge 16 yardes in every pole at 2d a yarde £3 6s 8d. The crosse gutter conteyninge 4 pole longe and 2 yardes over at 16d a pole 5s 4d. The gutter by the church is 5 yardes longe and a yarde over 10d. The markett place conteyninge 4 pole and 1 yard longe and 4 yardes and a halfe over 12s 10d. Geiven to the masons to mende theire wadges 18d. Alle that worke amowntinge to £15 2s 9d.

4 May for the pitchinge at the schoolehouse as followeth. For digginge of gravell 20d, carriage of 10 loades of gravell at 8d a loade 6s 8d, 6 loades of stone 2s 4d and for the carriag thereof 20d, 2 dayes digginge of gravell 18d, to a laborer for 6 dayes worke to serve the masons 4s, halfe a dayes worke to helpe to loade the cart with stones 5d. For the whole pitchinge beinge 135 feete at 2d a yarde. And 4d geiven to them in beere 32s 10d. The whole cominge to 51s 1d.

[Total of pitchinge]	17	13	10
[Marginated subtotal of f. 64r]	22	11	3
[f. 64v] As a rewarde to Mr Anslowe the clark of the assise for entringe of Mr Maiors appeerance at the assise 26 August	0	3	4
Geiven by Mr Harris maior to the poore prisoners at Oxon' this Christmas 1622	0	2	6
To Durbridge for a newe lock for the schoolehouse dore	0	2	2
To be deducted out of the rentrole for the rent of Mr Whittons greate house 15¹/₂d and for his kitchin that Mr Blunt hath 12d	0	2	3¹/₂
For a plancke for the almeshouse dore	0	0	6

To the muster master for his fee for this yeere 3s 4d. To Mr Almon highe constable of Wootton hundred for the marchalsies, the maimed souldiers and house of correction for this yeere 13 June 16s 10d.	0	20	2
All which Bennett Painter had a levy for of 36s			
Geiven to Mr Glover as geiven to poour souldiers	0	0	6
To Durbridge for an iron latch and a boult for the schoolehouse dore	0	0	18
[Marginated subtotal]	0	32	11½
Summ totall of all the disbursmentes	76	4	3
Summ totall of all the receiptes this yeere is	59	2	8
Remayninge due to the chamberlins	17	0	19

[Signature of] Ed. Hiorne towneclark

The names of those that were at this accompte. Joseph Harris maior, John Glover alderman, Edmond Hiorne, William Edwardes, Thomas Williams, Bennett Painter, Thomas Heathen, Roberte Bruce, Thomas Woodward, Thomas Bruce, Roberte Bignill, Nicholas Tayler.

[f. 65r] Md at the accompte the towne doe owe these debtes followinge which they are to be allowed interest for from this daye. To Mr Browne £5 4s. Mr Thomas Rayer £34 17s 7d. Summ   39 17 7

Debtes owinge to the towne

Mr Whitton for rentes 25s 9d. John Powell 10s. Bryan Stephens 15s. Thomas Warde 20s. George Frauncis 15s. Thomas Williams 5s.
Summ   4 10 9

[f. 65v] [blank]

---

[1] A new source of income in the accts.
[2] Bridget, wife of Edw. Kemp of Hampton Poyle, occurs on 24 Feb. 1613 in B 78/2.
[3] d. 16 Aug., bur. 17 Aug. 1622: Yarnton parish reg.; Williams, *Parl. Hist.* 198.
[4] Todman (d. 1624) was a keeper in Woodstock park: MS. Wills Oxon. 153/3/50.
[5] Nic. Crouch, undersheriff 1620: Davenport, *Oxon. Lords Lieut.* 61.
[6] The king needed a benevolence because Parl. failed to grant a subsidy for the German wars: *Acts of P.C.* 1621–23, 176–7. Subsidies granted 1621 were still being collected: see below; *Cal.S.P.Dom.* 1619–23, 225, 315, 379.
[7] Thos. Browne became rector of Bladon 23 Dec. 1621: O.R.O., Clerus, ff. 55r, 411v.

[f. 66r] **A true note of the men, woomen and children of Woodstock which doe receave the wickly benevolence of the right worshipfull Sir Thomas Spenser Knighte and baronett. And which did begin on Sunday the 26 February 1614[/15], Joseph Harris alderman, beinge then maior.**

Menn [numbered 1 to 10]
Richard Wright, Richard Coles, Richard Lowe, John Seely, Richard Private, Christofer Bowman, Gyles Coles, Water Wells, Thomas Belcher, John Gilbert. Every man hath 3d in bread delivered to him on everye Sonday.

Woomen [numbered 1 to 10]
Widdowe Pulchoe, John Wilkinson wife, John Masons wife, Katherine Dissell widdowe, widdowe Bowland, widdowe Maynard, widdowe Browne, widdowe meadowes, Joane Cope, widdowe Wilsden. Every wooman hath 2d in bread delivered to her on every Sonday.

Children [numbered 1 to 20]
Joane Gelly, Jane Gelly, the daughters of widdowe Gelly; Edward Barnes, William Barnes, Judeth Barnes, children of widdowe Barnes; Charles Barneshewe; William Gee, Winifrite Gee, children of Thomas Gee; Joseph Price, son of John Price; Thomas Rayer, son of William Rayer; William Homes, Richard Homes, children of widdowe Homes; Robert Coles, Jane Coles, Elizabeth Coles, children of Richard Coles; Milright Wilkinson, son of John Wilkinson; John Garter, Frisses Garter, sons of Frauncis Garter; John Newell, son of Richard Newell; Joan Vardam, daughter of widdowe Vardam. Every child hath a peny of bredd delivered to them on every Sonday.

The wickly some is 5s 10d.
The annual some is £15 3s 4d.
This yeere ended the 18 February 1615 [/16] £15 3s 4d.

Md he also gave 30s at Christmas 1615, the men 12d, the woomen 12d, the children 6d. All which hath beene delivered by the handes of Joseph Harris.

Witness Edm. Hiorne towneclark

[f. 66v] [memorandum of the sums which Hiorne received from Sir Thomas Spencer up to 1621, which can be summarized as follows]

27 Feb. 1615[16]	£7	10s	but	paid 3s 4d arrears
28 Sept. 1616	£11	10s	but	paid 45s 10d arrears
31 March 1617	£9	10s	and	2s 6d from last account
5 Oct. 1617	£10		and	5s from last account
[f. 67r] 27 Mar. 1618	£10		and	29s 2d from last account
1 Oct. 1618	£10		and	41s 8d from last account

[f. 67v]	28 April 1619	£10	and	12 s 6d from last account
	14 Oct. 1619	£10	and	£3 6s 8d from last account
	6 May 1620	£10	and	4s 4d from last account
	26 Oct. 1620	£10	and	£4 17s 6d from last account
[f. 68r]	16 April 1621	£10	and	£4 11s 8d from last account

[f. 68v] 22 December 1622 to 20 December 1623, Thomas Rayer and George Noble, chamberlains

[Disbursements]   £   s   d

Inprimis payed for guiftes and rewardes geiven by the towne at Christmas 1622 as followeth. In rewardes to Sir Jarratt Fleetwoodes servantes 7s. For fower cakes 10s a peece which were sente to the severall parties heereunder written at Christmas 1622, to the Lady Spencer, Sir Henry Browne, Sir Henry Lee, Sir Jarratt Fleetwood to eache of them one, 40s. For one suger loffe sent then to Sir Henry Lee wayinge 8lb 1 quarter and a halfe at 13d a pownde 9s 1d. Geiven to the officers at Sir Henry Brownes then in rewardes 13s. For a suger loffe sent then to the Lady Spencer 10s 2d. Spent at the eatinge of the taste cakes 2s 3d. Geiven to Sir Henry Lees servantes in rewardes 26s 6d. For a cake and sugerloffe sent to my lord cheife barron 19s 7d. In rewardes to theire servantes 9s 8d. To Mr Osbaston theire man when he came to invite us in wine 14d.   6   18   5

To George Greene for lopping 9 trees at Symon Colliers dore which was geiven to the almesepeople   0   0   6

Paied to certeine messengers that brought severall proclamations at severall tymes as heereafter followeth. To Mr Shockleges for one proclamation concerninge the releife of the poore 4s. Last day of December 1622 to Mr Edmond Pitcher messenger for 2 proclamations, one for publique greevances, the other for flessh 3s 10d. To William Edwardes a messenger for a proclamation concerninge pressinge of marriners 2s 6d. To Mr Shockleges concerninge gentry to reside in the contry at theire owne howses 2s 6d. To William Edwardes messenger for a proclamation concerninge regestringe of knightes 2s 6d. To Mr Shockleges for a proclamation about the apprehendinge of one Feild 2s 6d. To Mr Edwardes messenger for a proclamation concerninge gold wier 2s 6d. To Mr Edwardes messenger for 2 proclamations the one aboutes feltes the other about printinge of woodes [wordes].[1] All amowntinge to 24s 4d. [Marginated] 15 April 1623 for 1 proclamation about spices[2] and for a lettre for the cownsell 3s 6d. For another proclamation about munition 2s 6d. Summ totall   0   30   4

[f. 69r] Paied for wine geiven by Mr Maior and by his appoyntment at several tymes and to severall persons for severall uses this yeere as followeth. 1 quarte of sack to the justices that sate heere in January 12d. For wine to the justices that sate here 18 February 20d, in the midle of Lent 20d, in Aprill 20d. To Sir James Whitlock 17 June 2s 4d, 24 July 2s 8d, in August 20d, 4 November 20d.

1 quarte of clarrett to Mr Browne that dined at Mr Whittons 8d. For wine to Mr Twitty on Sunday after the last accompte 2s, to Mr Browne 29 January 10d, to Mr Haswell that preached in February 20d, Mr Browne in February 12d, Mr Harris 2 March 20d, Mr Browne 9 March 12d, Mr Hull 16 March 20d, Mr Saunderson that preached 23 March 20d, Mr Dod last day of March 2s 8d, Mr Sheppard 6 April 12d, Mr Browne on Easter Day 20d, Mr Birde on Sonday folowinge 20d, Mr Raunson 11 May 20d, Mr Browne on Whitsonday 20d, to him 15 June 20d, Mr Tayler for his 2 sermons 22 June 2s 8d, Mr Browne on Midsommer Day 12d, to him 6 July 12d, for the Irishe preacher 13 July 20d, Mr Raunson 2s 2d, Mr Sidnam 27 July 2s 8d, 10 August 1623 Mr Browne and Mr Potter of Oxon' whoe preached 2 sermons that day 3s 8d, Mr Duttons chaplin 17 Auguste 12d. For sack for Mr Browne last day of August 15d. For wine 7 September to Mr Wattes and to the ould minister 2s 8d, to Mr Hull 20d, Mr Browne 14 September 12d, for Sir James Whitlock 8 October 12d, to Mr Rowlandson 12 October 20d, Mr Browne 19 October 12d, Mr Shockledge the Kinges messenger 6d, Mr Potter 26 October 20d, Mr Browne 1 November 2s, to him 1 pynt of sack 5 November 6d. For wine to Mr Browne 14 December 12d. All amowntinge to the somme of   3 10 11

[f. 69v] Payed for monyes geiven by Mr Maior and by his appoyntment, and by others of the neighbours to diverse poore people and sowldiers as heereafter followeth. To a poore woman that had a passe 3d. To 2 poore travylinge men goinge to Lavington 3d. To a poore wooman that Mr Hiorne leid out 3d. To a poore souldier that came out of Gilderland with a passe 4d and to a poore criple the same day 3d. To a poore souldier named Erasmus Pope 4d. To a poore wooman that came from Brackly 2d. To 2 poore woomen of Wittney 6d. Paied to Henry Whiteside 2d which he gave to a poore boddy. Geiven by myselfe to 3 poore people 6d. To 2 poore people travylinge to the Bath 4d. To a lame man and a blinde man 3d. To poore Irishe people that came with severall passes 14d. To 3 poore people that came out of Cheschere 3d. As geiven by Mr Hiorne to 2 poore souldiers 6d. To 2 souldiers that came with a passe from Count Mansfeild 6d.[3] To 2 other souldiers that came from him allso 6d. To 2 other poore people 2d. As geiven by Mr Hiorne to a poore souldier 3d. To a poore wooman that came from Bewly 2d. Paied Henry Whiteside which he gave by Mr Maiors appoyntment to certeine Egiptians 6d. To a poore souldier 3d. To one Rowland Price that came with a passe 3d. By me to poore people at several tymes 12d. To a poore traviler 4d. To a poore man that had the Turkes passe 4d. At Christmas 1623 to the poore prisoners in Oxford 2s 6d. Paied to Mr Maior as mony geiven by him to poore people from 22 December 1622 till 15 September 1623 as appeereth by his note 38s 9d. More to a poore man 2d. Amowntinge to 51s 2d. [Marginated]

More geiven by Mr Maior to poore people 7s. In toto   0 58 2
To 2 wardsmen for 4 faiers   0   5 4

To Mr Hiorne which he gave to recorde Mr Maiors appeerance
at the 2 assises and for wine to Mr Ansloe the clarke of the
markett and to the judges cryer   0   7   8

To Morgan for deliveringe a lettre to the clarke of the cownsell
from the towne concerninge alehowses[4]   0   2   0

To Mr Glover for Mr Recorders entertaynement 14 August
for his dyet 17s, wine 4s 8d, horsemeate 3s. In toto   0   24   8

[f. 70r] Geiven to Mr Markereth of Chippingnorton to make up
his collection 10s   0   0   21

To Mr Harris maior his fee   10   0   0

Paied the fee farme to Mr Hugh Candishe undershreeve
to Sir Rowland Lacye 53s 4d, acquittance 6d   0   53   10

To the receaver for the cownty of Oxon' Sir Robert Lee for
the quitt rent £5 6s 8d, acquittance 18d   5   8   2

To Mr Lenthall our recorder his fee £3 6s 8d whereof he
appoynted the towne to reteyne 20s towardes the repayringe
of poor children. So paied   0   46   8

To Edmond Hiorne townclark fee, assises, accomptes   0   45   0

To Mr James schoolemaster his stipend   13   0   0

To Mr Glover for Mr Beale the clarke of the markett his
dinner 11s, wine 2s and in rewarde by Mr Maiors
appoyntment 10 December 1623   0   23   0

To be deducted out of the rent role for the rent of
Mr Whittons greate house and kitchine [as before]   0   2   3¹/₂

Summ totall of all the disbursmentes   53   18   8¹/₂
Summ totall of all the receiptes this yeere   50   15   4¹/₄
[corrected in ms. to]   51   3   4¹/₄
Remayninge due to the chamberlins this yeere   3   3   4¹/₄
[corrected in ms. to]   0   55   4¹/₄

[In latin] By me Edmond Hiorne common clerk of the aforesaid borough

[f. 70v] [blank]

[f. 71r] [Receipts]

Of Mr Doleman   8   0   0

Of Mr Thomas Rayer for interest of £50 in his handes of the
mony due to the schoolhouse and for the maytenance of the
schoolmaster which was recovered from Mr Doleman's father
which £5 was due the 20 June[5]   5   0   0

Of Thomas Heathen serjant at the mace for stallages   6   14   7

And for the standing of the coontry bakers 12d a peece for
every quarter, 9s of 3 for three quarters and for the standing of
certeine privileged butchers upon a yeerly rate by composition.   0   9   0

Of Edward Longe toleman for the tole	0	48	1
Rentes of this boughroughe	24	17	10
Of Alice Shad widdowe for rent of the wooll beame	0	24	0
Of Symon Collier for the lopp of 2 elmes and 2 asshes			
growing before his dore which lopp was sould unto him			
by the said chamberlyns	0	4	6
[f. 71v] For the seale of Thomas Williams fyne[6]	0	4	0
For the seale of John Woodwardes fyne	0	4	0
Of Edward Johnson tayler for his admission	0	30	0
Of Frauncis Druce alias White for his admission	0	0	20
Of John Bignill for his admittance	0	0	20
Of Clement Warren for the seale of a fyne from Richard			
Warren and his wife and Richard Puddenton[7]	0	4	0
Summ totall of the disbursementes is	53	18	8½
Summ totall of the receiptes is	51	3	4¼
Remaining due to the chamberlins is	0	55	4¼

A note of the buckettes receaved by Mr Rayer chamberlyn
which are to be accompted for. 4 August to buy buckettes
27s. Of Warde for his buckett 3s. [Bucketts at 3s 4d
each] Jerome Longe, Thomas Snapes, John Tassill,
Richard Browne, Thomas [Jackson] joyner, James Nickoles,
John Yonge, Roberte Belcher, Henry Whiteside junior,
Edward Johnson, Richard Hamond, Frauncis Druce alias
White, John Bignill and Francis Collingwood

[John Bignill deleted]. Somme is	3	16	8
Whereof he hath delivered into the hall 12 buckettes at 3s 4d			
a peece, 40s. So remains in his handes	0	36	8

[f. 72r] The towne oweth Mr Rayer £40 18s 7d.[8] Mr Browne
£4.[9]

Debtes due to the towne

Mr Whiton for rentes 27s. John Powell 10s. Bryan Stephens
15s. Thomas Ward 20s. George Francis 15s. Widdowe
Collingewood for her sone 10s. Richard Hamond 10s.
John Yonge 10s. Thomas Williams 5s.

At this accompte the 20s which Mr Rayer hath of the guift of
Mr Recorder for the clothinge of poore children is delivered
to Thomas Williams chamberlyn. [And to same] of the monyes
received upon the extreates 26s. [Both marginated] Paied.

Summ	0	40	0

[1] i.e. against the disorderly printing of books and works: *Stuart Proclams.*, i, no. 247.
[2] Issued 5 Nov. 1622: ibid. no. 232.
[3] Ernest, count of Mansfield, a professional soldier close to Prince Chas. and the duke of Buckingham, was recruiting in Eng. for the Continental wars: *Cal.S.P.Dom.* 1619–23, 287, 313. For impressing in Woodstock see below in 1624.
[4] The mayor informed the Privy Council that the town council had suppressed needless alehouses and immoderately strong beer, and would maintain vigilance: *Cal.S.P.Dom.* 1619–23, 532.
[5] This information in subsequent accounts in the MS. is omitted in this edition. For the acquisition of school money see above, Intro.
[6] For a house in High St: B 77/2, 5 Aug.
[7] Ibid. 19 Dec. 1623.
[8] Explained in B 81, f. 29r as £38 19*d*. laid out for the town and 57*s*. due to him on this acct.
[9] 'monye lent to the towne by his father': ibid.

[f. 72v] 20 December 1623 to 22 December 1624, Thomas Williams and George Noble, chamberlains

[Disbursements]   £   s   d

Wine. Inprimis payed for wine geiven by Mr Maiors appoyntment at severall tymes and to severall men for the credite of the towne. To a preacher 22 December 1623 in wine 12d. To Mr Browne on Christmas Day 1623 in wine 12d. For wine spent at the eatinge of 3 cakes last of December 1623 2s. Sent to Sir James Whitlock 11 January 1623[/4] 2s 8d. Geiven to the undershreive at the electinge of the burgesses for this boughroughe 12d.[1] To Mr Browne in January 12d, and 22 February at Mr James his house 20d, to him on Palme Sonday 12d. To Mr Ramsy 20d, to Mr Recorder 8 April 2s,[2] to the justices 14 April sittinge about alehouses 20d, to Mr Browne 18 April 6d, to Mr Coolin 25 April 20d. In wine to Mr Dod 2 May 20d, to Mr Browne on Whitsonday 6d. To a precher (beinge a traviler) that dyned at Mr Maiors 23 May 20d. 30 May to Mr Browne 20d, 6 June for wine to a preacher of Corpus Christi College in Oxon' 20d. To Mr Browne 13 June 8d, to Sir James Whitlocke and his lady 17 June 20d, to Mr Browne 24 June 6d. In wine to Mr Woodward for his 2 sermons 27 June 2s 8d. To the justices at the first sittinge of the subsidies 3s 8d.[3] To Mr Browne 25 July 20d. The same day to Mr Collingwood 2s. To Mr Browne 8 August 20d. To Mr Harris in wine to the Kinges Majesties officers at the Kinges Majesties beinge at Woodstock 16d.[4] To him in wine for the Kinges trumpeters 12d. To the Kinges justices in September 2s 4d. To Mr Recorder 12 September 6s 8d. To Mr Birde for wine at his sermon 19 September 2s 4d. To Mr Browne 29 September 6d. To Mr Hawkins preacher 29 September 20d.
To the justices at a sittinge about [f. 73r] subsidies 11 October 2s 8d. To Sir James Whitlock 13 October 20d. To Mr Browne last of October 20d. To Mr Stone for his sermon 19 November 12d. To the justices in wine at the pressinge of soldiers 26 November 20d.[5] To Mr Bird 28 November at his sermon 10d. To a strainge preacher 6 December 1624 6d.   3   6   4

Guiftes. Payed for guiftes and rewardes geiven by the towne at Christmas 1623. One cake 10s and one sugerloffe 6s 6d sent to Sir Jarratt Fleetwood, in rewarde to his servantes 5s 6d. One cake 10s and one sugerloffe 9s 6d sent to Sir Laurence Tanfeild knight lord cheife baron, in rewarde to his servantes 10s 3d. One cake 10s and one sugerloffe 5s 6d sent to Sir Henry Lee knight, in rewarde to his servantes 23s. One sugerloffe sent to Mr Browne our parson 10s 6d.   5 0 9

Proclamations and rewardes. To Mr Edwardes for bringinge 2 proclamations, one about corne, the other for dressinge of meate 3s 6d. To him for proclamations concerninge the bannisshinge of pristes 4s, for 2 other about golde, and silver mynes 4s. For bringinge the booke of subsidies 2s 6d, for 2 proclamations 4s, for 1 proclamation paied by Mr Maior 2s 6d. To Mr Shockleges for 1 proclamation 2s 6d.   0 23 0

[f. 73v] Guiftes to poore people. To a lame souldier 2d, a poore man and wooman 2d, a poore souldier 2d, a poore widdowe and her 2 sonnes 2d, a poore souldier 2d, other poore people 8 May 6d, a blinde man 6d, a poor creeple brought to the towne on horseback 6d. Paied Henry Whiteside which he paied to poor people 4d. To 3 poore people 3d, a poore souldier 4d, a poore souldier 3d. To Mr Harris maior as mony geiven to poor people in his maioralty 36s 4d. To Mr Meatcalfe maior [the like] 6s. To him for a shrewde for Raphe Symons 3s. To Mr Glover as leid out by him 18d. To George Noble as paied by him 12d. To the joayle at Oxon 2s. To the Princes players 2s. [Marginated] 55s 4d received for the towne.   0 55 4

For wood at the hall at the last accompte 6d. For wood for the sealinge of busshells 6d. Paied for chardges and workmanshipp about the coockinge stoole 18d. For slatt, nailes and workmanshipp about the schoolehouse 3s 2d. Paied to the wardsmen at eache of the 4 fayers 16d a fayer 5s 4d. For sending a lettre to Blechington to Mr Recorder 3d.[6] For wax to seale Mr Fletchers indenture between the Skinners of London and the towne 1d.[7] For mendinge a bedsteede in the litle house 2d. Paied to John Norman and Anthony Deverill surveyers[8] for carriages out of the hollowe way and about the towne 5s 6d. Paied Greene and Gee for 2 dayes worke about the highewayes 3s 4d. Stone, lyme and morter, and workmanshipp about the hall at the Kinges coming 5s 4d. For wallinge the pownde and about the holloweway and for stones and carriage thereunto 7s. Paied to Morgan for carrying a lettre to the Earle of Montgomery about the conveyance of water to the towne 12d. For sweepinge the almeshouse chimnyes 8d. For riddinge of rubbishe out of Peppers backside for the guildhall 7d.[9] For 1 bushell of lyme for that work 8d. Slattes and crestes for the schoolehouse 6d.   0 36 1

[f. 74r] Paied to Mr Hiorne which he laied out at the twoe assises to the clarke of the assise in mony and wyne 3s 4d a tyme and to the judges cryer 12d a tyme   0 8 8

Paied to him for a statute booke of the last parliament   0 3 0

Paied unto him which he payed to Mr Midleton the clark to the Company of Skinners for his paynes about Mr Fletchers guifte	0	20	0
To Mr Glover for Mr Recorders entertainment 10 April 6s 6d, his horsmeate 14 September 18d, his entertainment 11 December 3s.	0	8	11
Payed as geiven by Mr Harris maior at the Kinges beinge last at Woodstock in August to the Princes tru}peters 10s, the Kinges trumpeters 13s 4d. To the clarke of the markett of the Kinges Majesties houshold 10s. For a cake sent to the Earle of Montgomerye from the towne 10s and a sugerloffe to him 10s.	0	53	4
To Mr Harris maior fee £5 at Our Lady Day, Mr Meatcalfe maior fee £5 at Michaelmas	10	0	0
To Mr Langston, undershreeve to Sir William Ascue knight,[10] fee farme 53s 4d, acquittance 6d	0	53	10
To Sir Robert Lee recevor for quitt rent	5	8	2
To Mr Lenthall esq recorder his fee	3	6	8
To Edmond Hiorne towneclarke fee, assises, accomptes	0	45	0
To Mr James schoolemaster his stipend. [Deleted £14]	13	0	0
To be deducted out of the rent role for the rent of Mr Whittons greate house 15½d and for his kitchin that Mr Blunt hath 12d for this last yeere	0	2	3½
Paied to Henry Whiteside and Thomas Woodward constables which they payed 14 May to the high constables for maymed souldiers and marchallsy	0	16	10
[f. 74v] Summ totall of all the disbursementes	56	10	3½
Summ totall of all the receiptes this yeere	53	12	7
So remayninge to the chamberlins	0	57	8½

[In latin] By me Edmond Hiorne common clerk of the maior and cominaltye of the aforesaid borough

[f. 75r] [Receipts]

Of Mr Thomas Doleman	8	0	0
Of Mr Rayer alderman for interest of £50	5	0	0
Of Thomas Heathen serjant for stallages	7	18	6
Of Edward Longe toleman for the tole	3	8	3
Rentes of this boughroughe	24	17	10¼
Of Alice Shad widdowe for rente of the wooll beame	0	24	0
Receaved at the last accompt in monye	0	20	0

Of Thomas Rayer alderman which Mr Recorder gave to cloth poor children	0	20	0
George Noble receaved of Adderbury bakers 15s. And he receaved from Thomas Bruce constable which he receaved of Adderbury bakers 21 December 1624 9s, vizt of Roger Burbery 2s, Lester 2s, Smethes 2s, Cooper 12d, Anthony Burbery 2s. In toto	0	24	0

[f. 75v] Summ totall of this yeeres receiptes	53	12	7
Summ totall of all the disbursementes	56	10	3¹/₂
So remayninge to the chamberlins 22 December 1624	0	57	8¹/₂

The towne doe owe these debtes at this accompte

which they doe allowe interest for, Mr Rayer £45, Mr Browne £4, Thomas Williams 57s 8¹/₂d.	51	17	8¹/₂
Allso the debtes due at the last accomptes for admissions are owinge to the towne from the perticuler persons therein mentioned.			

[Signature of] Edmond Hiorne towneclarke

---

¹ Sir Phil. Carye and Wm. Lenthall. Parl. was summoned 20 Dec. 1623 and sat 12 Feb.–29 May 1624: *Handbook Chron.*
² Apparently Lenthall's first appearance at the local court since appointment as recorder in 1621: B 77/2, 8 Apr. 1624.
³ There was a parl. grant in Mar. 1624 of three subsidies and three tenths for the restitution of the Palatinate and for troops to go to Ireland for 'probable war': Act, 21 Jas. I, c. 33; *Cal.S.P.Dom.* 1623–5, 199; and see below.
⁴ Jas. I was at Woodstock from c. 23–7 Aug.: *Cal. S.P.Dom.* 1623–5, 330–1; Nichols, *Progresses,* iv. 1001–3.
⁵ Letters were sent 23 June to the Lords Lieut. and by them to the justices to press soldiers for service in the United Provinces, where the king's daughter and son-in-law were refugees; levies were authorized in Nov.: *Acts of P.C.* 1623–25, 249, 375, 385 sqq.
⁶ Lenthall's brother Sir John lived in Bletchingdon: Berks. R.O., Lenthall pps. D/E11, 218.
⁷ For indenture of 25 Nov. see benefactions book B 97, p. 3.
⁸ Of the highways, parish officers elected in the view court: e.g. B 78/3, 5 Apr. 1615
⁹ John Pepper, cooper, who had a shop by the High Cross: see rental above.
¹⁰ Sir Wm. Aishcombe of Alvescot, high sheriff 1623: Davenport, *Lords Lieut.* 44.

[f. 76r] 22 December 1624 to 21 December 1625, Thomas Williams and George Noble, chamberlains

[Disbursements]   £   s   d

Inprimis paied for guiftes and rewardes geiven by the towne at Christmas 1624 as followeth.

To Sir Gerrard Fleetwood knight one cake 10s and one suger loffe 9s 4d, in rewardes to his servantes 6s. To Sir Henry Browne one cake 10s, in rewardes to his servantes 11s. To Sir Henry Lee knight one cake 10s and one sugerloffe of 7 powndes 9s 4d, in rewardes to his servantes 23s. To Mr Parson Browne deceased one sugerloffe of 8 powndes 10s 8d.

All amownting to   4   19   4

Paied to soondry messengers for bringing of proclamations at severall tymes this yeere by Mr Maiors appoyntment as followeth. For one concerninge the restraint of people to come to the court 18d, one concerninge the faste 2s. To Mr Edwardes for proclamations 3s 6d, Mr Souche 3s, Pawlins[1] the messenger 3s, and more 2s. To Mr Edwardes for diverse proclamations at severall tymes 10s 6d, at one tyme for diverse proclamations by Mr Maiors appoyntment 10s, for 2 proclamations 3s 6d. To Mr Shockleges for proclamations 3s 6d, for 2 proclamations at twice 5s. To Mr Souche for a proclamation 3s, to Mr Shockleges deputy 3s 6d. To Mr Edwardes for 4 proclamations at twice 8s. In toto   3   2   0

[f. 76v] Wine. Paied for wine this yeere, as appoynted by Mr Maior in the behalfe of the towne as followeth. 3 quartes of sack and 3 quartes of clarrett sent to the justices at the quarter sessions for the cownty houlden at Woodstock at Michaelmas 1625 5s. Sent to the justices at the seasing of the subsidie 20d.[2] 1 pynte of sack for the messenger that came from the lordes of the privy cownsell with a lettre 6d.[3] A quarte of sack to Mr Evans when he preached and dyned at Mr Maiors 12d. A pynte of sack to Dennis when he came to invite the towne to Sir Henry Lees 6d. Wine to Mr Hodges a preacher that dyned at Mr Glovers 12d. To Mr Gregory when he sate to take recognizances for victulers and butchers 12d. To the justices that sate at the asseasinge of the seconde subsidies 20d. To Mr Edwardes that brought proclamations the last of March 6d. To a yong man of Penbrocke Colledge at Mr Maiors house 12d. To Mr Duncombe that preached in Aprill 20d. To Mr Doctor Prideux at his induction 20d, upon the publisshinge of his articles 22d.[4] To the justices in Aprill sittinge about the poore and alehouses 20d. To Mr Doctor Prideux when he preached 22 May 20d. To Mr Rowlandson the same day after his sermon a pottle of clarrett 16d. To a lame preacher of Hanwell 20d. To a preacher that came with Mr Harris his sonne in lawe beinge of Jesus Colledge on Whitsonday 20d. To a straunger preacher in wine on Whitson Tusday 1 quarte and a pynt of sack and a quarte of clarrett 23d. To Mr Hull 12 June 20d, Mr Meadreues of Exiter Colledge 19 June 20d, Mr Duncombe 26 June 20d. Mr Tayler and Mr Dickinson for 2 sermons 10 July 2s, Mr Doctor Price 17 July 20d. In July [for a preacher] that came from Rockston [Wroxton?] and   preached 2 sermons 2s 8d.   To Mr Kilby 21 October 20d, Mr Hull 9 October 12½d, Mr Kilby 23 October 20d, Mr Wheatly upon the fast 8d, Mr Kilby for his 2 sermons 11 December 1625 2s 10d. In the whole   0 48   1

[f. 77r] Mr Recorder. Paied for Mr Recorders chardges 22   December 1624 18d. To Goodman Dubber for goeinge with a letter to Mr Recorder 18d. For beere and horsemeate for Mr Recorder at Mr Glovers 12d, a quarte of sack 29 March 1625 12d. In toto   3 11   8

Expenses at the Kinges beinge here.[5]
Geiven to Mr Walker the clarke of the markett for the verge in rewarde 10s, wine for him 2s 2d, to his man 12d. In rewarde to the Kinges trumpiters 10s, wine for them 3s 4d. To the trumpiter that sounded the Kinges proclamation with the knight marchall 5s. Paied for the proclamation when Kinge Charles was proclaymed 10s, wine then spent at the townes chardges 3s. For one cake sent to the Earle of Montgomery 10s and for 3 cheeses sent to him 3s 4d. In toto   0 57 10

Geiven in rewarde to Mr Beale the clarke of the markett at lardge 30 July 10s and in wine 12d   0 11   0

Paied for wood at the last accompte 8d. For a newe markett busshell 2s and for the iron worke about the same 5s. 15 January geiven to the messenger that came to distreigne for the fee farme unpaied at Michaelmas 1624 14s, wine and beere to him 16d. To William Rayer and 2 laborers more for fillinge cartes with stones for the highe wayes and for spreading them 7 February 2s. For wax 1d. For stones and for mendinge the litle house 2s. 2 wardsmen at 4 faiers 5s 4d. To John Doe for goeinge to Aylesbury assises 2s 4d. For mendinge the table and barr at the guild hall 6d, nailes 4d. For riddinge of the litle house 8d. In toto   0 36   3

[f. 77v] Paied to Mr Hiorne as geiven to Mr Anslowe the clarke
of the assises and for wine to him at both the assises 6s 8d.
Geiven to the judges cryer of the courte at each assise
12d and 2s.   0   8   8
To Mr Meatcalfe maior as geiven to poore 24s, to one souldier
by Mr Glovers appoyntment 4d, another souldier 6d. To one
poore man which George Noble paied by Mr Hiorns
appoyntment 4d. In toto   0 25   2
To Mr Meatcalfe maior his stipende   10   0   0
To Mr Dunch[6] his undershreeve for fee farme 53s 4d,
acquittance 6d   0 53 10
Paied at Readinge by Mr Chesterman to Sir Roberte Lee
knight receaver for quitt rente £5 6s 8d, acquittance 18d   5   8   2
To Edmond Hiorne towneclarke fee [etc.]   0 45   0
To Mr James schoolemaster his stipende   13   0   0

Paied for the renewinge of the commission of the peace at Oxon', to the clarke of the crowne upon the death of King James[7]	0	44	6
Paied Mr Chesterman 8s which he paied to the clarke of the Parliament for the fylinge of the indenture for the burgesses of our towne at the last Parliament when Sir Jerratt Fleetwood and Sir Phillipp Carye were chosen[8]	0	8	0
[f. 78r] To be deducted out of the rent role for this yeere for the rent of Mr Whittons greate house 15^1/2d, for the house thereto adjoyninge which Mr Blunt nowe useth for a kitchin 12d. And for the rent of Thomas Gees house for that it is out of lease and in controversie 5s. The towne is to enter upon the house and to evict Thomas Gee out of it.	0	7	3^1/2
[Marginated subtotal]	56	6	9^1/2
Summ totall of all the disbursmentes [corrected in MS.]	57	6	9^1/2
Summ totall of all the receiptes this yeere	55	7	0
So remayninge to the chamberlins	0	39	9^1/2

[In latin] By me Edmond Hiorne common clerk of the maior and cominaltie of the aforesaid borough

[f. 78v] [blank]

[f. 79r] [Receipts]

Of Mr Thomas Doleman	8	0	0
Of Mr Rayer alderman for interest of £50	5	0	0
Of Thomas Heathen serjant for stallages	7	14	9³/4
Of Edward Longe toleman for the tole	3	19	8
Rentes of this boughroughe	24	18	10^1/4
Of Alice Shadd widdowe for rente of the wooll beame	0	24	0
Of Headdy for his admission to his freedom 20s and was to pay at Michaelmas 1625 10s more. So receaved	0	20	0
Allso he payed to the chamberlins for a buckett which is to be provided	0	3	4
[f. 79v] Of Edward Silver for his admission to his freedom 20s. And he was to pay more at Michaelmas 1625 10s. And he paied 3s 4d for a buckett which is to be provided. So receaved as nowe accompted for	0	20	0
Of John Barnes for his admission to his freedom 20d and paied then 3s 4d for a buckett. So accompted for	0	0	20
Of John Patterick for his admission to his freedom 5s and for his buckett 3s 4d which is to be provided for. So accompted for nowe but only	0	5	0

Of a tanner of Chippingnorton for a fyne for sellinge leather unsealed contrary to the statute[9]	0	4	0
Of John Norman for victualinge without licence	0	5	0
Benedict Norwood for the like	0	5	0
John Cotten for the like[10]	0	5	0
Of Mr Kyte upon a composition for the placeinge of his stone wall next to the highe way at hoggerill hill and for the increase of grownde then taken in as nowe the wall standeth	0	10	0
Of the bakers for standinge at the crosse, Smith 3s, goodwife Leister 3s, Roger Burbery 2s, Anthony Burbery 2s, William Cooper 2s, Roberte Leister 12d, Henry Cooper 12d	0	14	0
Summ totall of all the receiptes	55	7	0
Summ totall of all the disbursmentes [sum corrected]	57	6	9½
So remayninge to the chamberlins	0	39	9½

[In latin] By me Edmond Hiorne common clerk of the maior and cominaltie of the aforesaid borough

[f. 80r] Debtes owinge by the towne

To Mr Rayer £17 18s 7d. Mistris Browne £4.[11] Thomas Williams £5 2s. Summ	27	0	7

Owinge to the towne

Mr Whitton for rentes 29s 2½d. John Powell 10s. Bryan Steephens 15s. Thomas Warde 20s. George Frauncis 15s. Francis Collingewood and his mother 10s. Richard Hamond 10s. John Yonge 10s. Thomas Headdy 10s. Edward Silver 10s. Summ	6	19	2

[f. 80v] [blank]

[1] And. Pawlinges, king's messenger in ordinary: B 77/2, 17 Sept. 1625.

[2] Two subsidies were granted by Parl. in June, the first payable in Oct., the second by Apr. 1626. Letters were sent out to J.Ps.: *Acts of P.C.* 1625–26, 364; *Cal.S.P.Dom.* 1625–49, 28; Act, 1 Chas. I, c. 6.

[3] See *Acts of P.C.* 1625–26, 206–7, commending the corporation for taking Jas. Hall, an Oxf. tailor, into custody for uttering 'lewd and pernicious words'. Hall had said the king was gone to Scotland and a new king proclaimed: *Cal.S.P.Dom.* 1625–6, 104. Hall (d. 1630) had already been in trouble in Oxf.: *Oxf. Council Acts* (O.H.S. lxxvii, 1928), ed. H. E. Salter, 202, 263. The Thos. Hall below in 1626 may be the same man.

[4] John Prideaux became rector of Bladon 1 Apr. 1625: see appendix, biogs. He had in 1624 preached before the king in Woodstock 'a sermon directed against the Puritans': Nichols, *Progresses*, iv. 1002.

[5] Chas. I was proclaimed 27 Mar.: *Acts of P.C.* 1625–6, 5–6. He was in Woodstock from 28 July, and the court stayed there until 26 Aug. to escape plague in London: *Cal.S.P.Dom.* 1625–26, 84; cf. *Cal. S.P.Ven.* 1625–26, 138.

[6] Wal. Dunch of Newington: Davenport, *Lords Lieut.* 44.

[7] Ald. Thos. Rayer and Edm. Hiorne, town clerk, were added to the commission. Cf. 1621 n. 14.
[8] Chas. I's first parl., dismissed 12 Aug.1625: *Handbk Chron.*
[9] Thos. Wilks of Chipping Norton: B 77/2, 26 Sept. 1625.
[10] For cases see victuallers' sessions 26 Oct. 1625 in B 77/2.
[11] Susan, widow of Thos. Browne jun., rector of Bladon (d. 1625). The money had been owed in 1621 to her father-in-law Ald. Thos. Browne (d. 1621). She also held the £10 he left for sermons. By 1627 the debts were said to be owed to her second husband, Mr. Vernon: B 81, f. 30 and v; below in 1627.

[f. 81r] 21 December 1625 to 23 December 1626, Thomas Williams and George Noble, chamberlains

	[Disbursements]	£	s	d

Guiftes and rewardes at Christmas 1625.
To Sir Henry Lee one cake 10s and one sugerloffe wayinge 7lb 3 quarters and half at 17d per pownde 10s 7d. In rewardes to his servantes 21s 6d. To Sir Henry Browne one cake 10s. In rewardes to his servantes 11s 6d. To Sir Gerrard Fleetwood one cake 10s and 1 shugerloffe wayinge 7lb at 17d per lb 10s 4d. In rewarde to his servantes 6s 6d. To Mr Doctor Prideaux one shugerloffe of 9lb at 17d a pownde 12s 8d. All amowntinge to

	£	s	d
All amowntinge to	5	3	1

Stipendes and allowances annually.

	£	s	d
To Mr Meatcalfe maior his allowaunce at his feast at Our Lady Day	5	0	0
To Mr Thomas Rayer maior [the like] at Michaelmas	5	0	0
Paied quitt rent at London £5 6s 8d, acquittance 18d	5	8	2
Feefarme to Sir Richard Bluntes undershreeve 53s 4d, acquittance 7d [deleted 6d]	0	53	11
To Mr Lenthall esq recorder his fee	3	6	8
To Mr Hiorne towneclarke fee. assises, accomptes	0	45	0
[f. 81v] To Mr James schoolemaster his stipend. [Sum corrected in MS. from £13]	12	0	0

	£	s	d
Summ totall of annuall paymentes and allowances from the towne	35	13	9

Expences for the towne this yeere

	£	s	d
Payed to the shreeve for the returninge of the indenture of the burgesses into the Parliament[1]	0	8	0
Geiven in rewarde to Mr Beale the clarke of the markett 29 May 10s and payed for his dinner 5s	0	15	0
Geiven in rewarde to Mr Bryan for teachinge the trayned shouldiers in marchall dissepline[2]	0	5	0
To Thomas Screevin for mendinge the glasse windowes in the upper hall	0	3	6
To Richard Hamond for keepinge possession at Gees house	0	0	12

To George Greene for keepinge the current in the holloway
for 2 yeeres past at Michaelmas   0   3   0
Payed to severall messengers that brought proclamations this
yeere before the composition was made of 13s 4d per annum
to be payed at Midsomer yeerely as followeth. To Mr William
Meatcalfe maior 2s, to Woodruffe in rewarde and wine 20d.
For severall proclamations besides at severall tymes before the
composition 12s 6d.   0   16   2
Payed as geiven to the clarke of the assise at the 2 last assises
6s 8d. To the cryer 2s. For Pulchoe for his inditment 2s 6d.[3]
For the cryers 4d. For Newells inditment 12d.[4] For Thomas
Halls inditment for treasonable wordes 12d[5] and to the cryer 4d.
And for Thomas Heathens oath and Thomas Godfryes oath
4d a peece 8d.   0   14   2
Payed to Mr Alderman Glover for chardges at his house 2s 6d
and for wine 14d in entertayning Mr Lenthall recorder when he
came for his fee in December 1626   0   3   8
Leyed out by George Noble for newe worke done in the
scholehouse and making a newe dore at the almeshouse   0   4   0
[f. 82r] To twoe wardsmen at 4 faiers   0   5   4
To Richard Newell and Richard Hamond for goeinge with
a vagrant to the house of correction at Wittny the last fayer   0   0   16
For stringes for the towne skales the tastors use   0   0   4
To Mr Rayer maior 20s which he payed for keeping of
Jerom Longes child   0   20   0
Summ totall is   5   0   6

Almshouse. Expences bestowed upon the almeshouse.
To Francklyn the slatter for 6 dayes worke 6s, to his boye foure dayes 2s 8d.
Slattes 16d, lyme 8d. For throwinge away the earth from Archers 2d. For lyme
for the bayes and scholehouse 18d. For mosse and 2 hundred of slatt 2s 6d. 2
dayes worke for the slatter 2s. Pynns, nailes and lath 4d, mosse 2s, 5 crestes 15d,
lathnailes and slatpins 4d. For mendinge the scholehouse dore 4d and for the
office dore 4d and for slattinge and mosinge the office 2s   0   23   5
Holloway. Bestowed in pitchinge and mending the holloway and wooden
bridge there since Michaelmas 1626 as followeth. To William Evans for stone 2s
6d. Geiven to Steephens the mason in earnest 12d, for pitchinge of nyne score
and 6 yardes at 2½d a yarde 38s 9d, for 2 and ½ days worke there about the
walls 2s 11d. To Thomas Huggins for 2 dayes and a halfe of masonr[y] work
about the walls 2s 6d. To John Kent for carryinge of 26 loades of stone 8s 8d
after the rate of 4d a loade. To Phillipp Hawthorne for digginge the same 26
loades of stone 8s 8d after the rate of 4d a loade. 35 loades of gravill 35s.
Squaringe of a peece of tymber 4d and for the tymber for a planck, nayles, and
workemanshipp about the bridge 2s. To Mr Rayer for 2 peeces of tymber for
that worke 3s.   5   5   0

[f. 82v] Guiftes and rewardes to poore people.
As geiven by Mr William Meatcalfe 18s, by Mr Thomas Rayer 5s 11d, the chamberlyns and others 2s 5d. 6d by George Noble. [Marginated] 6d to Godfrey.
Summ totall   0 26   4

Expences about venison.
Leid out in expences of 2 buckes eating, 1 of the Earle of Montgomeries guift and 1 of the Lord Sayes[6] guift, this yeere as followeth. For beare at the eatinge of the taste cakes 12d. To Mr Whites[7] mann for bringinge of a doa 12d. To John White for goeinge to Tewe 6d. To the Lord Sayes keeper for bringing a bucke from my Lord Say 10s. Wine and beare upon him 12d. To William Bradshewe to give to the Lord Sayes 16d. For wine at the eatinge of the said 2 buckes (besides the keepers fee of 10s geiven) 10s. Paied for the chardges about the eatinge of one bucke from my Lord of Montgomery and Sir Gerard Fleetwood,[8] and 1 from the Lord Say: for 2 bushels of wheat flower 9s 6d, 30lb of butter 9s 6d, 2lb and 1/2 of pepper at 2s 4d, 5s 10d, egges 22d, beefe 4s, 4 legges of mutton 3s 4d. To Mary Bradshewe for buyinge of butter and egges 6d. 4 cuple of rabbettes 4s 8d. Capp paper 1/2d. Geiven to the keepers men that brought the buck from Woodstock Parke 12d in mony and 1d in beere. To Bignill for bakinge the 2 buckes beinge 9 pasties 2s. Bred and beare spent at the eatinge of the venison 4s 9d. Wood spent in boyling the beefe and mutton and rosting the rabbettes 6d. Wasshinge of lynnen about this busines 8d. 3lb and 3 quarteres of butter and 8 egges for the last pasty sent to Mr William Meatcalfe 17d. A pecke of flower 15d. Rose water 12d. To Richard Phillipps wife for makinge these 9 pasties 2s 6d. *[f. 83r]* The somme of Mr Rayer his bill is 54s 5d of which he receaved at the tables 19s and the towne is to pay 35s 5d. So all the whole chardge to the towne in this behalfe is   3   0   3

To be deducted out of the rent role for this yeere, for the rent of Mr Whittons great house 151/2d, for his kitchine 12d, for Thomas Gees house nowe in the townes handes 5s   0   7   31/2

Leyed out and payed for wine for the towne at severall tymes, and to severall uses followinge. To Sir Henry Lees man in cominge to envite the towne 12d. To a messenger 8 January 12d. [Sermons] Mr Hull 8 January 20d, Mr Hides brother January 20d. To Mr White in cominge to geive notice of the doa bestowed upon the towne in wine and beere 8d. For wine spent by the towne on the corronation daye 18d.[9] [Sermons] Mr Rawlinson 12 February 20d, Mr Richard Prideaux 5 March 6d. To the justices of 6 March sitting about recognizances 20d. To a preacher that dyned at Mr Frauncis Gregories 12d. To the justices 20 March sitting about subsidies 3s 4d.[10] [Sermons] Mr Garborne 26 March and upon a minister from Bandburyside the same day 22d, Mr Miller 2 April 12d, Mr Hodgettes upon Easter Day 11d. To the justices 12 April 3s 4d. [Sermons] Mr William Collingwood

23 April 14d, Mr Greene 7 May 14d, Mr Gee same day 18d, Mr Raunson 20d, Mr Binckes 4 June 20d, Mr Kinge 11 June 20d. To Mr William Meatcalfe mayor for wine to Mr Hodgettes 6d. *[f. 83v]* [Sermons] Mr Potter and a preacher of Cambridge 2s, Mr Hide 20d. To a messenger 5 July 8d. [Sermons] Mr Taylor 9 July 2s 4d, Mr Greene 16 July 14d, Mr Doctor Potter 13 August 12d. To the justices 16 Auguste sittinge about the bene-volence 3s 4d.[11] To a preacher of Exiter Colledge 20 August 20d. To the justices 13 September 20d. To Mr Stonehill for his sermon 24 September 20d. To Mr John Jeans in wine and beere for his 2 sermons 3s 1d. To Mr Gee for his sermon 22 October 15d, at his supper 7d. [Sermons] Mr Werrall 12 November 22d, a preacher 29 November 22d. In beere to a messenger that brought a proclamation 1d. [Sermons] Mr Doctor Prideaux in wine 2s 5d, Mr Hodgettes 16 December 1626 in wine 11d. For 1 pynte of sack to a stranger that dyned in Mr Hodgettes companye 7d.   3   2   1

Summ totall of all the disbursementes	60	0	20½
Summ totall of all the receiptes	59	13	11
So due to the chamberlins upon this accompte	0	7	9½

By me Edmond Hiorne

[f. 84r] [Receipts]

Of Mr Thomas Doleman	8	0	0
Of Mr Thomas Rayer alderman for interest of £50	4	0	0
Of Thomas Heathen serjant for stallages	7	0	1
Of him for bakers standinges about the crosse and priviledged persons	0	21	6
Of Edward Longe for the tole	4	0	6
Rentes of this borough	24	18	10¼
Of Alice Shad widdowe for rent of the wooll beame	0	0	24
[f. 84v] Of Fראuncis Townsend for his admission to his freedom £3 10s and 3s 4d for a buckett which buckett the chamberlaines are to provide. So they accompted for	3	10	0
Of Mr Robert Lee for his admission to his freedom 50s and 3s 4d for a buckett which the chamberlaines are to provide. So they accompte for	0	50	0
Of William Locton for his admission to his freedom 20s and 3s 4d for a buckett which the chamberlaines are to provide and Lockton is to pay Our Lady Day 10s more for his freedom. So they accompte for	0	20	0
Of Mr Blunte for a seale of a fyne which Mr Hiorne and his wife did acknowledge to Mr Horborne and Mr Newton of Mr Whittons greate house to the use of Mr Blunte[12]	0	4	0
Of John Kente for a stone coult which the towne sould him	0	45	0

Summ totall of all the receiptes	59	13	11
Summ totall of all the disbursementes	60	0	20½
So remayninge due to the chamberlins	0	7	9½

By me Edmond Hiorne

[f. 85r] 23 December 1626.

The towne oweth

To Mr Rayer maior £19 4s 9d, Mistris Browne £4 , Thomas Williams £5 17s 9½d.	29	2	6½

Owing to the towne

Mr Marriat £10,[13] John Powell 10s, Bryan Steephens 15s,
Frauncis Collingwood 10s, Richard Hamond 10s,
John Yonge 10s, Thomas Headdy 10s, Edward Silver 10s,
William Locton 10s, Thomas Warde 20s, John Patterick 5s.

Remaining in Mr Thomas Rayers handes towardes buying of buckettes	0	36	8
Thomas Williams oweth for 7 buckettes which are to be provided for Thomas Heddy, Edward Silver, John Barnes, John Patterick, Frauncis Townsend and Robert Lee gentleman	0	23	4

Rentes incresed by consent at this accompte

John Warrens house in the comon acre is chardged with 1d per annum at Michaelmas only	0	0	1
Edmond Hiorne to pay for Nedd Whittes house and close next to the parke wall at Michaelmas only	0	0	1
Nedd Hull is to pay at Michaelmas only 6½d for the increase of the rent of his house in settinge out his bulk and pentice	0	0	6 ½
John Durbridge is to pay yeerely at Michaelmas for his newe pentice and for his grownde incroched at the end of his house	0	0	6
Mr Harris is yeerely to pay 18d for his newe house newe built in the backe greene	0	0	18
[f. 85v] Baldwin Durbridge is to pay yeerely at Michaelmas an increase of rent for the incrochment of the grownde before his dore	0	0	6
The widdowe Porter is yeerly to pay 4d for the stripe of grownde walled in before his dore at Nedd Woollyes house	0	0	4
Mr Hull is to pay 6d yeerely at Michaelmas for the incrochment of grownde where his stable is newely bulit	0	0	6
Mistris Browne is to pay yeerely for her rayles before her dore at Michaelmas	0	0	6
[Marginated subtotal]	0	4	6½

[Signatures of] Thomas Rayer maior, Edmond Hiorne

Summ totall of the whole rentrole is   25   3   4³/₄

[Signature of] Edmond Hiorne

¹ Sir Gerard Fleetwood and Edm. Taverner, secretary to the high steward, the earl of Montgomery, were returned for Woodstock: Williams, *Parl. Hist.* 200.
² See Boynton, *Militia*, 244 sqq. for the invasion scare this year and increased efforts to improve local forces by training an 'exact' or 'perfect' militia. Sergeants were brought from the Low Countries to drill the trained bands. There was a general muster in Woodstock on 28 July: B 96, f. 33v.
³ John Pulchoe, slatter, probably for felony: B 77/2, 16 May 1626.
⁴ Ric. Newell of Woodstock, shoemaker, probably for stealing a sheep: ibid. 28 May 1626.
⁵ Perhaps the Jas. Hall above.
⁶ i.e. Wm. Fiennes. Perhaps connected with the election of his son Jas. as MP for Oxon. 1626.
⁷ Thos. White, gent., Woodstock park: *V.C.H. Oxon.* xii. 352.
⁸ Cf. *Cal.S.P.Dom. 1625–26*, 547: payment of 12*d.* a day to Sir Gerard Fleetwood for supervising the game for 10 m. around Woodstock manor.
⁹ 2 Feb. 1626.
¹⁰ See note above in 1625 for subsidies.
¹¹ For the benevolence, the equivalent of four subsidies, see R. Cust, *The Forced Loan and Eng. Politics* (Oxf. 1987); cf. T. G. Barnes, *Somerset 1625–1640*, 161–4.
¹² See B 77/2, 12 Dec. 1626: final concord between Edm. and Ann Hiorne and Symon Harborne and Wm. Newton. This signals the end of problems *re* the Whittons' rent: see above in 1609. Nic. Blunt (d. 1656), citizen and innholder of London and Woodstock, was John Whitton's father-in-law: P.R.O., PROB 11/257, f. 311.
¹³ A gift to the town from Mary Keene (d. 1626): see below in 1629. John Marriat must have acted for his wife Joan, Mary's niece and heir; her mother Joan Browne (d. 1625) was Mary's sister: MS. Wills Oxon. 5/2/9; 39/3/1.

[f. 86r] 23 December 1626 to 22 December 1627, Thomas Williams and George Noble, chamberlains

[Disbursements]   £   s   d

1. Guiftes and rewardes at Christmas 1626. To Sir Henry Lee knight and barronet one cake 10s, one shugerloffe of 8lb, 12s 8d, in rewardes to his servantes 23s 6d, in toto 46s 2d. To Sir Henry Browne knight one cake 10s, in rewardes to his servantes 11s 6d, in toto 21s 6d. To Sir Gerrard Fleetwood knight one cake 10s, one suger loffe of 8lb, 12s 8d, in rewardes to his servantes 8s, in toto 30s 8d. To Mr Doctor Prideaux one sugerloffe of 8lb 3 quarters and a halfe at 18d a pownde 14s 3d. All amowntinge to   5   12   7

2. Stipendes and allowances annuallie. To Mr Thomas Rayer maior his allowance £10. Quitt rents £5 6s 8d, acquittance 18d, £5 8s 2d. To Mr Bromlowe undershreeve to Sir Cope Doyly knight for fee farme 53s 4d, acquittance 6d, 53s 10d. To Mr Lenthall esq recorder his fee £3 6s 8d. *[f. 86v]* To Mr Hiorne towneclarke fee [etc] 45s. To Mr Symon Jeames schoolemaster his stipend £12. Summ totall for annuall rents allowances and fees   35   13   9

3. Expences to messengers and other businesses and workes for the towne this yeere as followeth. In rewardes to the clarkes of the assise and unto the judges cryers at the twoe assisses 8s 8d. To Mr Woodrooffe one of the Kinges Majesties messengers for bringinge of proclamations forthe last yeere endinge at Midsomer 13s 4d. To him in rewardes for bringinge 2 proclamations about golde 2s and salt petter 2s, for other proclamations 12d, and 2s in parte of payment of 13s 4d for this yeere to ende at Midsomer 1628, 5s. Payed for three horsse lockes for the townes use 4s. For mending the litle house dore 8d. For twoe wardsmen at 4 fayres 8d apeece per diem 5s 4d. To George Greene for his waydges due at Michaelmas for clensing the holloway 18d. For clensing the litle house prison at twoe tymes 8d. To a mason and a servitor for 2 dayes worke about Elizabeth Lynn's house 2s 6d. To Thomas Huggins mason for 3 dayes worke in mendinge the pownde wall 2s 6d. To William Evans for placinge the casementes in the schoole house windowes and for 1 loade of stones about the holloway 18d. [f. 87r] To John Saye for makinge and placinge three dozen of pinns in the guild hall to hange buckettes on 3s 3d. For mending the glasse windowes in the schoolehouse 6s. To William Hawten for one daies worke 8d. To Thomas Screevant 2 January for mendinge the glasse in the towne hall 15s 6d. For pickinge the holloway 5d. For sendinge twoe letters to London for the towne 4d. For a rayle and pinns and workemanshipp to hange upp the schollers hattes 18d. For mendinge the slattes of the cage 4d. For leade to fasten in the iron worke of the casementes in the free schoole windowes and for wood to mealt the same lead 12d. For a peece of tymber for the growndsill of Besse Lynns house 4d. To a mason for 2 daies worke about the garden wall of Gees house 2s. For brusshing the elme at Gees dore 2d. Summ of expences to messengers and for workes and other business   3 17   2

4. Guiftes and rewards to poore people. To Mr Rayer maior as geiven to poore people and souldiers 18s. By George Noble at Mr Hiornes appoyntment to 4 poore people at 2 tymes 6d. To souldiers by Mr Glovers appoyntment 6d, to 1 souldier 4d, to poore people 12d, to one souldier 2d, and to one souldier by Mr Harris his appoyntment 3d, 2s 3d. Summ   0 20   9

[f. 87v] 5. Expences about venison and other paymentes for the towne. About the eatinge of the buck geiven by my lord chamberlaine 21 Auguste more then 20s which the neighbours spent as by Mr Maiors note of perticulers appeereath, 23s 3d. To goodman Hayles of Thrupp for 1 daies worke with his carte and to George Coper for 3 quarters of a day with his teame to carry durte heapes out of the streetes against the Kinges last cominge 5s. For the keepinge of Jerome Longes child 20 weekes 30s 10d, whereof 20s was allowed at the last accompte which the chamberlains payed out of Mr Dolemans mony, 2s 8d Jerome Longe payed, 6s 8d Mr Rayer maior payed, 6s 8d. To Mr Chesterman for a writt and warrant for the towne against George Drewe 7s. To Mr Chesterman for his fee in procuringe a staye of the proces against the town by the clarke of the parcells in the Exchequer this Michaelmas terme wherein the towne is much behouldinge to Sir Henry Crooke knight 6s 8d and for a pynte of wine to him 7d. In toto 7s 3d. For carryinge and recarryinge the charter to and from London this last Michaelmas terme about that busines only 2s 6d. Geiven to Mr Champnies clarke of the markett for this cownty the last of March in rewarde 10s. Summ 3 0 20

6. Expences at the Kinges beinge heere 29 July. In rewarde to Mr Walker the clarke of the markett for the Kinges howshold 10s, to his man 12d. To the Kinges trumpiters 10s. For wine to them and to the Kinges garde and other the Kinges servantes by Mr Maior 6s 8d. Paid for 2 sugerloves waighinge 6lb, 9s 9d, for one cake 10s and 4 cheeses 3s 4d, which were sent by the towne to my lord chamberlaine our highe steward. 0 50 9

[f. 88r] 7. A note of wine spent this yeere by the towne. Wine sent to Mr Doctor Prideaux when he dyned at Mr James his sonne John christininge upon Innocentes Day 1 pottle of sack and 1 pottle of clarrett 3s 8d, upon Newe Yeeres Day 3 pyntes of sack 21d, 21 January 3 pyntes of sack and a quarte of clarrett 2s 5d, 18 March 1 quarte of sack and a quarte of clarrett 2s, 15 April 1 quart of clarret, 1 quarte and halfe a pint of sack 2s 3^{1}/$_{2}$d, on Whitsonday one quart of sack and 1 quarte of clarrett 2s, 16 September 1 pynt of sack and 1 quarte of clarret 17d, 25 November 3 pyntes of clarrett and 1 quarte of sack 2s 5d. Upon Mr Collingwood the last of December 1626 1 quarte of sack and a quarte of clarret 2s. Upon Porter Sir Henry Lees man for invitinge us to his master to dinner at Christmas and upon the undershreeve for bringinge a warrant about the lone[1] a quarte of sack 14d. Mr Hunte 7 January 1 quarte of sack and 1 quarte of clarret 2s. Upon the commissioners that sate 20 January about the Kinges loane 5 pyntes of sack and one pynt of clarrett 3s 3d. Mr Bryan Holland 18 January 1 pynt of sack 7d. Mr Readinge 4 February 1 quarte of sack and a quarte of clarret 2s. Mr Raunson 11 February 1 quarte of sack and 1 quarte of clarret 2s. *[f. 88v]* Mr Collingwood 18 February 1 quarte of sack and 1 quarte of clarrett 2s. A yonge preacher of Queenes Colledge 1 quarte of clarrett and 1 pynt of sack 25 February 15d. Mr Hodges 11 March 1 pynt of sack 7d. Mr Gowin Champnies when he sate as clarke of the markett 1 quarte of sack and 2 pyntes of clarrett 2s. Upon the justices 6 April in sittinge about victulers 1 quarte of sack, 1 quarte of clarrett 2s. Mr Hodges 22 April 1 pynt of sack and 1 pynt of clarrett and on a gentleman of Queen Colledge the same day at night a pynt of sack and a pynt of clarret 2s. Mr Hodges 10 June 1 pynt of sack and 1 pynt of claret 12d. A yonge man of Queens Colledge 24 June 1 pynt of sack and 1 pynt of claret 12d. Mr Ansloe the clarke of the assises at soomer assises 1 quarte of sack and 1 pynt of claret 15d. Mr Tayler 9 July at morninge and eveninge sermons that day 1 pynt of white wine, 1 pynt of sack, in suger 4d, 1 pynt of sack, 1 pynt of clarrett 2s 9d. Upon a preacher of Bayly Colledge 2 pyntes of sack, 1 pynt of white wine and suger and 2d in beere 23d. Mr Stonehouse 22 July and upon Mr Doctor Prideaux 3 pyntes of sack, 1 quart of claret, and 2d in tobacco 2s 10d. Mr Stone and Mr Vernon 13 Auguste 5 pyntes of clarret and 2 quartes of sack 4s 5d.

Upon the justices of the sheiere 17 Auguste 1 quarte of sack and 1 quarte of
white wine 2s. Mr Castell 19 August 1 pynt of sack and 3 pyntes of clarret 22d.
[f. 89r] Mr Osbaldston 26 August 1 quarte of sack and 1 quarte of clarret 2s.
Upon the justices about recusantes[2] 24 September a quarte of sack and a quarte of
clarret 2s. Mr William Woodward last of September in wine for his sermon 18d.
Mr Hoffman 7 October 18d. Mr Worrall 21 October 2s 8d. Mr Hodges 28
October 1 pynt of sack and 1 pynt of clarret 12d. Mr Vernon 4 November 1
quarte of sack and 1 pynt of clarret 19d.

Summ totall of all the wine this yeere	3	11	0$^{1}/_2$

8. Payed for expences. In newe makinge the benche about
the greate elme in Oxford streete 11s 8d, nayles 12d, 4 planckes
4s 8d, 8 postes 2s 8d, carpenters worke 2s 10d, laborer 6d.
[Total] 11s 8d. Receaved 6d so we receaved but 11s 2d. To
be deducted out of the rent role for this yeere endinge at
Michaelmas 1627 5s for the rent of Thomas Gees house for
that it was in the townes handes, and is noted sould to
George Drewe whoe is heereafter to pay the yeerely

rent of 5s to the towne for that house. Summ	0	16	2

9. To be allowed to Thomas Williams for one stone colte
which he sould to John Kent for 45s which colt was claymed
and delivered to the owners, and it is to be allowed back

againe to him[3]	0	45	0
Summ totall of the disbursmentes	58	8	10
Summ totall of the receiptes is	55	6	9$^{3}/_4$
So remayninge due to the chamberlains	3	2	0$^{1}/_4$

Cast up by me Edmond Hiorne

[Signatures of] Thomas Williams, George Noble

[f. 89v] [blank]

[f. 90r] [Receipts]

Of Mr Thomas Doleman	8	0	0
Of Thomas Rayer alderman and maior interest of £50	4	0	0
Of Thomas Heathen serjant for stallages	7	15	10
Of him for bakers standinges at the highe crosse and privileged persons	0	6	6
Of Edward Longe for the tole	3	5	5
Rentes of this boughroughe	25	3	4$^{3}/_4$
Of Alice Shadd widdowe for rent of the wooll beame	0	24	0
[f. 90v] For John Burgins admission 30s and he oweth 10s more due at Our Lady Day	0	30	0
Of Mr Nicholas Mayot for his admission	0	20	0

Of Josephe Fletcher for his admission	0	0	20
Of Gyles Francklyn for his admission	3	0	0
Summ totall of the receiptes is	55	6	9³/₄
Summ totall of the disbursmentes is	58	8	10
So remayninge due to the chamberlains is	3	2	0¹/₄

Cast upp by me Edmond Hiorne

Monye owinge by the towne 22 December 1627

[Entries cancelled in this paragraph]. To Mr Thomas Rayer
nowe maior £6 7s 1d. To Thomas Williams chamberlaine
£3 2s and £6 7s 1d, in toto £9 9s 1d. To Mr Vernon
which married Mistris Browne £4 .

To Mr Rayer maior £20 13s 9d. To Thomas Williams
£9 9s 1d. To Mr Vernon £4 . Summ   34   2   10

Monies owinge to the towne at this said accompte

Mr John Marriat oweth by a bill due at Michaelmas £10 .
[For admission] John Powell 10s, Bryan Steephens 15s,
Frauncis Collingwood 10s, Richard Hamond 10s, Jo.
Yonge 10s, [f. 91r] Thomas Heddy 10s, Edward Silver 10s,
William Locton 10s, Thomas Warde 20s, John Patterick 5s,
John Burgin 10s. Summ [sic]   15   0   0

Md after this accompt was finished Georg Drew⁴ paid 7s parcell of 47s which was
delivered to Thomas Williams chamberlin and he is to accompt for it at our
meeting at St Thomas Day next and he is to give bond to pay the other 40s at
Midsomer next.

[Signatures of] Thomas Rayer maior, John Glover, Joseph Harris, William
Meatcalfe, Thomas Williams, George Noble

It was also called to memorie at this meeting that Georg Noble is to accompt
with us for our pesthouse which he receaved into his handes which he did
acknowledg before us whose names are here subscribed and no monie paied unto
us for it as yet.

[Signatures of] Thomas Rayer maior, John Glover, William Meatcalfe, Joseph
Harris

Allso Thomas Williams is to accompte for all mony receaved for buckettes
savinge for 12 buckettes which he hath payed for. And Mr Rayer maior is dischardged of 40s which he had receaved in to his handes for buckettes for that he
payed for 12 newe buckettes which are nowe in the hall.

[Signatures of] John Glover, Joseph Harris, William Meatcalfe, Ed. Hiorne *[f. 91v]* [blank]

[1] Letters *re* the war loan were despatched 17 and 19 Jan. 1627, and commissioners came to Woodstock 20 Jan.: *Acts of P.C.* 1627, 21–22; *Cal.S.P.Dom.* 1627–8, 16, 25.
[2] Laws against them were strengthened in 1625: *Cal.S.P.Dom.* 1625–26, 551.
[3] The colt, claimed by Wm. Staploe of Blunham (Beds.), had strayed or been stolen from the common there: see above and B 77/2, 22 Sept. 1626, 27 Mar. 1627.
[4] *Alias* Gregory; and see below in 1628.

[f. 92r] 22 December 1627 to 20 December 1628, Thomas Williams and George Noble chamberlains

	£	s	d
[Disbursements]			

Guiftes and rewardes at Christmas 1627.
To Sir Henry Lee knight and baronett one cake 10s and one sugerloffe wayinge 6lb and a quarterne at 2s a lb, 12s 6d, in rewardes to his servantes 23s 6d. To Sir Henry Browne knight one cake 10s, in rewardes to his servantes 11s 6d. To Sir Gerrard Fleetwood knight one cake 10s and one sugerloffe wayinge 3lb 3 quarters and a halfe 7s 9d, in rewardes to his servantes 7s 6d. To Mr Doctor Prideaux one sugerloffe wayinge 6lb and a quarter at 23d a pownde 12s. All amowntinge to

	5	4	9

Stipendes and allowances annually

	£	s	d
To Mr Thomas Rayer maior and Mr Thomas Meatcalf maior £5 a peece allowance	10	0	0
Quitt rent £5 6s 8d, acquittance 18d	5	8	2
To Mr Langstone undershreeve for Sir Richard Wayneman knight for fee farme	0	53	4
Acquittance [changed from 6d]	0	0	7
[f. 92v] To Mr Lenthall esq recorder his fee	3	6	8
To Edmond Hiorne towneclarke fee, assises, accomptes	0	45	0
To Mr Symon James schoolemaster for his stipend, £8 from Mr Doleman and £4 from Mr Rayer for the interest of £50 in his handes	12	0	0

Expences for the towne
Paide as geiven to the clarke of the assise and to the judges cryer at the twoe assises this yeere 8s 8d. Geiven to Mr Gowin Champnies clark of the markett as a reward 20 March 10s. Paide to the undershreeve (Mr Langston) for the fee of the clark of the Parliament for the returninge of the indenture for the burgesses of the Parliament 8s.[1] For expences (at Mr Glovers) upon Mr Recorder, at his cominge 23 April 2s. For a statute book of the last Parliament 2s 4d and for a booke of actions for to remayne as a record for the towne 12d, 3s 4d. To Mr Woodruffe the Kinges Majesties messenger for his fee (agreed upon this yeere) for bringinge of proclamations 13s 4d and for wine upon him 7d, 13s 11d. To

the joyner for settinge a peece upon the stayer doore 3d. *[f. 93r]* Payed the messenger that brought a proclamation concerning artillarye 12d. To 2 watchmen at 4 faiers 5s 4d. For mendinge the scales to way butter 2d. Delivered to Henry Whiteside for expences at Deddington about the subsidies 3s 8d.² Payed for a haspe and stable for the pownde dore 6d. For making the grave for the souldier that died at Painters 4d. To Phillipp Hawthorne for sweeping the almeshouse chimnies 12d. To George Greene for his stipend for this yeere for clensing the watercourse in the holloway 18d.

Summ [town expenses]   0 59   8

Slatt and mosse for the repaire of the schoolehouse 2s, lath, pinns, and nayles 6d, crestes, lyme and heare 18d, to the slatter for one daies worke 12d, to a laborer to clense the schole court 4d. For mendinge the glasse of a casement in the guild hall 6d. Mendinge the greate wooden bridge and for tymber speekes and nailes 18d. Mending the pownde wales 7d. Nailes for the mendinge the bedsteede in the litle house 6d. A planck to newe leg the same 4d, and for the carpenters worke 4d. Payed the ploomer for mendinge the gutter of leade over the schoolehouse 2s. Expences about the usshers seate in the schoolehouse: for the greate tymber 5s 2d, halfe a hundred of bordes 5s, one plancke 4d, dustailes and nailes 8d, a lock and key 16d, the carpenters for 6 dayes worke 6s 6d.   0 30   1

To Mr Rayer for mony geiven by him to the poore from the last accompte to the ende of his maioralty 18s. To Thomas Metcalfe maior as geiven by him 6s, by the chamberlyns 13d.   0 25   1

Summ [town, school, poor expences]   5 14 10

[f. 93v] Expences about the eatinge of the buck which Sir Gerrard Fleetwood gave to the towne besides the 20s which he gave in wine as followeth

One pownde and quarter of pepper 2s 6d, capp paper 2d, 5 peckes of wheate 3s 4d, 20lb of butter 6s 8d, for baking 18d, for the cookes paines 3s 4d, 3 legges of mutton and 2 cropps of roste beefe 8s 6d, bread 18d, beere 3s 4d, wine over and above the foresaid 20s 3s 10d, for cheeses 8d. For Bradshewes attendance 6d. To Mr Whitton³ for his fee for killinge the buck 10s, to his man Henry for his paynes 2s 6d. All mowntinge to 48s 4d whereof the neighbours payed in mony 13s 6d. So the towne is chardged with   0 34 10

Wine spent this yeere by the towne

Upon Mr Hoffman for his sermon 26 December 1628 2s 3½d. Wine and beere upon Ned Porter at the inviting of the towne to Sir Henry Lee the last Christmas 9d. Wine to Mr Recorder 7 January 7d. Upon Mr Hollan at his sermon 13 January 15d. Wine and suger upon Mr Abraham Haynes 20 January 3s 4d. [Wine] upon Mr Fletchers sonnes of London 16d.⁴ Upon Mr Doctor Prideaux 17 February 2s 7d. 7 March sent to the justices at theire sitting about victuilers 2s. Geiven to Mr Gowin Champnies the clarke of the markett 10 March. Wine, beere and tobaccoe upon Mr Serjant Major, Mr Mannerringe and other officers of Collonell Mortons regiment at severall tymes 5s 2d.⁵ Upon

Mr Doctor Prideaux in wine 16 March 9d, on Palme Sonday 3s. Upon the justices 17 April about victulers 2s. [Sermons] upon Mr Woodward at his 2 sermons 27 April 2s 5¹/₂d, Mr Castell 25 May 12d. Mr Doctor Prideaux 1 June 2s
10d, Mr John James 8 June and a preacher of Magdalen Colledge the same day 2s
9d, Mr Smith and Mr Potter for theire 2 sermons 6 July 4s, Mr Tayler for his
[f. 94r] twoe sermons 13 July 2s 5d, Mr Hoffman for his sermon 25 July 2s.
Upon Mr Craddocke the clarke of the assises 2 August 2s, Mr Hodges 3 Auguste
12d, the justices at the asseasinge of subsidies 4 August 2s. 10 August upon Mr
Smith and Mr Potter for their 2 sermons 2s 9d, 14 September upon a preacher of
Exiter Colledge 2s, 21 September upon Mr Twittie 16d, 11 October to the justices at the subsidy sittinge 2s 4d. 26 October to a preacher that dined at Alice
Darlinges 2s. 23 November upon Mr Greene for his sermon 14d, Mr Hodges
the Sonday followinge 14d. 7 December upon Mr Butcher for his 2 sermons 3s
2d. 14 December for wine upon 2 preachers that dined at Sir Gerrard
Fleetwoodes 2s 4d. All amowntinge to the some of   3 7 9

To Mr Rayer as layed out by him for the fynnisshinge up
of the great beame which Mr Phillipp Dodwell the dyer of
Oxon' gave to the towne and for the carriage and recarriage
of it to and from London⁶   0 9 0
To be deducted out of the rent role for this yeere for the rent
of Gees house   0 5 0
Payed for expences about the hollowe way. To goodman
Cooper for carryinge of 5 loades of stone 20d, to Mr Lee for
carryinge stones to the highe way and for workemen 3s 8d.   0 5 4

Summ totall of the disbursmentes   52 15 3
Summ totall of the receiptes for this yeere is   50 6 2³/₄
So remayninge due to the chamberlyns   0 49 0¹/₄

Cast upp and examined by me Edmond Hiorne towneclark

[f. 94v] [blank]

[f.95r] [Receipts]

Of Mr Thomas Doleman   8 0 0
Of Mr Thomas Rayer alderman for interest of £50   4 0 0
Of Thomas Heathen serjant at the mace for stallages   6 13 4
Of him for the country bakers standinges   0 15 0
Of Nedd Longe toleman for the tole   0 58 6
Rentes of this bowroe   25 3 4³/₄
Of Alice Shadd widdowe for rent of the wooll beame   0 24 0
Of Roberte Bruce for admission of his freedom   0 6 8
Of Bryan Steephens in parte of payment of his admission
to his freedome   0 8 0

[f. 95v] Of John Meades, Gabrill Shadd, Allexander Johnson, and John Hiorne 20d a peece for theire admission to theire freedoms	0	6	8
Of George Drewe 7s which the towne allowed him at the last accompte for a writt and warrant at the towne suit against George Drewe	0	7	0
Receaved by George Noble chamberlaine for the tymber and boardes of the peste house which he sould to Henry Whiteside for 12s 2d, whereof he payed to John Yonge constable for Thomas Godferies levy 4s. Leyed out by himselfe for dyet while the poore people were shutt upp 4s 6d.[7] So remaininge to accompte for	0	3	8
Summ totall of the receiptes is	50	6	2³/₄
Summ totall of the disbursmentes is	52	15	3
So remayninge due to the chamberlyns	0	49	0¹/₄

Cast upp and examined by me Edmond Hiorne towneclark

[Marginated] Edmond Hiorne paied his £12 for Gees house at this accompte which was paied to Thomas Williams chamberlyn for mony due to him.

[Signatures of] Thomas Williams and George Noble chamberlins

A note of buckettes nowe due			
Thomas Williams chamberlyn hath mony for sixe [seven deleted] buckettes in his handes [23s 4d crossed out]	0	20	0
John Cotton, Roberte Bruce, John Homes and William Bradshewe each of them are to pay 3s 4d for theire buckettes	0	13	4
Edward Hull hath one buckett remaining in his house to be brought in to the halle			
Thomas Williams did pay at this accompte 3s 4d for a litle asshe sould out of Mistris Marriates backside	0	3	4

[f. 96r] 20 December 1628 monye owinge by the towne at this accompte

To Mr Rayer alderman £22 6s 9d. [A cancelled entry].
Mr Vernon £4.

[Added later: see below] Md Mr Marriott payed his £10 to Mr Rayer 22 April 1629	10	0	0

Monye owinge to the towne at this accompte

Mr John Marriat[8] oweth by a bill under his hand and seale £10 due at Michaelmas 1627 which Mary Keene gave to the towne, £10. Paied.

[For admissions]. John Powell 10s. Bryan Steephans, payed
by playing. [Interlined] allowed for his playing at Whitsontide
1629, 6s [changed from 7s]. Frauncis Collingwood 10s,
Richard Hamond 10s, John Yonge 10s payed, Thomas Heddy 10s,
Edward Silver 10s payed, William Locton 10s, Thomas Warde 20s,
John Patterick 5s, John Burgin 10s. John Cotton 6s 8d, [margin]
I think this was paied. John Homes 2s. James Keene is to pay
30s for his admission within this twoe yeeres.[9]
George Drewe upon a full accompte and all bills and reockninges
paied to him, and he is to pay at Our Lady Day 1629 10s.[10]

Summ   17   14   0

Md at this accompt delivered to Thomas Williams to accompte
for at the next accompte   0   18   0

Delivered to James Nickoles constable a boxe of wares which
was taken from John Tassill and the key remained with Thomas
Williams out of which Tassill is to have 3s 4d.[11]

[Signature of] Ed. Hiorne

[f. 96v] [blank]

---

[1] Sir Miles Fleetwood, nephew of Sir Gerard, and Edm. Taverner again: Williams, *Parl. Hist.* 200.

[2] Five subsidies were granted 1627: Act, 3 Chas. I, c. 8. For collection 1628–9 see *Cal.S.P.Dom.* 1625–49, 28–9, 731–2.

[3] John Whitton and his son Nic. Blunt Whitton were jointly named as Comptroller of Works and Surveyor of the Forests for Woodstock manor from Nov. 1628: ibid. 1628–9, 375.

[4] Hen. and Wm. Fletcher, sons of the town's benefactor: ex. inf. Mrs. C. Schwarz.

[5] Lt.-Col. Sir Thos. Morton. His was one of the regiments returned from the disastrous 1627 expedition to the island of Rhé which faced the govt. with the problem of returned soldiers and arrears of pay. Morton's troops were moved from Woodstock to Banbury in Feb. 1628 because of inconvenience to the park and town, though Woodstock was to 'contribute rateably': *Acts of P.C.* 1626, 262; ibid. 1627–8, 295; *V.C.H. Oxon.* x. 8

[6] See below 1631. Presumably a new woolbeam.

[7] Woodstock apparently shut up its poor in time of plague in a specially made pest house, which could be dismantled.

[8] See above in 1626.

[9] Bellfounder. He was also 'to caste a new bell for the towne at any time within this nine yeere having only but 30s allowed for it': B 81, f. 31v. For his Woodstock foundry see *V.C.H. Oxon.* xii. 363.

[10] *Alias* Gregory. He made final payment after the 1633 acct.: B 81, ff. 31v, 33v. Note writs against him in 1627 and above.

[11] The box was left with Tassill as surety for goods stolen from him. It was to be sold unless further sureties were given: B 77/2, 31 Aug., 2 Sept.; and below in 1629.

[f. 97r] 22 December 1628 to 23 December 1629, Thomas Williams and George Noble, chamberlains

[Disbursements]	£	s	d

Guiftes and rewardes at Christmas 1628.
Sent to Sir Henry Browne knight one cake 10s. And in
rewardes to his servantes, to the butler 2s 6d, the head cooke
2s 6d, the under cooke 6d, the inviter of the towne 18d,
the fueler 18d, the groome of the stable [18d deleted] 2s 6d,
the under groome 6d. [Total changed from 20s 6s]

	0	21	6

To Sir Henry Lee knight one cake 10s, one sugerloffe wayinge
7lb batinge 3 oz at 21d a pownde, 11s 10d. In rewardes to his
servantes, to the head cooke 5s, the under cooke 12d, the cheife
buttler 5s, the under buttler 12d, the ussher of the hall 3s, the
fueler 18d, the brewer 2s, the caterer 2s, the cheife groome 2s,
the under groome 12d. To Porter for invitinge the towne 2s 6d,
and for a pynte of sacke bestowed upon him 7d.

	0	48	5

To Sir Gerrard Fleetwood one cake 10s, one sugerloffe wayinge
7lb and a quarter at 21d a pownd 12s 8d. And in rewardes to
his servantes, to the buttler 2s 6d, the cooke maide 2s 6d,
William Lunn 12d, William Castell 12d, Nurth 6d.

	0	30	2

To Mr Doctor Prideaux one sugerloffe of £6 and a halfe
at 20d a pownde.

	0	10	10
Summ totall	5	10	11

[f. 97v] Stipendes and yeerly allowances payed by the towne as
followeth.
To Mr Thomas Meatcalfe maior at Our Lady Day £5 and
Mr Alderman Glover nowe maior at Michaelmas 1629 £5,
towardes the chardge of the twoe feastes for the towne

	10	0	0

Quitt rent £5 6s 8d, acquittance [18d deleted] 12d, wine 12d

	5	8	8

To Mr Langstone undershreeve to Sir Robert Dormer
for fee farme 53s 4d, acquittance 8d

	0	54	0

To Mr Lenthall esq recorder his fee

	3	6	8

To Mr Edmond Hiorne towneclarke fee, assises, accomptes

	0	45	0

To Mr Symon Jeames schoolemaster his stipend

	12	0	0
Summ totall	35	14	4

Expences for the towne this yeere at the Kinges beinge heere.
Sent to my Lord of Montgomery our highe steward one cake
10s, a sugerloffe of 8lb at 20d a pownde 13s 4d, and 6 cheeses
5s 8d. To Mr Walker the clarke of the verge 10s,[1] to his man
12d. And to Mr Glover maior 40s to bestowe upon the Kinges
trumpeters and garde as well in fees as in wine and dyet for them.

And geiven by Mr Mayor to the yeoman of the winseller at
Mr Maiors beinge there 12d.   4   0   12

[f. 98r] Expences for the towne this yeere.
Geiven in rewarde to the clarke of the assise at the twoe assises
this yeere 6s 8d, and to the cryer at eache assise 12d, 2s. For
drawing the inditement against Mr Cornishe concerninge the
bridge at Ould Woodstock mill 2s.[2] To the cryer for the oath
4d, spent with the officers about that busines 12d.   0   12   0
Geiven to Mr Gowin Champnies clarke of the market as a
rewarde 16 March   0   10   0
Payed Mr Woodroofe the Kinges messenger for his stipend
agreed upon for bringinge of proclamations for this yeere
endinge at Midsomer 13s 4d. And for expences upon him
by Mr Maiors appoyntment 12d.   0   14   4
To 2 watchmen at 4 faiers   0   5   4
Payed to a travilinge preacher that preached heere
8 November by Mr Maiors appoyntment   0   5   0
To George Greene for his stipend this yeere endinge
at Michaelmas for clensinge the water course in the holloway   0   0   18
To Mr Alderman Glover nowe maior for mony which he hath
geiven to diverse poore people in his maioralty since the death
of Mr Thomas Meatcalfe late maior 6 May 1629,[3] 13s 4d. By
the chamberlains at Mr Maiors appoyntment to certeine
travilers 12d. By Mr Hiorne to one gentleman like travilor 6d.
All amowntinge to   0   14   10

Reparations for the towne.
To the serjant ploomers men for mendinge the leades of the
crosse 5s, wood to heate theire irons 2s, beere for them 4d.   0   7   4
[f. 98v] To Edward Silver for mendinge the fann of the guild
hall 8d, the locke of the schoole house dore 4d, the chaine
of the markett busshell 2d, a casement at the towne hall 8d.
To George Greene for thetchinge of Besse Lyns roome at the
almeshouse 8d, strawe 12d.   0   3   6
For expences about the holloway and almeshouse, for stones
2s, for carriage of twoe loade of stones to John Slatter 12d.
To Thomas Huggins mason for 3 dayes worke 3s, for his boy
one day 8d. To Thomas Huggins for 3 dayes worke at the
almeshouse for himself and a day and a halfe for his sonne
4s. For 2 loades of stone for that worke 16d, carriage 12d.   0   13   0
For carriage and recarriage of waites to London to trye our
butter waites when Mr Cooper brought 2 writtes against
Nedd Longe and Richard Reade tastors this soomer. And
for newe waites for the selling of butter   0   0   14

Payed to James Nickoles, which he gave to the prisoners at Oxon' at Christmas 1628 by Mr Maiors appoyntment after the last accompte	0	2	6

Payed 8 June towardes the repayringe of the bridge at Ould Woodstocke mills (in case of necessity) till the title be tryed betweene the Kinge and Mr Cornishe whoe are to repayre the same, to the carpenters Humfry Bennett and William Wheeler for their paynes 2s 4d, Mr Thomas Williams alderman for 1 plancke 3s 4d, George Noble chamberlaine for 4 sleepers 6s 8d, John Norman for 1 plancke 2s 4d. The churchwardens James Nickoles and William Hitche are to be allowed for 5 planckes which were cutt out for the use of the church. For one loade of gravill 12d.　　　　　0　15　8

[f. 99r] Payed by Mr Maior and the aldermens appoyntment for the keepinge of the child that was leafte heere in the cage at the Kinges last beinge heere in August 1629 which is nowe with Prissilla Barnaby in the almeshouse　　　　　0　12　4

Payed unto Frauncis Townsend constable 20 July 10s which was ymployed to buy provision for the trayned souldiers at Bullington greene, and which Frauncis Townsend and James Nickoles constables are to geive an accompte for　　　　　0　10　0

Summ of expences and reparations　　　　　6　8　6

Wine spent this yeere

One quarte of sack for Mr Recorder at his cominge to Mr Maiors house 14d. A quarte of sack for Mr Chamberlaine that preached 21 December 1628 14d. Wine to the justices at the asseasment of the subsidy 23 December 1628 2s.[4] Upon Mr Chamberlaine that preched Christmas Day at eveninge prayer 14d, 27 December 1628 14d. Wine to Mr Doctor Prideaux 4 January 1628[/9] 2s, same day to Mr Tomalyn 14d. Upon Mr Doctor Prideaux when he preched 3 January 2s. Wine and tobacco upon Mr Chamberlaine preachinge twice 10 January 23d. Wine spent upon Mr Recorder and at the eatinge of the taste cakes 12 January 2s 4d. 2 quartes of sack upon Mr Chamberlyn of Martin Colledge 2s 4d. Quarte of sack for Mr Chamberlaine that preached 25 January 14d. [f. 99v] Wine upon Mr Raunson and another preacher that preched twice 23 February 2s 8d. 2 quartes of sack upon Mr Pope and Mr Watson that preched twice 8 Marche 2s 8d. Wine upon Mr Hodges the next Sonday 16d, the justices that sate about recognizances of alehowses 11 March 2s 2d, Mr Champnies the clarke of the markett 16 Marche 2s 1d, a preacher of Queenes Colledge 29 March 16d. Quarte of sack and a quarte of clarrett wine to the justices at the asseasinge of subsidies 9 April 2s 1d. Wine upon Mr Stone that preched twice on 12 April 2s 1d, the justices 22 April at the takinge of recognizances of victulers 2s 1d. [Preachers] Mr Watson 17 May 16d, the preacher 24 May 16d, Mr Chamberlaine and Mr Woodward both on 7 June 2s 9d. A quarte of sacke sent by Mr Maior to the lord busshopp of Oxon at the consecration of ministers 16d. A pynt of sacke and a pynte of white wine upon Mr Chamberlaine that preched 14 June 12^1/2d. Wine and beere upon Mr Doctor Prideaux that preched 22 June 18d. A quarte of wine upon the Kinges officers that came to inquire the state of our towne befor the Kinges cominge 16d. Wine sent to Sir William Spencer at his first cominge to the towne 30 June 2s 1d, at his second cominge to the towne 2s 1d.[5]

[f. 100r] A quarte of sacke and a quarte of clarrett to Mr Smith that preached 5 July 2s. Wine to [preachers] Mr Tayler the same eveninge 2s, Mr Hoffman 26 July 12d, Mr Wentworth and Mr Carpenter of Exiter Colledge both on 26 July 3s 8d, upon 2 other preachers that preached twice 9 September 2s 4d. Geiven by Mr Maiors appoyntment upon one of the Kinges servantes that had the oversight of the Kinges beere 13 August 12d. Bestowed upon Mr Walker the clarke of the markett of the Kinges howshold by Mr Maior and other neighbours at the Kinges last beinge heere in August 2s 6d.[6] 3 pyntes of wine geiven to the bisshopp of Bristowes chaplin that preched heere the Sonday before the Kinges coming 16d. A pynt of sacke for the knight marchalls men by Mr Maior and Mr Hiorns appoyntment at the Kinges beinge heere 8d. Wine upon [preachers] Mr Hodges 6 September 12d, Mr Nayler 29 September 8d, Mr Hodges 25 October 16d, Mr Tomalyn 1 October 16d, a minister 7 November 16d, Mr Hodges 15 November 16d, Mr Doctor Robertson on Sonday 13 December 1629 2s. [f. 100v] A quarte of sack for Mr Selfe that preached on Sonday night 13 December 16d. Sack bestowed upon Mr Doctor Prideaux and his wife on Sonday 20 December 1629, Mr Hodges that preached that daye 4s 8d. Summ totall for wine this yeere   4   4   4

Payed for worke about the scholehouse and almeshouse. For halfe a hundred of slatt for the scholehouse 10d, 8 crestes 2s, 2 bushells of lyme and heare 16d, lath pins and nayles 4d, mosse 6d. To the slatter for 2 dayes worke 2s. 2 crestes for the almeshouse 6d, a great payre of hinges for the great presse in the office 9d. For a mason to mende the pownde wall 12d.   0   9   3

For reparations about the litle house and the seller which Pudsey did breake, for 2 bordes 22d, nayles 9d. To the smith for iron worke of the stockes and for mendinge the lock of the seller dore 3s 4d. To the carpenter 20d. A peece to mende the stockes 6d. 1 daies worke for a mason 12d. Mendinge the quine [quoin] of the wale under the wooden bridge 4d. Grubbing and cleavinge and carryinge of an ould dead assh that grewe against Mr Jeames his dore.   0   9   10

Payed to Mr Chesterman for chardges for John Dubbers defence at Purdyes suit the bellfownder[7]   0   5   11

Summ totall of the disbursementes this yeere is	57	4	1
Summ totall of the receiptes for this yeere is	52	8	10^{1}/$_{2}$
So remayinge due to the chamberlains	4	15	2^{1}/$_{2}$

Cast upp and examined by me Edmond Hiorne towneclark

[Signatures of] Thomas Williams, George Noble chamberlains

[f. 101r] [Receipts]

Of Mr Thomas Doleman	8	0	0
Of Mr Thomas Rayer alderman for interest of £50	4	0	0
Of Thomas Heathen serjant at the mace for stallages	6	8	3
Of him for the standinges of the country bakers at the highe crosse	0	20	0
Of Nedd Longe toleman for the tole	3	5	9
Rentes of this boughroughe	25	0	2^{1}/$_{4}$
Of Alice Shadd widdowe for rent of the wool beame	0	24	0
[f. 101v] Delivered to Mr Thomas Williams at the last accompt in reddy monye to be accompted for	0	18	0
Of John Yonge owed for his admission unto his freedom	0	10	0
Of Edward Silver [the like]	0	10	0
Of John Collingwood [the like]	0	0	20
Of John Benn [the like]	0	20	0
Of Richard Gregorie alias Drewe [the like]	0	11	0
Summ totall of the receiptes this yeere is	52	8	10^{1}/$_{2}$
Summ totall of the disbursementes this yeere is	57	4	1
So remayinge due to the chamberlins	4	15	2^{1}/$_{2}$

Cast upp and examined by me Edmond Hiorne towneclark

[Signatures of] Thomas Williams, George Noble chamberlains

[f. 102r] A note of buckettes due to be brought in into the hall at this accompte 23 December 1629

Mr Thomas Williams hath 20s in his handes for 6 buckettes, quere whose they are	0	20	0
He hath received since the last accompte for buckettes, of William Lun[8] 3s 4d, John Collingwood 3s 4d, John Venn 3s 4d, Richard Gregorie 3s 4d	0	13	4

Buckettes behind. Md John Cotton, Roberte Bruce, John Homes and William Bradshawe each of them are to pay 3s 4d for theire buckettes

Md Edward Hull hath one buckett in his house to be brought in.

Wares. Md Jeames Nickoles constable is to bringe in a box of wares remaining in his handes

Debtes owinge to the towne 23 December 1629

For admission, John Powell 10s, Frauncis Collingwood 10s, Richard Hamond 10s, Thomas Headdy 10s, William Locton 10s, Thomas Warde 20s, John Patterick 5s, John Burgin 10s, John Homes 2s. George Drewe was to pay 10s 25 March.

[f. 102v] Debtes owinge by the towne at this accompte

At the last accompte the towne did owe to Mr Rayer
£22 9d the interest thereof till 22 April 1629 did amount
to 10s. Then Mr John Marriatt payed him in the £10 that
Mary Keene gave to the towne by her last will. So nowe
due of the principall is £12 9d and 11s interest from
22 April. So in the whole due to Mr Rayer at this
accompte is £12 11s 9d and for interest thereof till this day
beinge 8 monethes is 12s 9d.   13   4   6

More   0   6   0

To Mr Vernon as mony lent long since by Mr Browne
alderman deceased   4   0   0

To Mr Thomas Williams alderman, as mony leied out by
him in the last yeere of his chamberlainshipp for which
he is to be allowed interest for from this accompte   4   15   2½

[Signatures of] John Glover maior, Josephe Harris,
William Meatcalfe

Md at the end of this accompte the box of wares that were
leafte at Tassells by one that was to fetch his triall for them
were sould for 8s 10d whereof 2s was paied to Mr William
Meatcalfe for widdowe Coles her shrewed, the other 6s was
delivered to George Noble senior chamberlin to be
accompted for   0   6   10

And John Tassill is to be allowed his 3s 8d out of the extreates.

[Signature of] Edmond Hiorne towneclark

[1] The clerk of the verge of the king's household was also clerk of the market.
[2] For the mill see *V.C.H.Oxon.* xii. 334, 429. Hen. Cornish leased it from the Crown in 1616.
[3] Died in office 6 May: B 77/2, 11 May.
[4] One of the subsidies granted in 1627.
[5] Son of Sir Thos. Spencer of Yarnton. He came of age in 1629.
[6] *c.* 19–27 Aug.: Stapleton, *Three Oxon. Parishes*, 290, citing Gutch, *Annals*.
[7] John Dubber, shoemaker, common councillor; Ric. Purdue, itinerant bell-founder: Sharpe, *Church Bells of Oxon.* ii (O.R.S. xxx), 153, 479.
[8] A member of Sir Gerard Fleetwood's household, below, listed as freeman this year only and present at the mayor's election: B 96, f. 38.

[f. 103r] **23 December 1629 to 23 December 1630, George Noble and Thomas Woodward, chamberlains**

[Disbursements]   £   s   d

Guiftes and rewardes at Christmas 1629 and since.
Sent to Sir Henry Browne knight one cake 10s, in rewardes to his servantes 11s 6d. Sent to Sir Gerrard Fleetwood knight one cake 10s, in rewardes to his servantes 6s 6d, and allso sent to him one sugerloffe wayinge 4lb quarter and halfe quarter 7s 3 1/2 d. To Sir Henry Lee knight one cake 10s and one sugerloffe wayinge 5lb and a halfe 9s 2d, in rewardes to his servantes 26s. Geiven to my lord of Mownte-Garratt and his lady[1] to welcome them to Yearneton 10s, to their servantes in rewarde 5s. Sent to Mr William Lenthall our recorder one cake 7s, to Mr Doctor Prideaux one sugerloffe wayinge 5lb and 3 quarters at 20d per lb 9s 7d. Summ totall   6   2   0 1/2

Stipendes and yeerely allowances.
To Mr Glover maior fee £5, to Mr Alderman Williams nowe maior fee £5, £10 . To Mr Chesterman, quittrent £5 6s 8d, acquittance 12d, wine 12d, £5 8s 8d. To Mr French undershreeve to Sir William Cobb for fee farme 53s 4d, acquittance 8d, 54s. *[f. 103v]* To Mr Lenthall recorder his fee, £3 6s 8d. To Edmond Hiorne towneclarke fee [etc] 45s. To Mr Symon Jeames schoolemaster his stipende, £12. Summ totall   35   14   4

Expences and reparations for the towne this yeere. Geiven in rewarde to the clark of the assise at the twoe sessions 6s 8d, 3s 4d at each tyme, to the judges cryer at each assise 12d, [total] 8s 8d. Expences in repayringe the towne office with slattes, lyme, crestes, mosse and pynns 18d. Horsemeate and beere for Mr Recorder at his cominge to Mr Glovers at Michaelmas 1630, 2s. 3 April geiven to Mr Champnies in rewarde as clarke of the markett 10s and in wine upon him 18d, 11s 6d. Paied Mr Woodrooffe the Kinges messenger for bringinge proclamations this yeere endinge at Midsomer 13s 4d. To 2 watchmen at 4 faiers 5s 4d. For sweepinge the chimnes in almeshouse 12d, mendinge the mowndes in backside of almeshouse 6d, 18d. Geiven unto the Lord of Warrwickes trumpiters 2s 6d. Spent in cakes and bread at the birth of the yonge prince Charles 18d.[2] Expences about the woodden bridge, for an iron plate 3d, to the mason for 3 dayes worke 3s, for digginge of stone and carriage 10d, for mendinge the bayes 12d, 5s 3d. Beere for Mr Harris and Mr Triplett when they preached 4d and 6d, 10d. [Marginated subtotal]   0   53   11
[f. 104r] Leyed out for worke about the schoole house
For 5 dayes worke of the slatter in rippinge of the schoolehouse 5s. To a laborer to serve the slatter 16d, lath 2s 4d, nayles 16d, slatt pinns 12d, one loade of slatt 9s, mosse 20d, lyme, heare and sande 14d, makinge cleane the schoolehouse courte 6d, a new locke for the schoolehouse dore 2s.   0   20   4
10 July expenses about the slewce. To Richard Wollamm for 204 foote of elme planckes at 3d the foote to make the troffe for the conveyance of the water out of

the lee pooles 51s, for carriage 3s. For a lyntorne, elmeborde and a peece of oake
for the sluce 5s 10d, pinwood for the newe and owld worke 2s. To the said
Wollam and his man for dayeworke to fynnishe the same worke 8s 8d, 2 laborers
one day 20d, 3 laborers 2 dayes worke appeece 6s, 3 laborers for 3 dayes worke
apeece and a halfe day 9s 6d. 2 masons for one daies worke about the sluce and
mendinge the almeshouse mownde 2s 6d, a laborer to serve the masons one day
10d. To William Anthony for fellinge the elme at the almeshouse, for helpinge
about the sluce 12d. Twoe laborers for 2 dayes worke a peece to digge claye and
to scower the bayes 4s. 2 laborers for 5 dayes worke betweext them at the sluce 5s.
Carriage of 3 loades of claye 12d. 2 laborers 2 dayes a peece at same 6s. Beere
geiven at severall tymes to the carpenters, masons and laborers at same 14d. One
dayes worke at the sluce and bayes 12d. 5 bushells of lyme 3s 4d, 3 penyworth of
duble tenns and 1 penny worth of packthredd 4d.   5   13   11
Geiven in beere to my lord bisshopp of Bristowes chaplaine at
Mr Glovers house then maior   0   0   4
19 July expences about Hampton yeardes, mowinge for 15
yeardes in Hampton leyes 3s, one dayes worke 9d, 3 dayes
worke for 3 men apeece and one halfe day at 9d per diem
7s 2d, one wooman for 3 dayes at 5d per diem 15d,
expences which Mr Woodward layed out 7d   0   12   9
For mendinge the pownde gate 12d, lyme 3 bushells to
mende the litle house and the seller 2s, sande and candle for the
same worke 3d, a mason for 1 dayes worke for the same
service 12d, George Greene for his fee for this yeere endinge
at Michaelmas 1630 for clensinge the passage in the holloway
and at the bayes 18d   0   5   9
[Marginated subtotal for f. 104r]   7   18   1
[f. 104v] Bringinge the planckes from the mill bridge and
for planinge them in the guild hall   0   0   16
For 2 inditmentes against Michaell Collins the miller for
swipping the auncient watercourse in the mill haven   0   4   0
John Grainger for mendinge the schoolehouse wyndowes   0   5   0
Geiven to the prisoners of Oxon' by Mr Mayors appoyntment
10 December   0   2   0
A quarter of suger delivered to Thomas Heathen 5d. For 3 ells
of clothe for a shreewde for John Homes his wife 2s 6d. To
John Slatter for carriage of stones to the highewayes 3s 4d. For
expences for the neighbours that followed the cause against
Mr Cornishe in summer assises about the settlinge of the
repayringe of the bridge at Ouldwoodstocke mill which
Mr Cornishe was ordered by Mr Lyttelton to repayre and
which was this yeere 1630 by him accordingly repayred and
newe made 11s 4d.[3] To the clarke of the Petitions 2s 6d, and
in wine to him 2 January 7d   0   20   8

Geiven to 5 souldiers by Mr Hiorns appoyntment 8d.
To one souldier 2d, another 2d. To a poore minister by
Mr Maiors appoyntment 18d. To a poore souldier 2d,
2 poore souldiers 3d, another at Mr Hiorns appoyntment 4d.   0   3   3
To Mr Glover maior as geiven to poore people for 3 quarters
of his yeere at 6s the quarter 18s. To Mr Williams nowe maior
for one quarter 6s.   0   24   0
[Marginated subtotal]   3   0   8
Summ is   13   12   8

Wine spent this yeere.
A pynte of wine at the eatinge of the taste cake 7d. One pynte of wine geiven
to Mr Bullayne the muster master 7d. Wine to [preachers] Mr Raunson the last
of Januarie 14d, Mr Burkottes curat the same day 14d, to Mr Wattson 14
February 14d. Sent to the Bull to Mr Gregorie that there sate in busines for the
coontry 20 February 14d. To Mr Hill that preached 22 February 14d. Geiven
to Mr Fletcher and his brother 22 February 2 quartes of sack and a quarte of
white wine 3s. To the minister of Combe that preached the last of February
14d. Geiven to Sir Henry Browne knight 12 March 14d. For 2 quartes of sack
and 2 quartes of clarrett wine sent to Sir James Whitlocke knight 23 March 3s
8d. Wine to Mr Hutchins that preched heere 22d. A quarte of sack and 1
quarte of clarrett for Mr Recorder at his beinge heere 1 Aprill 22d. [f. 105r]
[Preachers] wine geiven to Mr Hodges 11 Aprill 11d, a quarte of sacke and a
pynte of clarrett for Mr Carpenter 25 Aprill 18d, 2 pyntes of sacke to Mr Doctor
Prideaux 9 May 14d, a quarte of sacke to Mr Hodges 16 Maye 14d. A quarte of
sacke and a quarte of clarrett sent to the justices 22 May 22d. Spent in wine
amongest the neighbours meetinge at the bonefire to rejoyce for the yonge
prince Charles 5s 6d. Wine to [preachers] Mr Harris of Yearneton 23 June 22d,
Mr Burcottes minister 24 June 14d, Mr Triplett 4 July 14d, Mr Tayler that
preched twice 11 July 2s 5d, the bisshopp of Bristowes chaplyn that preched
twice 25th July 2s 4d. A quarte of sack geiven to Mr Whisler the cownsellor by
Mr Maior and the aldermen 1 Auguste 14d. [Preachers] a quarte of sack to Mr
Butcher 19 September 14d, same to Mr Frith Michaelmas Day 14d and to Mr
Hodges 3 October 14d. A quarte of sacke and a quarte of clarrett upon Mr
Hodges by Mr Williams appoyntment for his sermon 10 October 22d. A quarte
of sacke for Mr Selfe 14d for his sermon. 2 quartes of sack spent upon Mr
Recorder at his cominge to Mr Maiors feast at Michaelmas 2s 4d. Wine sent to
the justices that sate at the Bull in service for the coontry 28 October 22d. Wine
bestowed upon the lord bisshopp of Oxon' and Mr Doctor Prideaux 7
November, the one cominge to confirme, the other preachinge 4s 7d. Upon Mr
Woodward 13 November for his sermon 22d. A quarte of sacke upon Mr Selfe
that preached 22 November 14d. Wine upon Sir Jerratt Fleetwoodes parson in
Hamsheir that preched heere 14d.   3   0   9
For felling, cleevinge and bringinge upp a dead asshe from the
almeshouse to the hall   0   0   5

Summ totall of the disbursementes	58	9	9$^{1}/_{2}$
Summ totall of the receiptes [corrected in MS. from £57 4s 5$^{1}/_{4}$d]	57	12	5$^{1}/_{4}$
So remayninge due to the chamberlins [corrected in MS. from 25s 4$^{1}/_{4}$d]	0	17	4$^{1}/_{4}$

Cast upp and examined by me Edmond Hiorne towneclark

[Signatures of] George Noble, Thomas Woodward chamberlains

[f. 105v] A note of buckettes due to be brought into the hall at this accompte 23 December 1630			
Mr Williams mayor hath in his handes before the laste accompte 20s for 6 buckettes and hath more for 4 buckettes in his handes 13s 4d for William Lun, John Collingwoodes, John Benns, and Richard Gregories. In toto	0	33	4
George Noble chamberlyn hath in his handes for 2 buckettes of John Hawtens and Thomas Paynters	0	6	8
John Cotton, Roberte Bruce junior, John Homes and William Bradshewe are owinge 3s 4d a peece for their buckettes	0	13	4
Edward Hull hath a buckettes of the townes in his handes which he is to deliver in or else pay	0	3	4

Debtes owinge to the towne 23 December 1630

For admission, John Powell 10s, Frauncis Collingwood 10s, Richard Hamond 10s, Thomas Heddy 10s, William Locton 10s, Thomas Warde 20s, John Patterick 5s, John Burgin 10s, John Homes 2s. George Drewe oweth 10s which he should have payed 25 March 1629. John Hawten is to pay 25s for his free-dom 25 March 1631. Mr Kyte oweth for his Puttgally rent for one yeere endinge at Michaelmas 1630, 6d. Jeames Nickolls hath 10s in his handes of Andrew Homes his mony.   Frauncis Druce alias White oweth for hay sould him out of Hampton leyes this soomer 8s. [Marginated] 5s geiven, 3s was paied.

Debtes owinge by the towne at this accompte

To Mr Rayer for which he is allowed interest for from this day £14 12s. To Mr Thomas Williams nowe mayor [likewise] £5 2s. The towne oweth £4 to Mr Vernon which ould Mr Thomas Browne alderman lent to the towne. It is agreed that Mr Vernon shall pay to the towne £5 and the towne is to be dischardged of the £4 and interest thereof. And wee are heereafter to dischardge Mr Vernon and Mr Brownes heiers and executors of the twoe sermons appoynted by Mr Brownes will. [Marginated] Md this £5 Mr Vernon paied to Mr Thomas Williams mayor at Michaelmas 1631 and since that tyme the towne is to pay for the twoe sermons.

[Signatures of] Thomas Williams maior, John Glover, Joseph Harris, William Meatcalfe, Ed. Hiorne towneclark *[f. 106r] [Receipts]*

Of Mr Doleman	8	0	0
Of Mr Rayer for interest	4	0	0
Of Thomas Heathen serjant at the mace for stallages	6	0	23
Of him for the standinges of 4 Adderbury bakers and 1 Deddington baker under the crosse at the rate of 12d a quarter each one for this yeere endinge on St Thomas Daye	0	20	0
Of Edward Longe toleman for the tole	4	3	6
Rentes of this boughroughe. [Interlined] Md 6d is denied for Mr Kytes Puttgallye, 2d for Hampton Lees is abated.	25	4	6¼
Of Alice Shadd widdowe for rent of the wooll beame	0	24	0
In reddie monye at the hall at the last accompte	0	6	10
For wooll sould that was taken upon Andrewe Homes⁴ a convicted felon 11s, besides 20s in mony of his is remaining in the handes of James Nickolls late constable	0	11	0
The haye of Hampton meade leyes sould to Frauncis White for £4 2s whereof Frauncis White yet oweth 8s. So receaved [sum changed from £3 14s]	4	0	12
[f. 106v] For John Hawtins admission to his freedom 25s in monye and his bill for 25s more to be paied at Our Lady Daye 1631. So receaved	0	25	0
Sealinge monye this yeere for Mr William Meatcalfes recoverie 4s, Edward Paynters fine 4s, George Nobles fine 4s, Mr Hulls fine 4s,⁵ Mr Rayers fine 4s, Henry Whitesides feoffment of his house from the towne 4s, Mr Thomas Woodwardes fine 4s, for a fyne to be sealed for Mistris Margery Gregorie of John Tassills house 4s.⁶ In toto received	0	32	0
Thomas Paynter for his admission to his freedom	0	0	20
And 3s 4d for a buckett			

Summ totall of the receiptes this yeere is [corrected in MS. from £57 4s 5¼d]	57	12	5¼
Summ totall of the disbursmentes this yeere is	58	9	9½
So remayninge due to the chamberlins [corrected in ms. from 21s 4¼d]	0	17	4¼

Caste upp and examined by me Edmond Hiorne towneclarke

[Signatures of] George Noble, Thomas Woodward, chamberlins

Md it was agreed this 23 December 1630 that the lector moved by Mr Woodward shalbe upon Wensday weekly.⁷ And the precher to be allowed 12d for his dinner only at the towne chardge to be payed by the chamberlains. And

WOODSTOCK CHAMBERLAINS' ACCOUNTS

Mr Hiorne is desired to procure the lord bisshopps consent
and approbation thereof which he is willing to undertake.

[Signatures of] Thomas Williams, John Glover, Joseph Harris,
William Meatcalfe, Robert Lee and Ed. Hiorne towneclark

[f. 107r] Md John Tassill was paied 18d of his 3s 8d, 23 December 1630.

[1] Marg., widow of Sir Thos. Spencer (d. 1622), married Ric. Butler, Lord Mountgarrett.
[2] 29 May 1630: *Cal.S.P.Dom.* 1629–31, 268.
[3] See above in 1629.
[4] A notable miscreant between 1623 and 1630: see B 77/2.
[5] Ibid 17 Nov. 1627
[6] Ibid 3 Dec. 1630.
[7] In fact held on Tuesdays in following years. For the fate of these combination lectures see below, 1633.

[f. 107v] **23 December 1630 to 21 December 1631, George Noble and Thomas Woodward, chamberlains**

[Disbursements]	£	s	d
Guiftes geiven at Christmas 1630 and afterwardes. For one cake 10s, one sugerloffe waying 5lb at 20d the lb, 8s 4d, sent to Sir Gerrard Fleetwood knight, in rewardes to his servantes 6s 6d. For one cake 10s and one sugerloffe 8s 6½d sent to Sir Henry Lee knight deceased, in rewardes to his servantes 26s 8d. 1 cake sent to Sir Henry Browne 10s and in rewardes to his servantes 11s 6d. One cake sent to Mr William Lenthall our recorder 7s. One suger loffe sent to Mr Doctor Prideaux 9s 7d. One cake sent to my lord chamberlaine[1] at the Kinges beinge heere 10s, one sugerloffe 10s 5d and for 4 cheeses 3s 4d. One cake sent to my Lady Lee at her first cominge into the coontry in soomer last 10s. In toto	7	0	22½
Stipendes and yeerely allowances from the towne.			
To Mr Thomas Williams maior his fee	10	0	0
To Mr Chesterman for quitt rent £5 6s 8d, 2 acquittances 12d, his paynes 12d.	5	8	8
To Mr Peeter Langston, undershreeve to Sir John Lacye knight, for fee farme 53s 4d, acquittance 6d.	0	53	10
To Mr William Lenthall recorder his fee	3	6	8
[f. 108r] To Mr Edmond Hiorne towneclarke fee [etc]	0	45	0
To Mr Jeames schoolemaster his stipend	12	0	0
Summ	35	14	2

Expences for reparations and other necessarie disbursementes
for the towne this yeere.

To Mr Maior for his extraordinary expences and rewardes geiven to the Kinges Majesties trumpeters and other his Majesties servantes at his Majesties beinge at Woodstock in August	0	40	0
To Mr Walker the clarke of the markett of the verge as a rewarde at the Kinges Majesties beinge heere 10s, his mann 12d. To Mr Gowin Champnies clarke of the markett at lardge as a rewarde 5 March 10s.	0	21	0
Paied Mr Woodruffe the Kinges Majesties messenger as a rewarde for bringinge proclamations 13s 4d for one yeere endinge 24 June upon a composition	0	13	4
To Mr Thomas Williams nowe maior as mony geiven by him to poore people at soondry tymes this yeere after the rate of 6s the quarter	0	24	0
Paied more extraordinarily by him and his appoyntment to 5 Irish gentlewoomen 12d, to a company of souldiers 16d, to one poore scholler by Mr Maior and Mr Hiornes appoyntment 6d	0	2	10
To twoe wardsmen at 4 faiers	0	5	4
For a messenger to goe with a lettre to Mr Recorder to bringe him to Woodstock at the Kinges Majesties last beinge heere 16d, his expences upon his entertaynement 3s 6d, horsemeate 6d	0	5	4
Rewardes geiven to the clarke of the assise at the 2 assises this yeere 6s 8d. To the judges cryer 2s as usually hath been geiven. Expences laied out by Mr Hiorne at Michaelmas quarter sessions in answeringe the justices to Sir Henry Brownes complainte 2s	0	10	8
[f.108v] For a litle booke of orders and directions to the justices concerninge corne buyers and sellers[2]	0	0	6
Expences in dressinge the buck which Sir Gerrard Fleetwood gave to the towne at Michaelmas to Edward Paynter the keeper for his fee 6s 6d, for the makinge and bakinge of the pasties 16s, expences at the eatinge of the taste cakes 2s	0	24	6
Summ	7	7	6

Sluce. Expences in repayringe the sluce. To John Durman for his paynes 20s, Claridge for one day 10d, 5 laborers one day 4s, for 8 furse faggottes to stopp the water 10d, fower laborers for 2 dayes a peece at 10 per diem 6s 8d, 2 laborers 2 dayes a peece 4s 2d, one laborer one day 8d, beere at the makinge of the bargaine 4d, Raphe Lucas to helpe John Hatter downe with a peece 1d. To one laborer for 1 dayes worke at the fynnisshinge of the sluce 10d, 2 laborers for 2 dayes worke apeece 3s 4d.   0   41   9

Hollowaye. For tymber to newe make the wherles at the hollowe waye 4s 6d, 23 foote of oaken borde to mende the woodden bridge 2s 2d, nayles 4d, 2 carpenters for 1 dayes worke 2s. To a mason for 2 dayes worke about the hollowe way and almeshouse 2s.   0   11   0

Guild hall and litle house. Expences in repayringe the towne hall. For slatt for the hall, the pennyles bench and the litle house 10s. Mosse 2s 6d, lath and nayles 2s 2d, slatt pynns 12d, 8 crestes 2s, 10 bushells of lyme at 9d the bushell 7s 6d, 2 bushells of heare 12d. To 2 slatters for 5 daies worke apeece 10s, a laborer for 5 dayes to serve the slatters 3s 4d, a mason for 1 dayes worke 12d and a laborer to serve him 9d. For a peece of tymber for the seller windowe 6d, 2 iron barrs wayinge 12lb, nayles to sett them on 3d. For mendinge the seller dore lock and settinge it on with speekes 2d. To the glasier for glasinge the upper hall windowes, mendinge the leades over the pennyles benche, newe payntinge the postes, nayles to sett upp the glasse 24s^1/2d. For a growndsill for the seller head 12d, a borde to mende the dore 4d, speekes and nayles 4d. To a mason for pitchinge worke 1 day 12d. To the carpenter for mendinge the seller dore 6d. Speekes and workemanshipp about the stockes 14d. Nailes and workemanshipp about the bedsteede in the litle house 4d.   3   10   10^1/2

New well. 18 July paied for expences in the newe makinge of the drawe well in Oxford Streete. To Humfry Bennett for 1 dayes worke about the fellinge and loadinge of the tree that Mr John Preedy gave to make the plumpe 12d. To John Symons for one daies worke about the plumpe 12d and in earnest for the makinge of the plumpe 6d. [f. 109r] To William Evans for 8 loade of stone to wall the well 4s. To John Hayles for carryinge away the cley and rubbishe from the well 5s, a laborer to helpe him 10d. 6 sleepers to lay over the well at 10 foote longe a peece 12s, 7 planckes of 8 foote longe, 12 foote in a planck 2 inches and halfe thick, at 2s a planck 14s. To 2 carpenters for 4 dayes worke a peece 8s. To the mason for 2 dayes worke in pitchinge the well 2s, a laborer 2 dayes to helpe him 20d. Gravill 12d, pinwood 6d, 4 peeces of oake to make standardes for the curbe 16d, 44 foote of borde to make the curbe 3s 4d, nailes for the curbe 5d. Paied by Mr Glover to William Evans for stones and planckes for the bottom and wallinge of the well 9s 6d, and for 2 daies wallinge 2s. To Kinge for 2 dayes wallinge worke 2s, John Hatter for 6 dayes digginge worke 6s, John Symons for boringe the plumpe 12d. In toto 20s 6d. Paied by Edward Silver more towardes this worke to John Damery for 5 dayes worke 5s, for his boy 5 dayes 2s 6d, John Randall for carryinge of stone 2 dayes 8s, William Abbott for 1 dayes carriage of stone 12d. For mosse 16d. To Richard Meades for 1 dayes worke 8d, Richard Homes for halfe a dayes worke 4d. In toto 18s 10d. Summ totall   4   15   11

Fludgates. For 3 planckes to make the fludgate at the bayes 9s, speekes and pynn wood 12d. To the carpenter for his worke 2s 6d. To George Greene for clensinge the ditche by the bayes 18d.   0   14   0

Paymentes and expences. To Phillipp Hawthorne for elmes sett at the townes ende 16d. To William Evans for 17 foote of stone and twoe quynes for the markett stone 4s 6d. Lyme and sande to poynt the same stone 12d. For expences bestowed upon the chaunce childe called Charitie when it was first placed with John Durman 19s 1¹/₂d, clothes against Easter 15d, 1 lace for her ¹/₂d. Paied to the churchwardens for planckes taken out of the church to mende the bridge at the mill 10s. To the churchwardens of Hampton Poyle for a levy for the repayre of the churche there for the towne leyes rated at the third parte of one yarde lande 20d. To Prissell Barnaby, John Seely and Joane Turner in time of theire sicknes 18d. For a shirte for Wardes boy by Mr Maiors appoyntment 12d. To Prissell Barnaby more in her sicknes 4d. For a shrewde for Joane Turner beinge 3 ells of callico 2s 6d. Geiven to a poore wooman that would have lyen in the towne to gett her away 6d. For widdowe Lucas her shrewde beinge 3 ells and a halfe and one peny worth of thred 3s, John Seelyes shrewde 2s 2d. For mendinge of Wardes boyes clothes 3¹/₂d. To Phillipp Hawthorne for sweepinge the almeshouse chimnies 12d. For mosse to mose the almeshouse 12d. In toto   0   52   3¹/₂

[f. 109v] Lecture.[3] Expences upon the preachers of the lecture which begann on Tusday 3 Maye for the expences of all the clergie men which came the first day beinge 13 in number, 19s 6d. [For dinners] for 2 servingmens that attended them 18d, 10 May for Mr Twitties 12d, 17 May Mr Harris 12d, 24 May Mr Palmers 12d, 31 May Mr Frenche 12d, 7 June Mr Woodwardes 12d, he preched my lord bisshopps turne, 14 June Doctor Prideaux chaplins 12d, 21 June Doctor Standardes 12d, 28 June Mr Smithes 12d, 5 July the vicker of Deddingtons 12d,[4] 12 July Mr Frithes 12d, 19 July Mr Palmers 12d, 26 July for a gentleman of Queenes Colledge in Oxon' that preached for Mr Woodward 12d, 2 August Mr Twitties 12d, 9 August Mr Palmers 12d, 16 August Mr Potters 12d. 23 August noe sermon was preached for that there was a sermon at the mannor before the Kinge.[5] 30 August for my lord bisshopps chaplaines dinner 12d, 6 September Mr Selfes that preached for Mr Doctor Prideaux 12d, 13 September Mr Doctor Standardes 12d, 20 September Mr Twitties 12d, 27 September Mr Woodwardes 12d, 4 October Mr Frithes 12d, 11 October Mr Butchers 12d, 18 October Mr Brinknells of Deddington 12d, 25 October Mr Twitties 12d, 1 November Mr Palmers 12d, 8 November Mr Robinsons 12d, 15 November Mr Franck 12d, 22 November Mr Harris 12d, 29 November Mr Selfes 12d that preched for Mr Doctor Prideaux, 6 December Doctor Standardes 12d, 13 December Mr Smithes 12d, 20 December Mr Brewikes of Deddington vicers 12d.
Summ totall   0   53   0

Wine. Upon Mr Doctor Prideaux on Christmas Eve [1630] 14d. Sent to the justices 29 December 1630 that sate about the prizes of corne 21d. To Mr Selfe that preched on Newe Yeers Day [1631] 14d, Sir Henry Lees man that invited the towne at Christmas 1630 7d, the justices that sate heere about corne busines 10 January [1631] 14d, Mr Rawnson that preched 23 January

22d, and Mr Butcher 30 January 14d. For wine spent at the eatinge of the Christmas taste cakes 12d. To the minister of Tewe that preched 27 February 12d. Sent to the clarke of the markett 27 February 2s 8d.
[f. 110r] Wine to a preacher of Penbrock Colledge that preched 27 March 2s 8d, the justices 3 April 12d, the recorder 7 April 12d, Mr Doctor Predeaux upon Easter Eve and Easter Day 3s, Mr Beard that preched heere 20d, a precher of Baylioll Colledge 12d. Sent to the justices 13 April 12d. Wine to [preachers] Mr Hide 17 April 22d, Mr Boucher 24 April 12d, Mr Selfe 1 pynte of sacke 1 May 6d. For wine sent to all the ministers that dyned at the Bull the first day of the beginninge of the lecture 3s 8d. To Sir Henry Brownes cominge to the towne 14 May 14d. To a yonge man that preched 22 May 12d. For a pynt of sack to Mr Selfe on the procession day 6d. For wine to the justices that sate about the poore the last of May 12d.[6] [Preachers] Mr Binckes and Mr. Greene that preached twice 5 June 2s 4d, Mr Butcher and Mr Doctor Standard in June 1631 2s, Mr Hodges 26 June 16d, Mr Taylers wyne at his 2 sermons 10 July 2s 10d, Mr Robinson 19 July 18d, the lord bisshopp of Oxon' when his chaplaine preched 21 July 18d, a precher of Queens Colledge 14 Auguste 18d, Mr Hodgettes that preched at the Kinges beinge heere 12d. Mr Walker the clarke of the markett of the Kinges howshold 12d. To Mr Tayler Sir Thomas Crewes chaplaine 11 September 2s, Mr Recorder 15 September 12d. [Preachers] Mr Hodges twice on 2 October 2s 6d. Mr Doctor Prideaux and a minister about Bissiter that preched 2 on 8 October 2s 8d, Mr Drake 16 October 18d, Mr Feild 4 December 12d. For wine spent at the eatinge of the buck at Michaelmas last which Sir Gerrard Fleetwood gave to the towne 8s 8d.

Summ totall is	3	9	10
Summ totall of the disbursementes is	70	12	2½
Summ totall of the receiptes is	59	5	5¼
So remayninge due to the chamberlains	11	6	9

[In latin] Examined by me Edmond Hiorne common clerk
of the maior and cominaltie of the aforesaid borough

[Signatures of] George Noble, Thomas Woodward chamberlains

[f. 110v] [blank]

[f. 111r] [Receipts]

Of Mr Thomas Doleman	8	0	0
Of Mr Thomas Rayer for interest	4	0	0
Of Thomas Heathen serjant at the mace for stallages	6	2	7
Of him for the standinges under the crosse	0	20	0
Of Edward Longe toleman for the tole	4	2	6
Rentes of this boughroughe	25	4	6¼
Of Alice Shadd widdowe for rent of the wooll beame	0	0	0
Of Roberte Hawkes sadler admission to his freedome	3	12	4

Of John Hawten upon his bill for his admission to his freedome	0	25	0
[f. 111v] For the haye of Hampton leyes this yeere sould to Phillipp Johnsson for	3	12	0
For the shrewde of fower elmes sould for 18s and of the trees at the crosse sould for 2s 6d	0	20	6
For the butt of elme which grewe in the almeshouse yarde which Mr Maior bought	0	8	0
Of John Meades for a straye bullock	0	10	0
Of Edward Silver for the seale of a fyne acknowledged by Humfry Silver and his wife, which was sealed at this accompte 4s.[7] Of Mr Thomas White for the seale of a fyne acknowledged by Mr William Hutchins and Mr Edmond Hiorne and Ann his wife 4s which was sealed at this accompte[8]	0	8	0
Summ totall of the receiptes is	59	5	5$^{1}/_{4}$
Summ totall of the disbursmentes is	70	12	2$^{1}/_{2}$
So remayninge due to the chamberlyns	11	6	9

Cast upp and examined by me Edmond Hiorne towneclark

[Signatures of] George Noble, Thomas Woodward chamberlains

Mr Gabrill Shad paied 24s for his rent due at Michaelmas last 1631, and the woollbeame is lett to him for one yeere from Michaelmas 1631 at 24s rent.

[Signature of] Thomas Williams maior, Edmond Hiorne

Md delivered to George Noble 20s in mony which is not entred into the ledger. And it is agreed that the tryangle for Mr Dodwells beame shall be bought and fynnisshed at the townes chardges

[Signatures of] Thomas Williams maior, John Glover, Joseph Harris, William Meatcalfe, Thomas Rayer, Ed Hiorne

[f. 112r] A note of buckettes due to the towne and are yet to be brought into the hall, collected at this accompte taken 21 December 1631.

Mr Thomas Williams nowe maior hath in his handes 20s for 6 buckettes and 13s 4d for 4 other buckettes, William Lunns, John Collingwoodes, John Venns and Richard Gregories	0	33	4

George Noble chamberlaine hath in his handes 10s
for 3 buckettes, John Hawtins, Thomas Paynters
and Roberte Hawkes   0   10   0
John Cotton, Roberte Bruce junior, John Homes and
William Bradshewe are owinge 3s 4d a peece for theire
buckettes yet to be brought in   0   13   4
Edward Hull hath a buckett of the townes in his handes
which he is to deliver in or else to pay   0   3   4
So there is yet 18 buckettes to be newe made and brought
into the halle

A note of debtes owinge to the town 21 December 1631

For admission, John Powell 10s, Frauncis Collingwood 10s,
Richard Hamond 10s, Thomas Heddy 10s, William Locton 10s,
Thomas Warde 20s [margin, g], John Patterick 5s, John Burgin
10s, John Homes 2s [margin g]. George Drewe was to pay 10s
25 March. Mistris Elizabeth Kyte oweth for 2 yeeres rent for
the putt gally due at Michaelmas 1631, 12s. Jeames Nickolls
hath 10s in his handes of Andrew Homes his monye.

Debtes owinge by the towne

To Mr Thomas Williams nowe maior £5 10s.[9] To
Mr Thomas Rayer alderman £16 4s 8d. Md it was
agreed that they shalbe allowed interest for theire monies
from this daye. Due to George Noble at the last accompte
17s 7d¹/₄d, and remayninge due to him at this accompte
£11 6s 9d. In toto 12s 4s 1d.

[Signatures of] Thomas Williams maior, Ed. Hiorne

[1] i.e. Woodstock's high steward, Phil. Herbert (d. 1650), earl of Montgomery and 4th earl of
Pembroke, Lord Chamberlain of the household 1626–41: *D.N.B.*
[2] One of the books of orders publ. by the govt. Sept. 1630: P. Slack, 'Books of Orders: Making of
Eng. Soc. Policy, 1577–1631', *T.R.H.S.* (1980), 2–4. Hiorne still had it in 1636: B 36, item 34. See
below for justices setting the price of corn.
[3] Tuesday dates for combination lectures.
[4] Wm. Brudenell, vicar 1630–41: O.R.O., Clerus, f. 428. Called Brincknell and Brewickes below.
[5] Chas. was in Woodstock in Aug.: *Cal.S.P.Dom.* 1631–3, 133–4.
[6] In 1631 the govt. sent out letters on the treatment of the poor, idle, and vagrant, and 223 books of
orders. Justices were to meet monthly to supervise the work of the constable and report to the
sheriff, and he in turn to the assizes: *Acts of P.C.* 1630–1, 214–7. See also below in 1634.
[7] For the house in Oxford St. occupied by Edw. Silver, Humf. and Alice's son, see B 77/2, 11 July
1626.
[8] Ibid. 4 Apr. 1631, where Wm. Hutchins is identified as a clerk, perhaps the preacher above.
[9] Mr Vernon's payment made on 24 Oct. with interest: see 1630 and B 81, ff. 32r–3v.

[f. 112v] 21 December 1631 to 21 December 1632, George Noble and Thomas Woodward, chamberlainsé

[Receipts]	£	s	d
Of Mr Thomas Doleman	8	0	0
Of Mr Thomas Rayer alderman for interest	4	0	0
Of Thomas Heathen serjant at the mace for stallages	5	19	10
Of him for the standinges of coontrye bakers	0	15	0
Of Edward Longe toleman for the tole	0	41	2
Rentes of this boughroughe	25	4	6¹/₄
Of Thomas Williams alderman for a fine of tenn yeeres from 25 March 1632 of his meadowe called le poole	13	6	8
Of Edmond Hiorne towneclarke the like fyne for the like terme of his parte of le poole meade¹	13	6	8
[f. 113r] Of Gabriell Shadd for rent of the wooll beame	0	24	0
Of Mr Danniell Warner of Midleton [Stoney] for the haye of Hampton leyes for this yeere endinge at Michaelmas	3	6	8
20d a peece for the admission of Thomas Glover, Richard Underhill, William Belcher, Henry Cooper and Mathewe Penn	0	8	4
Receaved at the hall in reddy monye at last accompte	0	20	0
Summ totall of the receiptes is [sic]	78	12	10
Summ totall of the disbursementes is	73	19	10
Summ remayninge due to the maior and cominaltye	4	13	0

[Signatures of] George Noble, Thomas Woodward, chamberlains

[In latin] Examined by me Edmond Hiorne common clerk of the mayor and cominaltie of the aforesaid borough

[f. 113v] [Disbursements]

	£	s	d
Guiftes geiven at Christmas 1631 and this yeere 1632. For one cake 10s and one sugerloffe 9s 7d sent to Sir Gerrard Fleetwood knight and in rewarde to his servantes 6s 6d. One cake sent to Mr Lenthall our recorder 6s 8d. One sugerloffe sent to Mr Doctor Prideaux 9s 4¹/₂d. One cake sent to Sir Henry Browne knight 10s.	0	52	1¹/₂
Stipendes and yeerely allowances. To Mr Williams maior fee £5. Mr Glover [same]	10	0	0
To Mr Chesterman for quitt rentes £5 6s 8d, 2 acquittances 2s, his paynes 12d	5	9	8

To Mr French undershreeve to Mr Horborne 53s 4d fee farme, acquittance 6d	0	53	10
To Mr Lenthall esq recorder fee	3	6	8
To Edmond Hiorne towneclarke fee, assises, accomptes	0	45	0
To Mr Jeames and Mr William Newman schoolemasters theire stipend[2]	12	0	0
Summ	35	15	2

[f. 114r] Expences for reparations and other necessary disbursementes for the towne for this yeere.

Paied as a fee sent to Mr Lenthall for the dischardge of the towne from the power of the knight marchall[3]	0	20	0
To Mr Selfe for preachinge of Mr Brownes twoe sermons	0	16	0
2 April geiven in rewarde to Champnies clarke of the markett 10s and in beere and wine to him 18d	0	11	6
Paied Mr Woodroffe the Kinges messenger for his fee due at Midsomer for bringinge proclamations	0	13	4
For chardges spent upon Mr Recorder and the neighbours to accompany him at his cominge to suppresse the victulers by Mr Justice Joanes his appoyntment[4]	0	16	4
To Mr Williams maior 18s, Mr Glover maior 6s, as geiven to poore at rate of 6s per quarter	0	24	0
As a rewarde to the clarke of the assise and to the judges cryers at the 2 assises this yeere	0	8	8
To 2 wardsmen at 4 faiers	0	5	4
Paied for clothes and other thinges for Lucas when he was hired at the last accompte to be beadle of the beggars.[5]			
For 3 yeardes and a halfe of redd and blue cloth 10s 6d, 1 yard and demi of the same to inlardge it 4s 6d, makinge of his coate and capp 2s, for his staffe 4d, cotton to lyne his capp 4¹/2d.	0	17	8¹/2

Almeshouse. Paied for reparations about the almeshouse.

12 sheets of mosse 2s, slatt pinns and 1 creste 18d, 2 bushells of lyme 18d. To the slatters for the newe mosinge of all the houses 6s 8d. For the repayringe of the almeshouse mownde and the pownde mownde 8d.	0	12	4
Sweepinge the chimnies there	0	0	12
2 dayes worke to dig stones for the almeshouse 20d	0	0	20

Litle house. A mason one day to mende the seller in the litle house and the almeshouse back side 12d. A peece of tymber to lay as a bonde in the wall 12d and to a laborer to serve him 6d and for candle 1d.

serve him 6d and for candle 1d.	0	2	7
A newe key for the litle house dore 18d and for a speeke to sett on the locke 2d	0	0	20
To George Greene for clensinge the ditch at the bayes	0	0	18

To John Durman for receavinge againe child Charity when goodwife Doa caused him to putt her away	0	10	0

To the messenger that brought newes of Mr Doctor
Barkers guifte of £20 to the towne 2s 6d.[6] For expences
leyed out by Mr Williams maior, Mr Alderman Harris and
Mr Hiorne at theire twice goinge to Oxon' for the mony

4s 3d.	0	6	9

Paied Mr Frauncis Gregory for 2 daies worke with his carte
to carry stones for the highewayes 8s, and for 3 laborers to

digg stones for the holloway and the sluce 5s	0	13	0

[f. 114v] To Richard Newell and Jerome Long for servinge

of writtes upon Carter and others at 2 severall tymes[7]	0	6	6

Sluce and holloway. To 2 laborers for 2 daies worke and a half to ridd the sluce 3s. To John Durman and Richard Redberd for 4 daies worke a peece about the sluce 8s. For a mason for 1 daies worke about the holloway 12d. 3 sleepers and one planck 4s 10d, 2 other sleepers and 1 planck for the sluce 5s 6d. To the carpenter for sawinge and squaringe the sleepers and fittinge them 18d. To Mr Gregory for one dayes worke with his teame to carry clay to the sluce and stones to the holloway 4s. To 3 masons for 2 dayes worke a peece about the holloway and the sluce 6s. 1 bushell of lyme for the sluce 9d. To John Durman and Richard Redberd for 4 dayes worke to clense the sluce and throw up the rubbishe and to digg claye 4s. To John Durman and Stone[8] for 2 dayes worke and halfe a peece for the fynnisshinge upp the worke at the sluce and to make it perfect 5s. To John Hale for one dayes worke with his teame to carry stones to the hollowe way and for a man to helpe to fill the carte 5s. To John Durman for his paynes about the sluce which was appoynted to be paied him at the last accompte 10s.   0 58 7

Paied 12d for horsse hier to ride to Burford to Mr Recorder[9] and geiven 6d to a messenger that brought a letter from Mr Recorder to Mr Maior   0   0   18

To John Hall for carriage of 3 loades of stone and morter to the sluce 12d and a peck of lyme 2¹/₂d   0   0   14¹/₂

Geiven to prisoners of Oxon' on Christmas Day last 2s and this yeere by Mr Maiors appoyntment 2s   0   4   0

Md 3s 8d for reparations and expences on the other side is cast in this somme.
Summ, the sluce and holloway besides 7d,   10   0   3

Wyne geiven this yeere.
To the minister of Stonsfeild that preached heere 1 January 18d. To Mr Doctor Prideaux and his wife 15 January, lyinge heere overnight that he preached heere and at his breakfast in the morning, 3s 6d Upon Mr Boucher that preached heere 29 January 18d, Mr Selfe and Mr Allexander that preached twice upon, 4 March 2s 6d. 28 March to Mr Cradockes clarke being the clarke of the assises 12d. Sent to Mr Selfe on Easter Day 12d.

[f. 115r] Sent to the deputy clark of the markett our Mr Harris by George Nobles appoyntment 2 April 18d. Upon Mr Recorder and the neighbours at his meeting 5 April 3s 6d. Sent to the justices 5 April at theire sittinge about ale-houses 20d. To Mr Feild 5 April at his preachinge heere then 14d. Upon Mr Selfe at his cominge home from the procession on Assenscion Day 6d. Upon one Mr Lovell that came to offer himselfe to be schoolemaster heere 18d. Upon [preachers] Mr Cooper 20 May 20d, Mr Smith 10 June 20d, Mr Hodges 19 June 20d, a straunger that preched in July in wine 20d. One pynt of wine to Mr Woodrooffe the Kinges messenger by George Nobles appoyntment 30 June 6d. To a minister that came out of Ireland and preached heere 15 July 18d. 2 August for one pynte of wine to Mr Woodrooffe the messenger by George Noble his appoyntment 6d. Geiven to Mr Selfe when he preched in August 10d, Mr Recorder and the neighbours in August 2s 2d, a preacher preached 22 August 20d, Mr Wentworth that preached twice 26 August 2s 6d, Mr Boutche that preched 7 October 14d. A quarte of wine to Mr Fletwood when he gave a warrant for a doa against Mr Glovers last feast 12d. Wine to [preachers] Mr Hodges 21 October 2s 2d, Mr Bowins sonne 4 November 14d, Mr Selfe for one quart of wine in December 1632 12d.

Summ of the wine is	0	44	8

[f. 115v] Lecture. To Mistris Williams for dyet of the lectures

that preached heere 48 sermons this yeere	0	48	0
To a messenger sent to Mr Watson to keepe his lecture day	0	0	8
Geiven to a scholler by Mr Williams mayor his appoyntment	0	0	6
To a mason for one dayes worke at the litle house and schoolehouse 12d, laborer to serve him 6d and a peece of tymber to laye in the litle house wall 12d	0	2	6
To Mr Thomas Williams maior as monye owinge to him by the towne at the last accompte	5	12	0

1 June expences and disbursementes concerninge the free schoole and reparations in the free schoole since the death of Mr Symon Jeames late schoolemaster as followeth. Spent in entertaynement of Mr Hatwell which came firste to make suit to be schoolemaster 2s. For makinge cleene the schoolehouse 3d. For a messenger to goe to Oxon' with a lettre to Mr Channell[10] for the sendinge of a schoolemaster in Mr Frithes absence 6d. For expences for Mr Newmans dinner and his freendes at the tyme of his entrance to examine the schollers and to take possession of the schoole 3s 6d. To Mr Williams maior for chardges bestowed upon Mr Lovell that came to make suit to be schoolemaster 11d. Summ   0   7   2
Reparations only of the schoolehouse.[11] Hundred and halfe of harte lath to seele the chamber in the schoolehouse 18d, 4 bushells and halfe of lyme 3s 4$\frac{1}{2}$d, one bushell and halfe of heare 9d, 4 hundred of lath nayles 8d, 2 dayes worke of the pargeter and his boye 3s. Makinge cleene of the schoolehouse 3d. One beame of 15 foote for the inlardginge of the schoolehouse chamber 6s 8d, 4 thick planckes to make gannies and studdes for the partition 8s 4d. [Subtotal]   0   24   6$\frac{1}{2}$

[f. 116r] 3 quarters of a hundred of bordes and one shorte peece of joyestes 6s 4d. Half a hundred of bordes 4s 6d. Tymber for the makinge of the dore postes and the sill for the clossett and for 4 joystes for the stayer head 2s 6d. To Richard Woollam carpenter for 7 dayes worke 7s, his man for 7 dayes worke at 10d per diem 5s 10d. 4 hundred of 8 penny nayles 2s 8d, duble tenns and single tenns used about the partition 18d. 7 hundred of harte lath at 12d the hundred 7s, 2 thousand of lath nayles 2s 8d. 6 bushells of lime unslacked 4s 6d, 3 bushells of heare 18d. A carpenter one day to mende the chamber flower 12d and for nayles 6d. 6 dayes worke of the pargeter and his boye 9s, a laborer 4 dayes to helpe him 2s. 8 hundred of sapp lath to seele the chamber 6s 8d, 1 hundred of hart lath 12d, 4 thousand of lath nailes 5s 4d, 1 hundred of 4 peny nailes 4d, 10 bushells of lyme 7s 6d, 6 bushells of heare 3s. To the pargeter for 5 dayes worke for himselfe and his boy 7s 6d, a laborer 4 dayes to helpe him 2s, a mason for 3 dayes worke to mende the stayers, pave the halfe part and make the back of the chimny 3s and to the laborer to helpe him 3 dayes 18d. 2 bushells of lyme 18d for the chinckes and stayers. Stones for the halfe part and hurthes of the chimnies 12d. To Mr Hobbs the ploomer for 8lb and a quarter of soder at 10d the pownd for the schoole house gutter 6s 10d. Wood to heate his irons and for a laborer to attende him 10d. To the pargeter and his boye for 1 dayes worke and a halfe 2s 3d. 1 bushell of stone lyme to make whiting 9d, size to size the chamber and schoolehouse 4d. Beere geiven to the workemen at several tymes 14d. A casement for the chamber wyndowe 2s 6d. To the glasier for glasinge of the chamber windowe and for culleringe the casement and the barrs 6s 4d. Glasinge and mendinge all the other windowes and for poyntinge upp the glasse of all the windowes 16s 8d. For the litle casement and wiringe of the litle windowe in the chamber, the hooke, hinges and boulte thereof, 18d.
[Subtotal]   6 18   0

[f. 116v] Nayles to sett upp the glasse and for lyme and heare to poynte the glasse 6d. To John Saye for a wainscott dore for the closett 3s 4d. For a lock and a pere of straite joyntes for the same dore 18d. To the joyner for a day and a halfes worke to sett upp shelves in the same closett 21d. For a waynescott dore at the stayre head conteyneinge twoe yeardes and a halfe at 2s 6d the yearde 6s 3d, the latch and hinges 2s. For the joyners tymber to make the windowe lyddes and the cubbord at the staiers head 4s 6d. Paied the joyner for 5 daies worke in makinge the windowe lyddes and the cubborde at the stayers head and for settinge upp of shelves in the schole house chamber 5s. 2 paire of hookes and hinges and one paire of duffetayles and for a bolte and stable for the windowe lyddes 20d. A bayborde for the chamber windowe 12d. 2 paire of straighte joyntes and for a locke for the cubborde dores 22d. Nailes and iron worke in the settinge upp of the shelves 14d. 2 paire of crosse gardners and a lock upon the settinge of the stayer foote dore 3s 10d. A sive for the plausterer to sifte his lyme and sande in 4d. To the carpenter for 1 dayes worke for himselfe and his man 18d. Nayles 3d, borde 6d, hookes and hinges for the dore under the stayers 6d. To John aye for a bedsteede for Mr Newman 13s. A matt and corde for same 2s 8d, curten

roddes and 4 iron pynns for the testorne 5s. For a table, chaier and stoolls in Mr
Newmans chamber 16s. A paire of andirons and one paire of dogges for the
schoole house chamber, wayinge 24lb at 3d the pownde 5s. 3 candlestickes in the
schoole 14d. Mendinge the lock of the schoolehouse outer dore 3d. A newe latch
and staple for the same dore 10d. [Subtotal]   3   19   4
[Total for school]   12   0   22½

[f. 117r] Summ totall of the receiptes is   78   12   10
Summ totall of the disbursementes is   73   19   10
Summ totall remayninge due   4   13   0

[Signatures of] George Noble, Thomas Woodward
chamberlains

[In latin] Examined by me Edmond Hiorne common
clerk of the maior and cominaltie of the aforesaid borough

[f. 117v] 21 December 1632 A note of buckettes due to the
towne and which are to be brought into the hall.
Mr Alderman Williams hath in his handes for 10 buckettes   0   33   4
Whereof he brought in at this accompte 4 buckettes which
were delivered into the hall. So he hath yet in his handes for
6 buckettes   0   20   0
George Noble chamberlaine hadde in his handes 10s at the laste
accompte for 3 buckettes. And since hath received 16s 8d for
5 buckettes yet to be delivered for Thomas Glover, Richard
Underhill, William Belcher, Henry Cooper and Mathewe Penn.
All which buckettes are yet to be delivered in.   0   26   8
These 5 laste buckettes were brought into the hall so 10s is
in George Nobles handes.

A note of debtes owing at this accompte to the towne

For admission, John Powell 10s, Frauncis Collingwood 10s,
Richard Hamond 10s, Thomas Heddy 10s, William Locton 10s,
John Patterick 5s, John Burgin 10s. George Drewe oweth 10s
which he shoulde have paied 25 March. Jeames Nickolls hath
10s in his handes of Andrewe Homes his mony. Summ   4   5   0

Debtes owinge by the towne at this accompte

To Mr Alderman Thomas Rayer £16 4s 8d with interest for
this yeere paste   17   10   3
To George Noble £12 4s 1d and for interest thereof nowe
agreed upon   0   40   0

[Signatures of] John Glover maier, Ed. Hiorne, Joseph Harris,
Thomas Rayer, William Meatcalfe

[f. 118r] Md 64 good buckettes in the hall at this accompte. Allso 2 owlde buckettes there. And Nedd [Hull] hath one in his hande. And allso 4 newe buckettes brought in by Mr Williams. In the whole 70 beside Hulls. All comitted to the chardge of Edward Longe.

[Signatures of] John Glover maior, Edm. Hiorne towneclark

[1] Lease and payment of fines noted in B 81, 16 Apr. 1635.
[2] Jeames d. 10 May 1632 and was succeeded by Wm. Newman. For the various applicants see p. 142.
[3] The Knight Marshall was marshall of the king's household and held the court determining suits arising in the verge: Jacob, *Dict.* Woodstock's 1453 charter granted that the borough was not to be questioned before the marshall: *Cal.Chart.R.* vi. 126.
[4] For list of victuallers see B 77/2, 8 Aug.
[5] The appointment seems to be in response to a govt. drive for more effective action on beggars: see above in 1631, n. 6. This is earlier than noted by Ballard, *Woodstock*, 91.
[6] Hugh Barker, archdeacon of Oxf. (d. 1632): *D.N.B.*
[7] John Carter, sued for £10 : B 77/2, 29 Oct. 1632.
[8] Bessill Stone, labourer: ibid. 29 Aug. 1634.
[9] Although Lenthall did not buy Burford Priory until 1634 he had family connexions there: *D.N.B.*; *Hist. of Parl. 1558–1603*, iii. 476, s.n. Tanfield.
[10] Perhaps Fras. Cheynell, Fellow of Merton Coll., Oxf.: Foster, *Alumni.*
[11] The largest expenditure on the school and house repairs in these accounts, caused by Mrs. Jeames continuing to live in the schoolmaster's house. Newman was eventually compensated: see below in 1636–9.

[f. 118v] 21 December 1632 to 21 December 1633, George Noble and Thomas Woodward, chamberlains

	£	s	d
[Receipts]			
Of Mr Thomas Doleman	8	0	0
Of Mr Thomas Rayer interest	4	0	0
Of Thomas Heathen serjant at the mace for stallages	6	18	10
Of him for the standinges of the coontrie bakers	0	20	0
Of Edward Longe toleman for the tole of beefe, sheepe and hogges	3	14	8
Rentes of this boughroughe	25	4	6¹/₄
Of Gabriell Shadd for rente of the wooll beame	0	24	0
Of Mr William Meatcalfe and Mr Thomas Williams aldermen for the lopp of the trees standinge upon hoggerill hill	0	10	0
Of Phillipp Johnson for the haye of Hampton leyes meade this yeere	3	3	4
[f. 119r] For the admission of Richard Stiles	0	50	0
For the admission of William Trewman	0	26	8
For John Slatter his admission	0	0	20
For William Kinge his admission[1]	0	0	20

Of Mr Thomas Williams alderman for the interest of £5
in his handes of Mr Vernons monye for one yeere
endinge at Michaelmas

Of Edward Silver for breache of the peace taxed upon him at
the sessions 3s 4d,[2] whereof laied out for wood cleavinge
for the use of the towne at the towne hall 7d. So due to the
towne

0	8	0
0	2	9

Summ totall of the receiptes is	58	6	1¼
Summ totall of the disbursementes is	61	2	6½
So remayninge due to the chamberlaines	0	56	5

[Signatures of] George Noble, Thomas Woodward

[In latin] Examined by me Edmond Hiorne common clerk
of the mayor and cominaltie of the aforesaid borough

[Signatures of] John Glover maior, Joseph Harris,
William Meatcalfe, Thomas Rayer

[f. 119v] [Disbursements]

Guiftes at Christmas 1632.
One cake 10s and one sugerloffe 9s 9½d, sent to
Sir Gerrard Fleetwood knight. One cake sent to
Sir Henry Browne knight 10s, in rewardes to his
servantes 11s 6d. Cake sent to William Lenthall esq
our recorder 10s. Geiven in rewardes to Mr Thomas
Coghills[3] servantes when Mr Shreeve invited them to
dinner at Christmas 1632 11s 6d.

3	2	9½

Stipendes and yeerely allowances.

To Mr Glover maior his stipend.	10	0	0
To Mr Chesterman quitt rentes £5 6s 8d, 2 acquittances 2s	5	8	8
To Mr Peeter Langstone undershreeve to Sir Thomas Coghill knight for feefarme 53s 4d, acquittance 6d	0	53	10
To Mr Lenthall esq recorder	3	6	8
To Edmond Hiorne towneclarke fee and accomptes	0	45	0
To Mr Newman schoolemaster his stipende	12	0	0
To Mr Selfe for preachinge Mr Brownes twoe sermons this yeere on St Steephens Daye and Easter Day	0	16	0

Paied on Good Fryday 4s and on the Friday before Christmas
1633 4s to the poore of the almeshouse by the guifte of

Mr Hiornes father deceased[4]	0	8	0
Summ of allowances	36	18	2

[f. 120r] Expences about the free schoole this yeere.
Paied for 203 foote of oaken planckes to make the newe deskes
with 12d geiven to the salesman for measuringe of them out 17s.
Expences in goeinge to the wood 3 tymes to buy the planckes
and geiven to the men that helped to loade them 2s 6d. To
Richard Hutt for the carriage of them home 5s 4, and for his
suger and horsemeate 18d. Sawinge those planckes 4s 6½d.
2 measuringe poles 2d. To John Symons carpenter for 13 daies
worke and a halfe at 14d per diem 15s 9d. To Jonathan his
sonn for 8 daies worke and a halfe at 12d per diem 8s 6d. To
George Symons for 17 daies worke and a halfe at 8d per diem
11s 8d. To John Woollam and his boye for 2 daies work 3s 4d.
To Nedd Hall the joyner for 1 daies worke 14d. Pinwood
used about that worke 12d. 32 foote of bordes for the makinge
of the table and deske 4s 2d. Nailes 2s 11½d. Total is
The deduction for offile and chipps allowed.

		3	14	5

Paied for the lecterers diett at the Bull from 8 January until
the 1 October. At which tyme the lector was geiven
over[5]

	0	36	0

To Mr Maior for a cake sent to the lord chamberlaine at the
Kinges beinge at Woodstock in Auguste 10s, a sugerloffe 13s 8d,
4 cheeses 3s 6d[6]

	0	27	2

To Mr Glover maior for allowance of monye geiven to the
poore and maymed souldiers

	0	24	0

To Mr Maior as monie allowed to him for entertainement of
straungers and for fees and allowences to officers at the
Kinges Majesties last beinge heere in August

	0	40	0

[f. 120v] 18 March to Mr Harris clarke of the markett of the
realme of England as a rewarde to him when he sate heere

	0	10	0

To Mr Walker clarke of the markett of the Kinges howshold
that sate heere at the Kinges last beinge heere in Auguste

	0	10	0

Geiven to his man for the coppie of the rates

	0	2	0

In rewardes to the clarke of the assise and the judges officers
at the 2 assises

	0	8	8

To Mr Woodroofe the Kinges Majesties messenger for
bringinge of proclamations for this yeere endinge at
Midsomer

	0	13	4

To 2 wardsmen at 4 faiers

	0	5	4

For Lucas his clothes beinge the beedle of beggers, for 4 yardes
and 3 quarters of blewe cloth for his capp and coate at 3s 4d the
yarde 15s 10d, halfe yarde and an nayle of redd cotton 12d, the
makinge of his capp and coate 2s

	0	18	0

Summ

	13	9	9

Expences and reparations for the towne this yeere.
For 1 loade of busshes for the almeshouse mownde 7s, makinge of the same
hedge 18d. A peece of tymber for the pitchinge of the hollowe waye 2s 6d.
Paied the workemen for pitchinge there 2s 10d. For a box staple for the seller
dore 6d. For mendinge of the towne ladders 6d. Geiven at severall tymes for
the releefe of John Warde 14d. For clensinge of the way at the wooden bridge
4d. 2 lockes and staples for the office dores 2s 2d. Paied upon a levy to
Hampton for Suttons roberie 2s. For the wooden bridge a rayle 12d, 1 dayes
worke of a carpenter 12d, nailes and speekes 14d, 2 oaken bordes 2s, 2 postes and
braces 16d, plancke 12d. Iron worke about the mendinge of the markett
busshell 2d. Busshinge of the elmes at the crosse 2d. To George Greene for
clensinge the watercourse at the bayes 18d. 1 dayes worke of a mason to mende
the pownde 12d. Mendinge the glasse of the schoole house windowes 4d. 2
daies thetchinge at the almeshouse 2s and for a laborer to serve the thetcher 4d.
[Marginated subtotal]   0 33   6
[f. 121r] Sweeping of the almsehouse chimnies 12d. Shickells and chaines for the
towne busshell 9d. Mosse, lyme and workemanshipp about the repayringe of the
towne office 2s. Twoe daies carriage of stones for the highewayes 9s. Settinge
of an elme at the crosse at the townesend and for busshinge of the other elmes
6d. One loade of strawe to thetche the almeshouse 9s, ealmeringe thereof 6d.
Mosse about the schoolehouse 6d. Fillinge the stone pitt by the pigion house
waye 18d. Lockes for the almeshouse dores 8d. In bred to the poore on the
Kinges hollyday 27 March by Mr Maior and the neighbours appoyntment 2s 6d.[7]
29 March for beere and fyer and Mr Recorders horssemeate at Mr Maiors house
16d. Delivered to the constables for the sendinge of a prisoner to Oxford goale
2s 6d. The guildinge, mendinge and overwaite of silver putt to the towne greate
mase, beinge broken at the Kinges Majesties beinge heere in Auguste 14s. Mr
Recorders horssemeate and fier 16 December 2s.
[Marginated subtotal]   0 47   9
[Total for town]   4   0 15

Summ   17 11   0

Wyne geiven and spent this yeere by and for the towne. Upon Mr Highe
Shreeve at his cominge to a sermon 12 February in wine, cakes and fire by Mr
Maior and the neighbours appoyntment 3s 9d. [Preachers] wine to Mr Doctor
Prideaux and his companie 16 February 2s 2d, Mr Smithe 24 February 16d, Mr
Selfe 17 February 12d, Mr Woodroofe 8 March 6d. To the clarke of the assise 9
March when Mr Maior and the neighbours went to see him at the Bull 20d, to
the clarke of the markett 19 March 20d. Mr Beesly that preached the last of
March 20d. Mr Recorder and the neighbours 30 March 5s 8d, Mr Boutcher
that preached heere 2 April 12d, Mr Woodrooffe the messenger 4 April 6d.
[Subtotal] 20s 11d.
[f. 121v] Mr Recorder 14 Aprill 2s. Wine and beere to my lord bisshopps gentleman on Easter Day 22d. Wine sent to the justices 22 April that sate about

alehouses 20d. Mr Hobbs that preched 28 Aprille 15d, Mr Recorder and his wife 29 April 3s 11d. Mr Woodrooffe the messenger 10 May 6d. Mr Hobbs and Mr Beaton ploomers upon the concludinge of the bargaine for newe castinge of the leades of the tower 2s 6d 17 May, Mr Doctor Prideaux that preched 26 May 3s 2d, the justices 12 June 20d. Mr Thorpe waterbaylife 14 June when he keepte his court heere 20d.[8] Mr Chesterman 17 June when he brought the towne acquittance 12d. Mr Twitty that preched the last of June 20d, Mr Greene 7 July 20d. The Kinges Majesties gentlemen usshers that came to veiwe the state of the towne before his last cominge to Woodstock 1 August 20d. The Kinges gentlemen harbengers 18 Auguste and upon the clarke of the markett of the Kinges Majesties howsholde 3s 4d. Mr Binckes and one other preacher that preched heere morninge and eveninge 3s 4d. Mr Beesly that preched heere 20d, Mr Harris that preched 15 September 20d. The justices that sate about the contribution of St Pawles Church 19 September 20d.[9] Wine and beere upon Mr Higgins that preched 7 October 2s. Wine to Mr Doctor Prideaux and Mr Kempe that preched morninge and eveninge prayer 20 October 2s 9d. Mr Allexander and Mr Selfe that preched morninge and eveninge prayer 27 October 2s 11d. Mr Turner after his sermon 17 November 20d. Mr Recorder beinge heere 16 December 2s 6d. [Subtotal] 47s 8d.

[Total]	3	10	7
Summ totall of the receiptes of this yeere	58	6	1¼
Summ totall of the disbursementes	61	2	6½
So remayninge due to the chamberlains	0	56	5
[Signature of] John Glover maior. [other expenses]	0	4	6

[In latin] Examined by me Edmond Hiorne common clerk
of the mayor and cominaltie of the aforesaid borough.

[f. 122r] Md 21 December 1633. A note of buckettes due to
the towne and which are to be brought into the hall.

Mr Alderman Williams hath mony in his handes for 6 buckettes.	0	20	0
George Noble hath monie in his handes for 4 buckettes this yeare for William Kinge, Richard Stiles, William Trewman and John Slatter 13s 4d which buckettes are to be brought in by him	0	13	4

There are nowe in the halle 70 buckettes besides the foresaid 10 buckettes to be brought in. And besides one buckett which Nedd Hull sadler hath in his handes.

[Entry cancelled] George Noble hath more in his handes 10s for 3 buckettes which he hath had in his handes these 2 yeeres and are yet to be brought into the hall, 3 buckettes to be brought in. [Marginated] 3 buckettes were brought into the hall at this accompte.

A note of debtes owinge to the towne

For admission John Powell 10s, Frauncis Collingwood 10s,
Richard Hamond 10s, Thomas Heddie 10s, William Locton 10s,
John Patterick 5s, John Burgin 10s. George Gregorie 10s
which should have been paied 25 March. Jeames Nickolls 10s
which he hath in his handes of Andrew Hockes his monie.   4   5   0

Md owinge. Monyes by the towne which they are to pay
interest for since the last accompte.
To Mr Thomas Rayer alderman £17 10s 3d. To George
Noble chamberlaine 40s.

[Signature of] John Glover maior

Examined by me Edm. Hiorne

[f. 122v] George Noble is to be allowed for the rent of
Henry Whitesides house due at Michaelmas which he
did accompte for at this accompte   0   8   4

[Signature of] John Glover maior

So the whole due to George Noble at this accompte with
the saide 8s 4d[10]   5   12   5

[Signatures of] John Glover maior, Edm. Hiorne

21 December 1633. Md it is agreed upon at this accompte that
Mr Rayer shall have a newe lease of the wooll barne upon the
oulde covenantes at 24s a yeere rent half yeerely for tenn yeeres
to beginn at Our Lady Day next. The lease to be made at his
chardge. And he payed all rent due till Our Lady Day next.[11]

[Signature of] John Glover maior

Md at this accompte there was delivered to Thomas Woodward
chamberlaine 20s in mony which was receaved of Mr Rayer
for the rent of the woolbarne   0   20   0

[Signatures of] John Glover maior, Edmond Hiorne

[f. 123r] Md 21 December Jeames Nicholls and Henry
Neweberry were elected collectours for the poore for the
yeare followinge, at which tyme there was delivered to Jeames
Nickolls in reddy mony 2s 7d, and more they are to receive
5s of Mr John Glover maior which he hath in his handes
as received of John Sattin.

[Signatures of] John Glover maior, Edm. Hiorne

[f. 123v] [blank save for odd sums]

[1] Apprenticed to Thos. Woodward, mercer, in 1623: B 77/2.

[2] For Silver's misdoings see ibid. 27 May, 16 Oct. This fine was for refusing to assist the constable and was to be paid for the use of the poor.

[3] Of Bletchingdon, high sheriff in 1632, i.e. Mr. Shreeve: Davenport, *Lords Lieut.* 46.

[4] In 1632 John and Edm. Hiorne, sons and executors of Edm. Hiorne (d. 1629), paid the borough £5 'for the best profite for ever to the almeshouse poore people'. The money paid off a debt to Noble and thereafter 8s a year was to be given to the almshouse poor: P.R.O., PROB 11/156, f.86; B 81, f. 33r.

[5] In 1634 Laud, who had been in Woodstock in Aug. 1633, noted that the lectures had ceased at his urging because they were not performed properly: *Works*, ed. J. Bliss (Oxf. 1847), v. ii. 330; *Cal.S.P.Dom.* 1633–4, 197, 246. In 1638 he assured the king that potentially dangerous lectures by private persons in the royal chapel at Woodstock had been suppressed: *Works*, v. ii. 356. It is not clear whether they represented a new attempt. The lectures were resumed in 1641: see below.

[6] Chas. left Woodstock 28 Aug. to visit the queen, but returned from 2 to *c.* 7 Sept., when he moved to Rycote: *Cal.S.P.Dom.* 1633–4, 176, 180, 196; *Cal.S.P.Ven.* 1632–6, 137n, 43n.

[7] Anniversary of Chas. I's accession 27 Mar. 1625.

[8] Not a Woodstock official.

[9] The repair of St. Paul's was a favourite project of Laud's: *Cal.S.P.Dom.* 1631–33, 514. A brief with note of sums collected in 1636 is in O.R.O., Woodstock churchwardens' accts., p. 25.

[10] The town borrowed £5 12s 5d at this audit from Thos. Rayer to pay Noble. It now owed Rayer £24 10s 7d plus interest: B 81, f. 33v; and 1634 acct. below.

[11] Wm. Rayer sen. had left the lease of the woolbarn to his son Thos. in 1619: P.R.O., PROB 11/134, f. 75.

[f. 124r] 21 December 1633 to 22 December 1634, Thomas Woodward and Bennett Paynter, chamberlains

[Receipts]	£	s	d
Of Mr Thomas Doleman	8	0	0
Of Mr Thomas Rayer alderman interest	4	0	0
Of Thomas Heathen serjant at the mace for stallages	5	15	5
Of him for the standinges of the coountry bakers 12d a peece by the quarter	0	15	1
Of Edward Longe toleman for the tole	4	2	3
For the rentes of this boughroughe	25	6	6¼
[Interlined] Mr Rayer is to paye for the wooll barne 24s per annum the seconde payment to beginn at Our Lady Day 1635.			
Of Gabriell Shadd for the rente of the wooll beame for one whole yeare endinge at Michaelmas	0	24	0
Of Bennett Paynter and Thomas Heathen for the haye of Hampton leyes for this yeare sould to them by the chamberlaines	3	3	4
For 300 and a halfe of slattes sould	0	5	4
[f. 124v] Of Mr Thomas Williams alderman for the use of five powndes in his handes of Mr Vernons monye for one yeere endinge at Michaelmas	0	8	0
In reddy monye at the laste accompte	0	20	0

For sealinge monye since the last accompte. Of Walter Baylies
for the seale of his fine 4s,[1] James Nickolls [the like] 4s,[2]
Raphe Symons for the seale of his recoverie 4s. In toto   0 12 0
For the admission of freemen this yeere, Thomas Smith 20d,
Walter Pepper 20d, William Hickes baker 20d,[3] James Blunden
smith 20d, John Wingfeild tayler 50s, Edward Parratt 30s,
Thomas Hawten 30s   5 16 8

Summ totall of all the receiptes	60	8	6¼
Summ totall of all the disbursementes	59	0	6½
So remayninge due to the maior and cominaltie	26s wanting ¼		

[In latin] Cast up and examined by me Edmond Hiorne
common clerk of the maior and comminaltie of the aforesaid
borough

[f. 125r] [Disbursements]

Guiftes geiven at Christmas 1633.
For one cake 10s and one suger loffe 10s 2½d to
Sir Gerrard Fleetwood knight, in rewardes to his servantes
6s 6d. One cake sent to Sir Henry Browne knight 10s.
1 cake sent to Mr Lenthall our recorder 10s. A sugerloffe sent
to Mr Doctor Prideaux our parson 12s 11d. In rewardes to
Sir Henry Brownes servantes 12s 6d. In toto
[Deleted 59s 7½d]   3 11 6½

Stipendes and yeerely allowances.

To Mr Glover maior £5, Mr Meatcalfe £5	10	0	0
To Mr Chesterman £5 6s 8d for quitt rentes, 2 acquittances 2s, his paynes 2s.	5	10	8
To Mr Goldesboroughe undershreeve to Sir Peeter Meller knight[4] for fee farme 53s 4d, acquittance 6d	0	53	10
To William Lenthall esq our recorder his fee	3	6	8
To Edmond Hiorne towneclarke his fee [etc]	0	45	0
To Mr Newman schoolemaster his stipende	12	0	0
[f. 125v] To Mr Selfe for preaching of Mr Brownes twoe sermons on St Stephens Day and Easter day	0	16	0
To the poore people of the almeshouse 4s on Good Fryday, 4s on the Fryday before Christmas 1634, as interest of £5 geiven the towne by Mr Hiorns father to continue for ever	0	8	0
[Marginated sum £39 19s 9½d]			
Summ	37	0	2

Expences for reparations and other things in this yeere as
followeth. About the schoole. 7 hundred of slattes 8s 2d,
carriage 2s 6d, mosse 20d, 3 hundred of hart lath 3s, 2 bushells
of lyme 20d, 9 hundred of lath nayles 15d, 2 hundred of 4d
nayles 8d, 4 crestes 10d, pecke and halfe of slatt pynns 9d.
To the slatters 6s. One hundred of hart lath 12d, a hundred
of 4d nayles 4d, 3 hundred of lath nayles 5d, a bushell of lyme
10d, mosse 4d, slatt pynns 6d, slatters worke 5s.   0   34   11
Paide Mr Woodrooffe the messenger for his agreed fee
for this yeere endinge at Midsomer for bringinge of
proclamations   0   13   4
To 2 wardsmen at 4 faiers   0   5   4
Geiven to the clarke of the assises and to the judges cryer at
the 2 assises   0   8   8
Paide to Mr Mates[5] and John Slatter surveyers of the
highewayes for cartes to carry stoones to the highe wayes
and for men to attende them   0   13   6
For Raphe Lucas his coate and makinge. For 5 yardes of
woollen cloth at 2s 9d a yarde 13s 9d, stuffe to face and lyne his
capp 19d, making 2s.   0   17   4
To John Homes for draginge flagges out of the brookes at
the bayes   0   0   8
To Mr Glover maior 6s a quarter for three quarters ending
Michaelmas as geiven to poore people   0   18   0
[f. 126r] To twoe pore ministers at twoe severall tymes at
Mr Selfes request 12d a peece   0   2   0
Geiven in rewarde to the clarke of the markett Mr Gowin
Champnies 10 March   0   10   0
Expences at Mr Maiors house upon Mr Recorder, cownsellors
and neighbours at the fowre tryalls 18 March[6]   0   22   6
Spent upon the officers that came to searche about ould soape
12d.[7] For suger sent to Doctor Prideaux and his wife in
Februarie 2d.   0   0   14
16 August geiven to Mr Filpott, Somersett and Blewmantell,
messengers out of the Court of Harraldrie for settinge out our
towne armes 30s, to their clarkes 10s, in expences upon
them 22d[8]   0   41   10
Paide to Mistris Williams for Mr Doctor Hackwells dinner that
Doctor Prideaux sent to preache   0   2   6
To George Greene for clensinge the water course at the
holloway   0   0   18
To ould Anthonye for sweepinge the almeshowse chimnies   0   0   12

To John Symons for makinge the coockinge stoole and the
stockes 28 October 40s. To William Hickes for 8lb and a halfe
of iron worke at 4d a pownde about same 2s 10d and iron
worke about the stockes 12d.   0   43   10
Paied for expences upon fower witches that were sent from
London to goe into Lankesheir by the Kinges appoyntment
at the coontries chardge which is to be allowed back to the
towne at the next quarter sessions after Christmas 1634.[9]
As by the perticuler bill thereof appeereth   0   23   0
For a paier of gold wayes and scales to bee as a standarde
for the towne by the Kinges proclamation   0   10   0
To poor prisoners in Oxon' at Christmas 1634   0   2   0
For makinge a wainescott presse in the schoole to laye
bookes in   0   20   0
To Edward Silver for 1 locke and key for the litle house dore,
1 for the stockes, a hinge for the hale dore, a key for the stayer
foote dore in the halle   0   6   6

[f. 126v] Wyne geiven and spente by the towne this yeere.
Wine spent at Mr Recorders beinge heere at Castells and others tryalls and for
the neighbours to keepe him company 2s 6d.[10] To the man that invited the
towne to dinner to Sir Henry Browne 12d. [To preachers] 2 preachers the
Sonday after Christmas 1633 3s 4d, Mr Selfe on Newe Yeeres Day 12d, a
preacher 18 January 20d. Upon Mr Harborne of Tacklie in February 2s 4d,
Mr Woodruffe 11 February 6d. [For preachers] Mr Raunson 16 February 20d,
Mr Doctor Prideaux 23 February 3s 6d, a preacher 28 February 12d. To the
clarke of the markett 10 March 20d. Sent to the justices that sate about measures 17 March 2s 2d. [Preachers] Mr Greene 30 March 14d, Mr Selfe on
Easter Day 12d, Mr Doctor Prideaux 4 May 3s 10d. To Mr Fleetwood upon
the cominge home of the maypole 12d. [Preachers] Mr Higgins 1 June 18d,
Mr Smith 15 June 20d, Mr Doctor Prideaux 29 June 2s 8d, Mr Selfe 27 July
1633 [sic] 12d, Mr Doctor Prideaux 31 July 2s 4d. Spent upon the harrold at
armes and his clarkes 15 Auguste 3s. [Preachers] Mr Doctor Prideaux 24
Auguste 2s 6d, Mr Doctor Hacwell last of Auguste 2s 6d, Mr Hewes 27
September 10d, Mr Beesly 2s, Mr Squire 14 September 20d. To the justices
about apprenticing yonge children in September 20d.[11] [Preachers] Mr Mates
kinsman 20d, a precher 5 October 20d, Mr Blakeborne 12 October 20d, Mr
Selfe 19 October 12d, Mr Higgins 26 October 20d, Mr Channell and Mr
Durant 2 November 3s 8d. For wine spent at the bonefire 5 November 12d.
[Preachers] Mr Marshall 9 November 2s, a precher 22 November 6d, Mr Selfe
7 December 6d. To the justices sitting about mony for Paules Church in
London 9 December 20d.   3   10   8

[f. 127r] Summ totall of all the receiptes   60   8   6¹/₄
Summ totall of all the disbursementes   59   0   6¹/₂
So remayninge due to the maior and cominaltie   26s wanting ¹/₄d

[Signatures of] William Meatcalf maior, John Glover,
Joseph Harris, Thomas Rayer, Thomas Williams

[In latin] Cast up and examined by me Edmond Hiorne
common clerk of the mayor and cominaltie of the aforesaid
borough.

[f. 127v] Md 22 December 1634 due and owinge to the towne

Mr Thomas Williams for 6 buckettes in his handes 20s.
George Noble for 4 buckettes in his handes 13s 4d.
Mr Thomas Woodward chamberlaine hath in his handes
these severall monyes for buckettes for Thomas Smith,
Walter Pepper, William Hickes, James Blunden, John Wingefeild,
Edward Parratt and Thomas Hawten 3s 4d apeece, 23s 4d.

Debtes owinge to the towne 22 December 1634

For admission, John Powell 10s, Frauncis Collingwood 10s,
Richard Hamond 10s, Thomas Heddye 10s, William Locton
10s, John Patterick 5s, John Burgin 10s, James Nickolls of
Andrew Homes his mony 10s. Mr Thomas Williams oweth
£5 which he received of Mr Vernon and is to geive interest
for it from this day.

Monyes owinge by the towne

To Mr Rayer at the last accompte £17 10s 3d. Interest
thereof for this yeere 27s 11d. More Mr Rayer paide to George Noble at the
last accompte for the towne debt £5 12s 5d. The interest
thereof is 8s 10d. So due to him at this accompte £26 9s 9d.

[Signature of] Edmond Hiorne towneclarke

It was agreed that Gabriell Shadd shall have the woolbeame for
one yeere at Michaelmas last for 16s a yeere.

[Signatures of] Ed. Hiorne, William Meatcalfe maior

---

¹ For the dwelling in Woolmarket St: B 77/2, 30 May 1634.
² For the dwelling in Oxford St: ibid. 2 June.
³ Probably Wm. son of John Hickes of Milton, by apprenticeship to John Glover on 27 Oct. 1617:
ex. inf. Mrs. C. Schwarz.
⁴ Called Sir John Meller in P.R.O. Lists and Indexes, ix, *Sheriffs*.
⁵ Alternative spelling for Mayott in B 77/2, 22 Oct. 1634.

[6] See Castell's trials below.

[7] In 1632 Chas. gave a monopoly of soap manufacture to a company that used only Eng. ingredients. It was unpopular since everyone was to buy 'new soap' and not make 'ould soap' at home: *Cal.S.P.Dom.* 1633–4, 433; 1634–5, 144–5.

[8] The heralds met at the Bull and the mayor had been ordered beforehand to collect names: ibid. 1634–5, 187–8; and see *Oxon. Visitations*, ed. W.H. Turner (Harleian Soc. v, 1871): 'the mayor and magistrates...bore us company to their Church and from thence to their Guildhall and shewed us the Auntient Armes of their Towne and also their comon seale'.

[9] There were several investigations into the Lancs. witches in 1612 and the 1630s. These were sent to London and back: *Somers Tracts*, ed. Wal. Scott (2nd ed. Edinb. 1810), iii. 95sqq.

[10] For suits over Castell property see *Cal.S.P.Dom.* 1629–31, 388–9; ibid. 1637–8, 436. Castell was accused of killing a man while defending the premises.

[11] Possibly connected with justices' returns of child apprentices and their masters, a sequel to letters and orders *re* poor relief: *Cal.S.P.Dom.* 1634–5, 445; above in 1631.

[f. 128r] 22 December 1634 to 23 December 1635, Thomas Woodward and Bennett Paynter, chamberlains

[Receipts]	£	s	d
Of Mr Thomas Doleman	8	0	0
Of Mr Thomas Rayer alderman for interest	4	0	0
Of Thomas Heathen serjant at the mace for the stallages of this borowe for 3 quarters of a yeere endinge at Michaelmas	3	11	4
Of him for the contrie bakers standinges at the highe crosse, 3 quarters of a yeere after the rate of 12d a peece by the quarter	0	15	0
Of Roberte Longe deputy to Edward Longe his father late deceased for the tole of the beafe, sheepe and hogges sould within this borowe for 3 quarters of a yeere from St Thomas day till Michaelmas	0	38	3
Of the widdowe Longe for the rente of the corne markett for one quarter of a yeere from Midsomer till Michaelmas upon an agreement	0	10	0
Of John Dissell and William Edwardes for the tole of the cornemarkett and beafe markett for one quarter of a yeere from Michaelmas till St Thomas Daye	0	40	0
Rentes of this borowe for this yeere	25	15	5¹/₄
Of Gabrill Shadd for the rent of the wooll beame for one yeere endinge at Michaelmas	0	16	0
[f. 128v] Of Bennett Paynter for the haye of Hampton leyes for this yeere sould to him by the chamberlaines	4	0	0
Of Mr Thomas Williams alderman for the use of £5 in his handes of Mr Vernons monye for one yeere endinge at Michaelmas	0	8	0

For sealinge mony since the last accompte for Christofer Smithes seale 4s and for Robert Nurthes seale 4s	0	8	0
Of John Durbridge for the fyne imposed upon him for speakinge uncivill wordes against William Edwardes one of the comon cownsell	0	3	4
For the admission of freemen Edward Meatcalfe 20d, Bartholomew Love 20d, William Hitch 20d, John Williams 20d, William Wright 20d and Edward Carter 20d.	0	10	0
In reddie monye at the laste accompte	0	26	0
Of Mr William Meatcalfe maior for the relinquishinge of his bargaine of stallages and for the receipt of the tole of one markett day	5	0	0
Of John Dissell for stallages from Michaelmas till this accompte beinge one quarter	4	8	6
Of him for stallages of the coontry bakers from Michaelmas till St Thomas Day	0	4	0
Summ totall of the receiptes this yeere is	63	13	10
Summ of the disbursementes this yeere is	66	8	1
So remayninge due to the chamberlains	0	54	3

[In latin] Examined by me Edmond Hiorne common
clerk of the mayor and community of the aforesaid borough

[Signature of] Thomas Woodward, Bennett Painter chamberlains

[f. 129r] Disbursements]

Guiftes geiven at Christmas 1634.

One cake 10s and one suger loffe 13s 9d sent to Sir Gerrard Fleetwood knight and rewardes to his servantes 6s 6d. One cake sent to Mr Lenthall our recorder 10s. Rewardes to Sir Thomas Coghills servantes at Christmas when Mr Maior and the aldermen dyned there 11s 6d. Beere at the eatinge of the taste cakes 8d. Bread and beere spent at the accompte 14d. One cake 10s, 3 cheeses 3s sent to the cowntis of Sussex to Ditchly 7 Auguste. 1 cake 10s, one sugerloffe 15s 5d, 4 cheeses 4s 8d, sent to the lord chamberlaine 28 Auguste. One sugerloffe sent to Mr Doctor Prideaux 11s 2d. In toto	5	17	10

Stipendes and yeerely allowances.

To Mr Meatcalfe maior his stipend	10	0	0
To Mr Chesterman quitt rent £5 6s 8d, acquittance 12d, his paynes for 1 payment 12d	5	9	8
To Mr Frenche undershreeve to Sir Peeter Wentworth knight of the Bath for fee farme 53s 4d, acquittance 6d	0	53	10

To William Lenthall esq recorder his fee	3	6	8
To Edmond Hiorne townclark fee [etc]	0	45	0
To Mr Newman schoolemaster his stipende	12	0	0
To Mr Selfe for preachinge Mr Browne's twoe sermons	0	16	0
[f. 129v] Paied to the poore of the almeshouse this yeere, guifte of Edmond Hiorne deceased	0	8	0
Summ totall	36	19	2

Expences for reparations and other thinges laied out for the towne this yeere.

To Mr Maior for cloth for Lucas his coate 14s 10^{1}/2d, stuffe for the facinge of the capp and coate 19d, makinge of the coate and capp 2s	0	18	5^{1}/2
Geiven to the constables at Christmas 1634 for the poore of the towne	0	6	0
To John Cooper for carryinge 3 loades of stone to mende the holloway 18d, Huggins for the same stone 18d. To Thomas Huggins and John Kinge masons for 3 dayes worke apeece about same worke 6s. To Henry Hamonde for servinge the said masons 9d.	0	9	9
To 2 wardsmen at 4 faiers	0	5	4
For John Glovers shrewde	0	2	8

For expences upon the repayringe of the highe way at the mill and the woodden bridge over the holloway as followeth. To Wheeler and Bennett for sawinge the tymber for the bridge 2s, Mr Rayer for raylepostes 4s 6d, William Abbott for carriage of twoe loades of stone 12d. Mr Williams for tymber for the bridge and millwaye 45s. To Thomas Huggins for 2 loade of stones for the wooden bridge 12d, 2 dayes mason worke there 2s 4d, laborers to attende him 18d. More to him for 2 dayes worke about the bridge 2s 4d and a laborer to serve him 18d. To John Symons carpenter for 2 dayes worke about the bridge 2s 2d, his boy for 2 dayes worke 2s. To John Symons for 3 dayes worke 3s 6d, his sonne for 4 dayes worke 4s. Nayles for the bridge 7d. Beere to those that helped to carry the bridge 6d. To John Symons for 3 dayes worke 3s 6d, his sonne for 3 dayes 3s, Morgan to serve them 1 daye 9d. To Raph Hamond for 3 dayes worke and a halfe 2s 7^{1}/2d. To Raphe Lucas for 1 dayes worke 9d. To Bryan Steephens for a peece of tymber for the causeway 5s. To Mr Williams for 27 foote of planckes for same at 3d a foote 31s 9d. [f. 130r] To Thomas Heathen for 3 planckes of 31 foote and a halfe at 3d a foote for same 7s 10^{1}/2d. To John Symons for worke 3d, Lucas for 1 dayes worke then 9d, Barneshalle for 4 dayes worke 3s, Henry Hamond for 4 dayes worke 3s, Richard Homes for 2 dayes worke 18d. To Parratt for 3 greate pinns for the wooden bridge 4s, 4 pinns more for the planckes at the mill 16d. To Mr Jefferies for carryinge stones to the highe wayes 12s. To John Bonnam for busshinge the elmes at Mistris James her dore 8d. To Nedd Silver for a showle for Lucas 12d. To masons and laborers to mende the litle prison house 18d. For a buisshell of lyme 10d. To ould Griffyn Tymes for cordes for the towne scales 9s 5d, William Hickes for 2 newe hookes for same 8d. To Raphe Lucas for wardinge 10 dayes in the courte tyme 6s 8d, Anthony Deverill for wardinge 10 dayes more same tyme at 9d per dyem 7s 6d. To Mr Rayer for expences leid out at the eatinge of halfe a bucke sent by Mr Wattson 16s 11d. A rayle at the wooden bridge, nayles and workemanshipp 12d. To Lucas to clense the channell at the hall dore 6d. For mendinge the seller dore and for a newe staple and nayles 5d. For a staffe beesom for Lucas 3d. A planck to mende the cage 12d. Nayles and workemanshipp 7d. 3 loades carriage of stones to the almeshouse 18d. To Keates a mason for 5 dayes worke in the almeshouse 5s, a laborer to serve him 5 dayes 3s 4d. For busshinge the gapp at the woodden bridge 4d. To Keates the mason for 2 dayes worke about the causeway 2s 1d, his boy to serve him 10d. To John Symons for mendinge the almeshouse dores and sills 12d. For a hinge for the almeshouse dore 5d. For a key for the dore under the stayer in the guild hall 4d. To Lucas for his quarteridge for clensinge the channell at the hall dore 6d. Beere spent at the Bull upon a preacher 8 February 4d. Beere to the workemen about the holloway 4d. To George Greene for his stipend for 1 yeere endinge at Michaelmas 1635 for clensinge the water course in the holloway 18d. Paied Mr Mates for the quarteridge for the poore 18s. 19 September geiven to a pursephant 12d. For a booke for John Dissells accomptes 12d. Mr Rayer for the tryangle 20s 6d and for carriage thereof by water and land 2s 3d. 8 April to Mr Woodruffe the messenger for bringinge proclamations for 1 yeere endinge 24 June 13s 4d.

	20	4	4

[f. 130v] For sweepinge the almeshouse chimnyes	0	0	12
To Mr William Meatcalfe maior for and towardes his fees and expences at the Kinges Majesties beinge heere in progresse in August[1]	0	40	0
Paied Mr Hiorne as geiven in rewardes to the clarkes of the assises and to the cryers at the 2 assises this yeere	0	8	8
Geiven to Mr Walker the clarke of the markett of the Kinges housholde at the Kinges beinge heere 10s, his man 2s, beere upon them 6d	0	12	6
Geiven to Mr Champnies clarke of the markett throughe the realme of England 17 January 10s, in rewarde 9 December 10s	0	20	0
To prisoners at Oxon' 15 December	0	2	0
For expences at Oxon' when Mr Rayer and I Edmond Hiorne went to Oxon' to pay the quitt rent upon the auditors firste proclamation	0	0	22
For nayles for the almeshouse 1 1/2d. To Humbard of Hampton for a levy to the churche there 6s. To Mr Maior for a shrewde for the blackamore wenche 2s 6d.	0	8	7 1/2

Wyne geiven and spent by the towne this yeere.

To Mr Fleetwood when he came to invite the maior and aldermen to diner at Christmas 1635 6d. The justices that sate about victulers and apprentices 20d. Sir Thomas Coghills man when he came to invite the towne to dinner at Christmas 1634 6d. [Preachers] Mr Higgins 4 January 13d, Mr Channell the same day 10d, Mr Bird 18 January 18d. Mr Champnies the clarke of the markett 17 January 12d. Spent at the eatinge of the taste cakes 12d. Mr Woodruffe the Kinges messenger 6d. Mr Smarte that preched heere 22d, Mr Selfe 1 March 6d. The justices that sate heere 10 March about recognizances for dressinge of flessh 12d. Mr Doctor Prideaux that preched 15 March 4s 2d and a prechere 22 March that came with Mr Durant 16d. Mr Justice Joanes at Mr Merrickes lodge 23 March 3s 6d, and the justices about the same tyme 20d. Mr Doctor Souche 2 April 12d. Mr Hobbs that preched 5 April 20d. 8 April upon Mr Woodrooffe the Kinges messenger 6d. Mr Trescott that preched 12 Aprille 12d. Mr Selfe 17 May 6d.

[f. 131r] [Preachers] Mr Doctor Prideaux 19 Aprille 3s 8d, a gente of Brasenose Colledge in the afternoone, Mr Selfe on the precession day 6d, Mr Durant last of May 12d. Upon servantes that came for a certificate against the Kinges Majesties cominge to Woodstock 23d. [Preachers] Mr Fleetwood 7 June 12d, Mr Bowman 14 June, Mr Bennett same day 3s 4d, Mr Doctor Prideaux 21 June 1632 [sic] 2s 2d. Upon the justices 23 June 1635 20d, Mr Craddocke the clarke of the assise 27 June 3s 8d. [Preachers] Mr John Hodges 29 June 20d, Mr Selfe 5 July 7d, Mr Higgins 19 July, Mr Selfe 26 July 6d. Mr Justice Joanes that dyned at Mr Merrickes lodge 27 July 3s 6d. Mr Flower that preched 9 August 14d. Mr Newton the Kinges Majesties gentleman ussher and other the Kinges servantes in wine and suger at the Kinges beinge heere 8d. Mr Recorder at his cominge to the towne at the Kinges last beinge heere 16d. Mr Rennolls that preched 13 September 20d. Mr Smith a messenger that brought proclamations 19 September 6d. Mr Merrideth that preched 20 September 20d, Mr Attland 11 October 20d. Mr Lynn the Lord of Danbies gentleman that came to search after Nicholas Aynchcombe 12d. A messenger that brought proclamations 10 November 3d. The Kinges Majesties players 22 November 7d. The highe shreeves man that came about the payment of the Kinges Majesties sheepe mony 4d.[2] Mr Fox that preched 13 December 20d, Mr Twitty preachinge 20 December 20d.   3   6   9

Summ totall of the disbursementes	66	8	1
Summ totall of the receiptes	63	13	10
So remayninge due to the chamberlains	0	54	3

[In latin] Examined by me Edmond Hiorne common clerk of the mayor and cominaltie of the aforesaid borough

[Signatures of] Thomas Woodward, Bennett Painter

[f. 131v] A true note of all such buckettes as are due to the towne at this accompte 23 December 1635

Mr Thomas Williams alderman hath monye in his handes for sixe buckettes 20s 10d, Mr George Noble for fower buckettes 13s 4d. Mr Thomas Woodward at the last accompte for seaven buckettes 23s 4d. Since he hath received monye for sixe buckettes which he is to bringe in unto the guilde hall 20s, for Edward Meatcalfe, John Williams, William Hitch, Edward Carter, William Wrighte, Bartholomew Edginge. 22 newe buckettes are to be brought in.

Md at this accompte 23 December 1635 Mr Williams brought in 3 newe buckettes at 3s 4d a peece, so in his handes in mony 10s. 4 newe buckettes are brought in which George Noble is to pay for, 13s 4d.

[Signatures of] William Meatcalfe maior, Thomas Woodwarde, Edm. Hiorne

[f.132r] A note of debtes due to the towne at this accompte 23 December 1635

John Powell 10s, Frauncis Collingwood 10s, Richard Hamond 10s, Thomas Heddie 10s, William Locton 10s, John Patterick 5s, John Burgin 10s, James Nickolls 10s. Henry Whiteside for rent of his house for twoe yeeres endinge at Michaelmas 8s 4d.
[Entry crossed through] Mr Thomas Williams alderman oweth £5 which he received of Mr Vernon for the towne and which he is to paye interest for towardes Mr Brownes sermon monye. [Marginated] Payed.

*Md the towne owe*d to Mr Thomas Rayer alderman at the last accompte 22 December 1634 £26 9s. 9d. The interest thereof for this yeere endinge at this accompte 23 December is 42s 4d. So there is due to him at this accompte £28 12s 1d. Allso to Mr Woodward £3 7s 4d. [Marginated] Payed.

Debtes owinge for rentes

For Raphe Bradshewes rentes 2s 1d. For Mr Sayes house in the Sheepesstreet 5s. For Mistris Wittnyes house 5s 1/2d. John Dissell is paied 7s 6d for his wages for St Thomas Dayes quarter.

[Signature of] William Meatcalfe maior

It was agreed at this accompte that Gabrill Shadd shall have the wooll beame at 8s rent from Michaelmas 1635 till Michaelmas 1636.

[Signatures of] William Meatcalfe maior, Thomas Woodward, Edmond Hiorne

---

[1] The king was at Woodstock c. 20 Aug.–2 Sept.: *Cal.S.P.Dom.* 1635, 330, 360, 365.
[2] Ship money was extended in 1634 and writs sent to corporate towns. Recs. of Woodstock's payments and of assessments of 70 townsfolk made 26 Sept. 1635 are in B 96, ff. 45 sqq.: Hiorne noted the money was paid within a month. Woodstock's £20 assessment was the lowest in Oxon. The

second payment, in 1636, was delayed in hope of a £5 abatement. At a meeting of corporate towns in 1637 Woodstock was rated at £15. It was reckoned 'backward' in payment that year: *Cal.S.P.Dom.* 1636–7, 494, 511.

[f. 132v] 16 March 1635[/6].[1]

There is remaining in the guildehall threescore and twelve buckettes in the chardge of John Dissell the cryer of the courte, 72 buckettes in the hall.

Mr Williams alderman hath 10s and Mr Thomas Woodward alderman 43s 4d of monyes in theire handes for buckettes yet to be brought in into the hall which monyes are ordered and appoynted by the maior and cominaltie to be ymployed for the buyinge of newe ladders and scalinge poles and irons for the use of the towne 16 March. For buckettes 53s 4d.

It is agreed upon this 16 March that the chamberlaines shall repayre the towne hall and almeshouse and the holloway this sumer at the towne chardge.

It is ordered that the leaes at Hampton Poyle shallbe demised by lease for 10 yeeres to such as will geive most for it.

It is agreed upon this 16 March that Lucas shall ympownde all the hogges that shall be fownde upon the markett hill upon the markett dayes heereafter and that he shall take a peny for everie hogge that he shall ympownde from thence or in any other parte of the streetes.

16 March due to Nicholas Mayott constable upon this accompte taken at the guild hall   0 55 3
To George Gregorie upon his accompte due at Michaelmas   0 6 6
For which monyes a levy was made at the hall for payment thereof.

[Signatures of] William Meatcalfe maior, Thomas Rayer, Thomas Woodward, Edmond Hiorne

[f. 133r] 23 December 1635 to 22 December 1636, Bennett Paynter and Robert Lee, chamberlains

[Receipts]	£	s	d
Of Mr Thomas Doleman	8	0	0
Of Mr Thomas Rayer alderman for interest	4	0	0
Of John Dissell and William Edwardes for the rent of the tole markett[2]	8	0	0
Of John Dissell for the standinges of the coontrie bakers at the highe crosse	1	7	0
Of John Dissell for stallages for one yeere	14	6	7
Rentes of this boughroughe	25	15	5¼
Of Gabriell Shadd for rentes of the wooll beame	0	8	0

Of Mr Rayer alderman for faggottes and wood sould him from the almeshouse this yeere	0	12	0
For morter sould upon the repayringe of the towne hall	0	0	3
Of John Fox pewterer for his admission	2	10	0
For his buckett	0	3	4
For a sorrell gealdinge sould unto him by the towne which was a waife	2	10	0
Of Wakefeilde for stones sould him	0	0	10
[f. 133v] Allowed for stones which I had my selfe	0	0	4
Of John Wakefeilde for the seale of the fine for the house which he bought of Mr Noble	0	4	0
Of Mistris James widdowe for woode and chipps sould to her upon the buildinge of Mr James his late dwellinge house	1	0	0
Of Thomas Paynter for the goodes and apparell of Mr Nicholas Ainshcombe sould unto him which fledd upon suspicion of felonye	0	7	0
Of Mr William Meatcalfe late maior for a fyne of 10 yeeres of Hampton leyes nowe lately demised unto him for tenn yeeres from Our Lady day 1636 at a 1d a yeere rent	18	0	0
Summ totall of all the receiptes	87	4	9½

[Signatures of] Bennet Painter, Robert Lee junior, chamberlains

[In latin] By me Edmond Hiorne common clark of the mayor and cominaltie of the aforesaid borough

[f. 134r] [Disbursements]

Payed for guiftes and rewardes geiven at Christmas 1635 as by the particulers may appeere in a booke under Mr Leyes hande	5	9	3
For stipendes and anuall allowances for this yeere endinge at Michaelmas 1636	36	19	2
For expences and reperations upon the towne hall, the schoolemasters house, the almeshouse, the highewayes and divers other necessarie thinges for the towne. Allso for other guiftes and rewardes.	35	15	1
For wine geiven and bestowed to divers persons for the townes use and by theire appoyntment for this yeere	4	12	2
Summ totall of all the disbursementes	82	16	8
Summ totall of the receiptes this yeere is	87	4	9½
So due to the towne upon this accompte is	4	8	0½

[Signatures of] Bennet Painter, Robert Lee junior, chamberlains, Thomas Rayer maior, Thomas Woodward, George Noble

Written and examined by me Edmond Hiorne towneclark of the saide boughroughe

[f. 134v] Md at this accompte Mistris Williams paied in £5 10s which her husband payd and owed to the towne[3]

Md James Nickolls was by Mr Thomas Rayer elected junior chamberlain for this yeere to come

Md the towne oweth to Mr Rayer only £24 which he is to have interest for from this day.

There remains in the churchwardens handes Henry Newbery and Gabrill Shadd to be presently bestowed upon the poore £2 13s 2d which was geathered at the church dore in the faste tyme 1636 besides the first dayes collection beinge 12s 1d which was geiven to the poore.[4]

Md Mistris James payed to Mr Newman parcell of her composition mony of forty shillinges,[5] 20s at Midsomer last and 20s at this accompte which the towne receaved beinge parcell of the 40s which Mr Lee payed unto him the saide Mr Newman for the townes mony. So Mr Newman received 20s more of Mistris James then he ought to have and the towne is receaved more 20s parcell of the £4 payed by Mr Lee chamberlain. The rentes owinge to the towne are in the ledger booke in the chest.

John Bignill promiseth to procure a sufficient surety in Kempsters behalf before Twelfeth Day after Christmas next or else to have the bonde to be put in suite.

Md noe mony was delivered to the chamberlains at this accompte.

Md Mr Rayer receaved of John Bignill 16s for interest mony and from John Norman 16s for interest mony. And Mr William Meatcalfe received of John Norman for interest mony 8s. So all interest paied from him till 6 November 1636[6]   0   40   0

[Signatures of] Thomas Rayer maior, Thomas Woodward, George Noble

---

[1] Rec. of a council meeting: see above, Intro. Constables' accts. were supposed to be made before quarter sessions.

[2] A new arrangement: see above, Intro. Dissell, who also succeeded Longe as cryer of the court, and Edwardes evidently tendered for them and the stallages in the last quarter of 1635: see above.

[3] See above in 1635. The chamberlains were now to pay £5 for Browne's sermons: B 81, f. 35r. The 10s was for three buttons Williams owed the town, presumably money he owed in Mar. 1636 above; the buttons were perhaps for the buckets: ibid.

[4] Proclamation 18 Oct. 1636 for a weekly fast in time of plague: *Stuart Proclams.* ii, no. 229.

[5] See settlement below in 1638 and 1639.

[6] Perhaps from town money out at loan.

[f. 135r] **22 December 1636 to 22 December 1637, Bennett Paynter and James Nickolls, chamberlains**

[Receipts]	£	s	d
Of Mr Thomas Doleman	8	0	0
Of Mr Thomas Rayer alderman for interest	4	0	0
Of John Dissell and William Edwardes for the rent of the tole markett	8	0	0
Of John Dissell for the standinges of the coontrie bakers at the highe crosse	1	4	0
Of John Dissell for stallages	14	4	0
Rentes of this boughroughe [total corrected in ms]	26	4	7
For the admission of freemen, Phillip Smith 40s, Peeter White 10s, Thomas Screevin[1] 20d, Roberte Flye 40s, Roberte Cooper 40s.	6	11	8
[f. 135v] Of Curtis the miller for ould broken tymber sould him by the chamberlains	0	7	0
Of Gabriel Shad for rent of the wooll beame	0	8	0
Summ totall of all the receiptes	68	19	3
Summ totall of all the disbursementes	75	1	6
Soe remayninge due to the chamberlains	6	2	3

[totals corrected in MS.]

This was cast upp by Mr George Noble

[Signatures of] George Noble, Edmond Hiorne towneclarke, Bennet Painter [and blank] chamberlaines

[f. 136r] *[Disbursements]*

Guiftes geiven at Christmas and at other tymes this yeere.
For 1 cake for Sir Gerrard Fleetwood 10s, 1 suger loffe
11s 8d, and in rewardes to his servantes 7s. 1 cake to Sir
Henry Browne knight 10s, rewardes to his servantes 14s.
A cake to Mr William Lenthall our recorder at Christmas
1636 10s. 1 cake and 4 cheeses to Sir William Fleetwood
knight 16s,[2] 1 cake to my Lord of Holland 15s, to
Mr Justice Joanes 1 cake 10s, 9 cheeses to them both 15s,
2 sugerloves to them both at the justice in eyres seate in
August 35s 6d. One sugerloffe to Doctor Prideaux at
Christmas 1636 13s 5d. To my Lord of Hollandes[3]
trumpiters at the saide justice seate 10s. To my Lord of
Hollandes footemen in wine 5s 4d, mony 5s. In rewardes
to Mr Gregories servantes at Christmas 1636 when Mr Maior
and the neighbours dyned there 5s 6d.

| | 9 | 13 | 5 |

Stypendes and yeerely allowances

To Mr Rayer maior his stipend	10	0	0
To Mr Chesterman for quitt rent £5 6s 8d, 2 acquittances 2s, his paynes 12d	5	9	8
To Mr Lodwicke Harris undershreeve to William Walter esq for fee farme rent 53s 4d, acquittance 6d	2	13	10
[f. 136v] To Mr Lenthall esq recorder his fee	3	6	8
To Edmond Hiorne townclark fee [etc]	2	5	0
To him as geiven in rewardes to the clarke of the assises and to the cryer and clarkes 4s 4d at eache assises	0	8	8
To Mr Newman and Mr Ringe[4] schoolemasters for theire stipende	12	0	0
To Mr Selfe for preachinge Mr Brownes twooe sermons	0	16	0
To the poor of the almeshouse, by guifte of Edmond Hiorne deceased	0	8	0
To 2 wardsmen at 4 faiers	0	5	4
To Mr Champnies the clarke of the markett as a rewarde upon his cominge at Michaelmas 10s	0	10	0
To Mr Woodruffe the messenger for his annuall stipend for this yeere endinge at Midsomer for bringinge of proclamations	0	13	4
To Raphe Lucas for sweepinge the towne gutters for this yeere endinge at Christmas and one quarter over 2s 6d and for 2 beesoms 6d	0	3	0
[f. 137r] To George Greene for clensinge the holloway gutterto the bayes for this yeere endinge at Michaelmas	0	1	6
To Phillipp Anthony for sweepinge the almeshouse chimnyes	0	1	0
To John Dissell for his fee for geatheringe of the stallage mony for one yeere endinge at this accompte	1	10	0
To Thomas Heathen serjant for his annuall stipend for the stallage monye of twoe fayers yeerely to be payed to the serjant yeerely for ever heere after	1	10	0
Summ	42	2	0

The chardge of the repaire of the highewaye at the mill.

To William Wheeler and a laborer to sett upp postes and rayles at the said way and for nayles for same 5d.	0	2	5
To Anthony Deverill for makinge cleane the holloway	0	0	10
To Steephen Damerye for makinge upp the parke wall that was pulled down to fetch stones out of the parke	0	1	6
To the laborers that digged stones for Mr Whitton in lewe of the stones the towne had in the parke for this worke	0	9	10
To Mr Jefferies for the carriage of stone and morter out of the parke for this worke	4	8	0
To James Gearlinge of Wootton for the like	0	15	0

To Mr Rayer maior for greate rugged stones for same	0	13	4
To the laborers for servinge the masons and to the workemen for mendinge the saide waye	2	5	10
To the same laborers for digginge of stones and rubbell and mendinge the saide waye	1	5	4
To same for fynnishinge of the saide causewaye	2	12	1
Summ totall	12	14	2

[f. 137v] Expences and disbursementes for the towne.

For cloth to make Lucas his coate and capp 18s 2d and for the makinge of it 2s 4d	1	0	6
To souldiers by Mr Hiorns appoyntment	0	0	4
Geiven to a Jerman [German] by Mr Maiors appoyntment	0	2	0
For firinge at the last accompte	0	1	6
To Prissilla Barnaby for wasshinge the towne buckettes	0	0	6
To a souldier by Mr Hiornes appoyntment	0	0	6
To a mason for mendinge upp the almeshouse wall	0	2	6
To Allexander Johnson and Mathewe Penn constables for twoe paymentes to the house of correction and for maymed souldiers	1	4	0
To John Symons for tymber, workemanshipp, nayles in settinge upp the benches at the greate elme	0	5	2
To a souldier by Mr Hiornes appoyntment	0	0	4
To a laborer for throwinge upp mudde at Mr Lees maulthouse	0	0	6
To Mr Jeffery for bringinge of stones out of Ouldwoodstock feildes into our highweayes by the surveyors appoyntment	0	6	0
And to William Abbott for the like	0	5	0
To a messenger that brought 5 severall proclamations against Sturbridge fayer[5]	0	2	0
To John Winckfeild for geivinge notice to the neighbors to clense the street against the justice seate	0	0	6
For 3 laborers to fill the dung cartes at the justice seate	0	2	0
Towardes repaireinge of the highe way in Stowe woode	1	10	0
[f. 138r] To a souldier by Mr Hiorns appoyntment	0	0	6
To Thomas Screevin for mendinge the schoolehouse wyndowes	0	9	0
For bread geiven to the poore on 5 November last by Mr Abrames appoyntment[6]	0	1	4
To the prisoners in Oxforde goale at Christmas 1636	0	2	0
For slatt, lyme and workemanshipp in mendinge of the slattes of the towne office	0	2	6
For mendinge the key of the schoole house dore	0	0	3
For a booke for the faste[7]	0	1	0
To Richard Huggins for mendinge the walle in the hollowaye	0	1	8
To prisoners of Oxon' at Christmas 1637	0	2	0

For firewood at this accompte	0	2	0
To Silver for 2 keyes for the schoole house	0	2	6
Summ	6	4	1

A note of wyne geiven and spent by the towne 1637. [For sermons] to Mr Warren 10 February 2s 2d, Mr Mason 18 February 1s 6d, Mr Selfe 20 March 1s. To a messenger that brought proclamations 5 March about the kinges evill 6d. To the justices 7 March 1s 8d. [For sermons] Mr Doctor Prideaux 12 March 2s 4d, a preacher 7 March 6d, Mr Doctor Potter 1s 11d, Mr Chapman 1s 8d, Mr Channell 26 March 10d, a preacher of Newe Inne 2 April 1s 8d. To the justices 11 April 1s 8d. [For sermons] Mr Langlie 23 Aprile 1s 7d, Mr Doctor Prideaux 7 May 2s 11d, Mr Holland same day 10d, Mr Selfe 21 May 11d, Mr Hollandes brother 28 May 1s 10d. To Mr Woodruffe the messenger 7d. [f. 138v] Upon Mr Throgmorton the recever of the Kinges rentes for the cowntie of Oxon' 11d. [For sermons] Mr Knightbridge 25 June 1s 8d, Mr Cooper 9 July 1s 3d. Upon the justices 11 July 1s 10d. Mr Chapman for his sermon 16 July 2s 2d. Upon Sir Gerard Fleetwoodes man that brought upp the pullpitt cloth and cussion, which his lady gave to the church 1s 4d.[8] Mr Selfe for his sermon 23 July 2s. Mr Pawlin the messenger for bringinge the proclamations 23 July 6d. A preacher of Universitie Colledge for his sermon 30 Auguste 3s. A messenger that brought proclamations to putt of Bartholomew's fayer 4d. Upon Mr Justice Joanes that laye at Mr Merrickes lodge 8 Auguste 3s 6d. Upon Mr Doctor Prideaux that preched 6 Auguste and dyned with Mr Branthwaites 6d.[9] Upon Mr Lenthall our recorder 1 September 2s 6d. To a messenger 21 Auguste 6d, another messenger 27 Auguste 10d. Sir William Fleetwoodes kinsmen, freendes and servantes at his firste cominge to the Lodge 2s 6d. [Sermons] 3 September 1s 7d, Mr Chapman 10 September 2s 8d. One of my Lord of Hollandes gentlemen 18 September 6d. The clarke of the markett by Mr Glovers and Mr Hiorns appoyntment 19 September 2s. Upon 2 of the Lord of Hollandes gentlemen 2 dayes before the lordes cominge 1s 8d. Mr Seely one of the clarkes of the assises about the same tyme 10d. Mr Lenthall at the tyme of his beinge at the justice seate 2s 6d. [f. 139r] [Sermons] a preacher 7 October 1s 8d, a preacher 15 October 10d, Mr Doctor Prideaux 19 November 3s 2d, Mr Warren 3 December 2s 5d. Mr Walford in wine, beere and suger at 3 severall meetinges 3s 10d. Mr Fleetwood when he came to invite Mr Maior and the neighbors at Christmas 1636 9d. Sir Henry Brownes man for the like service 6d. Mr Woodrooffe the messenger 30 December 1636 6d. [Sermons] Mr Mason 6 January 1636[/7] 1s 10d, Mr Chaplyn and Mr Mason 2 sermons 6 January 2s 6d. Spent at the eatinge of the taste cake 2s 4d. Summ   4   3   10

Summ totall of the receiptes this yeere is	68	19	3
Summ totall of all the disbursementes	75	1	6
So remayninge due to the chamberlains	6	2	3
[all sum totals corrected in MS.]			

This was cast upp by Mr George Noble

[Signatures of] George Noble, Edmond Hiorne towneclarke, Bennet Painter [and blank] chamberlaines

Bennett Paynter hath in his handes 16s 8d for 5 buckettes this yeere receaved, for Phillipp Smith, Peeter White, Thomas Screevin, Roberte Cooper, and Roberte Flye   0   16   8

[f. 139v] Md the chamberlains were paied at this accompte theire £6 2s 3d. And the towne oweth to Mr Rayer £32 7d which he is to be allowed interest for from this day. So owing to Mr Rayer   32   0   7

Debtes owing to the towne

From John Powell 10s, Richard Hamond 10s, Thomas Headdy 10s, William Locton 10s, John Burgin 10s.

[Signatures of] Thomas Rayer maior, John Glover, William Meatcalfe, Thomas Woodward, George Noble, aldermen, Edmond Hiorne towneclarke

[1] White, son of Jerome White, was apprenticed in 1612 to Ric. Philipps, weaver: ex inf. Mrs. C. Schwarz. Screevin was son of Thos. Screevin (d. 1637), glazier: MS. Wills Oxon. 86/1/30.
[2] Nephew of Sir Gerard Fleetwood, whom he succeeded this year at High Lodge as keeper, later ranger, of Woodstock park: *V.C.H. Oxon. xii.* 440, 447; *Hist. of Parl., House of Commons 1660–90*, ed. B.D. Henning (London 1983), ii. 331.
[3] Hen. Rich, earl of Holland, Chief Justice in Eyre south of the Trent, 1631–49: *D.N.B.*
[4] Thos. Ringe, appointed this year.
[5] Sturbridge fair in Cambridge and St. Bartholomew's fair in London were not held this year because of plague: *Stuart Proclams.*, ii, nos. 242, 245.
[6] Gift of Wm. Meatcalfe (d. 1608): see appendix, biogs.
[7] See above in 1636. Fasting was overseen by civic authorities in Stuart Eng. and recognizances on the sale of beer, ale, and meat returned to the Exchequer.
[8] The churchwardens accounted from now on for a velvet cushion and pulpit cloth, possibly a memorial gift since in 1635 they paid 6s 8d 'for breaking ground in the church to burye my Lady Fleetwood': O.R.O., Woodstock churchwardens' accounts.
[9] Ric. Brainthwaite of Ringwood (Hants.), father-in-law of Sir Thos. Spencer (d. 1622) and guardian of his children: Stapleton, *Three Oxon. Parishes*, 288-90.

[f. 140r] **22 December 1637 to 21 December 1638, Bennett Paynter and James Nickolls, chamberlains**

[Receipts]   £   s   d

Of Mr Thomas Doleman   8   0   0
Of Mr Thomas Rayer alderman for interest   4   0   0

Of William Edwardes and John Dissell for the rent of the tole markett	8	0	0
Of John Dissell for the standinges of the coontrie bakers at the highe crosse	1	6	0
Of John Dissell for stallages	11	4	8
Rentes of this boughroughe	26	4	7
[f. 140v] Of Gabriell Shadd for rent of the wooll beame	0	8	0
Of Mr Chadwell executor to Mr John Chadwell deceased £10 which he gave to the towne by his last will[1]	10	0	0
Summ totall of the receiptes this yeere is	69	3	3
Summ totall of the disbursementes this yeere is	78	6	6½
So remayninge due to the chamberlains	9	3	3½

[Signature of] Bennet Painter

Cast up by me Edmond Hiorne townclark

[f. 141r] [Disbursements]

Guiftes and rewardes geiven at Christmas and other tymes this yeere. 1 cake to Sir William Fleetwood knight 14s. 2 cakes to Mr Branthaite, one at Christmas of 14s, the other about Shrovetide of 8s, £1 2s. 1 cake to Mr Lenthall recorder at Christmas 14s, 1 cake to Sir Henrye Browne knight 14s, 1 cake to Sir Henrye Lee knight 14s. 1 cake to Sir William Spencer knight at his comminge into the coontrie about Easter laste 12s. 1 cake to my lord chamberlaine our highe steward at the Kinges beinge last at Woodstock 16s, a sugerloffe of 15s 6d, 6 cheeses of 6s, £1 17s 6d. 1 cake sent to Mr Tayler of the Midle Temple (clarke of the parcells) about Michaelmas last 15s, carriage to Morgan 3s 4d, the hoope and packthredd to bynde it to John Pepper 12d, 19s 4d. Geiven at Christmas laste to Sir Henry Brownes servantes 13s 6d, Mr Brainthaites servantes 8s, Mr Gregories servantes 5s 6d, Sir Henry Lees servantes 18s 6d, 1 sugerloffe to Doctor Prideaux 10s 6d. Summ

10	2	10

[f. 141v] Stipendes and yeerely allowances.

To Mr Thomas Rayer maior his stipend and allowaunce half yeere	5	0	0
To Mr Woodward [the like]	5	0	0
To Mr Rayer for the chauntery quitt rent for 1 halfe yeere endinge at Our Lady Day 53s 4d, acquittance 12d. Mr John Cole [the same] endinge Michaelmas.	5	8	8
To Mr John Ecles baylife under Mr Peeter Langston, undershreeve to Sir Thomas Peniston knight fee farme 53s 4d, acquittance 7d	2	13	11

To Mr Lenthall esq recorder fee	3	6	8
To Edmond Hiorne townclark fee [etc]	2	5	0
To him as geiven in rewardes to the clarke of the assises, cryers and clarkes, 4s 4d at each assises	0	8	8
To Mr Ringe schoolemaster stypende	12	0	0
To Mr Selfe preachinge twoe sermons for Mr Browne	0	16	0
To the poore people of the almeshouse, guifte of Edmond Hiorne deceased	0	8	0
[f. 142r] To twoe wardsmen on fowre faiers	0	5	4
To Mr Champnies deputie, the clarke of the markett, as a rewarde upon his cominge to sitt heere about Michaelmas	0	10	0
To Mr Woodrooffe a messenger for his stipend for this yeere endinge at Midsomer 13s 4d for bringinge of proclamations, a pynte of sacke 7d	0	13	11
To Raphe Lucas for clensing the towne gutters in the streetes for this yeere endinge at Christmas 6d a quarter 2s, and 1 quarter over and behinde in Mr Roberte Lees yeere 6d [1636]	0	2	6
To George Greene for clensinge the gutter at Mr Sayes gate to Mr Sayes puttgallye for this yeere endinge at Michaelmas	0	1	6
To Phillipp Anthony for sweepinge the chimnyes in the almeshouse for this yeere endinge at Christmas	0	1	0
To John Dissell for his stypend for this yeere endinge at St Thomas Day 1638 for geatheringe of the towne stallage monye	1	10	0
To Thomas Heathen the serjant for his annual stipende agreed upon to be paied to the serjant heereafter for ever for the stallages of his 2 faiers which heeretofore the serjant had for Mary Magdalen fayer and St Nicholas fayer	1	10	0
Summ	42	1	2

[f. 142v] Accedentall expences and paymentes in this yeere for the towne endinge at this accompte.

To William Randall for one day for carryinge of stones for the highewayes	0	5	0
For glasing work about the schoolehouse windowes	0	1	2
For Winckfeildes staffe which is to be for the tythingmens use	0	0	6
For one newe booke of assise remaining in the office	0	1	0
To Duke[2] to goe to Wootton to informe the towne of Wootton to prevent the cominge of one suspectede to be sick of the plauge	0	0	2
Mendinge of the towne scales which the tasters use	0	0	6
By Mr Woodwardes appoyntment now maior to goe into the coontry to fetch 2 coontry busshells	0	0	5

At the Bull 2 December for beere spent upon Mr Doctor Prideaux that came to preach	0	0	6
By Mr Rayers appoyntment for the newe matting of the maior and aldermans seates in the church	0	5	0
To Mr Andrewe Pollee a messenger that came about the busines of the clarke of the parcells	0	6	8
To one souldier 4d, 3 souldiers 6d	0	0	10
To Mr Meatcalfe for 3 yardes and a halfe of cloth for Lucas coate and coate [? cap] 17s, makinge 2s 4d.	0	19	4
For expences upon Mr Chadwell at his coming to the towne to pay Mr John Chadwells £10 which he gave to the towne	0	3	0
To Richard Newell to goe with a lettre to Mr Recorder for the towne	0	1	0
13 December to Mr Frauncis Gregorie for takinge out of a coppie of Mr Richard Nassh his will, whoe gave £100 to the towne: £20 for one sermon to be preached yeerely in Woodstocke church for ever, £80 to be lent to poore tradsmen and inhabitantes of Woodstocke gratis.[3]	0	12	0
[f. 143r] In August at the Kinges beinge at Woodstocke,[4] to Mr Walker clarke of the markett of the Kinges housould as a rewarde to him 10s and to his man for a coppy of the rates 2s.	0	12	0
To Mr Rayer maior for expences in entertaynement of Mr William Lenthall our recorder about Easter last and neighbors to beare him companie to bee advised in the schoolehouse busines and other towne affaiers	1	0	0
To John Pepper for a newe busshell for the markett place 2s 4d and for the ironworke about it 12d.	0	3	4
To Gyles Francklyn for settinge upp the dore in the lower halle and other worke there donn for the towne	0	1	0
To Mr Rayer maior £6 out of Mr John Chadwells £10 sent from the towne as a guifte to Mr Lenthall our recorder against his readinge in Lincolns Inn in Lent laste	6	0	0
To Mr Ringe schoolemaster of the free grammer schoole in Woodstocke for the rent of Mistris James her house in Woodstock for St Thomas Dayes quarter 20s, for Our Ladie Dayes quarter 20s, which she ought to have payed by her agreement 40s and she is to pay 20s a quarter from thence so longe as she dwelleth there	2	0	0
To Mr Dodsworthes man for the keepers fee for the bucke which my lord chamberlaine gave to the towne at the Kinges beinge at Woodstocke in August last 10s and for his mans paynes 12d	0	11	0
To the prisoners at Oxon' at Christmas 1638	0	2	0

For fire wood at this accompte	0	2	0
To be allowed to the chamberlaines for Mr Sayes rent of his house for this yeere 18d, for last yeer 18d. For the last yeeres rent for Mr Harris his maulthouse in the back greene which Mr Seimes should have paied 18d. 2 yeeres rent for Mr George Whitnyes house which his heier is to pay 11d.	0	5	5
For clensing the hall and for a staple for the backe dore and nayles	0	1	2
Summ	13	15	0

[f. 143v] Expences paied about the repayringe of the guild hall this yeere.
2 loades of slattes beinge 13 hundred and carriage 18s 4d, 1 loade of mosse and carriage 9s 4d. To Mr Woodward maior for lath, nayles, and crestes as by his booke appeereth £1 3s. 3 bushells of slatt pinns at 2s 4d a bushell 7s, 23 bushells of lyme at 10d a bushell 19s 2d. For 2 slatters wadges for 28 dayes at 12d apeece £2 16s. To the masons to pull downe the backe dore in the lower hall and wallinge it upp againe 2s 2d.

Summ	6	15	0

Expences layed out about the bakinge and eatinge of one bucke spent at Mr Maiors house 12 September which my lord chamberlaine gave to the towne.
In wyne to Mr Cockine the deputy raynger that came to knowe when the bucke should be killed 1s. To a messenger to goe to Oxon' to bringe a cooke to bake it 6d. 5 peckes of wheate flower 5s 6d, 1lb of pepper 2s 4d, 20 pownde of butter at 4^{1}/4d a pownde 7s 1d, 2 peeces of roste beefe 6s. 4 legges of mutton 7s, 1 coople of rabbettes 16d besides 3 coople of rabettes which Mr Cockin sent gratis to be spent at that tyme which he gave unto the companie 1s 4d, *[f. 144r]* capp paper 2d, 5 pottles and 1 quarte of clarrett wine 7s 4d, 2 pyntes of sacke 1s 2d, suger used about the pasties and disshes 8d. To the cooke for his paynes 5s. For breade and beere 5s 4d. For bakinge of the pasties 1s.

Summ totall is £2 11s 3d, whereof receaved at the 2 tables 17s. So the whole chardge for the eatinge of the bucke only from the towne is	1	14	3

The chardges of wyne spent this yeere by the towne.
24 December 1637 1 quarte of sacke and 1 quarte of clarrett to Mr Hobbes of Trinity Colledge in Oxon' 1s 10d. 1 quarte of sack to Sir Henry Brownes man that invited the townsmen to dinner at Christmas last and 1 pint upon Mr Branthaites man 1s 9d. 27 December 1637 to a preacher that dyned at Mr Glovers 1 quarte of sack 1s 2d. Wyne and beere upon Mr Andrewe Pawlinge the messenger that brought a warrant conceringe our busines in the Exchequer with the clarke of the parcells 1s 10d. 18 February 1 pint of sacke to Mr Woodrooffe the messenger which brought 2 proclamations 7d. 25 February 3

pintes of sack upon Mr Twitty that preached heere 1s 9d. 18 February 1 quarte of sacke and 1 quart of clarrett upon Mr Doctor Prideaux 1s 10d. 4 March 1 quart of clarrett and 1 pint of sacke upon the minister of Bissiter that preched heer 1s 3d. 12 March wine upon Mr Selfe that preched then 1s. 29 March 1 quart of sacke and 1 quarte of clarrett sent to the justices that sate heere about alehouses 1s 10d. [f. 144v] 1 April 2 pottes of beere upon a messenger and 9 April 1 pint of sacke upon Mr Woodruffe the messenger 9d. 1 pint of sacke upon Mr Doctor Prideaux 7d. Halfe pint of sacke upon another messenger 3 1/2d. To Mr Selfe 1 pint of sacke upon the precession day 7d. Wine upon Mr Ring that preched 15 April 1s 2d. To Mr Hiorns 22 April 1 quart of sack and 1 quart of clarrett 1s 10d. 6 May for wine sent to Mr Doctor Prideaux and his company 3s 2d, 13 May to Mr Selfe 1s 3d. 27 May a quart of sack and a quart of clarrett upon Mr Barker 1s 10d. 27 May to a minister that preached 1 quart of sack and a quart of clarrett 1s 10d. 2 June unto Mr Ringe a quart of sack and a pint of clarrett 1s 6d. Upon twoe of the Kinges servantes that came to inquire of the state of the towne before the Kinges last cominge hether 2s. Upon Mr Bearde 17 June 1 quarte of sack and 1 quarte of clarrett 1s 10d. 23 June upon Mr Selfe 1s 3d. 1 June spent upon the clarke of the parcells and Mr Cole about the towne busines 2s 9d. Upon Mr Doctor Prideaux 1 July when he dyned at Mr Branthaites 7d. Last of July upon Mr Branthayte upon is cominge home 1 pint of sack and a quart of white wine 1s 6d. 15 July 1 quart of sack and 1 quart of clarrett 1s 10d. 16 July upon the justices 1 quart of sack and 1 quart of clarrett 1s 10d. In wine to the recorder 16 July 2s 9d. 22 July upon Mr Selfe 1s 2d. 24 July upon Mr Justice Joanes a pottle of sack and a pottle of clarrett when he dyned at Mr Selfes 3s 8d. [f. 145r] Upon Mr Toser 29 July which preached twice that day 3 pintes of sack and 3 pyntes of clarrett 2s 9d. 4 August upon the Kinges servantes that came about the second certificate about the state of the towne against the Kinges cominge 1s. 19 Auguste in wine to Mr Selfe when he preached heere 1s 3d. 28 Auguste in wine upon Mr Recorder 1s 4d. 1 pint of sack and 1 pint of clarrett 11d which was sent to Mr Acland and an other preach-er of Exiter Colledge at Mr Hiornes house, 1 quart of sack at Mr William Meatcalfes house, at dinner one quarte of sack and 1 quarte of clarrett 22d, 3s 10d. 29 September 1 quart of sack and 1 quart of clarrett sent to the Bull to Sir Gyles Braye and Sir Robert Jenckins 1s. 7 October to Mr Woodward 1 quart of sack and 1 quart of clarrett wine 1s 10d. 14 October 1 quart of sack and 1 quart of clarrett upon Mr Sege that preached heere 1s 10d. 21 October upon Mr Doctor Prideaux 1 quart of sack and 1 quart of clarrett 1s 10d, the like upon an ould doctor that preached heere 1s 10d, 18 November upon a minister that preached heere 1s 10d. 25 November upon Mr Harris that preached heere 1 pint of sack and 1 pint of clarrett 1s. 2 December upon Mr Doctor Prideaux 3 pintes of sack and 1 quart of clarrett 2s 7 1/2d. 18 December 1 quart of sack and 1 quart of clarrett sent to the Bull to Sir Gyles Braye and Sir Robert Jenckins cominge about the swannimote court 2s.[5] 16 December 1 pint of sack to Mr Woodward that preached heere 7 1/2d. Summ   3   18   3 1/2

[f. 145v] Summ totall of the receiptes this yeere is	69	3	3
Summ totall of the disbursementes this yeere is	78	6	6½
So remayninge due to the saide chamberlains	9	3	3½

Md at this accompte the maior and cominaltie is indebetted
to Mr Thomas Rayer alderman £32 7d due at the last
accompte, and for the interest thereof due at this accompte
51s 2d. So in the whole owinge to him at this accompte   34   11   9

Md owinge to the towne for admittance of freemen,
John Powell 10s, Richard Hamonde 10s, Thomas Heddye
10s, William Locton 10s, John Burgen 10s.   1   10   0[sic]

Caste up by me Edmond Hiorne towneclarke

[Signature of] Bennet Painter

Md Bennett Paynter hath monie in his handes for 5 buckettes
16s 8d, Phillipp Smith, Thomas Screevin, Peeter White,
Roberte Cooper and Robert Flye.   0   16   8

Md at this accompte Mr William Meatcalfe paied James Nickolls
£5 parcell of the foresaid £9 3s 3½d and the other £4 is
owinge to the foresaid Bennett Paynter and he received his 3s
3½d so the towne oweth the saide £9 to Mr William Meatcalfe
and Bennett Paynter as aforesaid, which they are to [have]
interest for.   9   0   0

[Signatures of] Thomas Woodward maior, John Glover, George Noble, William
Meatcalfe

---

[1] See B 97, p. 13. He left £20 and presumably the other £10 was distributed. He was a resident of
the town: B 96, f. 13.
[2] Marmor or Norman Duke: B 96.
[3] See B 97, p.13. For Ric. Nash see appendix, biogs.
[4] The king was at Woodstock by *c.* 24 Aug., and at Michaelmas: *Cal.S.P.Dom.* 1637–8, 603–7; and
below in 1639.
[5] The forest court. Possibly when the king at Woodstock remitted fines imposed in 1637 at the
swainmoot court for Whittlewood (Northants.): *Cal.S.P.Dom.* 1638–9, 430; 1640–1, 411–12.

[f. 146r] 21 December 1638 to 21 December 1639, Bennett Paynter and Nicholas Mayott, chamberlains

[Receipts]	£	s	d
Of Mr Thomas Doleman	8	0	0
Of Mr Thomas Rayer alderman for interest	4	0	0
Of William Edwardes and John Dissell for the rente of the tole markett	8	0	0
Of John Dissell for the standinges of the coontrie bakers at the highe crosse	1	9	0
Of John Dissell for stallages	12	6	3
Rentes of the borowe	26	7	2³/₄
Of Gabriell Shadd for rentes of the wooll beame	0	8	0
[f. 146v] Of Peeter White for a fine for his garden which he holdeth by lease	0	25	0
Of Mr John Glover alderman for the lease of his house and gardens upon hoggerell hill	0	30	0
Of Frauncis Gregorie gentleman for his admission to his freedome	0	40	0
Of Henrie Newberrie [the like]	0	40	0
Of Mistris James for arrerrages of rent behinde at Michaelmas	0	13	4
Of Richard Rassh of Bladon for a fine in Michaelmas sessions laste for his abuse to Mr Maior and Henry Browne	0	5	0
Summ totall of all the receiptes is	68	3	9³/₄

Caste up by me Edmond Hiorne towneclark,

[Signatures of] Bennet Painter chamberline, Nicholas Mayott

[f. 147r] [Disbursements]

Guiftes and rewardes geiven by the towne this yeere at
Christmas and at other tymes.
One cake at Christmas 1638 sent to Sir Henry Browne
knight 14s and in rewardes geiven to his servantes 15s 6d,
£1 9s 6d. A cake at Christmas 1638 sent to Sir Henrie Lee
knight 14s and in rewardes geiven to his servantes 21s 6d,
£1 15s 6d. A cake at Christmas 1638 sent to Sir William
Fleetwood knight 15s and one other cake sent to his lady[1]
in August 1639 14s, £1 9s. A cake at Christmas 1638 sent to
Mr Lenthall our recorder 14s. A suger loffe at Christmas
1638 sent to Mr Doctor Prideaux 13s. 4 cheeses sent to
Sir William Fleetwoodes lady in August with the last cake

	£	s	d
3s 8d. Summ totall	6	4	8

[f. 147v] Stipendes and yeerely allowances.

To Mr Woodward maior his stipende	10	0	0
For the chaunterie quitt rente £5 6s 8d, two acquittances 2s	5	8	8
To John Eles Mr Doylies deputy undershreeve for fee farme rent 53s 4d, acquittance 7d in wine	2	13	11
To William Lenthall esq recorder his fee	3	6	8
To Edmond Hiorne townclark fee [etc]	2	5	0
More paied him which he gave in rewardes to the clarkes of the assises and cryer at the two assises this yeere 4s, and 4d at each assise	0	8	8
To Mr Ringe schoolemaster his stipende	12	0	0
To Mr Selfe for preaching of Mr Brownes twoe sermons	0	16	0
To the poore people of the almeshouse, guifte of Edmond Hiorne deceased	0	8	0
To 2 watchmen for warding 4 faiers	0	5	4
Geiven in rewarde to Mr Champnies deputy clarke of the markett about Michaelmas when he sate heere as clarke of the markett	0	10	0
Mr Woodroffe messenger for his bringinge of proclamations this yeere endinge at Midsomer 1639 upon an agreement made with him	0	13	4
[f. 148r] To Raphe Lucas skevenger for clensinge the towne gutters this yeere endinge on St Thomas Day 6d a quarter	0	2	0
To George Greene for clensinge the gutter and Mr Sayes puttgally for this yeere endinge at Michaelmas	0	1	6
To Phillipp Hawthorne for clensinge the almeshouse chimnyes for this yeere endinge at Christmas 1639	0	1	0
To John Dissell for his stipend for the geatheringe of the towne stallage monye	1	10	0
To Thomas Heathen serjant at the mace for his annuall stipend agreed upon to be paied to the serjant for ever heereafter for the stallages of twoe fayers which the serjant heeretofore had for St Mary Magdalen and St Nicholas faiers	1	10	0
Summ	42	0	1

Moreover there is yeerely heereafter to be payed by the chamberlaines £4 to the schoolemaster of the free scoole in Woodstock for the rent of Mistris James her house (during her husbandes lease), at Midsomer and at St Thomas day by equall portions the first payment to begin at Midsomer 1640.

	4	0	0
So the annuall stipend heereafter wilbe [sic]	46	0	1

[f. 148v] Accedentall expences and paymentes payed for the
towne this yeere endinge at this accompte.

Mr Rayer alderman 40s which should have beene allowed at the laste accompte for his extraordinerry expences at the Kinges Majesties beinge heere at Woodstock at Michaelmas 1637 when he was maior and which was forgotten at the last accompte he beinge then from home to clayme it	2	0	0
Spent upon Mr Wallford 3 tymes when he came to confer about security for Mr Richard Nasshe his hundred £ geiven to the towne 4s 4d, at the first meetinge 18d, at the second meetinge 16d, at the third meetinge 18d	0	4	4
For pickinge up stones in the hollowe way 6d, for a beesom for Lucas to sweepe the gutters in the streetes 3d	0	0	9
Mr Hiorne 6d for returninge the indenture of inquisition upon John Nickolls death which he paied to the clarke of the assise	0	0	6
For packthreed to measure Mr Glovers grownde upon Hoggerill Hill	0	0	1
For stones and for laborers to amende the holloway and the walls there 28 June	0	15	0
To the tincker that was preste from the towne to Scottland in somer 1639[2]	0	5	0
For makinge cleene the litle house and seller	0	0	4
To Jerom Longe for goeinge with a subpena to Sir William Spencer and Mr Knightly about the dole for the pore suite	0	5	0
To William Wheeler for 4 dayes worke and a halfe and for tymber to make slookes upon the highe wayes, 5s 6d for the tymber and 4s 6d for his labor	0	10	0
For glasinge of the broken peeces in the schoolehouse windowes	0	4	10

For expences about the almeshouse and schoolehouse. For one loade of slattes 7s. To the slatters for their labor 10s. 3 peckes of slatt pinns 21d. To the slatters for theire paynes for 9 dayes 9s. 10 bushells of lyme at 10d a bushell 8s 4d. Mosse for the almeshouse 20d, lath crestes and nayles 6s 8d. 4 crestes for the schoolehouse 12d. Summ	2	5	5

[f. 149r] For expences about the eatinge of the bucck geiven by Sir William Fleetwood knight in August 1639. To the keeper for his fee 10s and to his man 12d. For expences in eatinge and dressinge it: one bushell of wheate 4s 8d, 2 crops of beefe 8s, 17lb of butter 6s, halfe a lb of pepper 20d, egges 6d, a loyne of veale 3s, 1 coople of capons 4s 6d, 2 coople of chackin 2s 6d, a pigge 2s, peares, ploomes and turneupps 10d, 2 legges of mutton 3s, salte to salte the venison 4d, a pynte of white wine vinniger 3d, suger 5d, 3 dozen of brede 3s, beere 8s 4d. To

goodwife Phillipps for makinge the 3 pasties and dressinge the meate 2s 6d. For backinge the 3 pasties 18d. For helpers about the fire 12d. For a fine cheese 10d. For wasshinge the lynnen 8d. Wood to dresse the meate 4s. For the wine 19s 6d. Summ totale £4 10s 6d. Whereof receaved of the neighbors at the eatinge thereof 39s 6d. More paied to Mr Gregories man for bringing rabbett 6d which his master sent. So the towne is to pay   0   51   0

For expences about the eatinge of the doae which the yong lady Fleetwood gave to the towne 4 January. To the keeper for his fee 6s 8d, for his man 12d. For wine 7s 3d, a bushell of wheate 4s 6d, 18lb of butter 8s 6d, a dozen and halfe of bread 18d, a peece of powdered beefe 12d, a cropp of beefe and 2 legges of mutton 13s, pepper and salte and capp paper 20d, a quarter of suger 6d, for bieurr 5s 2d, egges 8d. For the cookes paynes 18d. For the bakinge 18d. For the wood to dresse the dynner 2s. Summ totall 56s 5d. Wheereof receaved of the neighbors at the eatinge thereof 19s.

So the towne is chardged with [sic]   0   36   11

More for strawe and laborers to thetch the widdow Privattes chamber or house in the almeshouse   0   4   4

For a showle and a beesome for Lucas to sweepe and shoule the streetes with   0   1   3

To the prisoners in Oxford castelle Christmas 1639   0   2   0

Wood to make a fire at this accompte   0   2   0

To Mr Mate for 5 yardes of cloth at 2s 8d a yard to make Lucas a capp and coate 13s 4d. To Trewman to make it 2s   0   15   4

Summ is   12   0   4

[f. 149v] Mr Cole his bill in Michaelmas terme 1639. Expences laied out by the towne in the suite depending in the chauncery against Sir William Spencer knight and barronett concerninge his fathers guifte of £18 13s 4d per annum to the poore of Woodstock as followeth. Inprimis for 2 subpoenas, 3 names 5s 6d. Drawinge the bill 10s, ingrossing it 6s. Mr Recorders fee for his hande to the bill 10s. To the six clarkes for filinge it 3s 4d. A subpena against the lady Muntgarrett 1s 6d, servinge it and oath 2s 6d. The drawinge that affidavit 1s. The coppy of Mr Branthawites answere beeinge 20 sheetes 18s. For the solicitors fee 6s 8d. For a recorde out of the office of please 3s 4d.

Summ totall is   3   7   10

Besides his paynes to the clarke of the parcells for 3 or 4 terms.

For 2 or 3 severall petitions [no total].

Mony paied to Mr Ringe. To Mr Ringe schoolemaster for the rent of Mistris James her house £4 for one yeere endinge at Our Lady day, more for three quarters of a yeeres rent endinge at St Thomas day.

So payed   7   0   0

To Mr Maior for his expences in goeinge to Madenhead and to Oxford about the asseasement of the laste sheepe monye £1 6s 4d.[3] More to him for 2 dozen of heare buttons for Lucas his coate 7d and for capp paper 2d, 9d. [Marginated] These 2 sommes are cast up in the accedentall expences and are parcell of the somme of £2 4d.

[f. 150r] The chardges of wine spent this yeere for the towne 23 December 1638 to Mr Smith that preached here 2s. Upon Mr Cockayne 3 January that came to geive notice of a doa geiven by Sir William Fleetwood knight 7¹/₂d. Upon Mr Woodrooffe for bringinge proclamations 7 January 6d. Upon Mr Lenthalls clarke and a gentleman of the guarde that came with him to visite his friendes and see the towne 13 January 1639 12d. Sent to the Bull 26 January 1638[/9] at the eatinge of the taste cakes 15d. Upon [preachers] Doctor Prideaux 3 February 2s 7¹/₂d, Mr Smith 10 February 2s, Mr Selfe 24 February 6d, Doctor Prideaux 3 March 2s 7¹/₂d, Mr Rumball 10 March 2s. Upon the justices at the Bull 11 March 2s. Upon Sir Roberte Jenckins and Sir Gyles Bray at the Bull 20 March 2s. Upon Mr Hobbs that preached heere 24 March 2s. Upon Mr Justice Joanes at Mr Merrickes house 24 March 4s. Upon Mr Toosen that preached heere on Sonday 11 Aprill 2s. Upon Capteine Ivey 13 April by Mr Maiors appoyntment 15d, more on Satterday 14 April 2s 6d.[4] For wine sent to Mr Maiors house 18 April 6s. Upon [preachers] Mr Write 21 April 2s, Mr Doctor Prideaux 26 April 2s 7¹/₂d, Mr Joanes 5 May 7¹/₂d, a yonge gente 12 May 2s, another preacher the same daye 2s, Mr Doctor Prideaux 26 May 2s 7¹/₂d, Mr Selfe 16 June 2s, the Lady Grantams chaplin 16 June 2s, Mr Snowe 23 June 2s. Upon Mr Woodroofe for bringinge proclamations 24 June, 7¹/₂d.

[f. 150v] Upon Mr Richard Prideaux that preched heere 30 June 2s. Sent to Sir Gerrard Fleetwood knight the same day 2s 3d. Upon the clarke of the markett 6 July by Mr Glovers appoyntment 22¹/₂d. Upon a Cambridge man that preached heere 7 July 2s 4¹/₂d. Upon serjant Cresswell 9 July 2s. Upon Doctor Prideaux that preched heere 11 August 2s 3d, Mr Chapman the same day 15d. Sent to Mr Justice Joanes to Mr Merrickes house 12 Auguste 4s 9d. Upon [preachers] Mr Hollan 18 August 2s and on a gentleman of Exiter Colledge the same day 2s. Sent to Mr Abrams house to Mr Doctor Standard by Mr Maiors appoyntment 12d. Upon Mr Busby 21 August 2s. Upon Mr Chapman 28 Auguste by Mr Mayor and Mr Hiornes appoyntment 16d. Upon a preacher of St Johns 1 September 7¹/₂d. Sent to the Lord Wayneman by Mr Maiors appoyntment 19 September 4s. Upon Doctor Predeaux that preched heere 22 September 2s 7¹/₂d. Upon Mr Recorder 24 September 19¹/₂d. Upon [preachers] Mr Knightbridge 6 October 2s, Mr Warren 17 October 2s, Mr Doctor Prideaux 10 November 2s 6d, Mr Fissher 17 November 23d, Mr Snowe 1 December 23d, Mr Fissher 8 December 23d. 17 December for the gentlemen hunters to Mr Maiors house 14d, for the preacher the same day 7d.   Summ   5   5   4

[f. 151r] Summ totall of the receiptes	68	3	9³/₄
Summ totall of the disbursementes	75	18	3
So remayninge due to the said chamberlaines	7	14	6¹/₄

Cast upp by me Edmond Hiorne townclark

[Signatures of] Bennet Painter chamberline, Nicholas Mayott

Md at this accompte the towne standes indebetted

To Mr Thomas Rayer alderman in the somme of £34 11s 9d which was due to him at the last accompte and allso the intereste thereof for this yeere 55s 2d. So in toto nowe due to him is £37 6s 11d which he is to be allowed interest for from this tyme	37	6	11
Md allso the towne standes indebetted to Mr William Meatcalfe alderman £5 due at the laste accompte and for the intereste thereof for this yeere 8s. So in toto now due to him is	5	8	0
Md allso the towne standes indebetted to Benedict Paynter chamberlaine £4 due at the last accompte. And for the intereste thereof for this yeere 6s 4d. So in toto now due to him is	4	6	4
Summ totall of the debtes owinge by the towne	47	1	3

Debtes due to the towne

John Powell 10s, Richard Hamond 10s, Thomas Heddy 10s, William Locton 10s. Summ 40s. Due for theire severall admittances.

[f. 151v] Buckettes due at this accompte unto the towne

Bennedict Paynter chamberlaine hath in his handes 23s 4d for 7 buckettes for Phillipp Smith, Peeter White, Thomas Screevin, Roberte Cooper, Robert Flye, Frauncis Gregory and Henry Newberries buckeates which are presently to be provided and broughte into the hall by him.	0	23	4
[Marginated Query] [Entry cancelled]. Md at the accompte 23 December 1635 payed in 10s, parcell of 20s in his handes for 6 buckettes. So nowe remaynes due	0	10	0

Md at the saide accompte 23 December 1635 Mr Thomas Woodward (now maior) had monye in his handes for 6 and 7 buckettes 43s 4d. For which he was then to pay it for the providinge of newe ladders, scalinge poles and irons for

the towne, then appoynted to be bought. It was in Mr
William Meatcalfes last maioraltie 16 March 1635[/6].
[Marginated] Query   0   43   4

Buckettes. Md 16 March 1635[/6] there were remayninge in
the towne hall 72 buckettes in the chardge of John Dissell,
the cryer of the courte. [Marginated] Query

[Signature of] Edmond Hiorne towneclark

Md at this accompte Mr William Meatcalfe alderman did turne over the five
powndes which the towne oweth unto him upon this accompte unto the maior
and cominaltie as a guifte geiven by his father Mr William Meatcalfe, late alderman unto the towne to provide one sermon to be heereafter preached in
Woodstock church once everie yeere in memorie of him. So the towne is
heereafter for ever to provide the saide sermon to be preached and to paye the
preacher for his paynes 8s.

[Signatures of] Thomas Woodward maior, Edmond Hiorne towneclarke

[f. 152r] Md allso at this accompte Bennett Paynter did turne over his debte of
£4 6s 4d due unto him at this accompte unto Mr Thomas Rayer alderman, allso
his debt of £6 21d due unto him from the towne upon this his last accompte,
allso his debt of 24s which he payed to the use of the poore, which was for the
intereste of Mr Chadwells £10 which he gave to the towne, which interest
monye of the saide £10 is heereafter to be payed to the poore by the maior and
cominaltie of this borowe. So the whole monye nowe due to the saide Mr
Rayer from the towne (Mr William Meatcalfe and the saide Bennett Paynter
beinge allowed and payed theire debtes, as aforesaide) is £48 19s which he is to
have intereste for from this accompte.   48   19   0

[Signatures of] Thomas Woodward maior, William Meatcalfe, George Noble,
Edmond Hiorne towneclark

[f. 152v] [blank]

---

[1] Sir Wm. married his second wife, Eliz. Harvey, c. 1638: Hist. Parl. 1660–1690, ii. 331. The gifts
were perhaps at her first coming to High Lodge.
[2] The Scots wars began in 1639.
[3] There were continuing problems over the collection of ship money, and the king sent out writs for
it as late as Dec. 1639: Cal.S.P.Dom. 1639–40, 158. See also below, in 1640.
[4] Possibly Wm. Ivie of Oxf., described in 1634 as 'now a captaine in the Low Countries': Turner,
Oxon. Visit. 260.

[f. 153r] **21 December 1639 to 21 December 1640, Nicholas Mayott and Bartholomew Love, chamberlains**

[Receipts]	£	s	d
Of Mr Thomas Doleman	8	0	0
Of William Edwardes and John Dissell for the rent of the tole markett	8	0	0
Of John Dissell for the standinges of the coontrie bakers at the highe crosse	1	12	0
Of John Dissell for stallages for this yeere	10	14	3
Of Gabriell Shadd for rentes of the wooll beame	0	8	0
Of Thomas Cotton for his admission to his freedom	0	1	8
Of William Drinckwater [the like]	2	0	0
Of Thomas Hawten for the common seale for his fyne from Raphe Bradshewe	0	4	0
[f. 153v] [Marginated] Md at this accompte Edmonde Hiorne paied 4s to the towne for Nedd Hulls fyne. Thomas Woodward maior.	0	4	0
From Mr Maior which he received of Mr Jafferies for expences formerly leied out by the towne about Mr Nasshes guifte, for the coppy of the will and the expences at Mr Wallferdes beinge at Woodstocke about it which the towne had formerly disbursed at the last accompte and no interest was allowed for the interest of the hundred pounds for the first yeere	1	0	0
14 February receaved of Bennett Paynter 10s which was allowed him at the last accompte and which Mr Lenthall our recorder gave to the towne out of his fee of the last yeere for his cownsell in Sir William Spencers suite	0	10	0
Of Bennett Paynter for trees sould by him to Thomas Forrest out of his back side	0	4	6
Of Mr John Williams for the rent of Brownes meade for one halfe a yeere endinge at Our Lady Day last upon the former lease	2	0	0
The like of Mr Thomas Rayer for his meade	2	0	0
Receaved of the chamberlaines for the rentes of the towne accordinge to the ould rates and upon the 2 leases, and for the rentes of the lee pooles latly leased to Mr Rayer and John Williams for 10 yeeres beinge at Our Lady Day £13 6s 8d a peece and for which they payed halfe a yeere before hande at the sealinge thereof. [Marginated] The ould rent role £28 15s 4³/₄d.	45	8	8³/₄
Of Mr Benjamin Merrick for a fine of his grownde before his doare graunted in fee farme to him from the towne 20s besides his rent of 4d per annum	1	0	0

21 October of Henry Hamond for his admission to his freedom   1   0   0
Of Bartholomew Love for the lopp of Robbin Hoodes elme 18s
and for 7 asshes sould out of Forrestes backside 36s. For the
shrewde of the trees 5s nexte to Richardsons house neere
the hollowaye.   2   19   0
Of Mr Rayer 26s which is the overplus of the some of £50
and the interest thereof which he and his father have longe since
owed to the towne as mony due to the free schoole of the saide
borowe which said 26s is due at this accompte which is in full
satisfaction of the saide £50 and of the interest thereof.[1] And
the maior and cominaltie of the saide borowe are heereafter
to paye to the schollemaster of the saide borowe the somme of
fowre powndes which is for the interest or profite of the
saide fyftie powndes.   0   26   0

Summ totall of yeeres receiptes is   88   8   1³/₄

Cast upp by mee Edmond Hiorne towneclarke

[f. 154r] [Disbursements]

Guiftes and rewardes geiven by the towne this yeere at
Christmas [1639] and at other tymes.
For one cake sent to Mr Peeter Browne[2] at Christmas 12s, in
rewardes to his servantes 14s 6d, £1 6s 6d, one cake sent to
Mr Lenthall our recorder 12s, a shuger loffe sent to Mr Doctor
Prideaux 12s 6d. 18 October for a cake sent to Sir William
Spencer knight barronet 13s 4d. Summ totall   3   4   4

Stipendes and yeerely allowances.
To Mr Woodward maior his stipend and allowaunces   10   0   0
For the chauntrie quitt rent £5 6s 8d, twoe acquittances 2s.   5   8   8
A messengers fee for cominge for it in that it was not payed
at the audite   1   0   0
To Mr Peeter Langston undershreeve to Mr Warcopp for fee
farme rent 53s 4d, acquittance 7d in wine.   2   13   11
To Mr Lenthall esq recorder his fee   3   6   8
[f. 154v] To Edmond Hiorne townclark fee [etc]   2   5   0
To him which he gave in rewardes to the clarkes of the assises
and to the judges cryer at the twoe assises this yeere   0   8   8
To Mr Ringe schoolemaster his stipende   8   0   0
To Mr Selfe for preachinge Mr Brownes twoe sermons   0   16   0
To poore people of the almeshouse, guifte of Edmond Hiorne
deceased   0   8   0
To twoe wardsmen at 4 faiers   0   5   4
[2 lines deleted]

	£	s	d
To Mr Woodroofe messenger for bringinge of proclamations for this yeere endinge at Midsomer	0	13	4
To Raphe Lucas for clensinge the gutters in the streete about the crosse and guilde hall for this yeere endinge at St Thomas Day 2s, at 6d a quarter	0	2	0
To George Greene for clensinge the gutter in the holloway this yeere endinge at Michaelmas	0	1	6
To Phillipp Hawthorne for clensinge the towne chimnyes in the almeshouse this yeere endinge at St Thomas Day	0	1	0
To John Dissell for his stipend for geatheringe the stallage mony for the towne for this yeere ending at St Thomas Daye	1	10	0
Mr Ringe scholemaster for this yeeres stipend for the rent of Mistris James her house £4 at Midsomer and St Thomas Day by equall portions, endinge at St Thomas Day	4	0	0
26 January paied Mr Selfe 8s for preachinge Mr William Meatcalfes fathers sermon which is to be paied by the towne for ever heereafter, this beinge the first payment	0	8	0
To Thomas Heathen serjant for his stipend for 2 fayers for ever to be paied	1	10	0
Summ totall of annuall stipendes and allowances	42	18	1

[f. 155r] Accedentall expences this yeere endinge at this accompte.

	£	s	d
To Mr Hiorne for his expences 2 dayes at Abbington assises by the judges comaunde to attende the triall of Humfry Edwardes for killinge of Leiuetant Moone 5s and for the inditement and cryer 16d[3]	0	6	4
For lettres for the towne twice	0	0	5
For candles at the last accompte	0	0	2
Mending widowe Privates dore	0	0	2
Mendinge of 24 lether buckettes	0	14	0
To Bennett Paynter 33s 4d for the repayer of Forrestes house, and to George Symons for 4 dayes worke there 4s, appoynted by the towne to be paied	1	17	4
Allowed to Bennet Paynter for the rent of Chawcers house 4s 6d passed in his accompt to the towne	0	4	6
Sendinge for a lettre from Mr Cole	0	0	3
Paied Pleevy for carryinge a lettre to my lord chamberlaine from the towne	0	6	0
Wax to seale indenture of the first burgesses[4]	0	0	1
Archer for mendinge gapps of Mr Rayers meade	0	0	3
Wheeler and his sonne for takinge upp and settinge Mistris Williams bridge	0	1	8
For a pole to make newe pinns for it	0	0	3

19 May paied Besse Gelly in part of 16s which she is to have for keepinge Battes childe	0	5	0
21 May paied to Mr Maior for his chardges at Oxon' about the batement of the lat sheepe monye[5]	0	1	4
19 July geiven to a sowldier that lost his coate and snapsack at Durbridges	0	5	0
2 August paied Peeter White for bear when Mr Doctor Preadeaux preached	0	0	2
18 October for carryinge a lettre to Oxon' for payinge the rent at Maidenhead	0	0	4
26 October for carrying a lettre to Mr Recorder	0	0	3
27 October to a messenger that brought a lettre from Oxon' about burgesses[6]	0	1	0
10 November for carriage of a lettre to London	0	0	3
For 2 stock beesoms for Lucas to use	0	0	6
20 November to a messenger that roade to the towne with a lettre for Mr Carter for the towne business	0	1	0
8 December paied Mistris Williams for Mr Toseyes expences and horssemeat when he preached at the fast[7]	0	5	8
For crying our markett at Norton and Wittny	0	0	8
Spent on the messenger that brought a lettre from Mr Recorder	0	0	5
For 5 yeardes and a halfe of cloth to make Lucas his coate and capp 14s 8d, buttons and thredd 4d, makinge thereof 2s	0	17	0
[Marginated subtotal]	5	10	0

[f. 155v] Expences about the office.

36 yeardes of mattinge at 18d a dozen 4s 6d, a new table and a wanescott cubborde 14s, 30 turned pinns and placinge them in 1s, 1 dayes worke for John Say and his sonn 1s 8d, threed and redd leather 4d, nayles 5d, 1 paire of hinges for the cubborde 9d, 4 joyned stooles and exchanginge the table 9s, mattinge the seates and nayles and thred and lether 10d. To Mr Ball for writinge the table of fees 8s. Summ	0	40	6

Expences about the highe crosse and newe buildinge of February. To Lyddam for 4lb of soder 4s. For 1 dayes worke 1s 2d, a laborer 1 day 8d. For bordes and wood 3s 4d, 12 lb of newe lead 2s. 27 April for repaires at the newe buildinge and the crosse, 32 foote of borde for the gutters 3s 6d, mosse, lyme, pins and heare 12d, 4s 6d. 11lb of soder and 2 dayes worke to Lyddom 13s 4d. To Pulchoe for 1 dayes worke and a halfe 1s 6d, a laborer 2 dayes 1s 4d. For clefte wood to heate the irons 2 dayes 8s. To Mr Maior for lyme, lath, nayles, slattes and 20lb and a quarter of leade. Beare 4s 7d. Summ	2	4	5

Expences about the pownde.
For 15 foote of bordes 19d, postes and ledges for the dore
2s 9d, 1 paire of hinges 8d, 1 iron hooke 2d, 1 iron spike 1d,
nayles 5d, 2 staples and a haspe 4d, and to George Symons
for 1 dayes worke 12d, 7s. For a horselock for the dore 1s 4d.
To Thomas Huggins for stone, carriage and workemanshipp
for the walls 10s. To Deaverill for digginge in the pownde
about the walls 1s. Summ   0   19   4

Expences about the towne hall.
7 June to John Say for wether borde for mendinge the
windowes and the longe table, frame and formes and for
14 turned pinns for the buckettes and mendinge the stayer
fote dore, 12s 6d. To Mr Maior for white leade 9d, 1 quarte
of oyle 12d, lambe black 3d, nayles 11d, 2s 11d. Summ   0   15   5

[f.156r] Expences about the repayringe the hollowe wayes
10 November to Richard Huggins for 3 dayes 3s 6d,
Thomas Huggins 3 dayes 3s 6, Thomas Bradshewe 4 dayes
4s 8d, Anthony Deverell 2 days and a halfe 1s 8d,
Dick Coles 4 dayes 2s. Pickinge and carryinge of stone 9d.
Summ   0   16   1

Summ totall of all accedental expences   12   5   9

Expences this yeere about the towne suit against Sir William
Spencer knight barronet concerninge the dole of bread and
mony of £18 3s 4d per annum for ever which his father
Sir Thomas Spencer gave to the poore of Woodstocke in his
life tyme. 8 February to Jerome Longe for goinge to London
to make affidavit that he served Sir William with
a subpena   0   7   6
27 April for sendinge the bill and answer to London   0   0   4
14 June paied Richard Meades for servinge Sir William Spencer
with a subpena to examine wittnesses   0   1   6
21 July to Mr Cole for chardges laied out by him, as by his
bill appeereth   6 19   0
1 August for expences which Mr Hiorne and Mr Mate layed
out in ridinge to Sir Thomas Peniston and Sir Roberte
Jenckinson to procure them to come to our commission 23d
and for Mr Mates his horsse hire 12d   0   2 11
10 August for sendinge a lettre to Mr Branthayte with a warrant
therein to warne his comissioners and wittnesses   0   0   6
19 August for the hier of a horsse for Mr Mate to ride to
Oxford to procuer a clarke at the comission   0   1   0

26 August paied the keepers fee 10s for a buck geiven by Sir William Fleetwood to be spent at the comission and upon the maior and aldermen, and to the keepers man 12d	0	11	0
Geiven to ould Hickes for his attendance as a wittnes	0	1	0
To a messenger to seek him at Cassington and Yearneton	0	0	6
26 August for expences upon the commissioners, wittnesses, clarkes, servingmen, and for Mr Branthaites chardges, and theire horssemeate, and for the neighbors that were wittness and keept them company	3	15	11
[f. 156v] For wine spent at dinner at the commission, and before and after dinner and at Mr Glovers house upon Sir William Spencer and his company	0	15	9
Paied and geiven to Mr John Church and Mr Elssinge clarkes to the comission	1	0	0
To Thomas Heathen junior for riding in to Warwicksheire[8] to warne wittnesses and to Yarneton and Oxon'. For ridinge to Sir Thomas Peniston and Sir Robert Jenckinson to geive them notice of the commission, and for warning all the wittnesses in the towne.	0	8	0
Geiven to Jerom Longe to carry a lettre to Mr Recorder about this busines	0	1	0
Summ	14	5	11

Expences for wine, payed this yeere, which was spent by the towne as followeth. Upon Mr Adkins of Waddome Colledge that preached on Neweeres daye 1s 11d. For wine at the eatinge of the taste cake the same day 7d. Upon Mr Recorder 9 January and the neighbors with him that dined at Mr Hiornes 4s 10d. 4 February upon the justices 1s 11d. [Preachers] Mr Smith 9 February 11d, for preachinge in the afternoon 7d, 16 February Mr Raunce 11d. To the justices 26 February 1s 11d. Mr Selfe that preached heere 22 February 11d. Upon Mr Recorder 28 February 3s 8d. [Preachers] 8 March Mr Doctor Predeaux 2s 6d, Mr Hollan 22 March 1s 2d. Upon the justices 9 April 1s 11d. Upon Mr Woodroffe the messenger 11 Aprile 7d. [Preachers] Mr Sotherton 19 Aprile 1s 11d, Mr Selfe 17 May 7d. 17 June upon the captaines at the Bull by Mr Maiors appoyntment 3s 10d. [f. 157r] Upon a captaine at Mr Glovers 21 June by Mr Maiors appoyntment 2s 10d. Upon 3 captaines 22 June at Mr Glovers upon the examination of Humfry Edwardes and divers other, which examinations were sent to the Kinge 1s 2d.[9] 27 June upon 2 captaines at Mr Glovers by Mr Glover and Mr Hiorns appoyntment 1s 2d. Upon Mr Sealfe that preached 9 July 7d. Upon the clarkes of the assises 6 July 1s 7½d. Upon Mr Harris of Yearneton that preached heere 12 July 1s 6½d. 19 July upon a captaine at Mr Glovers by Mr Glovers appoyntment beinge deputy maior 3s 10d. More upon the same captaine and his company by Mr Glovers appoyntment 3s 5½d. Same day upon one of the comaunders by Mr Hiorns appoyntment 4½d. 19 July upon a preacher of Exiter Colledge by Mr Selfes appoyntment at the Bull 7d. 19 July upon 2 preachers that did preache heere 1s 11d, more upon them at Mr Abrams the same day 11 1/2d. 21 July upon Mr Cole, by Mr Glover, Mr Abrames and Mr Hiornes appoyntment 1s 1/2d. 23 July upon Mr Bastvin the highe constable 4 1/2d. 26 July upon Mr Fissher that preched heere 1s 11d. 28 July upon the cuntry justices 1s 11d. 2 August upon Mr Doctor Prideaux that preached heere 7d. 3 August upon Mr Justice Joanes at Mr Merrickes at the night and morninge 5s 9d. 9 August upon Mr Cordiall and a Cambridge man that preched heere 2 sermons 23d at Mr Abrams house and afterwardes to them at the taverne the same day 2s, 3s 11d. Upon Mr Doctor Hobbes and Mr Chapman at Mr Maiors howse when they preached 1s 11d. Upon Mr Branthayte 18 August 1s 1d. 22 August upon Mr Cockin in wine and beere when he sent in the bucke against our commission 9d. 23 August upon Mr Woodward that preached heere then 11 1/2d. 24 August upon Mr Beck a messenger that brought proclamations 7d. [Preachers] 30 August upon Mr Chapman and a gentleman of Brasennose 11 1/2d, 6 September upon Mr Selfe and Mr Ringe 1s 2d. Upon Mr Cowey 13 September 1s 4d. 14 September upon the leiuetenantes of the cownty at Mr Maiors howse 3s 10d. [f. 157v] 20 September upon Mr Wattson that preached heere 1s 11d. 22 September upon Mr Gardner the recorder of London[10] that came to adjorne the justices seate 3s 10d. [Preachers] 27 September Mr Bowen 11 1/2d, 4 October Mr Doctor Prideaux 2s 6d, 16 October the Bisshopp of Coventrie and Litchfeild 3s 10d, 1 November Mr Doctor Prideaux 2s 6d. 10 November upon one of my lord chamberlains gentlemen by Mr Hiornes appoyntment 7d. 20 November to Mr Woodrooffe the messenger by Mr Maiors appoyntment 7d. 6 December upon Mr Doctor Prideaux that preached heere 2s 6d. Upon Mr Toser that preached 2 sermons 8 December, being the generall fast day throughout the whole kingdome 7d. More to the justices 18 December 1s 11d. Summ

	5	0	6
Summ totall of the receiptes this yeere	88	8	1 3/4
Summ totall of the disbursementes	77	14	7
So remayninge due to the towne	10	13	6 3/4

Cast upp and examined by me Edmond Hiorne towneclark.

[Signatures of] Nicholas Mayott and Bartholomew Love chamberlains

[f. 158r] Md 21 December 1640. A note of buckettes to be brought in for the use of the towne
Md Mr Thomas Woodward maior hath 43s 4d in hand
for 13 buckettes. [Marginated] Payed

	2	3	4

[Inserted] Md this 43s 4d was payed in this manner, to Mr Woodward for his paynes in ridinge about Sir William Spencers busines 13s 4d, and 10s a peece to him and Mr Hiorne in riding to London about the burgesshipp in the Parliament 20s, and the rest was paied in at this accompte.

Md Mr Nicholas Mayott chamberlaine hath 23s 4d for 7
buckettes which he receaved of Bennett Paynter late
chamberlaine. Allso hath in his handes 10s for 3 buckettes
more for Thomas Cottons, William Drinckwalters and
Henry Hamondes. [Marginated owinge] In toto   1   13   4
Summ   3   16   8

Debtes[11] owinge to the towne .

For his freedome Richard Hamond 10s, Thomas Heddy 10s,
William Locton 10s, John Powell 10s. Summ   2   0   0

By me Edmond Hiorne towneclarke

[Signatures of] Thomas Woodward maior, John Glover, William Meatcalfe,
Thomas Rayer, George Noble, Edmond Hiorne

[f. 158v] [blank]

[1] See above, Intro.
[2] Of Kiddington: see above in 1613.
[3] This and entries below for wine for captains were in connexion with the mutiny at Abingdon in
May and June of Dorset men pressed for the Scots war. They refused to go beyond Oxf. but were
persuaded to continue to a rendezvous at Woodstock: *Cal.S.P.Dom.* 1640, 323–4, 334–5.
[4] Wm. Lenthall and Sir Wm. Fleetwood for the Short Parliament, summoned 20 Feb., sat 13 Apr. to
5 May: Williams, *Parl. Hist.* 202; *Handbk. Chron.*
[5] See above in 1639.
[6] This and letters to and from Lenthall and journeys to London at the end of the acct. may be connected with the disputed election for Woodstock. After a double return on 27 Oct. Fleetwood and
Benj. Merrick were struck out and Lenthall and Wm. Herbert, younger son of the earl of Pembroke,
chosen 'by the unanimous vote of the mayor and commonalty'. Herbert decided to sit for
Monmouthshire and was replaced by Sir Rob. Pye: *Parl. Hist.* 202; M. Keeler, *Long Parl.*
(Philadelphia 1954), 60; *V.C.H. Oxon.* xii. 401. See also above, Intro.
[7] A fast this Tuesday was proposed by the Long Parl. and proclaimed 11 Nov.: *Stuart Proclams.* ii, no.
314.
[8] To Spencer property at Claverdon.
[9] See above, n.3.
[10] Sir Thos. Gardiner, Recorder of London, presumably acting at the quarter sessions instead of
Lenthall.
[11] In B 81, f. 36v. The debts owed, or, rather,the capital sums held on trust by the town were: to the
schoolhouse, £50; upon Chadwell's gift to the poor, £10; Browne's two sermons yearly, £10;
Meatcalfe's sermon, £5; Hiorne's gift, £5. Total, £80. Fletcher's and Nash's bequests would not be
included as they were invested elsewhere.

[f. 159r] 21 December 1640 to 22 December 1641 Nicholas Mayott and Bartholomewe Love, chamberlains

[Receipts]	£	s	d
Of Mr Thomas Doleman	8	0	0
Of William Edwardes and John Dissell for the rent of the tole markett	8	0	0
Of John Dissell for the standinges of the countrie bakers at the highe crosse	1	10	0
Of John Dissell for stallages this yeere	11	6	8
Of Gabrill Shadd for rent of the wooll beame	0	8	0
Of Nicholas Mayott for a fine sealed from Raph Bradshewe to him	0	4	0
[A deleted entry]			
[f. 159v] In reddy mony as a remaynder due to the towne at the last accompte	10	0	0
More receaved at the same accompte for monyes which then came to the townes handes	1	10	0
Of Mathewe Penn for the fine of his lease which he sould to Peeter White	1	0	0
Of Laurence Williow and Leonard Witham 20d a peece for theire admission to theire freedome, haveinge beene both apprentices, 20d a peece. But theire buckettes of 3s 4d a peece is yet to be determined whether it shalbe paied or not. [Marginated] Query	0	3	4
Of Hughe Weller baker for his admission to his freedome	2	10	0
Of John Wakefeild for the lopp of 10 trees in the almeshouse garden sould and demised to him for 40 yeers at the rent of 5s per annum from Our Ladye Day. A lease to be made him under the towne seale for the terme of 40 yeeres	0	10	0
Of the said chamberlains for the rentes of the towne for this yeere upon the newe alterations of the rentes of John Williams and Mr Rayers meades and of the almeshouse garden and Mr Merrickes rent	45	11	2³/₄
Summ totall of the receiptes this yeere is	90	13	2³/₄

Cast upp by me Edmond Hiorne towneclark

[Signatures of] Nicholas Mayott, Bartholomew Love chamberlains

[f. 160r] Md of Bennett Paynter for 7 buckettes 23s 4d which remained at the last accompte in the chamberlains handes. Remained allso in theire hands at the last accompte for 3 buckettes, Thomas Cotton, William Drinckwater and Henry

Hamond 10s. And since receaved for 2 buckettes for Mr
William Parker and Hughe Wellers 6s 8d. Which 12 buckettes
were brought in and delivered into the hall. Md there are
remayninge in the towne hall 86 buckettes at this accompte
committed to the custody of John Dissell cryer and keeper of the
hall. Md the chamberlaines brought into the hall 12 newe
buckettes which they had receaved, so that they have noe
buckettes in theire handes at this accompte.

[Signature of] Edmond [Hiorne] towneclark

Md at this accompte the said chamberlains had delivered to them in reddy mony £10 10s whereof £10 is presently appoynted to be sett out to interest for the benefite of the towne.[1]	10	30	0
Md allso they had delivered unto them 16s in mony, which John Norman paied for the interest of his £10 then due. Which 16s was before paied by the towne to Elizabeth Norman for keepinge of John Battes daughter, which 16s they are to accompte for at the next accompte	0	16	0
So in theire handes	12	6	0

[Signature of] Edmond Hiorne

[f. 160v] [blank]

[f. 161r]   [Disbursements]

Guiftes and rewardes geiven by the towne this yeere at
Christmas and at other tymes.

For one cake sent to Mr Peeter Browne at Christmas 1640 12s and geiven unto his servantes then in rewarde 15s 6d, £1 7s 6d. For one cake sent to Mr Speaker[2] to London at Christmas 1640 18s and for packinge and carriage of the same to London 6s 3d, £1 4s 3d. For a shuger loffe sent to Mr Doctor Predeaux at Christmas 1640 12s 4½d. For a cake sent to Sir William Fleetwood 10s. For 3 other cakes sent, one to the Earle of Carnarvan and one to the Lorde Saye, one to Mr Speaker at 12s a peece, £2 6s 0d. Summ totall	5	10	1½
[f. 161v] Stipendes and other annuall allowances payed as followeth. To Mr Woodward for his maiors stipend for this last halfe yeere endinge at Our Lady Day beinge the laste for ever heere after to bee allowed in that kynde. [Total £10 deleted]	5	0	0
For the chauntrie quitt rent for this last yeere endinge at Michaelmas £5 6s 8d, 2 acquittances 2s.	5	8	8
To Dutton to cary and pay the last halfe yeeres rent	0	1	0

To John Eeles deputy to Mr Brombly undershreefe to Mr Lybb highe shreeve of the cownty of Oxon' for fee farme rent 53s 4d, acquittance 7d in wine.	2	13	11
To Mr Lenthall esq recorder his fee	3	6	8
To Edmond Hiorne townclark fee [etc]	2	5	0
Geiven to the clarke of the assises for this cownty at the 2 assises and to the judges crier this yeere as aunciently heeretofore	0	8	8
19 Auguste paied for John Morris his inditement 2s 6d, to the cryer and baylife for examination of wittnesses 2s.	0	4	6
To Mr Selfe for preachinge Mr Brownes 2 sermons	0	16	0
To the poore people of the almeshouse 8s, guifte by Edmond Hiorne deceased	0	8	0
To twoe wardsmen at each of 4 fayers	0	5	4
To Mr Woodrooffe messenger for bringinge proclamations this yeere endinge at Midsomer	0	13	4
[f. 162r] To Mr Ringe schoolemaster for his stipende	8	0	0
For his stipend this yeere for the rent of Mistris James her house £4 at Midsomer and St Thomas Day	4	0	0
To Raph Lucas for clensinge the gutters and streetes about the crosse and the guildhall for this yeere endinge at St Thomas Day after the rate of 6d the quarter	0	2	0
To George Greene for clensinge the gutters in the holloway way this yeere endinge at Michaelmas	0	1	6
To Phillipp Hawthorne for clensinge the towne chimnies in the almeshouse this yeere endinge at St Thomas Day	0	1	0
To John Dissell for his stipend for geatheringe the stallage monye for the towne this yeere, endinge at St Thomas Daye	1	10	0
To Mr Selfe for preachinge Mr William Meatcalfes sermon geiven to the towne by his father, which is to be continued for ever	0	8	0
To Thomas Heathen serjant at the mace for his annuall stipend for 2 fayers, for St Mary Magdalen and St Nicholas fayers, for this yeere which is to be continued for ever	1	10	0
To Mr Ringe scholemaster for the interest of £50 nowe in the townes handes, which Mr Rayer formerly held, which was due at St Thomas Day and is yeerely heere after then to be paied which £50 was of Mr Dolemans guifte[3] towardes the maintenance of the schole master of the free gramer schole of Woodstocke	4	0	0
[f. 162v] Payed as geiven to the prisoners of the goale of the county of Oxon' at Christmas 1641 by Mr Maiors appoyntment	0	2	0

To George Sheires, armiger, lord of the mannor of Hensington
for an annual quitt rent due to him from the maior and
cominaltie of Woodstock 7s 8¹/₂d for 13 yeeres behinde unpaied
at Michaelmas 1640 as by his acquittance appeereth £5 2¹/₂d
and more paied unto him 7s 8¹/₂d for this one last yeeres
rente due at Michaelmas.⁴ In toto   5   7   11
July 10 to a messenger for bringinge 1 proclamation 12d. To
Mr Woodrooffe for a booke concerninge pole mony 12d,⁵
26 July for 1 other proclamation and a booke concerninge
souldiers 2s, 29 October for 1 proclamation 12d, for 3
proclamations 17 December 2s.   0   7   0
Paied at the Bull on the leete and sessions day at Michaelmas
(being the first payment of the newe order concerninge the
maiors dinners) for the dyet of the aldermen, justices and
chamberlains after the rate of 18d apeece beinge but 7 spoken
for, 10s 6d.⁶ For the jury and officers beinge 25 provided for
and spoken for at 12d a peece, 25s. In toto   1   15   6
22 December 1640 for 5 yardes and a halfe of grey cloth at
2s 6d a yarde for Lucas coate, buttons and threed 4d, the
makinge of it 2s.   0   16   1
To Mistris Williams 3 Auguste for the chardges of Mr Tosier,
twoe men and theire horsses for one night that came to preach
the first sermon of the lecture in Doctor Prideaux his place⁷   0   5   6
For the lectors dyet from the first day 3 August untill St Thomas
Day, 21 weekes at 12d a weeke, 21s. Mr Doctor Standardes
mans dyett twice, Mr Toshers man once, 6d a day, 18d.
[Sum sic]   1   0   6
To John Williams and Richard Hiorne constables as monye for
them to lye dormant to geive to poore people and to
bringe it in theire accomptes   0   12   0
[Marginated total]   51   10   1

[f. 163r] Accedentall expences this yeere.
To William Hawthorne for 9 yonge asshes sett at Forrestes
garden   0   2   6
For sendinge a lettre to Sir William Spencer 8d   0   0   8
For a beesome for Lucas 3d. Sendinge a lettre to London to
Mr Speaker 3d. A crest on Forrest house 3d. Carriage of
writinges to London by the carrier 6d. To Elizabeth Norman
for keepinge of John Battes dawghter 16s. Mendinge the
almshouse garden wall 2s, removinge of goodes from one
chamber to an other in the almeshouse 12d. For worke, tymber
and nayles about the almeshouse dores and partition in the entry
2s 8d. For a mason for 2 dayes work there 2s, tymber and
workmanshipp 18d. Mendinge and settinge on 2 lockes there

6d. For a borde 8d, nayles 2d, a pole 2d, a hinge and nayles
4d. For the carpenters worke one day 12d. For a staple and
mendinge 2 lockes and setting them on 10d. In toto   1 10 7
For a beesom to Lucas   0 0 3
For sendinge 3 lettres to London to Mr Cole
To Lyddam for mendinge the glasse windowes in the upper hall
agreed upon   0 17 6
Mr Tosiers horsemeate when he preached heere 9 May   0 0 6
For expences about the schole house and the chamber there
17 May, 500 of slatt and charriage 8s 8d, 9 bushells of lyme at
9d a bushell 6s 9d, heare 8d, 3 hundred and a halfe of hart
lath 3s 6d, moss 1 loade and charadge 7s 6d, 4 rafters 16d,
nayles and slatt pins 8s, a beesome 1d. For Batt for 8 dayes
and a halfe slattinge worke 9s 11d, Anthony Turner 5 dayes and a
halfe 6s 6d, Belcher 8 dayes and a halfe 7s 1d. For 2 crestes 5d.
In toto   2 19 5
20 May for reparations about the cadge and the pillory.
For planckes and tymber 8s, nayles 2d. To the carpenters
3s 4d, 1 hundred and halfe of slattes 2s, lath 6d, mosse 12d,
2 crestes 5d. To the slatters and laborers 6s. Nayles and
slattpinns 2s 10d. In toto   1 4 3
[f. 163v] For a laborer to keepe the water of the streete out
from the bayes 3 dayes   0 1 4
For a statute booke 20d and for leaden waites 20d   0 3 4
For a beesome for Lucas   0 0 3
To the ringers when the lordes and Mr Speaker were heer
20 September   0 2 0
For a hinge for the almeshouse streete dore 6d, mendinge
the lock of the hall dore 7d, iron for hanginge up the table
of fees in the hall 5d   0 1 6
For a messenger to goe to Mr Doctor Standard[8] to come
with Mr Speaker to Woodstock   0 0 3
To Henry Cooper and Christofer Smith which they had laied
out for the poore   0 9 11
For pickinge of stones out of the holloway   0 0 6
For a staple and brick for the markett busshell   0 0 4
To a mason to mende the wales in the prisons   0 6 6
For a trapp dore for the seller and a dore for the litle house,
for planckes 5s 4d, bordes 4s 3d, a planck 14d, 4 staples,
1 haspe, a hinge, 24 spikes and mendinge 3 hinges 2s 6d, nayles
2s 1d, carpenters worke 3 dayes 3s, makinge cleene the litle
house and the seller 6d, in beveridge to the workemen 2d   0 19 0
16 November a mason and a laborer 1 day 20d, stones 4d to
mende Nann Gyles house in the almeshouse   0 2 0

Geiven 19 November to William Tayler of Twixter[9] parke in County Yorke, that was robbed at the slayde	0	5	0
20 November to Thomas Screeven for ploomers worke about the crosse	0	3	6
Him for glasse worke about the scholehouse windowes	0	3	0
For a beesome for Lucas	0	0	3
17 September expences in eatinge and dressinge of the buck which Mr Speaker gave, more then was receaved	1	4	0
[f. 164r] 31 September paied at the eatinge of the doa which my Lord of Carnarvan gave more then what was receaved the wine of the buck and doa beinge paied for	2	3	1
For candles at the last accompt and at the last leete at Michaelmas	0	0	4
To 2 wardesmen on St Mathewes fayer to keepe out Adderbury bakers from the market because of the sicknes ther	0	1	4
To Thomas Huggins mason for his mason worke and stones to repayer the causeway by the pigion house, agreed upon	1	3	4
15 December 1641 geiven to 3 poore men of Wittny that had theire howses burned 2s by Mr Maiors and Mr William Metcalfes and Mr Hiornes appoyntment for that they should not begg the towne	0	2	0
[Marginated total]	14	3	7

[f. 164v] A perticuler note of wine spent this yeere for the towne as by Mr Rayers bill appeereth.

To Mr Joanes when he preached heere 13 June 7d, 4 July 11$\frac{1}{2}$d, 11 July 11$\frac{1}{2}$d, 1 August 11d, 8 August 11d, 7 September 18d, 10 October 14d, 24 October 7d, last of October 14d, 7 November 14d, 28 November 14d, 5 December 18d, 12 December 19d, 18 April 11$\frac{1}{2}$d, 2 May 11$\frac{1}{2}$d, 16 May 11$\frac{1}{2}$d, 6 June 11$\frac{1}{2}$d. Upon Mr Jerome Joanes when he preached heer 30 May 11$\frac{1}{2}$d, 22 August 11d, 17 October 11d, [total] 2s 9d. Mr Chapman that preached 20 December 1640 1s 9d, 27 December 3s 1d. 16 January for wine sent to Mr Maiors 7d. [Preachers] 17 January upon the parson of Combe 1s 2d, 24 January upon Mr Doctor Prideaux 1s 11d. 3 February upon Sir William Spencers man that came about the dole 1s 2d, 13 February upon one other of his men that came about the dole 7d. 14 February to Mr Cole that came to the towne on purpose about the bookes of the dole monye 1s 2d. *[f. 165r]* [Preachers] 28 February Mr Coxiter 1s 11d, 21 March Mr Downer of Charlebury 1s 6$\frac{1}{2}$d, 28 March Mr Southerton 1s 11d, 3 April Mr Adkins 1s 11d, 11 April Mr Fowler 2s 6d, on Easter Day to a preacher of Exiter Colledge 1s 11d. Same daye upon Mr Ringe for his paynes about the communion 11$\frac{1}{2}$d. [Preachers] 9 May upon Mr Tosyier 1s 11d, in the afternoone 7d, 23 May a preacher of Newe Inn Hall 1s 11d. 2 June upon Mr Glover and Mr Hiorne in ridinge to Yarneton about the dole busines to Sir William Spencer 7d. [Preachers] 13 June Mr Knitebridge in the afternoone 11$\frac{1}{2}$d, 20 June Mr Quaterman 11$\frac{1}{2}$d, same day a gentleman of

Exiter Colledge in the afternoon 11¹/₂d, 4 July [the same] 1s 11d. 17 July upon
Mr Woodrooffe the messenger for proclamations 8d. [Preachers] upon 18 July a
gentleman of Exiter Colledge 1s 10d, 24 July Mr Muncke 1s 10d, Mr
Quaterman at afternoone 7d, 3 August Mr Tosyer and his freend when Mr
Tosyer preched heere 3s 8d, Tewsday 10 Auguste upon Mr Doctor Standard
heere. 18 August upon Mr Cradocke the clarke of the assises and his clarkes, as
they were ridinge to the assises 1s 2d. [Preachers] 29 August Mr Doctor
Lawrence 1s 10d, same daye Mr Hallon 11d, 26 September Mr Burton 7d.
[f. 165v] 17 October Mr Craftes 1s 2d. 20 October upon Mr Eeles the undershreeves deputy when he came to receive the fee farme rent mony 7d. 27
October upon Sir William Fleetwood knight when he dyned at Mr Maiors on
the leete daye 1s 10d. 21 November upon Mr Quaterman that preched heere
then 1s 2d. 18 November upon Mr Captaine Warburton¹⁰ when he brought his
first £60, 2s 7d at Mr Maiors house, at the taverne 22 November upon the
deliverie of the other £40, 4s 2d in wine, beere and fire, 26 November when he
came to bringe his bondes of the first £60, 14d, [total] 8s 10d.
Sente to the Bull, 13 March to the justices 1s 11d, to Doctor Standard and Mr
Chamberlaine justices 30 April 1s 11d. Upon the justices at the Bull, 7 May 3s
10d, about the pole monye 27 July 5s 6d, upon the comissioners at the Bull 3
Auguste sittinge about the pole monye 1s 10d [and] an other tyme 1s 10d. In
toto to them 16s 11d.
16 September in wine sent to Mr Speaker and his wife when they laye heere and
when he gave his buck 8s 11d. Then sent to the lordes, knightes and gentlemen
to the Bull, that came about the forreste busines 8s 3d.¹¹
Summ totall of the wine mony this yeere   5   16   8¹/₂

Summ totall of the disbursementes   77   0   0
And the totall of all the receiptes   90   13   2³/₄
So there remains due to the towne from the chamberlains upon
this accompte   13   13   2³/₄

Caste upp and examined by me Edmond Hiorne towneclark.

[Signatures of] Nicholas Mayott, Bartholomew Love, chamberlains

---

¹ Mr. Chadwell's gift of £10. The next entry may also be connected with this bequest: see above in 1638.
² i.e. Wm. Lenthall: see above in 1640.
³ For Doleman's relationship to the original benefactor, Ric. Cornwell, see above, Intro. The entry
in accts. following has been shortened for this edition.
⁴ Money reserved in 1565 charter. There is no information about payment before 1641. In 1640 the
chamberlains were allowed to retain £10 at the acct. 'till Mr Sheares be payed', so this may be a
recent demand: B 81, f. 36v. For the original grant to Jerome Westall see *L & P Hen VIII*, xxi. 151.
⁵ The unpopular poll tax imposed by Parl. in June 1641 to pay off the Scots and the army in the
North: *Cal.S.P.Dom.*1641–3, 16, 19; Act, 16 Chas. I, c. 9.
⁶ Presumably an effort to cut the cost of the mayor's feast: see above, Intro.
⁷ The first indication that the sermons had been revived, probably because of parl. approval and the
attack on Laud. The rate was that of 1630 and they were again held on Tues. Toser, a noted Puritan
preacher, was Fellow of Exeter Coll. and vicar of Yarnton: *D.N.B.*

[8] Speaker Lenthall's brother-in-law, rector of Tackley: Turner, *Oxon. Visit.*
[9] Reading unclear. The place has not been identified.
[10] Capt. Thos. Warburton. The £100 bequest was for three-year loans to burgesses: B 83, pp. 95 sqq.; B 97, p. 13; see below in 1647.
[11] Perhaps measures to restrict operation of forest laws: cf. *Cal.S.P.Dom.* 1641–43, ix, 44.

[f. 166r] 22 December 1641 to 21 December 1642, Nicholas Mayott and Bartholomew Love, chamberlains[1]

[Receipts]	£	s	d
Of Mr Thomas Doleman	8	0	0
Of William Edwards and John Dissell for the rent of the tole markett	8	0	0
Of John Dissell for the standinges of the coontrie bakers at the highe crosse	1	8	6
Of John Dissell for stallages this yeere	10	13	7
Of Gabriell Shad for rente of the wooll beame	0	8	0
For the quitt rentes, and rentes by lease this yeere for the lee pooles, the almeshouse garden and Mr Merrickes rent, as appeereth upon the newe alteration of the rentes of the meadowes	46	3	8³/₄
[f. 166v] More at the last accompte in reddy mony which the chamberlains brought in £11 10s and 16s which John Norman paied in for interest of £10 for 1 whole yeere	12	6	0
Summ totall of the receiptes this yeere is	86	19	9³/₄

[Signatures of] Nicholas Mayott, Bartholomew Love, chamberlains

Edmond Hiorne: cast upp

[f. 167r] [Disbursements]

Stipendes and annuall allowances.

	£	s	d
To the undershreeve for the chauntery quitt rent for the yeere endinge at Michaelmas £5 6s 8d and for the twoe acquittances 2s. As by the acquittances appeereth. To Dutton the carrier for carryinge the said twoe halfe yeers quitt rent 12d a tyme 2s. In toto	5	10	8
For the fee farme rent for this last yeere endinge at Michaelmas. This was paied to Mr Langstone undershreife	2	13	4
To Edmond Hiorne townclark fee [etc]	2	5	0
To him as geiven to the clarke of the assises at the 2 assises and to the cryer 4s 4d at each assise	0	8	8
To the officers of the garison at Oxon' upon a generall muster[2]	0	0	6

To Mr Thomas Joanes for preachinge Mr Thomas Brownes
sermone on Sonday after Christmas Day 1642 8s.[3]
And to Mr Stutfeild for preachinge his seconde sermon on
Easter Day 1643 8s 16s.[4]   0   16   0
To Mr Stutfeild for preachinge Mr William Meatcalfes sermon
on Sonday 27 February 1642[/3][5]   0   8   0
To the poore people of the almeshouse, guifte of
Mr Edmond Hiorne deceased   0   8   0
To 2 wardsmen for wardinge at the 4 fayers   0   5   0
[f. 167v] To messengers for bringinge of proclamations at severall
tymes this yeere as by the perticulers in Mr Mayottes
booke appeereth   0   13   2
To Thomas Ringe schoolemaster his stipende   8   0   0
For his stipende this yeere for the rent of Mistris James house
£4, at Midsomer £2 and St Thomas Day 1642 £2.   4   0   0
To him for the use of £50 of Mr Dolemans monye nowe in
the townes handes £4 endinge on 21 December 1642 for the
yeere now last past   4   0   0
To Raph Lucas for clensinge the gutters about the crosse and
towne hall for this yeer endinge on St Thomas Day   0   2   0
To George Greene for clensinge the gutters in the hollowe
way this yeere endinge at Michaelmas   0   1   6
To Phillipp Hawthorne for clensinge the almeshowse
chimnyes this yeere endinge at St Thomas Day   0   1   0
To John Dissell for his stipend for geatheringe the stallages
this yeere endinge at St Thomas Day   1   10   0
To Thomas Heathen deceased, serjant at the mace for his
annuall stipend for 2 fayers, for St Mary Magdalen and
St Nicholas fayers, for this yeere endinge at St Thomas Day,
this to be continued for ever   1   10   0
To Mr Sheires lorde of the mannor of Hensington as a quitt
rent due to him from the maior and cominaltie for this
yeere endinge at Michaelmas   0   7   8 1/2
To Mistris Williams 19 April for dyet at the leete £1 18s 6d,
for 7 at 18d a peece and for 28 at 12d a peece   1   18   6
To her for the like at the leete 19 October, for 9 at 18d a
peece and for 28 at 12d a peece   2   1   6
To her for makinge and bakinge of 2 pasties of venison
then geiven by Sir William Fleetwood knight   0   6   0
[f. 168r] 19 November for 5 yardes of grey cloth at 2s 6d a
yard for Raph Lucas his coate, buttons and silke 6d,
the makinge 2s   0   15   0

To Mistris Williams for the lecturers dyet from 11 January till
18 October at 12d a daye as by Mr Mayottes
note booke appeereth[6]   2   10   3
Summ totall   40   12   6$^{1}/_{2}$

Guiftes and rewardes geiven this yeere.
1 January for 1 cake 12s sent to Sir William Fleetwood
knight   0   12   0

Accedentall expences.
2 Auguste payed for expences about Sir William Spencers
deedes of the poore. Geiven to his servantes at the sealinge 5s.
For wax 2d. To Mr John Hopkins for ingrossinge the deedes
£1 10s. To John Say for a newe box to putt the writinges
in 10d. Geiven to Mr Thomas Leighe as a rewarde upon
Mr Branthwaites motion £3. For Mr Woodward and
Mr Hiornes expences in ridinge to Oxon' about the busines
21d. For beere for the ringers at the sealinge the deedes 12d.   4   18   9
Mony for the poore upon Mr Thomas Fletchers guifte
when the monyes from London could not be receaved.
15 November 1642 to the poore 16s, 25 December 1642 16s,
25 March 1643 [sic] 16s. Mr Thomas Joanes for preachinge
Midsomer sermon 1643 16s.   3   4   0
For expences upon Collonell Ennyes[7] and the souldiers that
came to fetch Mr William Meatcalfes last cloth, to
Mistris Williams £1 17s 5d, to Mr Noble maior as by their
severall notes appeereth 5s 4d. The rest was paied by the
chamberlains.   3   10   0
[f. 168v] To Thomas Bruce constable for expences layed out
by him, at the appoyntment of Mr Noble maior at 2
severall tymes   0   15   0
To Mr Noble maior as mony geiven by him to the Kinge and
Princes foote men upon his cominge from Edge Hill as by
Mr Maiors note appeereth[8]   1   0   0
More paied him as geiven the Kinges trumpeters at the same
time 5s 6d and to his Majesties padman 5s. To the Duke of
Yorkes footemen 12d. To the trumpeters that sownded at the
readinge of the Kinges proclamation 2s. To a guide to goe to
Kidlington 6d.   0   14   0
To William Norman to goe as a guide in the night to
Charlebury   0   1   0
Summ [for four entries above] £2 10s.
24 December 1641 paied for tymber and workemanshipp about
the highe wayes to keepe of horsses, for tymber 6s, the carpenter
2s 8d, and to the mason 9d   0   9   5

30 December 1641 geiven by Mr Maiors appoyntment to a
poore minister   0   0   6
For sendinge a lettre to Mr Cole 2d. Geiven to a poore man of
Marson that had his house burnt 2s 6d.⁹ To an Irishe minister
1s 6d. To 2 Irishe gentlemen 1s 6d. To Pulchoe for 1 dayes
worke about the schoolehouse 1s. For mosse 3d, nayles and
slatt pins 3d.   0   7   2
9 February 1641[/2] paied Dutton the carrier for bringinge
bookes from Mr Cole 6d. For mendinge the bridge at the
holloway 4d   0   0   10
12 February paied to Elizabeth Norman for Battes child
3 yardes and a halfe of greene cloth at 2s 2d a yarde 7s 7d,
1 paire of shoes 1s 2d, making a petticote and wastcott 1s,
4 ells of lynnen cloth 3s 7d   0   13   4
Geiven to her to keepe the child   0   10   0
[f. 169r] To Screeven for mendinge the schoolehouse windowes
1s 6d. Geiven 2 souldiers 1s. 2 March geiven to an Irishe
gentleman and his wife and children 3s. Geiven to make upp
the some collected for Strattford that was burnt 9s 9d.¹⁰ Geiven
to 2 Irishmen and 2 children 1s.   0   16   3½
3 March 1641[/2] for 20 foote of planckes 3s 4d. For 12
spikes 1s. For single tenns 3d. To Symons 2 dayes about the
repayringe of the floodgates at the bayes [2s].   0   6   7
Paied to John Williams and Richard Hiorne as mony to geive
to the poore   1   4   0
9 April geiven to 3 souldiers by Mr Maiors appoyntment 1s. For a beesom for
Lucas 3d. To a mason for 2 dayes worke at the holloway 2s. For mendinge the
gapps in the meades 1s. 6 May to Roberte Fly for to make upp a somme for
the pole mony 7s. To Hickes for mendinge Ann Price her lock and for nayles
and a hoock 6d. For sendinge a lettre to Mr Cole 2d. 6 July paied for beere at
Mr Rayers when the muskettes were spoke for 6d. 12 July paied to one to
watch the proclamation against the Earle of Essex 4d.¹¹ 12 Auguste for
mendinge the stoopes upon the holloweway 6d. 31 August geiven the wardsmen that warded that day 12d to drincke. To John Lowe to goe to the high
constables to bringe in strawe for the souldiers 6d. Paied for a showle to Lucas
6d. 17 October to Gabriell Shadd overseere which he payed for mendinge the
holloweway 16s 4½d.   1   11   7½
26 October paied to Robert Fly collector for the royal subsidies asseased upon
the towne £1.¹² 26 October paied to Edward Silver and William Drinckwater
trayned souldiers for theire chardges £1. Paied for a beesom for Lucas 3d. Payed
for beere at Mr Glovers maiore when Sir William Fleetwood examined Pulchoe 1s.
For sweepinge the towne halle 2d. Paied to Mr Hiorne for reparations bestowed in
slattinge and weaxinge the towne office 17s 7d.   2   19   0
18 March paied 2 Irishe women and children   0   1   0

[f. 169v] To Thomas Bruce constable from 11 December 1642 till 19 March
1642[/3] for candles for the court of garde and sentries as he fetched them from
the chandlers[13]   2   15   0
30 November 1642 paied for expences upon the souldiers. For wood the first
night 1s. To Mr Freeman for 150 faggottes £1 10s. To Mr Jeffery for bringinge
1 loade of them to the towne 1s 6d. To Thomas Archer for cleavinge wood 1s.
To William Anthony 4 dayes, Greene 3 dayes, 2 souldiers 2 days 9s 8d. To a
souldier for carryinge in of wood 4d. Geiven to the souldiers at the George 6d.
Geiven to the souldiers at the first makinge of the bullworkes 10s.[14] 19
December 1642 paied to John Lowe, Richard Homes and William Norman
when they went first to worke at the bullworkes at Oxon' 3s. To William
Norman to goe with a warrant to Mr Drake to sende in wood 8d. To Mr
Noble maior for tymber and bordes for the horsse and gibbett 8s 4d, and to
Symons the carpenter for makinge them 2s. To Archer, Anthony, Lowe,
Clarridge, Fleckman and Homes for workinge at the bulworkes at Oxon 5s. To
William Yeates for 1 hundred of cheese taken and sent to Bandbury £1 13s 4d.[15]
To the widdowe Nickolls for faggottes and hard woode 8s. To William
Norman to goe as a guide to Bandbury 1s. To Thomas Archer for cleavinge of
wood 1s 6d.
Some totall   31   13   10

Summ totall of the disbursementes this yeere is   72   18   4½
Summ totall of the receiptes this yeere is   86   19   9¾
Summ totall remayninge due to the towne   14   1   5¼

Md this was caste upp and examined by me Edmond Hiorne towneclark

[Signatures of] Nicholas Mayott, Bartholomew Love, chamberlins

[1] The acct. belongs to mayor John Glover's time, but because of the Civil War it was audited with
the 1643 acct. by mayor Thos. Woodward: B 81, f. 37r. It contains items for 1643 when Geo.
Noble was mayor after Glover's death. See p. 203 and 1643 audit in B 81.
[2] Possible ref. to the unsuccessful attempt 10–15 Aug. to execute the king's commission of array in
Oxon., or to the parl. muster in Oxf. in Sept.: A. Fletcher, *Outbreak of Eng. Civil War* (London
1981), 361–2; *V.C.H. Oxon.* iv. 79.
[3] 1 Jan. 1642/3.
[4] Date changed in MS. from 1642. Easter Day 1643 was 2 Apr.
[5] A date outside the accounting period.
[6] Tues. lecture series.
[7] Col. John Innis, commander of royal dragoons at Edgehill, Gov. of Cirencester Mar. 1643: *Royalist
Ordnance Papers*, ii, ed. I. Roy (O.R.S. xlix, 1975), 433. For Meatcalfe (d. *c.* 1644), see appendix,
biogs.
[8] After the battle of Edgehill the king 'marched to his own house, to Woodstock', probably on 28
Oct., and to Oxf. next day: E. Hyde, earl of Clarendon, *Hist. of Great Rebellion*, ed. R. Lockyer (Oxf.
1967), 70.
[9] Marston: Stapleton, *Three Oxon. Parishes*, 258.
[10] Ibid.
[11] Proclam. of 9 Aug. 1642. It was for issuing that as well as for handing over the town armour to the
royalists that Hiorne was summoned to the Bar of the House of Commons 4 Oct.: *Commons Journals*,
ii. 792.

[12] Granted 1640 for relief of the army in the North: Acts, 16 Chas. I, cc. 2–4, 9.

[13] An example of expenses running into 1643 because of the war. Soldiers were quartered in Woodstock for several years.

[14] This reads as if they were at Woodstock but may refer to the fortification of Oxf., as in the following entries. For work done by outside labour see Roy, *Ordnance Pps.*, ii. 468.

[15] Banbury castle became a royalist garrison after Edgehill: *V.C.H.Oxon.* x. 9. 200 men are said to have returned from Banbury to the garrison at Woodstock by Christmas: C. Alwyne, 'Notes on Civil War and Siege of Banbury', *Trans. of N. Oxon. Archaeol. Soc.* (1853–5), 30. Despite few refs. to cheeses in these accts., the Woodstock cheese fair was important: *V.C.H Oxon.* xii. 372.

[f. 170r] **Md the accompte of the said chamberlains was taken 18 March 1643[/4] at the office, from 22 December 1642 till 21 March 1643[/4] which was in the tyme of George Noble gentleman maior before Thomas Woodward gentleman maior the aldermen and comon cownsell of the foresaid borowe for rentes and other accomptes then accompted for, whereof they were dischardged.**[1]

Md the receiptes this yeere was	58	7	10½
The disbursementes this yeere was	59	4	2
So 13s 4d for 4 buckettes beinge payed by the chamberlains there remayneth due to them	0	3	0

[Signatures of] Thomas Woodward maior, Edmond Hiorne towneclark.

Md 18 March 1643[/4] it was consented unto by the maior aldermen and comon cownsell of the said borowe that Mr Thomas Rayer alderman, Bartholomew Love, and John Williams shall joyntly hould and enjoye all the comon le poole meadowes for one whole yeere from the 25th day of this instant March 1643[/4] untill 25 March 1645 [1644 deleted] for £9 rent to be payed the first day of Maye next cominge. And them to keepe the banckes in good repaire and clense the brookes sufficiently, and preserve the mowndes and trees in and about the premisses to theire uttermost power.

[Signatures of] Thomas Woodward maior, Edmond Hiorne towneclark

Bartholomew Love, Edward Silver elected chamberlains to begin and take theire place from St Thomas Day [21 Dec.] 1643.

[Signatures of] Thomas Woodward maior, Edmond Hiorne towneclark

[f. 170v] Md Mr Mayott payed Mr Hiorne £2 8s 8d, Mr Rayer 5s 6d, Mr Noble 2s, more due to himselfe which is entred into the ledger booke 3s. Which mony was payed out of these monyes followinge that was payed by the parties followinge, from Gabrills rent mony 10s, from John Disselles mony entred in the ledger booke £2, from John Williams 12s, from Roberte Hattly for rent 20s.

Md delivered to Bartholomew Love chamberlyn 18 March 1643[/4] to be accompted for by him and Edward Silver £2 12s 1d. And a note delivered to him of the arrerrages of rentes yet due to the towne.

[Signatures of] Thomas Woodward maior, Edmond Hiorne

[1] Heading given in full because of the importance of the dates. The acct. was audited with its predessor with the same chamberlains, Nic. Mayott and Bart. Love. Their year ran 22 Dec. 1642–21 Dec. 1643, the date of the next acct. and of the election of new chamberlains: below, and B 81, f. 37r. The audit named Geo. Noble as mayor that year. The brevity of the acct. and the decline in receipts and expenditure reflect the Civil War's impact, with hundreds of soldiers at Woodstock. Rents, school money, and other payments were difficult to obtain: cf. 1646. For military activity around Woodstock see *Cals.S.P.Dom.* 1641–6, indexes; *Journal of Sir Sam. Luke*, ed. I.G. Philip (O.R.S. xxix, xxxi, xxxiii, 1950–3); *Letter Books of Sir Sam. Luke, 1644–5*, ed. H.G. Tibbut (Lond. 1965); *V.C.H. Oxon.* xii. 329.

The accompte of Bartholomewe Love and Edward Silver chamberlains of the said borowe, taken at the guild hall of the said borowe the 22nd daye of December, anno domini 1643 untill 21 December 1644, anno regni regis Caroli etc vicesimo. Before Nicholas Mayott gent. maior, Thomas Rayer, Thomas Woodward, George Noble, and Bennett Paynter alderman, Edmond Hiorne gent towneclark, and the major parte of the comon cownsell of the saide boughrough, for rentes and other accomptes then accompted for, whereof they were at this accompte dischardged.[1]

	£	s	d
Receiptes	29	4	0½
Disbursementes	31	0	8
Due to chamberlains	1	16	8
Due to town for rents in arrears at Michaelmas 1644	0	2	6
	1	14	6

as by a note entered in the chamberlains book this yeere
appeereth besides the rentes in arreares
unpayed the yeere before when Mr Mayott was chamberlaine
as by his accomptes appereth   5   15   9

[Signatures of] Nicholas Mayott maior, Thomas Rayer,
George Noble, Bennett Painter, Edmond Hiorne towneclarke

[1] Audit acct. taken from B 81, f. 37v. B 79 lacks a 1644 acct.

[f. 171r] 22 February 1645[/6] Bartholomew Love and George Gregory chamberlains[1]

[Receipts] £ s d

[3 lines deleted]

A note of the severall receiptes of the chamberlyns this yeere
Of Mr Doleman £8. Mr Fletchers money £12. Of three
freemen £1. Of the brasier for his freedome £2 3s 4d. Of
Edwardes for halfe a yeeres rent att St Thomas Day £2.
Of him for a quarters rent beforehand £1. For the old
tymber £2. Of John Dissell for halfe a yeeres rent for the
tole £2.   30 3 4
For stallidge £8 11s 11d. Upon the rent role £24 1s 10d.

Soe the totall of the receiptes   62 17 1

[f. 171v] [Disbursements]

To Mr Jones for preachinge Mr Fletchers sermon on Christmas Day 1644 16s.
For preaching Mr Brownes sermon the Sunday followeinge 8s. For Mr
Meatcalfes sermon 8s. Att Oxon' about the removeinge of Collonell
Windebancke £1 3s 6d.[2] For the removeinge of the exciseres 7s.[3] For takeinge
downe the signe att the White Heart 1s. For wardinge at Our Lady Day fayre 1s
4d. To Lucas for his wages 6d. For tymber for the crosse 3s 9d. Mr Thomas
Glover for goeinge to Sir William Spencers 2s 6d. Takeinge in the gate att the
townesend 4d. The sarjeant a quarters wages 7s 6d. Mr Fletchers sermon 16s.
Mr Brownes sermon 8s. For the leete dynner £1 17s 6d. To the glasier and the
carpenter for mendinge the crosse 10s 8d.   7 11 7
To the poore Mr Hiornes gift 4s. For moseinge the schoole £1 1s 9d. The
clarke for his halfe yeares wages 15s.[4] Lucas for his wages 6d. For horse hire
and draweinge a petition 4s 6d. *[f. 172r]* For preachinge Mr Fletchers sermon
1645 16s. The Kings trumpetter 5s. Mr Gregorie for draweinge a bill for
quarteringe souldiers 2s 6d. The schoolemaster att Our Lady Day last £10.
For quarteringe Collonel Howardes souldiers 8s.[5] Mr Mayott maior £5 4s 2d.
For a cake geiven to the governor 10s[6]. The serjeantes wage 7s 6d. For a key
for the hall dore 1s.   19 19 11
For sweepeinge the hall 1s. For slatt for the schoole 1s 6d. For bordes to mende
Oxon' gate 3s. For poles had of Mr Maior 1s 6d. Lucas for his wages 6d. For
keepeinge Brownes childe £1. The clarke for halfe yeares wages 15s. Mr Maior
for the poore £4. For quarteringe Bristoll souldiers goeinge to Farrington £1 16s.[7]
For Mr Fletchers sermon 16s. For wardinge at Michaelmas fare 8d. For sweepeinge the hall 1s. For preacheinge Mr Fletchers sermon 5 November 1645 16s.
For mendinge the wainscott and other worke about the hall 4s. 10 16 2

For a booke for the aletasters 6d.   For wyne to Mr Maiors 5s 4d.   For wardinge the last fare 8d.   For chardges att Oxon' 6s.

[f. 172v] For the dynner the laste leete £1 2s 8d.   Due to mee since the last accomptes £2 1s 2d.   To the poore for Mr Hiornes gift 4s.   For horse hire att severall tymes 3s.   The serjeant for gatheringe the stallidge halfe a yeare 15s.   For his wages halfe a yeare 15s.   For Mr Fletchers sermon on Christmas Day last 1645 16s.   Mr Hiorne for his fee and the two assises £2.   For the turnepike 10s.   For makeinge upp the accomptes 5s.   George Gregorie for severall thinges as appeares by his bill £1 18s 4d.   For wood this day 2s 2d.   For beare att the accomptes 1s 6d.

[Total £11 4s 10d corrected]	11	6	4
The totall of all the disbursementes	49	14	0
Soe that here remayneth to the towne the summ of	13	3	5

Since to Silver for wares 6s 5d, paied to Mr Hiorne 8s 5d.   The towne after-wardes allowed Mr Love £2 which hee receaved short of Mr Dolemans money which he promiseth to procure to the use of the towne.[8]

Remayneth to the towne the summ of	10	8	3

[f. 173r] 29 December 1645

Md that I Bartholomewe Love doe acknowledg my selfe to bee indebted unto the towne upon this accomptes the some of tenn poundes eight shillinges and three pence which I doe promise to pay to the chamberlyns of this boroughe the tenth day of February next witnes my hand.   Witnes hereunto [signatures of] Bartholomew Love   John Williams

4 May 1646 Md this day Mr Bartholomewe Love payd to George Gregorie to the use of the towne the somme of £10 8s 3d accordinge to the bill above writ-ten.

[Signature of] John Williams towneclarke

[f. 173v] [blank]

---

[1] Date of audit.   The year of acct. given in B 81, f. 38r was from 22 Dec. 1644 to 29 Dec. 1645. There was a decline in toll and rents, no woolbeam receipts, no payment for fee farm or chantry rents or recorder's stipend.

[2] Col. Fras. Windebanke, shot 3 May for surrendering Bletchingdon House to Cromwell, had been in Woodstock in Feb. and Mar.: *Letter Books of Sir Sam. Luke*, 323, 687, 693; *Diary Kept by Ric. Symonds*, ed. C.E. Long (Cam. Soc. 1959), 163–4.

[3] Excise duty, introduced by the Westminster Parl. 22 July 1643 and by the royalist Oxf. Parl. in Apr. 1644, became essential to raise money for troops.   Excisers were generally disliked: *Acts and Ordinances of Interregnum*, ed. C.H. Firth and R.S. Rait (Lond. 1911), i. 202; *Stuart Proclams.*, ii, no. 489; R. Hutton, *Royalist War Effort, 1642–46* (Lond. 1982), 93, 156.

[4] Presumably John Williams, who took over from Hiorne this year and signed below as town clerk, though Hiorne was still paid for court duties.   The town was alarmed at possible parl. victory, especially when the king left Woodstock 8 May and was defeated at Naseby in June.

[5] Col. Thos. Howard's royalist horse brigade: P. Young, *Naseby*, 33; *Symonds Diary*, 182.

[6] Capt. Sam. Fawcett of the royalist ordnance became governor of Woodstock in Mar.: *Ordn. Pps.* ii. 448; *Letter Books of Sir Sam. Luke,* 693.

[7] On 19 Sept. the Privy Council at Oxf. ordered most of the horse, which came from Bristol after Prince Rupert's surrender 10 Sept., to Woodstock: *Cal.S.P.Dom.* 1645–7, 145.

[8] B 81, f. 38r notes that he was paid short by Humf. Gillet of Faringdon. The Doleman estate at Childrey was close to fighting around Newbury, and that may explain why Woodstock did not get its regular payment: *Symonds Diary,* 3, 145, 148.

[f. 174r] Accounts taken 25 January 1646[/7], George Gregorie and Allexander Johnson, chamberlains[1]

[Receipt]s	£	s	d
12 January halfe a yeare of Mr Fletchers money £6. Of John Durman for a fyne for Hitches house £3. Of William Edwardes a quarters rent of the tole 13s. Of Mr Love 4 May due to the towne upon his accomptes £10 8s 3d. Of Mr John Meatcalfe for halfe a yeare of Mr Fletchers money due att Our Lady Day last £6. Of William Edwardes for a quarters rent £1. Of Joseph Fletcher for 2 postes 1s. Of Edward Silver for two beames of the old malthouse 17s. Of John Parsons for his freedome £3. Of John Hitche for his freedome 1s 8d. Of Thomas Browne for his fee 1s 8d. Of John Slatter for his fee 1s 8d. Of Edward Glover for his freedome £2 10s. Of Austen Geringe for his fyne £2 10s. Of Francis Druce for the seale of his fyne 4s.	36	8	3
[f. 174v] Of William Edwardes for a quarters rent of the tole due at Michaelmas last £1. For Hampton leas £2. For Mr Fletchers money due att Michaelmas last £6. Of William Edwardes quarters rent £1.	10	0	0
Of Thomas Heathen for stallidge this yeere £7 8s 1d. Of him for the chuntrey bakers standinges 10s 9d. For 6 buckettes £1. Upon the rentrole by George Gregorie £17 16s 10½d. Of old arreres 10s 7d. [Deleted subtotal]	28	16	9½
The totall of all George Gregorie his receiptes [corrected from £75 15s 0½d]	73	15	0½

[f. 175r] [Disbursements]

The severall disbursementes of George Gregorie this yeare. To Mr Francklyn 31 December 1645 by the appoyntment of the major part of the companie £2. Payd Mr Jones for preaching Mr Brownes sermon 20 December 1645 8s. Payd

Lucas for makeinge cleane the towne hall 2d. 8 January 1645[/6] payd for Mr Towneclarkes chardges and myne when wee went to the lord cheife justice 6s 6d. For cloath and makeinge Lucas his coate 18s 6d, paire of shooes 3s 6d. To Mr Browne 16 January 1645[/6] for one yeare and a halfe for St Maries quit rent due att St Michaell last as appeareth by the acquittances £8. For 3 aquittances 3s. For my expences then 1s.

[Marginated subtotal]   12   0   8

To William Hickes for a key for the towne hall dore 1s. 6 February to Mr Widdowes for one quarter due on St Thomas Day last past of Mr Fletchers money 20s and 20s of the towne, £2.[2] Payd Mr Jones for preachinge Mr Meatcalfes sermon 18 February 8s. Thomas Holland for puttinge barrs into the hall windowe 10d. By Mr Mayors appoyntment for carrieinge the tymber of the White Hart to James Keenes house 3s.

[f. 175v] Mr Williams for his chardges and Edward Parrett when they went to Oxon' to Collonel Palmer 5s.[3] James Blunden for 2 boltes and staples on the towne hall dore 2s 2d. Richard Meades for carrieinge a lettre to the governor of Gaunt and another to the governor of Compton 3s 6d.[4] 10 Marche to Mr Witt for 2 yeares rent due att Michaelmas last £5 6s 8d.

[Marginated subtotal]   8   10   2

Goodwife Richardson for wages for keepeinge the sicke people 18s. Francis Richardson for watcheinge about sicke peoples dores 14s, for carrieinge a lettre to Gaunt and another to Compton 3s. Mr Maiott for money layd out about the petition for quartereinge Collonel Palmers men 1s 6d. Francis Richardson for goeinge to Gaunt with a lettre 1s 6d. 4 souldiers for carrieinge the timber of the White Hart 1s 4d. 26 Marche to Mr Widdowes £4. Lucas for one quarters keepeinge the crosse gutter and for wardeinge 1s. Old Hickes the money given by old Mr Hiorne for the poor of the almeshouse, 4s. Mr Jones for preacheinge Mr Brownes sermon on Easter Day 8s. 23 Aprill to Mr Williams when hee went to London about Compton busines £1.[5]

[Marginated subtotal]   7   12   4

[f. 176r] To him more for the same jorney 10s. For his horse hire 8s. For bringeinge the tymber out of the parke 2s. To George Greene for 5 dayes about the lea pooles 5s. Payd Mr Jones for preacheinge Mr Fletchers sermon 3 May 16s. To Thomas Scriven for glazeinge the schoole windowes 2s. For a newe bushell with irons and chaines 8s. Harris for mendinge the towne buckettes £1. Meades for carrieinge a lettre to the generall to remove the sicke souldiers 1s 6d.[6] Him for goeinge to the generall againe 1s 6d. For expences when I went to Yarneton about the dole 1s. Mr Jones for preacheinge Mr Fletchers sermon on Midsomer Day 16s.

[Marginated subtotal]   4   11   0

For mendinge the bridge over the hollowe way 8s 3d. To Mr Widdowes att Midsomer £5. For a shovell and besomes for Ralphe Lucas 1s 6d. For a quart of sacke and pinte of white wine for Mr Marrit 1s 10d. Lucas for wardeinge att Maudlin fare 8d. For chardges when went to Banburie to the comittee 13s 4d.[7] The sarjeant for halfe a yeares wages due att Midsomer 15s.

[f. 176v] Him then for gatheringe the stall money 15s. For makeinge cleane the hall 3 tymes 6d. To Lucas by Mr Maiors appointement 2s beinge part of Mr Fletchers dole 2s. 6 August to Mr Recorder for his fee for 5 yeares at Michaelmas next £16 13s 4d.

[Marginated subtotal]   24   11   5

26 August for Mr Woodwardes chardges and myne when wee went to London about the lecture £2 11s 4d.[8] For a peece of tymber to mende the 2 paire of stockes 6s. The carpenter for worke 1s 6d. For clensinge the little house 6d. Joseph Fletcher for horse hire when I went to Mr Lewis 6d. For wine and beare when Mr Lewis came to Mr Maiors 1s 3d. Harris for mendinge the bucketes 16s. For wine bestowed on Mr Cole 3s 2d. For waxe for Francis Druce his fyne 2d. Lucas for wardeinge on St Mathias Day 8d, for the cross gutter at Michaelmas last 6d. For my horse and chardges when I went to Einsham about the £80,000, 2s 8d.[9]

[Marginated subtotal]   4   4   11

1 October 1646 for makeinge the wall of the White Hart 8s. A laborer for 4 dayes 3s 4d. Mr Jones for preacheinge Mr Fletchers sermon on Michaelmas Day last 16s. *[f. 177r]* Mr Williams for his yeares fee due att Michaelmas last £1 6s 8d. 20 October to Mr Twyford[10] for halfe a yeares rent for chantrey quit rent due att Michaelmas £2 13s 4d, an acquittance 6d. For my horse hire and chardges when I went to pay it 2s 6d. Gave Lucas for makeinge cleane before the hall at 4 tymes 1s. For a rope for the hall bell and mendinge about the bell 1s 2d. Spent on Mr Lane when I receaved the rent of Hampton leas 1s. For bordes for mendinge the hall windowe 2s. Mr Jones for preacheinge Mr Fletchers sermon 5 November last 16s. To the poor then 16s. The sarjeant for a quarter due att Michaelmas last 7s 6d and for gatheringe the stallidge 7s 6d, 15s.

[Marginated subtotal]   8   2   6

Coles for carryeinge the tymber and the slattes from the White Hart 2s. Lucas for wardeinge att Michaelmas fare last 8d. For repaireinge the roofe of penniles benche 9s 2d. For wine sent to the generall 9s 4d. For 1 quart of sacke bestowed on Mr Ferrers 1s 4d. For mendinge the schoole gutter 1s 6d. For 1 pint of sacke bestowed on a preacher 8d. Geven to Lucas 4d. Durbridge for a haspe and a staple for the White Hart dore 4d.

[Marginated subtotal]   1   5   4

[f. 177v] Payd 22 December 1646 the money which old Mr Hiorne gave to the poore of the almeshouse 4s. Lucas for sweepeinge the crosse gutter 6d. 26 December last for a coate and cap for Lucas £1 1s 6d. Payd Mr Jones for preacheinge Mr Fletchers sermon on Christmas Day last 16s. Payd then which was geven to the poore the Sunday before Christmas last beinge of Sir Thomas Spencers dole £1 10s. For a pinte of sacke bestowed on the preacher 8d. The serjeant for a quarters wages due att St Thomas Day last 7s 6d and for gatheringe the stall money 7s 6d, 15s. For goeinge to Oxon' about the souldiers 1s 6d. For Brownes childe in full of all £1. Mr Glover for his chardges to Einsham 2s 8d. The towne clarke for writeinge theise accountes 5s. For fyre att thacountes 3s.

[Marginated subtotal]   7   3   10

The totall of George Gregories disbursementes	78	2	2
The totall of his receiptes [corrected from £75 15s 0¹/₂d]	73	15	0¹/₂
Soe that there remaynes due to him [corrected from £2 17s 1¹/₂d]	4	7	1¹/₂

[f. 178r]   The receiptes of Allexander Johnson this yeare

7 September of John Whitaker for his freedome £2 10s, for his buckett 3s 4d. Of Walter Bayleyes for his freedome 10s 6d, for his buckett 3s 4d. Of Hughe Lardner for his freedome £2 10s, for his buckett 3s 4d. Of John Durman upon the rent roll £1.

[Marginated subtotal]	7	0	6

The disbursementes of Allexander Johnson this yeare

Francis Richardson 1 Marche for goeinge to Oxon' with a lettre 1s 6d. For paper for thoffice 6d. To Plivie for goeinge to Mr Doleman with the receiptes 1s 6d.[11] Spent att my goeinge to Einsham about towne busines 2s 8d. To Mr Twyford the last of September for one halfe yeares rent due att Michaelmas last £2 13s 4d. For the receipt 6d. For expences that jorney 4s 6d. To Mr Marrit for Hitches house for halfe a yeares rent due at Michaelmas last 16s 8d.
[f. 178v] Paper for thoffice 6d. For Michaelmas leete dinner £1 18s. For the towneclarkes jorney to Banbury 3s. To 6 laborers 2 dayes for throweinge downe the bullwharkes 8s.[12] For a case of waites and scales and carriage of them 17s. Thomas Paynter for his horse and himselfe goeinge to Einsham 2s 8d.

The totall of his disbursementes is	7	10	4
His receiptes are	7	0	6
Soe there remaynes unto Allexander Johnson	0	9	10

The totall of both their disbursements is [corrected total in margin of MS.]	85	12	6
The totall of both theire receiptes [corrected total in MS.]	80	15	6¹/₂
Soe that there remaynes to them both [corrected total in MS.]	4	16	11¹/₂
To George Gregorie	4	7	1¹/₂
To Allexander Johnson	0	9	10

[f. 179r]   The names of the severall persons who have made default of payement of theire rentes and for stallidge this yeare.[13]

+ Mr Hiorne for his severall rentes £1 9s 3d.   Henry Hammonde for his house 10s and 10s for the former yeare, £1. Henry Whiteside for 2 yeare 16s. + Edward Silver for his house 7s. Gabriel Shad for the wooll beame 2 yeares 16s. The heires of William Walford for the dove house close 2 yeares 1s. Mr Vernon for severall rentes 10s 8d. For George Gregories house 6s 8d. + Matthew Pen for his house 2 yeares 3d. Robert Symons for John Colliers

house 2 yeares 11d. John Norman for his house and pales 9d. John Wakefeild
for the house where Belcher dwelt and the towne garden 2 yeares 10s 8d. Mistris
Harris for the Bull 2 yeares 11s. The heires of George Witney for 3 houses in
Oxon' streete 5¹/₂d. And for a former yeare 5¹/₂d. Richard Manninge for his
house and garden adjoyneinge to Petty Johns lane 8d. Thomas Meatcalfe for the
houses where Scurrier dwelleth 3³/₄d. William Tomlins for Spittle house close
2d. William Lardner for the George 2 yeares 8d. Kirby for Holmes and
Newells house 2¹/₂d.

[Marginated subtotal]   6   13   1¹/₄

[f. 179v] The heires of William Walford for the house where Joan Harris
dwelleth 4¹/₂d. Widdowe Warren for a house in the common acre 1d.
Widdowe Ray for her house in Pettie Johns lane ¹/₂d. Thomas Frayne for
Thomas Bruce his house 3d. Mistris Glover for a halfe yeares rent of her part of
the common pooles 4 yeares since £3 6s 8d.

[Marginated subtotal]   3   7   5¹/₄
The totall of theise arreeres   10   0   7¹/₂

The arreers of stallidge followeth.

Allexander Johnson for 14 stalls 1s 2d. Christofer Woodburne for severall stalls
3s 4d. Thomas Paynter for 6 stalls 6d. Mistris Glover for severall stalls 6s.
Robert Hatly for stalls 3s 10d. William Seare for severall stalls 4s 8d. Mr Noble
behinde 6d.   1   0   4

George Gregorie his marke.[14] [Signature of] Alexander Johnson

This accountes was examined by mee John Williams towneclerke

[1] This acct. shows some recovery of rents and an effort to make back payments despite the siege of
Woodstock from Mar. until its capture on 26 Apr.
[2] Thos. Widdowes must have become schoolmaster in 1645. He resigned in 1653. He is the reputed
author of *The Just Devil of Woodstock* (London 1660), about the disturbances at the manor house in
1649. His account can most easily be found in the appendix to Sir Wal. Scott's *Woodstock*.
[3] Lt.-Col. Ric. Palmer, Provost Marshal for royalist forces in Oxon. His troops were in Woodstock
at this time: *Ordnance Pps.* ii. 457; see below.
[4] Gaunt House, Standlake, was captured 1 June 1645: C.H. Firth and G. Davies, *Regiment. Hist.
Cromwell's Army* (Oxf. 1940), i. 92, citing J. Sprigg, *Anglia Rediviva* (Oxf. 1854), 25. Compton
Wynyates (Warws.) had fallen to Parl. in 1643: *V.C.H. Warws.* v. 60–61; P.E. Tennant, 'Parish and
people: S. Warws. and Banbury Area in Civil War', *Cake and Cockhorse*, xi. (1990), 143–8.
[5] Cf. below in 1650, ref. to £4 lent to Compton House. The garrison there took contributions from
Oxon. 1645–6: Tennant, 'Parish and People' 144; A. Hughes, *Politics, Society, and Civil War in
Warws. 1620–1660* (Camb. 1987), 188.
[6] Gen. Fairfax, who took Oxf. on 24 June, or perhaps Commissary-Gen. Ireton, who received the
submission of the royal forces there: Sprigg, 255.
[7] Banbury was in parl. hands from 27 Apr. Note the town clerk's journeys there, below.
[8] Presumably Fletcher's sermon paid for by the Skinners Co. of London: see above, Intro.
[9] Perhaps the money, despite the discrepant amount, which Luke's scouts had reported in 1643: 'Mr
Abraham of that towne informeth that there is £8,000 in the town and will give directions how to
take that money': *Journal*, 29. Abraham was still an alternative name for the Meatcalfe family:
O.R.O., Woodstock churchwardens' accounts, 1644.
[10] Edw. Twyford of Northmoor, active in town affairs in the following accts.
[11] There is no record of money paid by Doleman this year in these accts.

[12] Presumably around Woodstock: see above in 1644.
[13] Evidence of disruption to town revenues caused by the war. The crosses may relate to the problem of collection.
[14] The only chamberlain in these accts. unable to sign.

[f. 180r] Taken 8 January 1647[/8], George Gregorie and Allexander Johnson, chamberlains[1]

The Receiptes   £   s   d

Of Mr Norman for his arreares of rent 9d. Of Gabriell Shad for his arreares of the woole beame 5s. Of John Wakefeild for 2 yeares arreares of the almeshouse garden 5s, for his dwellinge house 2 yeares 5d. 17 February 1646[/7] of Peter Silver for parte of his freedome money 14s 5d, for a buckett 3s 4d. 26 March 1647 of Thomas Scriven for the seale of his fyne 4s. Of William Edwardes 1 quarters rent of the tole £1. Of Mr Doleman one halfe yeere £4. 26 May of Mr Banger in parte of Bignells money £8 12s.[2]

[Marginated subtotal]   15   4   11

23 June of Mr Love att the sealeinge of his lease for one halfe yeares rent before hand £2 15s. Of Mr Fletchers money for one halfe yeare due att Our Lady Day £6. Of Thomas Glover att the sealeinge of his lease for one halfe yeares rent before hand £2 15s.

[f. 180v] Of Robert Hatley in parte of his fyne for his freedome £1, for his buckett 3s 4d. Of William Edwardes halfe a yeares rent for tole £1. Of the money which came from Yarneton £10 8s 2d. Of Mr Rayer for makeinge the moundes of his meade 19s 6d. Of Mr Doleman half a yeare £4. Of Christofer Woodburne for his chardges and composition 10s. 20 November for 3 yeares use of £10 of Anthony Carter £2 8s.[3] For halfe a yeare of Mr Fletchers money due att Michaelmas last £6. Of William Edwardes 1 quarters rent for tole £1.

[Marginated subtotal]   39   19   0

Of Mr Norman for his parte of the use of £10 for 3 yeares £1 4s. Of Thomas Heathen for stallidge and shewe money ending this day £7 8s 10d and contrey bakers standinges 10s 5d, £8 5s 3d. 25 November received by my partner of Mr Jefferies for 3 yeares use of his parte of £10 of the poores money £1 4s. The rest of Joseph Enslowes money for chardges £1 9s 6d.

[Marginated subtotal]   12   2   9
Upon the rent roll   31   4   9½

The totall of all the receiptes this yeare is   98   11   5½

[f. 181r] [3 lines deleted, rest blank]

[f. 181v] Disbursementes by George Gregorie .

For candles att the last accountes 2d. John Durman for keepeinge Trewmans boy due to the same day £1. Lucas for makeinge cleane the hall 2d. 28 January for a coate for the childe which Odell Bayleyes kept 9s. Christofer Smyth for rent for his house taken for the sicke 10s. Left due unto mee from the towne upon the last accountes £4 7s 1½d. 29 January a quart of sacke for the preacher 1s 4d. Paied Mr Jones for preacheinge Mr Meatcalfes sermon 7 February £8.

[Marginated subtotal]   6   15   9½

8 January 1646[/7] our chardges and 2 horses when wee went to Oxon' about the souldiers 12s 6d. For a besome for Lucas 3d. 17 February to an Irishe gentlewoeman by the appoyntment of Mr Maior 3s 4d. 19 February Booden and Dissell for 2 dayes worke att the White Hart 3s 8d. 24 February Mr Rayer for wine 2s 2d. Lucas his quarters wages 6d. Quarteringe 48 horse and men of Collonel Fleetewoodes regiment £4 16s.⁴ 17 March the towneclarke for his chardges att thassizes and to the clarke of thassizes and the clarke of the petitions 13s 2d. Waxe for Scrivens fyne 1d. Mr Jones for preacheinge Mr Fletchers sermon 25 March 16s.

[f. 182r] Paied the poore of Mr Fletchers money 16s. Lucas for wardeinge on the fare 8d.

[Marginated subtotal]   8   4   4

Mr Rayer which he gave unto Irishe people 6 April 2s 6d. Mr Widdowes for his quartridge due att Our Lady Day £5. Mr Sheeres for 4 yeares quitt rent due att Our Lady Day att 7s 8½d per annum, £1 10s. 13 April Plivie for fatcheinge one halfe yeares rent from Mr Doleman 3s. 15 April paied Mr Williams for the leete dinner £2. Paied William Hickes Mr Hiornes his money geven the poore on Good Friday 4s. Paied the money which Sir Thomas Spencer gave to the poore on the Sunday before Easter £1 10s. Mr Jones for preacheinge Mr Brownes sermon on Easter Day 8s. For carryeinge a lettre to Mr Mancell about the poll money 1s.⁵ Gave Lucas 1s. Paied the sarjeant for a quarter due 25 Marche and for gatheringe the stall money 15s.

[Marginated subtotal]   11   15   4

22 May paied Redhead for carryeinge 8 loades of stones 3s 4d. 8 loades of stone 8s. The mason for 3 dayes worke 3s 6d. A dore and a post for the pounde and for whimwhoms 6d.⁶ 2 loades of thorne 10s and for carriage 6s, 16s. John Woodes for stoppinge a gap against the malthouse 3d. 23 May gave by Mr Maiors appoyntment to one Mistris Carie an Irishe woeman 3s 6d.

[f. 182v] 24 May Mr Rayer for wine 5s. 26 May paied att Oxon' for entringe an action against Joseph Onslowe and tharest fee 1s 6d. Richard Meades for goeinge about Trewmans childe 1s 6d. George Greene and William Hawthorne for hedgeinge the meades 4s. 5 June for my chardges and Thomas Paynters for goeinge to Mr Higgins with the money 4s. For cuttinge the weedes in the brooke 4s. 8 June Mr Rayer for wine 1s 10d.

[Marginated subtotal]   3   11   11

13 June unto Robert Busbie in parte of the money which hee was to have with Trewmans boy £2 5s. Lucas for his quartridge due 25 June 6d. Mr Jones for preacheinge Mr Fletchers sermon 24 June 16s. Paied then to the poore 16s. July 5 carryeinge a lettre to London 2d. Paied Mr Widdowes his quarters rent due 24 June £5. 3 dayes worke for scowreinge Thomas Glovers ditches 3s 6d, moweinge his grasse 1s 2d, makeinge his hay 3s 6d. Lucas for wardeinge att Maudlin fare 8d. Lockton towardes the kinges benche and maymed souldiers 10s. Weedle for makeinge cleane the celler 1s. 2 August Mr Williams for thassizes, the clarke of thassizes and the clarke of the petitions 13s 2d, for writtes 8s 4d.

[f. 183r] 9 August to Nathaniel Hanckes for 1 dayes worke in the little house 1s 2d. Wine 1s 4d. 21 August to Mr Rayer for wine 8s. 26 August halfe a yeares of the chauntrey quitrent £2 13s 4d. To the messenger and for the acquittance 5s 6d. Wine 5s 4d.

[Marginated subtotal]   14 13   8

6 September to Christofer Smyth for worke done att the bayes and the holloway £1 10s 4d, September 11 for worke 19s 1d, 12 loades of stones 12s, £1 11s 1d. 22 September Mr Maior when hee and Mr Glover went to Oxon' for chardges 3s 3d. For Mr Glovers horse 1s, Mr Mayottes horse when he went to Norton to the comittee 1s, his chardges 1s 6d.[7] Lucas for wardeinge on St Mathewes fare 8d, Peter Silver for staple and hapses for the little house dore 1s. Hanckes and his boy for 3 dayes worke about the holloway 5s 6d. 28 September Holmes to serve the writt on Mr Jefferies 1s. Mr Jones for Mr Fletchers sermon on Michaelmas Day 16s. Lucas for 1 quarter 6d. Richard Underhill for a cake for the Lady Spencer 12s. Mr Widdowes his quarteridge due at Michaelmas £5. The sarjent for halfe a yeares wages and gatheringe the stallidge then due £1 10s. More to Holmes 1s.

[Marginated subtotal]   12 11 10

[f. 183v] 17 October our chardges when wee went to Mr Dolemans and for horse hire 12s. 16 October Mr Rayer for wine 13s 7d. 18 October Locktons sonne for goeinge to Barton 1s. 21 October Thomas Scriven for mendinge the schoole windowes 2s 6d. 25 October Peter Silver for a key to the little house and mendinge the stockes 1s 7d. 26 October to the receaver att Oxon' for one whole yeare of the chauntery quitrent due att Michaelmas last £5 6s 8d, two acquittances 1s. A copie of the record 3s 8d. Entringe an action att Oxon' 1s 6d. My chardges and horse hire the same time 3s. Withdraweinge the action 4d. 5 November Mr Jones for preacheinge Mr Fletchers sermon 16s. To the poore the same day 16s. Bestowed on Mr Boxe the attorney and the sarjeant att Oxon' 1s 4d.

[Marginated subtotal]   9   0   2

Paied Mr Williams 1 December for the leete dinner £2 5s, his yeares fee £1 6s 8d, his chardges att Hayley 3s 10d, his chardges att Norton 1s 6d, his horsehire 1s, for a writt 5s 1d. 7 December Edward Glover for 3 yeares interest of Captain Warbertons money £1 16s.

[f. 184r] Lucas for wardeinge on the fare 8d. Robert Busbie in full of his money with Trewmans childe £2. To goodwife Bryan for 3 yeares use of £10 of Captain Warbertons money £1 16s. Mr Widdowes for one quarter due att St Thomas Day last £5. 18 December for our chardges when wee went to Oxon' to the governor 4s.[8] 19 December to the poore the Sunday before Christmas of Sir Thomas Spencers dole £1 10s. Lucas for one quarter due att St Thomas Day 6d. James Pyman for 3 yeares use of £10 of Captain Warbertons money 16s. To the poore of the almeshouse geven by old Mr Hiorne 4s.

[Marginated subtotal]   18   10   3

24 December 1647 to William Batt for repaireinge the schoole 3s 4d. Mr Love for hay for the calves 1s 6d, for a horse to Oxon' 1s. A paire of shooes for Lucas 3s 4d. Mr Jones for Mr Fletchers sermon on Christmas Day last 16s, for Mr Brownes sermon the same day 8s. To the poore the same day 16s. Robert Cooper hapses, hinges and staples for the pounde 1s 8d. 3 January 1647[/8] paied the sarjeant for one quarters wages due att St Thomas Day 7s 6d. And for 1 quarter for gatheringe the stalls 7s 6d.

[f. 184v] Mr Marrit for halfe a yeares rent due att Michaelmas 16s 8d. For Lucas coate, cap and makeinge £1 4s 3d. Gyles Francklyn for the wainscott in the hall £3, for tymber nayles and workemanship £2 0s 10d.

[Marginated subtotal]   10   7   7

Sir Thomas Spencers. A note of the chardges for the recoverie of the dole. 22 August to Richard Meades for goeinge to the windmill feild to looke for a distresse 6d. The same day to 4 bayliffes 2s. 26 August Mr Holloway for his fee 10s. For writinge thassignement 2s 6d. For chardges then 3s 10. For our horsemeate 1s 8d. For 3 horses hire 3s 6d. 6 baylifffes for goeinge to distrayne 6s. 27 August 5 bayliffes when they were beate 13s. For the chamberlyns chardges goeinge to councell 3s 10d. 29 August horse hire 1s. A man to goe to Northleigh 8d. For chardges att Oxon' and geven to the councells clarke and horse hire 4s 2d. 30 August for my chardges spent on the leftenant ensigne and souldiers 4s 10d.

[f. 185r] 31 August Woodes for goeinge for the warrant 2s. 5 bayliffes to goe to distrayne 5s. Woodes for carryeinge a lettre to the councell 1s. 3 bayliffes for goeinge 2 tymes to Yarneton 6. Hughe Jones for carryeinge a lettre to the councell 1s. Whitacres Locktons sonne and William Heathen for goeinge 2 dayes to Yarneton 16s 2d. Sam Allen for goeinge 2 dayes to see whether there were anie cattle on the grounde 1s 4d. For expences at Yarneton 1s. Paied when Mr Maior and the aldermen went to the lady 8d. For a horse for Mr Williams to Clarden 3s.[9] 29 September Mr Holloway for his councell 10s. Spent at Yarneton that day 2s. Payd Mr Williams which hee disburst 3s 10d. Paied my partner Johnson which hee disburst in that busines £1 13s 3d. Spent att Yarneton when wee fatched the money 1s 2d. Paied for 3 horses hire 3s.

[Marginated subtotal]   7   7   11

[f. 185v] To my partner which was due to him since the last accountes 9s 10d. For a sheete of pastbord for the table of articles 4d.[10] For 3 quires of paper for the three bookes 1s 3d.   1 May to Mistris Marrit for halfe a yeare rent due att Our Lady Day last 16s 8d.   15 May for £8 of brasse weightes and for carriage troy waytes 8s 10d.   To Mr Cooper for layeinge out the grounde att the White Hart 1s.   John Hayles for carryeinge 1 loade of stones and 1 loade of morter to the towne hall 1s 6d.   Thomas Rayer for a day and a halfe worke there 1s 9d.   Thomas Archer for one day there 1s.   Hanckes for 1 loade of stones 1s.   To Woodes and Barnewshawe for clensinge the little house 1s.   Paper 5d.   A horse hire for my partner 2 dayes to Mr Dolemans 2s.   1 December att Oxon' for 4 warrantes 8s.   Expences att Oxon' about the cuntrey petition 2s 5d.[11]   For 2 horses hire then 2s.   Delivered to Mr Maior 16s which hee was to pay of old Nell 16s.

[Marginated subtotal]   3   15   0

Payd Mr Williams for 5 warrantes 10s.   My partner Johnson which was layed out by him £1, 5 January 17s 7d.   Mr Rayer in full for wine to this day 4s 6d.   For expences att makeinge up thaccountes 3s.

[f. 186r] For fyre att the hall 3s.   The towneclarke for writinge out thaccountes 5s.

[Marginated subtotal]   3   3   1

The totall of all the disbursementes   109   16   10¹/₂
The totall of the receiptes is   98   11   5¹/₂
Soe that there remaynes from the towne to the chamberlyn
Mr Gregorie   11   5   5

This is a true and a just accountes to this day George Gregorie his marke, [signature of] Alexander Johnson

Delivered to Thomas Glover chamberlyn, 36s 6d.
[Signature of] John Williams

[f. 186v] The names of those that made defalt of payment of theire rentes this yeare [1647]
Mr Hiorne for his rentes £1 9s 3d.   Mistris Glover for hoggerill hill 5s.   + Edward Silver 7s.   Gabriell Shad 8s.   + Thomas Glover for le poole 5s. Edward Carter 13s 4d.   + The heires of Mr Say 3s 1d.   Mr Vernon 4s 10d. John Bignell 2s 4d.   + Thomas Glover for the crowne close 1s 6d.   Kirby 6d.   The heires of William Walford 6d.   Mistris Meatcalfe 3d.   +Edward Silver 3d.   Mr Vernon 6d. George Gregorie 6s 8d.   Francis Druce 5d.   Mathewe Pen 1¹/₂d.   Robert Symons 5¹/₂d.   John Wakefeild 2¹/₂d.   More from him 5s.   John Bignell 2d. Mistris Harris 5s 6d.   The heires of George Witney 5¹/₂d.   Thomas Heathen 6d. Walter Bayleyes 9d. Thomas Meatcalfe 3³/₄d.   William Tomlyns 1s 2d.   William Lardner 4d.   Kirby 2¹/₂d.   The heires of William Walford 4¹/₂d.   Widdowe Rayer ¹/₂d.   Thomas Frayne for Thomas Bruce his house 3d.
[Marginated subtotal]   5   15   3¹/₄

[1] Note the restoration of town finances, receipt of Doleman's money, and back payments of stipends and quitrents.
[2] Possible ref. to surety and bond noted in the 1636 acct.
[3] This and sums below were left by Capt. Warburton: see above, Intro.
[4] His regiment was part of the New Model Horse: above, in 1646; Firth and Davies, *Reg. Hist.* i. 91-101
[5] See above for poll money.
[6] i.e. trifles. Cf. Shropshire meaning of turnsticks: ex inf. Dr. D.M. Barratt.
[7] Chipping Norton. Perhaps the Committee for Compounding, which was active at this time.
[8] In 1647-8 Lt.-Col. Thomas Kelsey, in the absence of his superior, Col. Ric. Ingoldsby: *Reg. Hist.* i. 376.
[9] Claverdon (Warws.).
[10] Probably the Oxf. Articles of War ordered to be printed 24 June. They allowed royalists in Oxon. to compound for their estates: F. Madan, *Oxf. Books 1641–50*, ii, no. 1880.
[11] From the county of Oxford, presented to Parl. 14 and 15 Sept. 1647: B.L., Thomason Tracts, i. 437.

[f. 187r] Accounts taken [17 deleted] 22 January 1648[/9], Thomas Glover and Francis Druce, chamberlains[1]

Receiptes	£	s	d
8 January [1647/8] in money	1	16	6
6 March of Richard Phillips for the shred of elme by the cage	0	8	0
Of Mr Edwardes for a quarter for the corne tole	1	0	0
8 May of Mr Doleman	4	0	0
16 February of Mr Love in parte of Mr Nashes £20	10	0	0
10 May Mr Fletchers money	6	0	0
Of Thomas Heathen for stall money St Thomas Day to Our Lady Day	1	11	5
13 June of John Saunders of the dole money	1	10	0
25 June of Mr Love more of Mr Nashes money	2	10	0
10 July of Thomas Heathen for stall from Our Lady Day to this day	1	1	1
5 October of William Edwardes	1	10	0
12 October the dole money from Yeardington	1	10	0
18 October towards the repaire of the cage	0	10	0
10 November Mr Dolemans money	4	0	0
20 November more of Mr Love of Mr Nashes money	2	10	0
13 December Mr Fletchers money	6	0	0
[f. 187v] 16 December of William Edwardes	1	10	0
20 December of Robert Hatley	1	0	0
9 January [1648/9] of Thomas Heathen 20 July to this day	2	1	6
Upon the rent role	48	12	4
More upon the rent role	0	3	10
More on the rent role	0	0	9
The whole of the receiptes [corrected in MS. from £99 4s 6d]	99	5	5

[f. 188r] Theire disbursementes

8 January 1647[/8] to George Gregorie £11 5s 5d, Mr Woodward £10. 11 January Morgan for bringeinge downe the mortmaine 2s 6d.[2] 13 January Mr Maior and Mr Rayer for a levie for the towneland £1 16s.[3] 14 January wine for Captain Meservie 2s 4d.[4] 16 January Thomas Haughten and Thomas Cotten £1 12s.

6 February Mr Jones for Mr Meatcalfes sermon 8s. 8 February delivered to Gyles Francklyn of Mr Nashes money 10s. 16 February Thomas Scriven for glazeinge the schoole windowes 1s 6d.

1 March wine for the comittees 2s 4d, a pinte of sacke for Mr Lester 8d,[5] a quart of sacke for Mr Kecke a preacher 1s 4d. Hanckes for amendinge the almeshouse wall 1s. 2 March the towneclarke for lent assizes and a writt 15s. To him for John Jeffes a prisoner 10s. 16 March Mr Mayottes chardges and myne owne and horse hire twice to Barton 5s. 18 March in money for the dole £1 10s.
[Subtotal]   38 13 1
25 March Mr Widdowes his quartridge £5. 26 March Mr Jones for Mr Fletchers sermon 16s. Payd then to the poore 16s.

[f. 188v] 26 March for 3 monethes taxe[6] for the towne land 12s. 28 March Lucas for wardeinge and makeinge cleane the gutter 1s 2d, wood for the guarde 3s. 31 March payd Hixe that was gave to the poore by old Mr Hiorne 4s.

3 April payd Mr Jones for Mr Brownes sermon 8s. 7 April spent on Mr Lester 1s. 17 April the leete dinner £2 15s. 20 April widdowe Duke by Mr Maiors order 2s. 21 April for my horse hire and expences goeinge to Yeardington 1s 6d. 29 April Mr Marrettes halfe yeares rent 16s 8d.

1 May my chardges and horse hire to Yeardington [Yarnton] 1s 6d. 6 May 2 horses hire two dayes to Mr Dolemans 5s, theire meate 3s, our expences 9s. 16 May Edward Glover £5. 18 May Peeter Silver for worke in the little house windowe and dore 2s 2d. 22 May Mr Maior for a levie for the towne land 16s. Mr Jones for Mr Nashes sermon 16s. 1 June payd Mr Woodward for 2 horse hire 4s.
[Subtotal]   19 13 0
[f. 189r] 8 June a paire of floodgates 16s. 10 June 2 horse hire for Mr Woodward and Mr Mayott to Adderbury 2s. Thomas Heathen for Lady Dayes quartridge and gatheringe the stallidge 15s. 22 June horse hire to Yeardington 1s. Wine for Mr Prideauxe 1s 4d.   24 June two horse hire and my owne and my partners expences to Banbury 4s 4d. 28 June Mr Widdowes his quartridge £5. 29 June Lucas his quartridge 6d. 1 August Edward Silver for a levie for the towne land 18s. 2 August a quart of sacke geven to Mr Knightbridge 1s 4d. 6 August Mr Johnson and Mr Gregories chardges to Oxon' 4s 4d. 8 August my horse hire and Gabriell Shaddes and our chardges goeinge to the comitee 4s 4d. 13 August Woodes for makeinge cleane the gutter of the crosse and hall 6d. 18 August Richard Holmes for goeinge with a warrant to the highe constable 1s 2d. 23 August Thomas Heathen for his quartridge and the stallidge 15s.

4 September wine for Mr Knightbridge when hee preached 2s 2d. Mr Jones for Mr Fletchers sermon 16s. 16 September a quart of sacke and beare for the quarter master that came with the prisoners from Colchester 1s 10d.[7]
[Subtotal]   11   17   4

[f. 189v] 18 September Richard Meades for goeinge towardes London 2s 6d. 21 September for quarteringe 18 horses one night with fyre and candle 9s. 23 September Lucas for wardeinge 8d. 28 September Richard Meades for goeinge to St Albons 8d.[8] 29 September Mr Widdowes his quartridge £5. Lucas for makeinge cleane the gutter 6d.
1 October payd Mr Fletchers money to the poore 16s. 2 October Mr Jones his sermon 16s. For a cake for Sir Thomas Spencer 10s. For horse hire to carry it 1s. 7 October Mistris Marrit her halfe yeares rent 16s 8d. 18 October wine for Captain Grymes and Captain Shrimpton 4s 4d.[9] Whitacre for cleansinge the churche £1 6s 8d. 20 October for the leete dinner £2 10s. To Mr Lee of Yeardington 15s. 21 October for repareinge the stockes and pennyles benche 4s. The workemen for veweinge the churche 5s. Scriven for the same 1s. 24 October lathe nayles and pins for the cage 2s 8d. Batt for workemanship and mosse 4s.
[Subtotal]   14   13   0
29 October Symons for a bell wheele 10s.
5 November the sheriffe for the quitrent £2 13s 8d. 5 November Francis Druce and Gabriel Shad for horse hire to St Albons and to London 16s.
[f. 190r] 5 November payd the poore Mr Fletchers money 16s. Payd Mr Jones for his sermon 16s. Our chardges goeinge to St Albons and London £3 4s. Gave to Mr Rushworthes[10] clarke 5s. Spent on Mr Twyford 2s 8d. 6 November John Archer for a loade of slatt 8s 10d. 8 November Dissell for carryeinge them 2s. 12 November for a messenger from Alscott to Childrey[11] and my chardge and horse hire 5s 4d. 14 November Christofer Smyth the overseer for repaire of the highewayes 2s 6d.
24 November lyme and worke and nayles and cresste for the cage 3s 4d. Lucas for wardeinge 8d.
13 December cloath for Lucas his coate £1. 20 December Mr Widdowes his quartridge £5. Edwardes for mendinge the bushell 3s. Robert Hatley for goeinge betweene Lockidge and Childrey 2s. Mr Lucas for wardeinge 6d.
[Subtotal]   16   10   8
Payd Hickes Mr Hiornes money 4s. 22 December George Symons for 2 dayes worke and a halfe in the churche 2s 6d. 23 December the poore the dole money £1 10s. Mr Jones for Mr Fletchers sermon 16s, for the poore 16s. Makeinge Lucas his coate and buttens 2s 6d. Horse hire for the towneclarke and Francis Druce to Daddinge and Oxon' and Francis his chardge 6s 10d.
[f. 190v] 4 January 1648[/9] two horse hire and chardge for Mr Mayott and my owne to the comitte 4s 6d. Geven to Mr Appletrees[12] clarke 2s. 6 January Mr Jones for Brownes sermon 8s. Thomas Heathen for halfe a yeares wages and gatheringe the stall money £1 10s.
[Subtotal]   6   2   0

The towneclarke which hee layd out by Mr Maiors appoyntment £2 4s. To
him which was oweinge upon the booke £1 9s 4d, his yeares wages due at
Michaelmas £1 6s 8d, for the sumer assizes 11s 4d, for his chardges to Adderbury
and Oxon' 2s 4d, for writinge this accountes 5s.   5   18   8
16 January a quart of sacke 1s 4d.
Expences att makeinge this accomptes 2s, fyre the
accountes day 2s 6d.   6   5   10

The totall of the receiptes [corrected in MS. from £99 4s 6d]   99   5   5
The disbursementes   113   13   11
Soe there remaynes to the chamberlyns [corrected in MS.
from £19 8s 0d]   14   8   6

*[f. 191r]   The names of those who have made defaulte of payment of theire rentes this
yeare [1648]*

[First entry crossed out] Mr Woodward for Hampton leas £1. Mistris Glover for
hoggerill hill 5s.   Henry Whiteside for his house 8s.   + Edward Silver for his
brothers house 7s.   + Mr Love for the common pooles £5 10s. Edward Carter+
for his house 6s 8d.   Mr Vernon for the greate house 4s 10d.   Mr Love for his
house 7d.   Edward Silver for his dwellinge house 3d.   John Vernon for the house
where William Batt lately dwelt 6d.   + George Gregorie for his dwellinge house
2d.   And for the poores + rent 6s 8d.   + Francis Druce for Dissells house 5d.   Mr
Selfe for his house 1½d.   And for his pales and porche 6d.   Robert Symons for
Collyers house 5½d.   The heires of George Witney 5½d.   Thomas Heathen for
his house 6d.   Mr Manninge for Kentes house 4d.   Mr Thomas Meatcalfe for
[deleted, his] Scurriers houses ¾d.   And for the garden 1½d.   And for one other
house next to it 1½d.   William Tomlyns for Spittle house close 2d.   William
Lockton for the George 4d.
Summ totall [blank]

[f. 191v] [blank]

¹ Receipt of £15 from Nashe's money and regular receipts of the Spencer dole money and
Doleman's school money helped continue the town's financial recovery, despite the loss of some
rents.
² Presumably the grant of mortmain obtained 1599 to enable the town to buy £100 of land for the
school and the poor: B 81, f. 16v; *Rep. Char. Com., 1815–39*, 489. It would have been needed for
the Commission for Charitable Uses which was considering Woodstock charities: see below, 1650.
³ Presumably the govt's three-monthly assessment levy as below, although it could be a local poor
rate as recorded in churchwardens' accts. from the 1650s. There is no mention here of paying the
assessments in 1646 or 1647 despite being under parl. control; in 1645 Luke's men mistakenly arrested a Bicester man for an unpaid Woodstock assessment: *Letter Books* p.504. For parl. taxes see *Acts
and Ordinances*, iii. 12; Gardiner, *Hist. of the Great Civil War*, i. 96.
⁴ Capt. Fras. Messervey of Jersey, a parl. officer: *Cal. Cttee. for Compounding, 1643–60*, iii. 2245.
⁵ Possibly the same local cttees. as below. Rob. Leicester or Lester of Adderbury was a member of
the county cttee. for sequestrations : *Cal. Cttee. for Compounding, 1643–60*, i. 172. He and Appletree
were active in Woodstock in 1649 also: below.
⁶ Above.

[7] In June and July Colchester was besieged by a parl. army that included Fleetwood's regiment formerly at Woodstock: *Reg. Hist.*, i. 94; above. The church had to be cleaned and repaired after the prisoners had been kept in it: below.
[8] St. Alban's was the army HQ from 21 Sept.
[9] Capts. John Grymes and John Shrimpton of the New Model Foot regiment occupying Oxf.: *Reg. Hist.* i. 375, 379, 382, 383.
[10] John Rushworth, historian, secretary to the army council in St. Alban's: *D.N.B.*
[11] To collect Doleman's money.
[12] Thos. Appletree of Deddington, member of the county cttee. for sequestrations which had sat in Woodstock in 1646: *Cal. Cttee for Compounding*, 1643–60, ii. 1441.

[f. 192r] Accounts taken 28 December 1649, Thomas Glover and Francis Druce, chamberlains

[Receipts]	£	s	d
22 January 1648[/9] receaved that day in money	1	7	0
20 February of Mr Norman	0	8	0
12 April Mr Dolemans money	4	0	0
13 April of Sir William Spencer money	1	10	0
12 May Mr Fletchers money	6	0	0
20 July the old arreares of Mr Smyth	6	17	4
2 October for Salters fyne	0	4	0
18 October Mr Dolemans money	4	0	0
16 November of Sir William Spencers money	1	10	0
Then Mr Fletchers money	6	0	0
Of Mr Rayer of Mr Loves money	1	0	0
Of William Edwardes yeares rent of tole	4	0	0
16 December of Thomas Heathen for stall money	4	8	0
[Marginated subtotal]	41	4	4
Upon the rent role	53	2	8
Summ totall	94	7	0

[f. 192v] [blank]

[f. 193r] Disbursements

1648 remayneinge to the chamberlyns since the last accountes £14 19s 6d. 22 January 1648[/9] Christofer Smyth for worke and carryeinge stones for the repaire of the holloway 4s, William Drinkewater which the towne owed him 9s, Thomas Cotten £2. 24 January George Gregorie for a levie for the towne £1 12s. 29 January Hankes for worke about the hollowe way 9s, a pint of sacke for Mr Draper 8d, geven Mr Prideauxe a quarte sacke 1s 4d.
4 February Mr Jones for Mr Meatcalfes sermon 8s.

20 February glazeinge the schoole windowes 13s 6d. 22 February Mr Norman for slatt and carriage 8s 8d. 23 February worke and materialls for repaire of the schoole £1 3s 4d. 24 February Mr Twyford for one yeare for the chauntrey £5 6s 8d, a quart of sacke to him 1s 4d, acquittances and charges 5s. 25 February a spout of lead for the schoolhouse 1s 9d. 2 March payd goodwife Bryan 1s. 4 March Thomas Haughten for Lucas his shooes 3s 8d. Wine for a preacher 1s 4d. 4 March payd widdowe Morris 1s.

[Marginated subtotal]   27   19   9

[f. 193v] 14 [March] payd goodwife Batt 1s, goodwife [Weadle deleted] Lowe 6d. 3 pintes of sacke and a pint of clarrett for Mr Dobson 2s 5d. 18 March Sir William Spencers dole £1 10s. 23 March old Mr Hiornes dole money 4s. 25 March Mr Jones Mr Fletchers sermon 16s, and to the poore then 16s.

[Marginated subtotal]   3   9   11

25 March Mr Widdowes his quarteridge £5. 26 March Mr Jones Mr Brownes sermon 8s. Geven Henrie Lowes daughter 6d. 28 March Lucas his quarteridge and clensinge the gutter 1s 2d. 29 March a pint of sacke and beere for Mr Eles 1s 2d. 31 March Christofer Smyth for the holloway and the bridge 7s 9d.

6 April a quart of sacke for Doctor Prideauxe 1s 4d. 9 April horse hire and chardges goeinge to Mr Dolemans 5s 4d. 20 April Mr Marrittes rent 16s. 21 April the towne leete dinner £3. 23 April a quart of sacke for the comittees 1s 4d. 24 April Phillip Smythes wife 7s. A pint of sacke for Mr Lester 8d. 26 April Gabriell Shad a levie for the towne 12s.

Payd Mr Lester £3, gave Mr Appletree a pint sacke 8d.

4 May beere for Mr Eles 4d. 24 May Mr Jones for Mr Nashes sermon 8d. 3 June a quart of sacke for Mr Knightbridge 1s 4d. 14 June payd Thomas Paynter a levie for the towne £1. 16 June for 4 quartermasters for breade and beare 1s 8d.

[Marginated subtotal]   15   14   11

[f. 194r] 16 June Robert Wilsden for worke att the schoolehouse 3s. 24 June Mr Jones for Mr Fletchers sermon 16s, and to the poore then 16s.

[Marginated subtotal]   1   15   0

26 June Mr Widdowes his quarteridge £5, Lucas his quarteridge 6d, for a pint of sacke and a pint of clarrett for Mr Knightbridge 1s 1d. 28 June wine for Mr Hoffeman 2s.

10 July goeinge to Yeardington to Mr Smyth 1s.   16 July Peter Silver for a paire of fetters 3s 6d. 18 July wine for Mr Kempe 1s 8d. 20 July horse hire and chardges to Yeardington when I had tharreares 1s 8d. 24 July Lucas for wardeinge 8d.

8 August a cake for Judge Adkins 10s, wine and beare eateinge the tast 1s, Mr Rayer a 3 monethes taxe £1 8s 6d. 9 August beare and horsemeate for the sheriffes deputie 1s 6d. 10 August wine for Doctor Darton.[1] 22 August mosse and pins 2s 6d, nayles 1s 8d, lead for the gutter 1s 4d, lyme and haire 3s 4d, lathe 1s, a dozen of cresse 3s. 8 September workemanship about the penniles benche 13s. Beare and horsemeate for Eles 6d. 10 September wine for 6 quartermasters 2s 8d. 22 September Lucas for wardeinge 8d.

[Marginated subtotal]   9   3   5

[f. 194v] 29 September Mr Widdowes his quarteridge £5, Mr Jones for Mr Fletchers sermon 16s, the poore then 16s. 30 September Sam [Allen] for goeinge to Oxon' 1s 4d.

1 October Lucas his quarteridge 6d. Payd Mr Marrittes rent 16s 8d. 15 October horse hire and chardges to Yeardington 1s 6d. 16 October for the leete dinner £3. Charges goeinge to Childrey 11s 8d. 29 October payd Mr Johnson for a 3 monethes taxe £1 10s.

5 November Mr Jones for Mr Fletchers sermon 16s, the poore then 16s. From September 12 to October 16 payd Mr Rayer for wine for the lecturers 5s 5d. 12 November for wine for Mr Sherlocke 2s 3d.

14 November for a showell for Lucas 1s 2d. 16 November for carrieinge Adrie away 5s. For cloath for Lucas his coate 17s 8d. 22 November carryeinge the almeshouse wood 6d. 26 November making Lucas his coate and buttons 2s 6d. Payd Newberry Hensington quitrent 3s 10d and for thacquittance 4d. 27 November a quart of sacke for Mr Woodward 1s 6d.

6 December Lucas for wardeinge 8d.

16 December Mr Widdowes his quarteridge £5, Goodman Edwardes for mendinge the hall bell 4d, Batt for repaireinge the almeshouse £1 1s 8d, beveridges to the workemen 1s 6d.

[Marginated subtotal]   22   10   0

[f. 195r] 9 December a pint of sacke and a pint of clarrett for Mr Jones 1s 3d, 16 December him a quart of sacke 1s 6d. 18 December Liddam for glazeinge the hall windowes 12s 8d. 20 December payd the poore Mr Hiornes money 4s, Lucas his quarteridge 6d, a pint of sacke for Mr Astyn 9d. 23 December payd the poore Sir William Spencers dole money £1 10s, shooes for Lucas 3s 8d. 25 December Mr Jones for Mr Fletchers sermons 16s, the poore then 16s. Mr Jones for Mr Brownes sermons 8s. For besome for Lucas 3d, Thomas Heathen for his yeares wages £1 10s, and for gatheringe the stall money £1 10s. Payd the towneclarke his wages £1 6s 8d, for 2 assizes £1 2s 8d, for Cornewells will[2] and his chardges and his horse to Oxon' 4s 6d, payd him which hee layd out to Mr Astyn 10s. Layd out in chardges for the towneclarke and my selfe to Oxon' 4s. Payd him for writeinge this accountes 5s. For expences att makinge up this accountes 3s.

[Marginated subtotal]   11   10   5

Summ totall receiptes	94	7	0
The disbursementes	92	3	5
Soe there remaynes to the towne	2	4	5

This accountes was examined by me John Williams towneclarke

[f. 195v] [blank]

[f. 196r] The names of those that have made defaulte of payement of theire rentes this yeare 1649

Mr Woodward for Hampton leas £2. Mistris Glover for hoggerill hill 5s. Henry Whiteside for his house 8s. Henry Hammond 5s. + Edward Silver for the house where his brother Peter dwelleth 7s. Mr [Vernon deleted] Browne for his great house 4s 10d. John Kirby for Edward Harris his house 6d. The heires of William Walford for the dove house close 6d. + Edward Silver for his dwellinge house 3d. Mr Vernon for the house where William Batt lately dwelt 6d. + George Gregorie for his dwellinge house to the poore 6s 6d. Mr Woodward for his dwellinge house 3d, his house next to it 3d. Christofer Smyth for his dwellinge house 3d, his pales 6d. Henry Nurth for William Seares house 5d, and for his penthouse and bulke 7d. Mathew Pen for his house 1¹/₂d. Robert Symons for John Colliers house 5¹/₂d. John Norman for his dwellinge house 3d, and for his pales 6d. Mr Sheires for the Bull 5s 6d, hee for 3 houses in Oxon' streete 5¹/₂ d. Thomas Meatcalfe for his 2 houses 2³/₄d. William Tomlyns for the Spittle house close 2d. [Total]   4   8   2¹/₄

[f. 196v] 28 December 1649 Md this day it was agreede by Mr Maior Mr Rayer Mr Noble and the major parte of the common councell that Christofer Woodburne should bee admitted a free comeburgesse of this boroughe. Hee for a fyne is to take George the childe of George Day and give in a bond of £40 to save the towne harmelesse from any chardge that shall come to the towne by reason of the said childe and the towne to forgive him all arreares for stallige which hee oweth unto them.[3] Provided that if the parentes of the sayd childe shall within two or three yeares after this day take to them the sayd childe then the sayd Christofer hath promised to pay to the towne forty shillinges (in money).

[Signatures of] Nicholas Mayott maior, John Williams towneclarke

[1] Nic. Darton (1603–1649), noted presbyterian divine: *D.N.B.*
[2] Again needed for the commission considering the Woodstock charities this year: below, 1650.
[3] Presumably an apprenticeship. For his arrears see 1646.

[f. 197r] Accounts taken 17 January 1650[/1], Thomas Glover and Francis Druce, chamberlains

Receipts	£	s	d
4 April 1650 receaved of Mr Love	5	1	6
Of Mr John Hopkins the gift of his brother Mr Henry Hopkins to the use of the poore[1]	5	0	0
The dole money	1	10	0
3 June of Thomas Slatter towardes the money disbursed at Oxon'	0	19	0
For the one eyed sorrell horse	4	8	0

22 June Mr Fletchers money	6	0	0
10 July from Childrey	4	0	0
9 September of Mr Noble	5	0	0
5 November from Yeardington	1	10	0
12 November from Childrey	4	0	0
12 December Mr Fletchers money	6	0	0
20 December for the bay horse	1	17	0
Of William Edwardes for one yeare for tole	4	0	0
Of Thomas Heathen for one yeare for stallidge	4	10	0
Upon the rent role	51	6	7
[Marginated total]	105	2	1

[f. 197v] [blank]

[f. 198r]   Disbursements

28 December 1649 payd William Drinkewater 6s. For fyre the last accountes 2s 6d. 1 January 1650 widdowe Richardson 1s 10d, Thomas Bruce 2s 6d, Francis Druce 4s. 5 January nayles and worke about the cage 1s 4d. 12 January Mr Eles the fee farme £2 13s 4d, his chardges and acquittance 5s 6d.² For sweepeinge the almeshouse chimneyes 10d. 14 January mendinge the holloway and tymber 8s 10d. Wine for the two Mr Woodwardes 3s. 15 January Christofer Smyth 16s 9d. John Morgan for carryeinge Hulls children to London 6s. 22 January wine for a preacher 1s 6d. To Mr Twyfordes man for 1 yeares for chauntreyes £5 6s 8d, acquittances and charges 6s 10d. 28 January horse hire and charges to Dadington 3s 4d. Paper 5d. 2 February payd the undersheriffe the feefarme £2 13s 4d, charges and acquittance 2s 8d. 4 February Mr Jones for Mr Meatcalfes sermon 8s. 6 February wine for Mr Trumball 1s 6d. For Mr Nashes sermon £1. For the jeame of the towne hall 17s 6d, the jeames and steire 6s 6d, carryeinge morter and bemes 7s.

[Marginated subtotal for f. 198r]	17	8	2

[f. 198v] 22 February wine for Mr Ferrers 9d. The 3 monethes taxe to Mr Noble £1. For Mistris Marrittes house 1s. For carrieinge rubble from the hall 6d. 23 March payd Mr Widdowes his quarteridge £5. Edward Silver for 3 crestes 9d. Wine for Mr Crooke,³ Mr Woodward and Mr Ferrers 5s 6d, for Mr Twyford 1s 6d. 25 March Mr Jones Mr Fletchers sermon 16s, to the poor 16s. Wine for Mr Knightbridge 1s 6d. Lucas for wardeinge 8d, his quarteridge 6d. 2 April Mistris Marrittes rent 16s 8d. 5 April Mr Loves horses meate att Oxon' 1s 10d. The sarjeantes fees of tharest 2s 4d. Horse hire and charges thether 2s 6d. 7 April the poore the dole money £1 10s. 10 April payd Mr Rayer for hay for Mr Loves horses 8s 6d. 12 April Mr Hiornes money for the poore 4s. A cake for Judge Adkins 10s. Mr Butlers entrance for Mr Loves horses 2s. 16 April Mr Jones for Mr Brownes sermon 8s. 18 April for councell and other charges and dinner att Oxon' £4 13s.

[Marginated subtotal for f. 198v]	17	3	6

[f. 199r] 18 April wine for a preacher 1s 6d. Hay for Mr Loves horses, hay 3 nightes and oats 6s 6d, shooeinge them 1s 2d. Horse hire for Mr Hiorne 1s 6d. Mendinge the office windowes 3s 3d. 22 April goeinge for the dole money 1s 6d. 24 April a sessions booke 5s. A shooe for Mr Loves horse 6d. Mr Banger for the decree 3s 4d, to his clarke 1s. 26 April Richard Phillips the 3 monethes taxe 16s 6d. 29 April horse hire to goe to Oxon' for Mr Hopkins 2s 6d. Payd Francis Pyman £3. Henry Newberry for halfe a yeares rent for Hensington 3s 10d, an acquittance 2d.

1 May Richard Phillips for Mistris Marrites house 1s. 2 May a rope for the hall bell 1s 4d. Joseph Fletcher the leete dinner £2 5s. Gabriell Shad the britishe taxe £1 10s.[4] 6 May Thomas Heathen 6s. 13 May Richard Underhill £2. 16 May for Mr Loves horses meate when they were bloodded 1s 8d, blooddinge and fatcheinge up 10d. Robert Cooper the collector 16s.

[Marginated subtotal for f. 199r]   12   10   1

[f. 199v] 26 May mendinge and glazeinge the hall windowes next to Robert Coopers 6s 8d. Wine for Mr Knightbridge 1s 6d. 28 May repaireinge parte of the hall and all materialls 12s 6d, beveridges for workemen 9d. 18 June Mr Nashes sermon £1. For Mr Loves horse grasse 12s 6d. Wine for Mr Woodward 1s 6d. Payd Goodwife Durbridge 12s, Weller the collector 3s 2d. 24 June Mr Widdowes his quarteridge £5. Mr Jones Mr Fletchers sermon 16s, the poor then 16s. Lucas his quarteridge 6d. Wine for Mr Hawes 1s 6d. For twice goeinge to Childrey 6s. 1 July mendinge the towne bushell 1s 6d. To him that brought Childrey money 2d. 13 July wine for a preacher 1s 6d. 22 July Lucas for wardeinge 8d. 22 August riddeinge the bayes 1s 6d. 6 September Mr Rayer a 3 monethes taxe £1 6s. 12 September mendinge the wall of the holloway 9s 8d. 24 September Mr Widdowes his quarteridge £5. For mendinge the hall bell 1s 4d. Wine for Mr Twyford 1s 6d. Lucas for wardeinge 8d. Wine for the minister of Hampton 1s 3d. 26 September Mr Draper £2 13s 4d. 29 September Mr Fletchers sermon 16s, to the poore 16s. Lucas for his quarteridge 6d.

[Marginated subtotal for f. 199v]   22   2   2

[f. 200r] 4 October Mr Rayer for bullet and powder 8s 8d. 6 October Thomas Paynter and George Gregories charges to the highe constable 8s 3d. 18 October the towne dinner £2 10s. 22 October goeinge for the dole money 1s 6d. Wine for Mr Woodward 1s 6d, for the comissioners 3s.[5] 24 October Captain Butler[6] the fee farme £2 13s 4d, acquittance 6d. 30 October the 3 monethes taxe 16s.

4 November a pint of sacke 9d. 5 November Mr Fletchers sermon 16s, to the poore 16s. Mistris Marrittes rent 16s 8d. 12 November goeinge to Childrey 8s 8d. Oweinge to mee since I was constable 12s 8d. 10 December Lucas for wardeinge 8d. 13 December a locke for the little house. 16 December to Robert Bruce £1 10s. 18 December to William Dissell £1 10s. Mr Widdowes his quarteridge £5. Parchement for the engagement 6d. To the poore Mr

Hiornes money 4s. My brother Williams for timber £1 6s. Workemanship, nayles, hookes and hinges for the cage and woodden bridge £1 4s 8d. Francis Druce for a loade of stone 1s. 25 December the poore the dole money £1 10s. Mr Fletchers sermon 16s, to the poore 16s. Lucas for his quarteridge 6d. For Mr Brownes sermon 8s.

[Marginated subtotal for f. 200r]   25   2   10

[f. 200v] Payd the towneclarke for 2 actions and two arrestes at Oxon' 3s. Him more which Mr Maior had for Hulls children £1. For 2 writtes and 5 warrantes £1 2d, for his charges to Oxon' one night 4s, for the searche of 3 wills 3s, an extract of Cornewells will and the coppie of the probate 2s 6d. Payd him which he delivered to Thomas Heathen 2s 6d. For his charges to Oxon' 3s. Delivered to old Anthonie 2s. His charges to Oxon' 2s. Payd him for a messenger that [rode] all night from Oxon' to Daddington for the Comission of Charitable Uses 5s.[7] Payd him Mr Crookes charges att Our Lady Day leete 1s. Payd him for the 2 assizes £1 2s 8d. His yeares wages at Michaelmas £1 6s 8d. Payd him for entringe the decree in the pettibagg 2s 6d. For Mr Crookes charges the last leete 1s. Payd him for writinge this accountes 5s.

[Marginated subtotal for f. 200v]   6   6   0

[f. 201r] January 1650[/1] Thomas Heathen his yeares wages £1 10s. Payd him for the gatheringe the stall money £1 10s. Mr Rayer for timber 17s. For Lucas his coate and makeinge 18s, a paire of shooes 3s 8d. Spent att makeinge thaccountes 3s. For fyre and spent att thaccountes 5s.

[Marginated subtotal]   5   6   8

[Entry crossed through] Soe that that totall of all the receipts this yeare is £105 2s 1d. The totall of the disbursements £105 19s 5d. Soe there remaynes to the chamberlyns £1 19s 7d. The defaulters this yeere £6 3s 6¾d. This accountes was examined by me John Williams towneclarke.

Oweinge by the chamberlyns the last accountes	2	4	5
His receiptes	105	2	1
The disbursementes	105	19	5
Soe there remaynes to the towne	1	7	1

This accountes was examined by mee John Williams towneclarke

[Entry cross-referenced to last line of accounts] Mr Glover to pay more upon old arrears 12s.

[f. 201v] 17 January 1650[/1] Md then all accountes were made even betweene Mr Woodward and the towne for all rentes due and all other accountes betweene the towne and him and upon this accountes it appeares that the towne is indebted unto him £1 9s 8d which is to be allowed him. The foure poundes hee lent to Compton House excepted.

Md this day it was agreede that Joseph Fletcher shall have the pitche and shewe of all stalls hee shall sett before his dore where hee nowe dwelleth for the terme of foure yeares if hee shall dwell soe longe there payeinge 20s a year dureinge suche tyme hee shall holde it the money to bee payd halfe yearly. He is to begin from St Thomas Day last.

[Signature of] George Noble maior

[f. 202r] The names of those that made defaulte of payement of theire rentes this yeare 1650

Mr Thomas Woodward for Hampton leas £1. Mistris Glover for hoggerill hill 5s. + Francis Druce for the garden 2s. For Trewmans house 3s 4d. Richard Underhill for his house 5s. + Francis Druce for Maudlin house 5s. For the other little garden there 6d. + John Bradshawes heires for Gabriell Shades house 10s. + Henry Hammond for his house 10s. + Henry Whiteside 8s. + Edward Silver for his brothers house 7s. + Gabriell Shad for the wooll beame 8s. Edward Carter for his house £8 13s 4d. Mr Vernon for the house where William Edwardes dwelleth 4s 10d. Edward Harris for Kirbies house 6d. Mr Love for his house and pales 7d. The heires of William Walford for the dove house close 6d. Mistris Meatcalfe for Privates house and the barne 3d. + Edward Silver for his dwelling house 3d. Edward Glover for hoggerill hill 3d. Mr Vernon for Fletchers house 6d. + George Gregorie for his house 2d. + For the poores money 6s 8d. Mr Woodward for his house 3d, and for the next house to it 3d.

[Marginated subtotal for f. 202r]	5	10	2

[f. 202v] Francis Druce for William Dissells house 5d. Christofer Smyth for his dwellinge house 3d, and for his pales 6d. + Henry Nurth for Thomas Brownes house 5d. + For his penthouse and bulke 7d. + Edward Silver for Locktons house 1$\frac{1}{2}$d. + Robert Symons for Colliers house 5$\frac{1}{2}$d. + John Norman for his house 3d, + his pales 6d. Mr Sheires for the Bull 5s 6d. +Francis Druce for his dwelling house 4d. Mr Sheires for the houses where William Hickes, James Pyman and the widdowe Hitche dwell 5$\frac{1}{2}$d. Widdowe Heathen for her house 6d. + Richard Manninge for the house next Pettie Johns lane 4d. + For a little garden adjoyneinge to the same lane 4d. Thomas Meatcalfe for his 2 houses and garden 3$\frac{3}{4}$d. William Tomlins for Thomas Cottens house 1s, and for Spittlehouse close 2d. Kirby for the houses where Holmes and Newell dwelt 2$\frac{1}{2}$d. The heires of William Walford for 2 houses let to Joane Harris 4d. Widdowe Warren for the house in the common acre 1d. Widdowe Raye for Busbies house in Pettie Johns lane $\frac{1}{2}$d. Thomas Scriven for his house 3d.

[Marginated subtotal for f. 202v]	0	13	7$\frac{3}{4}$

Totall [for uncollected rents]	6	3	6$\frac{3}{4}$

[ff. 203r–211v] [blank]

[1] A Good Friday bread charity left by Hen. Hopkins (d. 1643) of Exeter Coll., Oxf.: MS. Wills Oxon. 32/2/29; B 97, p. 14. The war must account for this late payment.

[2] First of three payments for the fee farm this year, probably including one for 1649 and one for the Civil War period.

[3] Ric. Crooke, dep. recorder of the town, dep. steward of the manor, and brother of a 1649 parl. commissioner, was frightened out of the manor house by the supposed hauntings: Widdowes, *Just Devil*. In Jan. 1652 the town voted him 40s, 'for his love in assisting the corporation with his advise and councell and for his great paynes taken in the behalf of the town'. In Aug. he was admitted freeman without payment of fees or dues, and on 2 Sept. he was elected common councillor: B 83, pp. 97–9. The dissenting votes of Thos. Rayer, Edm. Hiorne, Geo. Noble, Thos. Glover and Fras. Druce reflect the tensions of the period.

[4] Presumably the same tax as levied in 1644 for the relief of the British army in Ireland: see *Cttee. at Stafford 1643–5*, ed. D.H. Pennington and I.A. Roots (Manch. 1957), xl, 336.

[5] Perhaps for the commissioners in the previous accts.

[6] Capt. John Butler of the New Model Horse: *Reg. Hist.* i. 209. By 1647 he was living in a park lodge, and by 1649 claimed dues as deputy-steward of Woodstock manor. As lessee of the manor in 1650 he used materials from the manor house to rebuild Begbroke House. See Wootton bapt. reg. 1647–51; Bodl. MS. Top. Oxon. c 85, p. 6; *V.C.H. Oxon.* xii. 8, 439.

[7] The Commission for Charitable Uses sat in Deddington from 1649 and considered Woodstock charities: P.R.O., *Lists and Indexes*, ix. 8, inquisition bundle 20, no. 10.

APPENDIX 1

Totals of receipts and disbursements 1608 to 1650[1]

End of year	Receipts			Disbursements			Remaining + Deficit −			
	£	s	d	£	s	d	£	s	d	
1609	67	3	1	61	4	10¹/₂	5	18	2¹/₂	+
1610	64	16	0¹/₄	65	6	7¹/₂	0	10	7¹/₄	−
1611	63	17	9¹/₄	73	6	9¹/₂	9	9	0¹/₄	−
1612	87	4	5	109	9	11	22	5	6	−
1613	80	9	5³/₄	99	2	10¹/₂	18	13	10	−
1614	63	4	2	65	19	1	0	54	11	−
1615	58	14	11	61	11	10	0	56	11	−
1616	55	8	2	62	0	21	6	13	7	−
1617	50	13	2¹/₄	50	17	9¹/₂	0	4	7¹/₂	−
1618	54	11	5¹/₄	52	18	0¹/₂	0	33	4¹/₂	−
1619	61	14	2¹/₂	67	8	6¹/₂	5	14	4	−
1620	49	17	7¹/₄	52	10	9¹/₂	0	53	2¹/₄	−
1621	50	19	10	77	18	5	26	18	7	−
1622	59	2	8	76	4	3	17	0	19	−
1623	51	3	4¹/₄	53	18	8¹/₂	0	55	4¹/₄	−
1624	53	12	7	56	10	3¹/₂	0	57	8¹/₂	−
1625	55	7	0	57	6	9¹/₂	0	39	9¹/₂	−
1626	59	13	11	60	0	20¹/₂	0	7	9¹/₂	−
1627	55	6	9³/₄	58	8	10	3	2	0¹/₄	−
1628	50	6	2³/₄	52	15	3	0	49	0¹/₄	−
1629	53	8	10¹/₂	57	4	1	4	15	2¹/₂	−
1630	57	12	5¹/₄	58	9	9¹/₂	0	17	4¹/₄	−
1631	59	5	5¹/₄	70	12	2¹/₂	11	6	9	−
1632	78	12	10	73	19	10	4	13	0	+
1633	58	6	1¹/₄	61	2	6¹/₂	0	56	5	−
1634	60	8	6¹/₄	59	0	6¹/₂	0	25	11³/₄	+
1635	63	13	10	66	8	1	0	54	3	−
1636	87	4	9¹/₂	82	16	8	4	8	0¹/₂	+
1637	68	19	3	75	1	6	6	2	3	−
1638	69	3	3	78	6	6¹/₂	9	3	3¹/₂	−
1639	68	3	9³/₄	75	18	3	7	14	6¹/₄	−
1640	88	9	1³/₄	77	14	7	10	13	6³/₄	−
1641	90	13	2³/₄	77	0	0	13	13	2³/₄	−

End of year	Receipts			Disbursements			Remaining + Deficit −			
	£	s	d	£	s	d	£	s	d	
1642	86	19	9³/₄	72	18	4¹/₂	14	1	5¹/₄	−
1643	58	7	10¹/₂	59	17	6	0	3	0	−
1644	29	4	0¹/₂	31	0	8	1	16	8	−
1645	62	17	1	52	8	10	10	8	3	+
1646	80	15	6¹/₂	85	12	6	4	16	11¹/₂	−
1647	98	11	5¹/₂	109	16	10¹/₂	11	5	5	−
1648	99	5	5	113	13	11	14	8	6	−
1649	94	7	0	92	3	5	2	4	5	+
1650	105	2	1	105	19	5				
	2	4	5 (owed by chamberlains)				1	7	1	+

[1] The totals are as given in the accounts, and no attempt has been made to correct them.

APPENDIX 2

Biographies

These are notes on local men connected with Woodstock council during the period of the accounts. For national figures such as the high stewards, recorders, and tenants of the royal park see biographical dictionaries such as the *Dictionary of National Biography*; for preachers see identifications in the index below, and see also *Alumni Oxonienses 1500–1714*, ed. J. Forster (Oxf. 1888–92).

Unless otherwise stated, the information has been taken from the following sources: death (d.), inventory (inv.), son (s.), wife (w.) from probate (prob.) records in the Oxfordshire Archives or in the Public Record Office (P.C.C.); burial (bur.) from Woodstock or Wootton parish register transcripts by Brig. G. Goadby; details of aldermen (ald.), junior and senior chamberlains (jun., sen., chamb.) and mayors, from Woodstock Borough Mun. B 79, B 81; sergeants (serg.), constables (con.), tithingmen, victuallers (vctl.), and innkeepers (innk.) from B 78/1, 2, 3 (court books), B 79; admission to freedom (adm.) from B 79, B 81; membership of the common council from B 96; churchwardens (chw.) from the Woodstock churchwardens' accounts in Oxfordshire Archives. The Justices of the Peace for Woodstock (J.P.) are taken from the sessions in B 78/2, and from the 1621 and 1625 commissions as detailed in the footnotes to these accounts; note that the mayor was a J.P. by virtue of his office.

Abraham (Abram), see Meatcalfe.

Bradshewe, Thos.: d. 2 June 1613 (inv.); w. Mary d. by 2 Oct. 1619; innk. of the Bull, opposite the market cross; gent.; jun. chamb. 1595–6; sen. chamb. 1596–7; mayor 1604–6, 1608–10; J.P. 1608; inv. £242 13d; books in inv. included *Marcus Aurelius, Holinshed, Bible, Common Prayer.*

Bradshewe, Wm.: d. 1616; s. of Ralph; w. already dead; mercer; jun. chamb. 1612–1613; sen. chamb. 1613–14; inv. £299 9s 6d.

Browne, Thos: d. 1621 (P.C.C.); w. Joan Keene d. Feb. 1624/5; her inv. £222 13s; ald. by 1588; chamb. 1588; mayor 1591–3, 1597–9, 1601–2, 1608; J.P. 1608; sold house at Park gate to town; in will left £200 and Fletcher's House to his w., 40s to poor of Woodstock, £5 to poor of Wootton-under-Edge (Glos.), 40s to poor of Chipping Norton, £10 to endow sermons in Woodstock, £5 for the same in Chipping Norton.

Browne, Thos.: d. 1625; B.A. Oxf. B.N.C.; s. of above; w. Susan; rector of Bladon 1621–5.

Cooper, Rob.: bur. 15 Mar. 1660/1; w. Eliz.; cooper; adm. 1637; jun. chamb. 1652–5; sen. chamb. 1657–9; chw. 1656–7; inv. £480 16s 8d.

Dissell, John: d. 1646; w. Jane; fuller; clothworker; innk. 1608; chw. 1635–6; tollman with Wm. Edwardes from Mich. 1635 to the end of 1645; collected stallages 1635– c. 1645; crier of the court 1636.

Drewe, Geo., see Gregory.

Drinckewater, Drinckwater, Wm.: bur. 16 Nov. 1659; w. Eliz.; vctl.; innk. of the Rose and Crown in 1652 rental; adm. 1640; trained soldier 1642; chw. 1650–4; surveyor of highways 1654; jun. chamb. 1657–8; inv. £80 17s 8d.

Druce, alias **White, Fras.:** bur. 11 May 1663; adm. 1623; chw. 1646–7, 1649–50; jun. chamb. 1647–50.

Edginge, Bart., see Love.

Edwardes, Wm.: vctl. 1616, 1619; con. 1618; common council by 1619; chw. 1623–5; tollman with Dissell from Mich. 1635 to 1645; and on own until end of accounts in 1650.

Evans, Edw.: d. 1621; M. A. New Coll., Oxf.; rector of Bladon 1610–1621.

Flye (Fly), Wm.: c. 1623; w. Ann Fauxe; glover; woolman; con. 1610; jun. chamb. 1605–7; ald. 1608–22; mayor 1618–20.

Franklinge, Giles: bur. 17 July 1665; w. Eliz. bur. 10 Nov. 1683; chw. 1660–2; jun. chamb. 1664.

Glover, John: d. by 25 Sept. 1643 (inv.); w. Joan d. 1655 (P.C.C.); gent.; baker; innk. of the Crown; jun. chamb. 1607–8; sen. chamb. 1608–10; ald. from 1611; mayor 1612–14, 1620–2, 1629–30, 1632–4, 1641–3; J.P. 1621; inv. £201 4s 6d.

Glover, Thos.: bur. 3 Oct. 1683; w. Anne; gent.; innk. of the Crown; adm. 1632; chw. 1641–2, 1655–6; sen. chamb. 1647–50; ald. 1658; mayor 1660–1; inv. £19 3s.

Gregory, Fras. Nash: bur. 3 Jan. 1654/5 (Wootton reg.); gent. of Hordley and Old Woodstock; relative of Jerome Nash; adm. 1613; attorney in Woodstock courts; J.P. 1621.

Gregory, alias **Drue or Drewe, Geo.:** bur. 7 Oct. 1658; w. Dorothy bur. 16 May 1661; gent.; cutler; kept town armour 1628; con. 1634; chw. 1637–9, 1654–5; jun. chamb. 1644–5; sen. chamb. 1645–7; ald. 1655; mayor 1655–7.

Harris, Jos.: d. by 9 Mar. 1634/5; gent.; mercer; innk. of the Bull; tithingman 1607–8; common council 1609; con. 1609–10; sen. chamb. 1610–13; ald. 1613; mayor 1614–16, 1622–24; J.P. 1621; inv. £124 2s.

Hatley, Rob.: bur. 11 Oct. 1674; gent.; w. Joan bur. 11 Jan 1685; adm. 1647; chw. 1657–60; jun. chamb. 1660–2; ald. 1662 as replacement for Commonwealth ald.; mayor 1664–5, 1673.

Heathen, Thos.: d. 1642 (B 79); chandler; adm. 1612; con. 1616; sergeant-at-the-mace from Feb. 1617/18 to 1642; probably the Thos. Heathen *alias* Hearne (bur. reg. and adm. acct.), d. by 18 Mar. 1646/7 with inv. £36 8s 10d. Delay in presenting inventory possibly due to the war and the problem of collecting debts, as his s. Thos. said that some of his father's debtors had died or gone abroad (adm. acct.).

Heathen, *alias* **Hearne, Thos.:** bur. 1 Aug. 1695; sergeant-at-the-mace, probably from 1642, but so named from 1646 to death.

Hiorne, Edm., senior: d. 1629; w. Eliz.; yeoman; left household property and sheep in Great Tew and household property in Woodstock to family, and £5 for poor of Great Tew and £5 for poor of Woodstock almshouse.

Hiorne, Edm.: bur. 27 June 1669; w. Ann Rawlins bur. 20 Sept. 1673; children Thos., Geo., Lady Ann Fleetwood, Mrs. Susan Wright (in Ireland), Mrs. Rebecca Waters (in Ireland); adm. 3 July 1605; town clerk 10 Dec. 1607 to sometime in 1645, restored in 1662, retired by 1664; J.P. 1625; dep. steward of Woodstock manor.

James (Jeames), Symon: d. 1632 (B 79); w. Eliz., perhaps daughter of Edm. Hiorne senior; gent.; schoolmaster; attorney in Woodstock court; adm. 3 July 1605; appointed schoolmaster 1608; common council Sept. 1608.

Johnson, Alex.: bur. 28 July 1681; w. Ann Williams, sister of John Williams, town clerk; mercer; adm. 1621; chw. 1639–41, 1644–6; jun. chamb. 1645–6, 1646–7; sen. chamb. 1651–6; mayor 1658–9, 1661–2; removed from council 1662.

Jones, Thos.: M.A. St. John's Coll., Oxf.; curate at Woodstock 1641–6, 1652–60: *V.C.H. Oxon.* xii. 408–9.

Kyte (Keyt, Kite), Jerome: d. 3 Dec. 1631 (monument in ch.); w. Eliz. d. 1648; Esq.; B.C.L.; ex-Fellow of St. John's Coll., Oxf.; lived in Chaucer's House, owned the Talbot Inn; J.P. 1621; inv. £348 19s.

Lee, Rob.: d. 1636; gent.; adm. 1626; chw. 1632–5; jun. chamb. 1635–6; inv. £215 14s.

Longe (Long), Edw.: d. before Mich. 1635; lastmaker; adm. 1608; made crier of court and clerk of church for life in Sept. 1608; taster 1611; tollman by 1609 to death.

Love, *alias* **Edginge** (chw. accts.), **Bart.:** bur. 12 Mar. 1654/5; brother of Thos. Love, woolman; adm. 1635; chw. 1625–6; jun. chamb. 1639–43; sen. chamb. 1643–5; ald. 1646; mayor 1646.

Lucas, Raphe: d. *c.* 1654 (when new scavenger appointed: see B 83); same or namesake confessed theft as servant of Rob. Bignill, baker, on 8 April 1612 in B 78/2; town scavenger and beadle of the poor 1632– *c.* 1654.

Mayott (Mates), Nic.: bur. 26 Jan. 1659/60; haberdasher; adm. 1627; chw. 1631–2; con. 1636; jun. chamb. 1638–9; sen. chamb. 1639–43; ald. 1645; mayor 1644–5, 1649–50, 1654–5.

Meade (Meades), Ric.: d. by Sept. 1620; w. Joan; yeoman 1620 but innk. 1608 and held the Geo. Inn 1609; jun. chamb. 1608–10; inv. £96 17s 4d.

Meatcalfe, Thos.: d. 6 May 1629 (B 79); s. of Wm. (d.1608); gent.; woollendraper; con. 1609; jun. chamb. 1610–12; ald. 1621; mayor 1628 to 6 May 1629; inv. £165 16s 8s.

Meatcalfe, *alias* **Abraham, Abram, Wm.:** d. 22 Jan. 1607/8 (B 78/2); draper, with shopbooks in Bicester and Woodstock in will; chamb. 1589–90; ald. 1591; mayor 1595–7, 1602–4, 1606–8; left £5 for sermon in Woodstock, 40s for new bell and £3 towards a water conduit for the town. The family was also called Abraham or Abram, perhaps after Abraham Metcalfe who was mayor in 1563: see B 81, f. 5r.

Meatcalfe, Wm.: d. *c.* 1644; will proved 12 July 1648 (P.C.C.); son of Wm. (d. 1608); w. Margaret in probate; woollendraper; adm. 1607; con. 1609, 1610, 1611; chw. 1614–15; jun. chamb. 1614–15; sen. chamb. 1615–19; ald. 1619–43; J.P. 1621; mayor 1624–6, 1634–6.

Meatcalfe, Wm.: overseer of the poor 1662–3; sen. chamb. 1663–9; perhaps the nonconformist of 1672 and 1678, which would account for his not appearing as an office-holder later. See also *V.C.H.Oxon.* xii. 381, 415.

Nash (Nasshe), Jerome: d. by 2 Oct. 1623 (inv.); of Old Woodstock; gent., M.A. 1581; B.C.L. 1588; Fellow of St. John's Coll., Oxf.; inv. £354 11s 9d.

Nash (Nasshe), Ric.: d. 1637; of Old Woodstock; gent.; brother and heir of Jerome; left Woodstock £20 for an annual sermon and £80 loan for poor tradesmen and inhabitants.

Newman, Wm.: schoolmaster 1632–7.

Nickolls (Nicholls), Jas.: d. by 22 May 1641 (inv.); baker; w. Eliz. d. 1648; adm. 1622; con. 1628; chw. 1631–2; jun. chamb. 1636–8; inv. £149 17s 4d.

Noble, Ant.: d. 1617; clerk; curate by 1577 (MS. Wills Oxon. 185, f. 57v); poss. schoolmaster ; w. Ursula, sister of Wm. Meatcalfe (d. 1608), d. by Feb. 1636/7 (prob.). See also *V.C.H. Oxon.* xii. 408, 416.

Noble, Geo.: bur. 26 Mar. 1657; cooper; s. of Ant.; w. Rose d. 1669; adm. 1610; tithingman 1610; con. 1612, 1613; chw. 1615–16, 1626–9; jun. chamb. 1619–29; sen. chamb. 1629–33; ald. 1636; cast up accounts in 1637; mayor 1643, 1647–9, 1650–1.

Norman, John [poss. *alias* **Munck]:** perhaps the John Norman d. 1653 (P.C.C.); butcher; tithingman 1610; adm. 1610; con. 1611; jun. chamb. 1615–17; chw. 1627–9.

Paynter (Painter), Bennett: d. 1646; w. Edie in 1632 will; glover; vctl. 1608, 1616, 1617; innk. of the Three Cups; adm. 10 Nov. 1602; con. 1619–21; chw. 1620–3; jun. chamb.1633–5; sen. chamb. 1635–9; ald. by 1644.

Paynter (Painter), Thos.: d. 1654 (P.C.C.); w. Priscilla d. 18 May 1694; glover; vctl. 1611; innk. of the Three Cups; probably the Thos. adm. 1630; chw. 1644–6; some refs. may be to the Thos. d. 1619 or to his s. in the next entry.

Paynter (Painter), Thos.: bur. 14 Apr. 1711; s. of Thos.; chandler; jun. chamb. 1651; sen. chamb. 1661, 1662; ald. 1662; mayor 1663-4, 1668-9, 1672, 1674, 1678, 1680, 1685, 1692, 1693, 1703–4.

Phillipps, John d. by 28 Oct. 1608 (inv.); w. Mary; innholder in 1584; glover; adm. 1584; ald. 1597; mayor 1586-8, 1589–91, 1593–5, 1599–1600; occupied Chaucer's House; inv. £119 1s 8d.

Prideaux, John: d. 1650; D.D.; rector of Bladon 1625–41; rector of Exeter Coll.; Regius Prof. of Divinity: *D.N.B.*

Raunson (Raunce), John: d. 21 Jan. 1610/11 (inv.); w. Marg.; glover; chamb. 1583–5; ald. *c.* 1608; mayor 1610–11; inv. £66 7s.

Rawlins, Thos.: d. 1633 at Cassington; adm. 1597; town clerk 1598 to 10 Dec. 1607; dep. steward of Woodstock manor; cousin of Jas. Chesterman of Oxf., who acted in legal matters for Woodstock; son-in-law Edm. Hiorne, town clerk; inv. £342 16s.

Rayer, Thos.: bur. 7 Mar. 1661/2; s. of Wm. (d.1619); vctl. 1620; vintner; innk. of the Bear, and of the Swan (1652); adm. 1613; con. 1614–16; chw. 1616; common council by 1617; jun. chamb. 1617–19; sen. chamb. 1619–23; ald. 1623; J.P. 1625; mayor 1626–8, 1636–8 1645–6, 1652–4, 1657–8.

Rayer, Wm.: d. 1619 (P.C.C.); w. Alice d. by Sept. 1626; her inv. £218 17s 8d; vctl. 1608; innk. of the Bear; sen. chamb. 1602–8; ald. 1608; mayor 1611–12, 1616–18.

Ringe, Thos.: schoolmaster 1637–42.

Rudgate, Edm. or Edw.: d. by 7 Oct. 1617 (B 79); shoemaker; son of Hen. (d.1613); w. Ellen; con. 1607–9; sergeant-at-the-mace 1612–17; inv. £12 9s 7d.

Rudgate, Hen.: d. by Aug. 1613; w. Anne; cordwainer; vctl. 1608; sergeant-at-the-mace from at least June 1594 to 1611; inv. £49 16s 8d.

Ryly (Ryley), Wm.: d. 1609; chamb. 1560–1, 1563–4, 1565–6; ald. *c.* 1570; mayor 1570–1, 1581–2.

Ryves, Geo.: bur. 9 July 1677; w. Joan, granddaughter of Edm. Hiorne, bur. 22 Feb. 1677; gent.; town clerk after Hiorne from 1664.

Selfe, Geo.: d. 1675; M. A. Pembroke Coll., Oxf.; ordained 1629; curate of Woodstock 1632–41.

Shadd, Gabriel: con. 1634; chw. 1636–8, 1646–7, 1649–50; rented wool beam 1630 to 1650 when he was still paying arrears.

Shadd, Ric.: d. 1617; chandler (MS. Wills Oxon. 4/4/1); w. Alice; chw. 1614–15; taster 1614–18; rented wool beam from 12 Dec. 1606 and his widow after him to 1630.

Silver, Edw.: bur. 7 July 1686; w. Eliz.; ironmonger; adm. 1625; chw. 1642–3, 1656–7; jun. chamb. 1643–4; ald. 1662.

Sparrowe, Thos.: bur. 23 Oct. 1678; w. Eliz. bur. 8 Dec. 1693; mercer; collector for the poor 1658–9; jun. chamb. 1658–9; sen. chamb. 1659–60; ald. 1661; mayor 1662–3, 1665–6, 1676–7; inv. £666 11s 7d.

Underhill (Undrill), Ric.: bur. 17 May 1676; w. Mary bur. 7 July 1676; baker; adm. 1632; collector for the poor 1657–8.

White, Jerome: d. 18 Feb. 1617/18 (B 78/3); w. Alice; vctl. 1608, 1616; adm. 1599; sergeant-at-the-mace from 7 Oct. 1617 until death.

White, Fras., see Druce.

Whiteside, Hen., senior: d. by 4 Jan. 1631/2; w. Anne; shoemaker; adm. 1619; con. 1620, 1624, 1627.

Whiteside, Hen.: bur. 19 Jan. 1675/6; w. Marg. bur. 6 Feb. 1675/6; adm. 1622.

Widdowes, Thos.: schoolmaster from *c.* 1646–53; possibly minister; author of *The Just Devil of Woodstock: V.C.H. Oxon.* xii. 408.

Williams, John: bur. 16 Sept. 1663; s. of Thos. (d. 1636); w. Amy d. by Nov. 1631; adm. 1635; chw. 1639–41; con. 1641; town clerk 1645 until removed 1662; inv. £184 10s.

Williams, Thos.: d. 1636; w. Eliz. bur. 14 Sept. 1654; baker in 1605; vctl. 1608; innk. of the Rose and Crown; adm. 1605; common council by 1608; con. 1607-9; jun. chamb. 1613–14; sen. chamb. 1614–15, 1623–29; ald. 1629; mayor 1630, 1631; inv. £464 15s 11d.

Woodward, Thos.: d. 1668 (P.C.C.); mercer; innk.; adm. 1619; con. 1621, 1624; chw. 1625-26; jun. chamb. 1629–33; sen. chamb. 1633–35; ald. 1635; mayor 1638–40, 1644, 1651–2; removed from council 1662.

APPENDIX 3

Aldermen

There were five aldermen, including the mayor. They were elected for life, save for exceptional circumstances as in 1662 when the town council was purged at the Restoration. In the list below the date of the alderman's death which led to the next vacancy is given.

1599–1601   Thos. Browne, Wm. Meatcalfe, John Phillipps, Wm. Ryley, John Williams (d. by 1602).

1602–7   Thos. Bradshewe, Thos. Browne, Wm. Meatcalfe, John Phillipps, Wm. Ryley.

1608–9   Thos. Bradshewe, Thos. Browne, Wm. Flye, Wm. Meatcalfe (d. 22 Jan. 1607/8), John Phillipps (d. by 28 Oct. 1608), Wm. Rayer, John Raunson, Wm. Ryley (d. 1609).

1610–12   Thos. Bradshewe, Thos. Browne, Wm. Flye, John Glover (after Raunson), Wm. Rayer, John Raunson (d. 21 Jan. 1610/11).

1613   Thos. Bradshewe (d. 2 June 1613), Thos. Browne, Wm. Flye, John Glover, Jos. Harris (after Bradshewe), Wm. Rayer.

1614–19   Thos. Browne, Wm. Flye, John Glover, Jos. Harris, Wm. Rayer (d. 1619), Wm. Meatcalfe (after Rayer).

1619–20   Thos. Browne (d. 1621), Wm. Flye, John Glover, Jos. Harris, Wm. Meatcalfe.

1621–2   Wm. Flye (d. *c.* 1623), John Glover, Jos. Harris, Thos. Meatcalfe, Wm. Meatcalfe.

1623–8   John Glover, Jos. Harris, Thos. Meatcalfe, Wm. Meatcalfe, Thos. Rayer (after Flye).

1629–34   John Glover, Jos. Harris, Thos. Meatcalfe (d. 6 May 1629), Wm. Meatcalfe, Thos. Rayer, Thos. Williams (after Meatcalfe).

1635   John Glover, Jos. Harris (d. 9 Mar. 1634/5), Wm. Meatcalfe, Thos. Rayer, Thos. Williams, Thos. Woodward (after Harris).

1636–42   John Glover, Wm. Meatcalfe, Geo. Noble (after Williams), Thos. Rayer, Thos. Williams (d. 1636), Thos. Woodward.

1643–4   John Glover (d. by 25 Sept. 1643), Wm. Meatcalfe (d. *c.* 1644), Geo. Noble, Bennett Paynter, Thos. Rayer, Thos. Woodward.

1644–5   Nic. Mayott, Geo. Noble, Bennett Paynter (d. 1646), Thos. Rayer, Thos. Woodward.

1646–54   Bart. Love (d. 12 Mar. 1654/5), Nic. Mayott, Geo. Noble, Thos. Rayer, Thos. Woodward.

1655–6   Geo. Gregory, Nic. Mayott, Geo. Noble (d. by 26 Mar. 1657),

	Thos. Rayer, Thos. Woodward.
1657–8	Alex. Johnson, Geo. Gregory (d. 7 Oct. 1658), Nic. Mayott, Thos. Rayer, Thos. Woodward.
1659–60	Rob. Cooper (d. by 15 Mar. 1660/1), Alex. Johnson, Thos. Glover, Nic. Mayott (d. by 26 Jan.1659/60), Thos. Rayer, Thos. Woodward.
1661	Alex. Johnson, Thos. Glover, Thos. Rayer (d. by 7 Mar. 1661/2), Thos. Sparrowe, Thos. Woodward.
1662	Alex. Johnson (removed), Thos. Glover, Rob. Hatley (d. 1674), Thos. Paynter (d. 1711), Edw. Silver (d. 1686), Thos. Sparrowe (d. 1678), Thos. Woodward (removed).

Mayors

Elected annually on the Monday before St. Matthew's Day (21 Sept.) and took office at Michaelmas (29 Sept.). The term of office therefore took in part of two years.

1601–2	Thos. Browne
1602–3	Wm. Meatcalfe
1603–4	Wm. Meatcalfe
1604–5	Thos. Bradshewe
1605–6	Thos. Bradshewe
1606–7	Wm. Meatcalfe
1607–8	Wm. Meatcalfe (d. 22 Jan. 1607/8)
1608	Thos. Browne (Jan.–Sept.)
1608–9	Thos. Bradshewe
1609–10	Thos. Bradshewe
1610–11	John Raunson (d. 23 Jan. 1610/11)
1611–12	Wm. Rayer (from Jan. 1610/11)
1612–13	John Glover
1613–14	John Glover
1614–15	Jos. Harris
1615–16	Jos. Harris
1616–17	Wm. Rayer
1617–18	Wm. Rayer
1618–19	Wm. Flye
1619–20	Wm. Flye
1620–1	John Glover
1621–2	John Glover
1622–3	Jos. Harris
1623–4	Jos. Harris
1624–5	Wm. Meatcalfe

1625–6	Wm. Meatcalfe
1626–7	Thos. Rayer
1627–8	Thos. Rayer
1628–9	Thos. Meatcalfe (d. 6 May 1629)
1629–30	John Glover (from May 1629)
1630–1	Thos. Williams
1631–2	Thos. Williams
1632–3	John Glover
1633–4	John Glover
1634–5	Wm. Meatcalfe
1635–6	Wm. Meatcalfe
1636–7	Thos. Rayer
1637–8	Thos. Rayer
1638–9	Thos. Woodward
1639–40	Thos. Woodward
1640–1	Thos. Woodward
1641–2	John Glover
1642–3	John Glover (d. by 25 Sept. 1643)
1643	Geo. Noble
1644	Thos. Woodward (by 18 Mar. 1643/4)
1644–5	Nic. Mayott
1645–6	Thos. Rayer
1646–7	Bart. Love
1647–8	Geo. Noble
1648–9	Geo. Noble
1649–50	Nic. Mayott
1650–1	Geo. Noble
1651–2	Thos. Woodward
1652–3	Thos. Rayer
1653–4	Thos. Rayer
1654–5	Nic. Mayott
1655–6	Geo. Gregory
1656–7	Geo. Gregory
1657–8	Thos. Rayer
1658–9	Alex. Johnson
1659–60	Thos. Glover
1660–1	Thos. Glover
1661–2	Alex. Johnson
1662–3	Thos. Sparrowe
1663–4	Thos. Paynter
1664–5	Rob. Hatley

Town Clerks

Appointed by Council

1598–1607	Thos. Rawlins
1608–45	Edm. Hiorne
1645–62	John Williams
1663	Edm. Hiorne
1664–	Geo. Ryves

Sergeants-at-the-Mace

Elected annually on 21 Sept. at the same time as the mayor.

By 1594–1612	Hen. Rudgate
1612–17	Edm. Rudgate
1617–18	Jerome White
1618–42	Thos. Heathen senior
1642–95	Thos. Heathen

Chamberlains

Elected annually at the audit. Their year ran from *c.* 20 Dec. of the first year given. The senior chamberlain, elected by council, is named first; the junior, chosen by the mayor, is second.

1599–1600	John Dubber, Mic. Nurse
1600–1	John Dubber, Mic. Nurse
1601–2	Wm. Rayer, Mic. Nurse
1602–3	Wm. Rayer, Mic. Nurse
1603–4	Wm. Rayer, Wm. Flye (audit 20 Jan. 1603/4)
1604–5	Wm. Rayer, Wm. Flye
1605–6	Wm. Rayer, Wm. Flye
1606–7	Wm. Rayer, Wm. Flye
1607–8	Wm. Rayer, John Glover
1608–9	John Glover, Richard Meades
1609–10	John Glover, Richard Meades
1610–11	Jos. Harris, Thos. Meatcalfe
1611–12	Jos. Harris, Thos. Meatcalfe
1612–13	Jos. Harris, Wm. Bradshewe
1613–14	Wm. Bradshewe, Thos. Williams
1614–15	Thos. Williams, Wm. Meatcalfe

1615–16	Wm. Meatcalfe, John Norman
1616–17	Wm. Meatcalf, John Norman
1617–18	Wm. Meatcalfe, Thos. Rayer
1618–19	Wm. Meatcalfe, Thos. Rayer
1619–20	Thos. Rayer, Geo. Noble
1620–1	Thos. Rayer, Geo. Noble
1621–2	Thos. Rayer, Geo. Noble
1622–3	Thos. Rayer, Geo. Noble
1623–4	Thos. Williams, Geo. Noble
1624–5	Thos. Williams, Geo. Noble
1625–6	Thos. Williams, Geo. Noble
1626–7	Thos. Williams, Geo. Noble
1627–8	Thos. Williams, Geo. Noble
1628–9	Thos. Williams, Geo. Noble
1629–30	Geo. Noble, Thos. Woodward
1630–1	Geo. Noble, Thos. Woodward
1631–2	Geo. Noble, Thos. Woodward
1632–3	Geo. Noble, Thos. Woodward
1633–4	Thos. Woodward, Bennett Paynter
1634–5	Thos. Woodward, Bennett Paynter
1635–6	Bennett Paynter, Rob. Lee
1636–7	Bennett Paynter, James Nickolls
1637–8	Bennett Paynter, James Nickolls
1638–9	Bennett Paynter, Nic. Mayott
1639–40	Nic. Mayott, Bart. Love
1640–1	Nic. Mayott, Bart. Love
1641–2	Nic. Mayott, Bart. Love
1642–3	Nic. Mayott, Bart. Love
1643–4	Bart. Love, Edw. Silver
1644–5	Bart. Love, Geo. Gregory
1645–6	Geo. Gregory, Alex. Johnson
1646–7	Geo. Gregory, Alex. Johnson
1647–8	Thos. Glover, Fras. Druce
1648–9	Thos. Glover, Fras. Druce
1649–50	Thos. Glover, Fras. Druce
1651	Alex. Johnson, Thos. Paynter [audit 20 Feb. 1651/2]
1652	Alex. Johnson, Rob. Cooper [audit 22 Jan. 1652/3]
1653	Alex. Johnson, Rob. Cooper [audit 23 Jan. 1653/4]
1654	Alex. Johnson, Rob. Cooper [audit 26 Jan. 1654/5]
1655	Alex. Johnson, Rob. Cooper [audit 26 Jan. 1655/6]
1656	Alex. Johnson, Ric. Underhill [audit 19 Feb. 1656/7]
1657	Rob. Cooper, Wm. Drinckewater [audit 1 Mar. 1657/8]
1658	Rob. Cooper, Wm. Drinckewater [audit 31 Jan. 1658/9]
1659	Rob. Cooper, Thos. Sparrowe [audit 30 Jan. 1659/60]

1660   Thos. Sparrowe, Thos. Paynter [audit 19 Feb. 1660/1]
1661   Thos. Paynter, Rob. Hatley [audit 7 Mar. 1661/2]
1662   Thos. Paynter, Rob. Hatley [audit 23 Feb. 1662/3]
1663   Wm. Meatcalfe, Giles Franklinge [audit 10 June 1664]
1664   Wm. Meatcalfe, Giles Franklinge [audit 23 Mar. 1664/5]

Tollmen

1609–35   Edw. Longe
1635–45   John Dissell and Wm. Edwardes
1646–50   Wm. Edwardes

INDEX OF PERSONS AND PLACES

Abbreviations: adm., admitted freeman; ald., alderman; bro., brother; chamb., chamberlain; chw., churchwarden; clk., clerk; con., constable; dau., daughter; ld., lord; pr., preacher; prop., property; s., son; sis., sister; w., wife; wid., widow.

Standard abbreviations have been used for names and places. Places are in Oxfordshire unless otherwise stated. Leading townsmen are identified by **biog.** *refs. Institutions, occupations, officers and offices are indexed under subjects.*

INDEX OF SUBJECTS